Communications in Computer and Information Science 476

More information about this series at http://www.springer.com/series/7899

Cyrille Artho · Peter Csaba Ölveczky (Eds.)

Formal Techniques for Safety-Critical Systems

Third International Workshop, FTSCS 2014
Luxembourg, November 6–7, 2014
Revised Selected Papers

 Springer

Editors
Cyrille Artho
National Institute of Advanced Industrial
Science and Technology
Amagasaki
Japan

Peter Csaba Ölveczky
University of Oslo
Oslo
Norway

ISSN 1865-0929   ISSN 1865-0937   (electronic)
Communications in Computer and Information Science
ISBN 978-3-319-17580-5   ISBN 978-3-319-17581-2   (eBook)
DOI 10.1007/978-3-319-17581-2

Library of Congress Control Number: 2015937953

Springer Cham Heidelberg New York Dordrecht London
© Springer International Publishing Switzerland 2015

Printed on acid-free paper

Springer International Publishing AG Switzerland is part of Springer Science+Business Media (www.springer.com)

Preface

This volume contains the proceedings of the *Third International Workshop on Formal Techniques for Safety-Critical Systems* (FTSCS 2014), held in Luxembourg on November 6–7, 2014, as a satellite event of the ICFEM conference.

The aim of FTSCS is to bring together researchers and engineers who are interested in the application of formal and semi-formal methods to improve the quality of safety-critical computer systems. FTSCS strives to promote research and development of formal methods and tools for industrial applications, and is particularly interested in industrial applications of formal methods. Specific topics of the workshop include, but are not limited to:

- case studies and experience reports on the use of formal methods for analyzing safety-critical systems, including avionics, automotive, medical, and other kinds of safety-critical and QoS-critical systems;
- methods, techniques, and tools to support automated analysis, certification, debugging, etc., of complex safety/QoS-critical systems;
- analysis methods that address the limitations of formal methods in industry (usability, scalability, etc.);
- formal analysis support for modeling languages used in industry, such as AADL, Ptolemy, SysML, SCADE, Modelica, etc.; and
- code generation from validated models.

FTSCS 2014 received 40 regular paper submissions and two position/work-in-progress paper submissions. Each submission was reviewed by at least three reviewers; based on the reviews and extensive discussions, the program committee selected 14 of these regular papers and both position/work-in-progress papers for presentation at the workshop. This volume contains revised versions of those 14 regular papers, as well as invited papers by Klaus Havelund and Thomas Noll. As was the case for FTSCS 2012 and FTSCS 2013, a special issue of the *Science of Computer Programming* journal is devoted to extended versions of selected papers from FTSCS 2014.

Many colleagues and friends contributed to FTSCS 2014. We thank Klaus Havelund and Thomas Noll for accepting our invitations to give invited talks and the authors who submitted their work to FTSCS 2014 and who made this workshop an interesting event attracting more than 30 participants. We are particularly grateful to the members of the program committee, who all provided timely, insightful, and detailed reviews.

We also thank the editors of Springer's *Communications in Computer and Information Science* (CCIS) series for publishing the proceedings of FTSCS 2014, Bas van Vlijmen for accepting our proposal to devote a special issue of *Science of Computer Programming* to extended versions of selected papers from FTSCS 2014, Jun Pang and Magali Martin for their help with local arrangements, and Andrei Voronkov for the excellent EasyChair conference systems.

January 2015   Cyrille Artho
                                                                                                    Peter Csaba Ölveczky

Organization

Workshop Chair

Hitoshi Ohsaki   AIST, Japan

Program Committee

Erika Ábrahám   RWTH Aachen University, Germany
Musab AlTurki   King Fahd University of Petroleum and Minerals,
                                Saudi Arabia
Toshiaki Aoki   JAIST, Japan
Farhad Arbab   Leiden University and CWI, The Netherlands
Cyrille Artho (Chair)   AIST, Japan
Kyungmin Bae   Carnegie Mellon University, USA
Saddek Bensalem   Verimag, France
Armin Biere   Johannes Kepler University of Linz, Austria
Ansgar Fehnker   University of the South Pacific, Fiji
Mamoun Filali   IRIT, France
Bernd Fischer   Stellenbosch University, South Africa
Klaus Havelund   NASA JPL, USA
Marieke Huisman   University of Twente, The Netherlands
Ralf Huuck   NICTA, Australia
Fuyuki Ishikawa   National Institute of Informatics, Japan
Takashi Kitamura   AIST, Japan
Alexander Knapp   Augsburg University, Germany
Yang Liu   Nanyang Technological University, Singapore
Robi Malik   University of Waikato, New Zealand
Frédéric Mallet   Université Nice Sophia Antipolis, France
César Muñoz   NASA Langley, USA
Thomas Noll   RWTH Aachen University, Germany
Peter Csaba Ölveczky (Chair)   University of Oslo, Norway
Charles Pecheur   Université catholique de Louvain, Belgium
Paul Pettersson   Mälardalen University, Sweden
Camilo Rocha   Escuela Colombiana de Ingeniería, Colombia
Ralf Sasse   ETH Zürich, Switzerland
Oleg Sokolsky   University of Pennsylvania, USA
Sofiène Tahar   Concordia University, Canada
Carolyn Talcott   SRI International, USA
Tatsuhiro Tsuchiya   Osaka University, Japan
Chen-Wei Wang   McMaster University, Canada

| Mike Whalen | University of Minnesota, USA |
| Huibiao Zhu | East China Normal University, China |

Additional Reviewers

Dunchev, Cvetan	Hung, Dang Van	Limbrée, Christophe
Enoiu, Eduard Paul	Jansen, Christina	Mentis, Anakreon
Fang, Huixing	Jansen, Nils	Mu, Chunyan
Gao, Sa	Johnsen, Andreas	Siddique, Umair
Hatvani, Leo	Kremer, Gereon	Soualhia, Mbarka
Huang, Yanhong	Li, Qin	Wu, Xi

Contents

Experience with Rule-Based Analysis
of Spacecraft Logs

Klaus Havelund$^{(\boxtimes)}$ and Rajeev Joshi

Jet Propulsion Laboratory, California Institute of Technology, Pasadena, USA
havelund@gmail.com

Abstract. One of the main challenges facing the software development
as well as the hardware communities is that of demonstrating the correctness of built artifacts with respect to separately stated requirements.
Runtime verification is a partial solution to this problem, consisting of
checking actual execution traces against formalized requirements. A related activity is that of humans attempting to understand (or *comprehend*)
what the system does when it executes, for validation purposes, or for
simply operating the system optimally. For example, a key challenge in
operating remote spacecraft is that ground operators must rely on the
limited visibility available through spacecraft telemetry in order to assess
spacecraft health and operational status. In this paper we illustrate the
use of the rule-based runtime verification system LogFire for supporting such log comprehension. Specifically, LogFire is used for generating
abstract events from the concrete events in logs, followed by a visualization of these abstract events using the D3 visualization framework.

1 Introduction

1.1 Motivation

Demonstrating the correctness of a software or hardware artifact is a challenging
problem. In the ideal case we want to prove the artifact correct for all possible
input. Unfortunately, full verification is still cost-prohibitive for complex systems (especially those with tight deadlines), so practitioners typically use less
formal, but cheaper, alternatives to build confidence in their systems. One such
alternative is runtime verification, which checks a particular execution against a
formal specification, which in this case becomes the test oracle. However, runtime verification systems can be used during deployment as well, to monitor the
actual execution of the system in the field. Such monitoring can happen *online*,
as the system executes, or *offline* by analyzing log files generated by the running
system. Violations of the formal specification can be flagged by the runtime verification system, either leading to automated behavior modification in the case

The work described in this publication was carried out at Jet Propulsion Laboratory,
California Institute of Technology, under a contract with the National Aeronautics
and Space Administration.

© Springer International Publishing Switzerland 2015
C. Artho and P.C. Ölveczky (Eds.): FTSCS 2014, CCIS 476, pp. 1–16, 2015.
DOI: 10.1007/978-3-319-17581-2_1

of online monitoring, or human driven systems modification in the case of offline monitoring (as examples).

In this paper we suggest yet a slightly different use of a runtime verification system: namely that of *system comprehension*. One of the key challenges in operating remote spacecraft is that the only knowledge ground operators have of the spacecraft behavior is the telemetry sent down to earth. Such telemetry typically consists of logs of system events and sensor measurements (such as battery voltage or probe temperature). A log may be viewed as a sequence of time-stamped records with named fields. Current practice at NASA's Jet Propulsion Laboratory (JPL) is to develop ad-hoc tools using various scripting languages, resulting in a growing collection of scripts that are hard to maintain and modify, which becomes a concern for long-running missions that last many years. A more desirable solution is a specification-based approach where *comprehension rules* are formulated in a human readable DSL (Domain Specific Language). In this paper, we present such an approach applied to the telemetry received from the Curiosity rover currently on Mars, and part of the MSL (Mars Science Laboratory) mission [31].

1.2   Contribution

More concretely, we illustrate the application of the LOGFIRE runtime verification system [25] and the D3 visualization system [14] to support *human comprehension* of logs sent down to earth from Curiosity. Although illustrated on such logs, the approach is fully general. LOGFIRE is a rule-based monitoring framework, a concept extensively studied within the artificial intelligence community. It is implemented in the SCALA programming language as an internal DSL (essentially an API), and its core algorithm is a modification of the RETE algorithm [19], to support event processing as well as fast indexing, as described in [25]. RETE is one of the original algorithms for rule-based systems, optimizing rule-evaluation, and known for its complexity.

Rules have the form: $condition_1, \ldots, condition_n \Rightarrow action$. The state of a rule-system can abstractly be considered as consisting of a set of *facts*, referred to as the *fact memory*, where a fact is a mapping from field names to values. A condition in a rule's left-hand side can check for the presence or absence of a particular fact. A left-hand side matching against the fact memory usually requires unification of variables occurring in conditions. In the case that all conditions on a rule's left-hand side match (become true), the right-hand side action is executed, which can be any SCALA code, including adding and deleting facts, or generating error messages. The DSL allows domain specific constructs to be mixed with SCALA code, making the notation very expressive and convenient for practical purposes, one of the reasons that LOGFIRE is used daily on the MSL mission.

LOGFIRE was originally developed for verifying execution traces against formal specifications. A main focus was monitoring of events carrying data, what is also sometimes referred to as data parameterized monitoring. The purpose was to understand how well rule-based systems fare for this form of task. In the work presented here, we instead use LOGFIRE for generating abstract facts from low level events occurring in a log. Such facts are generated as a result of executing actions of rules triggered by lower-level events and facts. The rule-based approach is particularly suited for this form of fact generation, compared to other forms of runtime verification logics, such as temporal logics, regular expressions or state machines. The collection of facts built in this manner is then fed into a visualization tool implemented using the D3 library. The system is currently in use by the Curiosity operations team. A main core message of this work is that runtime verification as a field should embrace a wide range of technologies for not only verifying systems but also for learning and comprehending their behavior.

1.3   Related Work

In [26] we describe an attempt to build a DSL on top of LOGFIRE in order to make it even easier to formulate abstraction rules for log comprehension and visualization. That work, however, is still a research prototype, and not (yet) used in mission operations, as is the case with the work presented here.

Numerous systems have been developed over the last decade for supporting monitoring of parameterized events, using various formalisms, such as state machines [2,5,11,21,32], regular expressions [1,32], variations over the μ-calculus [4], temporal logics [4,5,8,9,15,22,32], grammars [32], and rule-based systems [7,25]. LOGFIRE itself was in part inspired by the RULER system [7]. Other rule-based systems include DROOLS [17], JESS [27] and CLIPS [13]. Standard rule systems usually enable processing of facts, which have a life span. In contrast, LOGFIRE additionally implements events, which are instantaneous. DROOLS supports a notion of events, which are facts with a limited life span, inspired by the concept of *Complex Event Processing* (CEP), described by David Luckham in [28].

Two other rule-based internal DSLs for SCALA exist: HAMMURABI [20] and ROOSCALOO [33]. HAMMURABI, which is not RETE-based, achieves efficient evaluation of rules by evaluating these in parallel, assigning each rule to a different SCALA actor. ROOSCALOO [33] is RETE based, but is not documented in any form other than experimental code. The DROOLS project has an effort ongoing, defining functional programming extensions to DROOLS [18]. In contrast, by embedding a rule system in an object-oriented and functional language, as done in LOGFIRE, we can leverage the already existing host language features.

TRACECONTRACT [5] and DAUT (Data automata) [23,24] are internal SCALA DSLs for trace analysis based on state machines. They allow for multi-transitions without explicitly naming the intermediate states, which allows for temporal logic like specifications, in addition to data parameterized state machines. TRACECONTRACT was deployed throughout the LADEE mission [29], checking command sequences (similar format as logs) sent to the spacecraft, as documented in [6] at an early stage of that project.

1.4   Contents

The paper is organized as follows. Section 2 introduces the rule-based system LOGFIRE, illustrating how it can be used for verifying the correctness of program/system executions. The example is that of general deadlock potential detection between any number of tasks, chosen since it illustrates the expressive power of rules. Section 3 presents the application of LOGFIRE to abstract and visualize telemetry from the Curiosity rover. Finally, Sect. 4 concludes the paper.

2   The LogFire Runtime Verification System

LOGFIRE [25] is an API in the SCALA programming language, also here referred to as an internal DSL, created for writing rule-based runtime monitors. A monitor is specified as a set of rules, each of the form: $lhs \Rightarrow rhs$, which operate on a database of facts, called the *fact memory*. Rule left-hand sides test on incoming events, as well as presence or absence of facts in the fact memory. Right-hand sides (actions) can add facts to the fact memory, delete facts, issue error messages, and generally execute any SCALA code. A monitor takes as input a sequence of events, consumed one at a time, and for each event executes the actions of those rules whose left-hand sides evaluate to true. Monitors can be used to analyze the execution of a program as it executes or to analyze logs produced by the program. LOGFIRE is an implementation of the RETE algorithm [19], specifically as it is described in [16], modified to process instantaneous events (in addition to facts that have a life span), and to perform faster lookups in the fact memory. We will illustrate LOGFIRE using the example of detecting deadlock potentials [10] in a program by just analyzing a single execution trace generated by an instrumented version of the program. This example illustrates the flexibility of using a rule-based system. The reader is referred to [25] for more details about the implementation of LOGFIRE.

2.1   The Deadlock Potential Detection Problem

Deadlock potentials in a program can very easily be detected by analyzing single execution traces generated by an appropriately instrumented program. We consider traces that only contain two kinds of events: $lock(t, l)$, representing that task t takes the lock l; and $unlock(t, l)$, representing that task t releases lock l. As described in [10], the standard technique for detecting deadlock potentials is to build a *lock graph*, where nodes are locks and where there is an edge between two nodes (locks) l_1 and l_2, labelled with task id t, if task t at some point holds lock l_1 while taking lock l_2. Nodes and edges are only added to the graph (never deleted). If at some point the graph contains a cycle it indicates the potential for deadlock, although not necessarily an actual deadlock. The algorithm can typically be made efficient in practice since it only needs to check for deadlock *potentials*, in contrast to, say, a model checker, which typically has to search the reachable state space for *actual* deadlocks.

$T_1 : lock(l_1); \ lock(l_2);$
  $\langle critical \ section \ 1 \rangle$
  $unlock(l_2); \ unlock(l_1)$

$T_2 : lock(l_2); \ lock(l_3);$
  $\langle critical \ section \ 2 \rangle$
  $unlock(l_3); \ unlock(l_2)$

$T_3 : lock(l_3); \ lock(l_1);$
  $\langle critical \ section \ 3 \rangle$
  $unlock(l_1); \ unlock(l_3)$

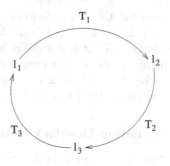

Fig. 1. Example illustrating three tasks T_1, T_2, and T_3, taking three locks l_1, l_2, and l_3 in a cyclic manner, opening for a deadlock potential. This is detected as a cycle in the corresponding lock graph

Figure 1 shows an example illustrating how the algorithm works. The left-hand side shows three tasks (say, threads in a multi-threaded program), each taking two locks, then entering a critical section, and then releasing the locks. The locks are taken in a circular manner: a deadlock can occur if the tasks are scheduled such that each gets to take their first lock, but not the second. After that point none of the tasks can take the second lock since it is already held by one of the other tasks. Testing may not reveal this deadlock which only happens with certain schedules. For example, if we run these tasks in a sequential manner (first task T_1, then T_2, and then T_3), no deadlocks will occur. However, we can record the lockings and unlockings in a graph, as shown on the right of Fig. 1. Each node is a lock, and an edge is drawn from a lock l_x to a lock l_y, labelled with task T_z if task T_z at some point holds lock l_x while taking lock l_y. If this graph ends up containing a cycle, as in this case, we have detected the potential for a deadlock.

Traditional implementations of such deadlock-potential checkers are coded as algorithms in a programming language [10]. An alternative is to formulate such a checker in a logic as a monitor specification, expressing that there must be no such cycles. The general case involves a cycle between any number n of tasks. It turns out, however, that traditional temporal logic is not expressive enough for the case where n is unknown (it can vary at execution time). Temporal logic solutions for exactly two tasks are shown in [3,34]. For example, the solution provided in [34] has the following form (with some minor changes for presentation purposes) expressed in linear temporal logic (LTL) extended with data, and stating the property that no cycles should exist between two tasks and locks:

$\forall t_1, t_2 : Task, l_1, l_2 : Lock \ \bullet$
  $\mathbf{G} \ ($
    $\neg lock(t_1, l_2) \ \mathbf{U} \ (lock(t_1, l_1) \wedge (\neg unlock(t_1, l_1) \ \mathbf{U} \ lock(t_1, l_2)))$
    $\rightarrow$
    $\mathbf{G} \ \neg(\neg lock(t_2, l_1) \ \mathbf{U} \ (lock(t_2, l_2) \wedge (\neg unlock(t_2, l_2) \ \mathbf{U} \ lock(t_2, l_1))))$
  $)$

This formula can be read as follows: always (**G**), **if** task t_1 does not take lock l_2 until (**U**) it takes lock l_1, and from then on does not release l_1 until (**U**) it takes l_2, **then** always (**G**), it is not the case that task t_2 follows the opposite pattern. Besides being cumbersome to read, it only captures the situation for two tasks and two locks. As we show in the next section, using a rule-based logic makes it possible to express the property for an arbitrary number of tasks.

2.2 Formulating Deadlock Detection in LOGFIRE

Assume that our traces contain the two events: lock(t,l) and unlock(t,l). The cycle detection property (that no cycles should exist) is shown in Fig. 2. The main component of LOGFIRE is the **trait**[1] *Monitor*, which any user-defined monitor must extend to get access to the constants and methods provided by the rule DSL. The *events* lock and unlock are short-lived instantaneous observations about the system being monitored, those submitted to the monitor. In contrast, *facts*, in this case Locked and Edge, are long-lived pieces of information stored in the fact memory of the rule system, generated and deleted explicitly by the rules. The monitor contains five rules. Each rule has the form:

$$name -- condition_1 \& \ldots \& condition_n \longmapsto action$$

Event and fact names, as well as parameter names are values of the SCALA type *Symbol*, which contains quoted identifiers such as 't. The rules read as follows. The first rule, named lock, states that on observation of a lock('t, 'l) event we insert a Locked('t, 'l) fact in the fact memory, representing the fact that task t holds the lock l. The second rule, named unlock, states that if a task t holds a lock l (represented by Locked('t, 'l)), and an unlock('t, 'l) event is observed, then that Locked fact is removed from the fact memory. The third rule, named edge, states that if a task t holds a lock l1 (represented by Locked('t, 'l1), and a lock('t, 'l2) event is observed, then an edge from l1 to l2 is drawn. The fourth rule, named close, performs the transitive closure of the edge-relation. Note that LOGFIRE for each event first evaluates all left-hand sides, recording which evaluate to true. Then it deletes the event from the fact memory, evaluates all the corresponding right-hand sides, and continues evaluating rules until a fixed point is reached (infinite loops are possible to program by a mistake). Only hereafter is the next event is consumed. This special handling of events is one difference wrt. the original RETE algorithm described in [16,19]. The last rule, named cycle, detects cycles in the graph. It states that if there is an edge from a lock to itself then it is considered a deadlock potential. Symbols representing bindings of parameter values must be accessed with special get functions.

A monitor can be applied as shown in Fig. 3. Since the trace exposes a deadlock potential, an error trace is produced as shown in Fig. 4. Each entry in the error trace shows the number of the event, the event, the fact that it causes to be generated, and the rule that triggers.

---

[1] A **trait** in SCALA is a module concept closely related to the notion of an *abstract class*, as for example found in JAVA.

```
class NoLockCycles extends Monitor {
  val lock, unlock = event
  val Locked, Edge = fact

  "lock" —— lock('t,'l) ⟼ insert(Locked('t,'l))

  "unlock" —— Locked('t,'l) & unlock('t,'l) ⟼ remove(Locked)

  "edge" —— Locked('t,'l1) & lock('t,'l2) ⟼ insert(Edge('l1,'l2))

  "close" —— Edge('l1,'l2) & Edge('l2,'l3) & not(Edge('l1,'l3)) ⟼
    insert(Edge('l1,'l3))

  "cycle" —— Edge('l1,'l2) ⟼ {
    if (get('l1) == get('l2)) fail("cycle detected on " + get('l1))
  }
}
```

Fig. 2. No-lock-cycles property in LOGFIRE

2.3   Improving the Specification

The deadlock potential detection specification shown in Fig. 2 can be improved in three ways. Firstly, it can yield false positives. It will for example report a deadlock potential for a single task that accesses locks in a cyclic manner, although a single task cannot deadlock on its own (assuming reentrant locks). In order to exclude such false positives (although it can be argued that any cycles should be avoided), edges in the lock graph should be labelled with task ids, and a cycle is only reported in case all the task ids on the edges of the cycle are different. Secondly, the monitor will report the same deadlock potential multiple times due to the fact that different cycles (starting in different locks) represent the same problem. Thirdly, lock(t,l) and unlock(t,l) events are assumed to have exactly two arguments. Events in general may have many arguments, and instead of referring to them in a positional style as shown, we may want to pick out those arguments we are interested in by name, as for example with the notation unlock('task → 't, 'lock → 'l). The alternative specification shown in Fig. 5 is an attempt to make these improvements and to illustrate additional features of LOGFIRE.

As can be seen, event arguments are referred to by name, as in unlock('task → 't,'lock → 'l). Each edge now also includes a set of task ids, namely those involved in forming the edge. A check in rule close is now performed that two edges can only be composed (transitive closure) if their task ids differ. We see here the use of set operations and sets as arguments to facts. Finally, in order to avoid a deadlock between a set of tasks to be reported multiple times, a

```
object ApplyMonitor {
  def main(args: Array[String]) {
    val m = new NoLockCycles

    m.addEvent('lock)(1, "11")
    m.addEvent('lock)(1, "12")
    m.addEvent('unlock)(1, "12")
    m.addEvent('unlock)(1, "11")

    m.addEvent('lock)(2, "12")
    m.addEvent('lock)(2, "13")
    m.addEvent('unlock)(2, "13")
    m.addEvent('unlock)(2, "12")

    m.addEvent('lock)(3, "13")
    m.addEvent('lock)(3, "11")
    m.addEvent('unlock)(3, "11")
    m.addEvent('unlock)(3, "13")
  }
}
```

Fig. 3. Applying the lock pattern monitor to a trace corresponding to executing the three tasks in Fig. 1 in sequential order

variable is declared in the monitor, storing the sets of tasks that have so far been reported being involved in a deadlock potential. The rule `cycle` avoids to report a deadlock potential between a set of tasks in case a such has already been reported for those tasks. This illustrates how rules can be mixed with SCALA code, including declaration of variables and methods.

3   Analyzing Telemetry from the Curiosity Rover

In this section, we describe how we have used LOGFIRE to process telemetry received from the Curiosity rover on Mars. Our focus here is on building tools based on LOGFIRE for processing telemetry in order to generate summaries that can be used for creating effective visualizations for use by the daily operations team. Our tools are integrated into the mission ground data system, and receive and automatically process telemetry from the rover several times a day. As this telemetry is processed, the tools generate summary files, typically in comma separated values (CSV) format. These summary files are in turn used by visualizations built using the D3 library [12]; these visualizations are used as part of a "dashboard" that is regularly monitored by mission operators and science planners.

```
[1]   'lock(1,"11") ⟹ 'Locked(1,"11")
      rule : "lock" −− 'lock('t,'l) ⟼ {...}

[2]   'lock(1,"12") ⟹ 'Edge("11","12")
      rule : "edge" −− 'Locked('t,'l1) & 'lock('t,'l2) ⟼ {...}

[5]   'lock(2,"12") ⟹ 'Locked(2,"12")
      rule : "lock" −− 'lock('t,'l) ⟼ {...}

[6]   'lock(2,"13") ⟹ 'Edge("11","13")
      rule : "close" −− 'Edge('l1,'l2) & 'Edge('l2,'l3) & not('Edge('l1,'l3)) ⟼
              { ... }

[6]   'lock(2,"13") ⟹ 'Edge("12","13")
      rule : "edge" −− 'Locked('t,'l1) & 'lock('t,'l2) ⟼ {...}

[9]   'lock(3,"13") ⟹ 'Locked(3,"13")
      rule : "lock" −− 'lock('t,'l) ⟼ {...}

[10]  'lock(3,"11") ⟹ 'Edge("13","11")
      rule : "edge" −− 'Locked('t,'l1) & 'lock('t,'l2) ⟼ {...}

[10]  'lock(3,"11") ⟹ 'Edge("11","11")
      rule : "close" −− 'Edge('l1,'l2) & 'Edge('l2,'l3) & not('Edge('l1,'l3)) ⟼
              { ... }

[10]  'lock(3,"11") ⟹ 'Fail("ERROR cycle detected on 11")
      rule : "cycle" −− 'Edge('l1,'l2) ⟼ {...}
```

Fig. 4. An error trace representing a lock cycle

In the following subsections, we give two examples of telemetry processing tools and show how they are used in building useful visualizations.[2]

3.1   Monitoring Sequence Execution Status

The first example shows a tool that monitors execution of spacecraft *sequences*. A sequence is a list of commands that perform specific spacecraft actions such as taking an image, or deleting a file, or possibly even invoking another sequence. The operations team typically uplinks a list of sequences every other day containing the commands that the rover should perform over the next two days.

---

[2] In the interests of readability, and to comply with NASA restrictions on publishing mission data, we have simplified the examples and modified the actual names and times from actual telemetry.

```
class NoLockCyclesImproved extends Monitor {
  val lock, unlock = event
  val Locked, Edge = fact

  def getset (s: Symbol) = get[Set[Int]]( s)

  var cycles : Set[Set[Int ]] = Set()

  "lock" −− lock('task → 't ,' lock  →  'l) ⟼ insert(Locked('t ,' l ))

  "unlock" −− Locked('t,'l) & unlock('task → 't ,' lock  ↦  'l) ⟼
    remove(Locked)

  "edge" −− Locked('t,'l1) & lock('task  →  't ,' lock  →  'l2) ⟼
    insert (Edge(Set(get[Int ]('t )),' l1 ,' l2 ))

  "close" −− Edge('s1,'l1,'l2) & Edge('s2,'l2 ,' l3) & not(Edge('_,'l1 ,' l3 )) ⟼
  {
    if ( getset ('s1). intersect ( getset ('s2 )). isEmpty)
      insert (Edge(getset ('s1). union( getset ('s2 )),' l1 ,' l3 ))
  }

  "cycle" −− Edge('s,'l1,'l2) ⟼
  {
    if (get ('l1) == get('l2) & !cycles . contains ( getset ('s)))
      fail ("cycle detected between tasks" + get('s))
    cycles += getset('s)
  }
}
```

Fig. 5. Improved no-lock-cycles property in LOGFIRE

This includes mobility requests (such as driving to a specific location), science requests (such as taking a panorama or firing a laser), as well as engineering requests (such as deleting old data files to free up space on flash memory).

Figure 6 shows the rules for processing telemetry related to sequence execution. These rules rely on processing an *event log* which is generated on board and sent to the ground periodically. The event log consists of a list of EVRs (short for "event reports"); each EVR has an associated timestamp (indicating the sclk, or *spacecraft clock* time when the event occurred), a unique identifier, and a text *message* describing the event. The SeqMonitor class extends the trait EvrMonitor, which itself extends trait Monitor, and in addition defines various utilities, such as the EVR event. The rule start_seq is triggered by the log event EVR_SEQ_START and adds a fact SeqStart to the fact memory, recording the name and start time

```
class SeqMonitor extends EvrMonitor {
  val SeqStart, SeqDone = fact
  def seq_name(s:String) = words(s)(2) // Helper function

  "start_seq" —— EVR('id → "EVR_SEQ_START", 'sclk → 'S, 'msg → 'M) ⟼ {
    val w = words('M.s)
    val seq_name = w(15).slice(1, w(15).length−2)
    insert (SeqStart(seq_name, 'S.d))
  }

  "end_seq_ok" —— EVR('id → "EVR_SEQ_SUCCESS", 'sclk → 'E, 'msg → 'M)
               & 'SeqStart('name, 'S) ⟼ {
    if (seq_name('M.s) == 'sname.s) {
      replace(SeqStart)(SeqDone('name.s, 'S.d, 'E.d, "OK"))
    }
  }

  "end_seq_fail" —— EVR('id → "EVR_SEQ_FAILURE", 'sclk → 'F, 'msg → 'M)
                 & 'SeqStart('name, 'S) ⟼ {
    if (seq_name('M.s) == 'name.s) {
      replace(SeqStart)(SeqDone('name.s, 'S.d, 'F.d, "FAIL"))
    }
  }

  "print" —— SeqDone('name, 'S, 'E, 'stat) ⟼ {
    updateCSV('name.s, 'S.d, 'E.d, 'stat.s)
    remove(SeqDone)
  }
}
```

Fig. 6. Rules for sequence execution

of the sequence. A sequence may terminate either successfully or unsuccessfully. A successful termination is denoted by the event EVR_SEQ_SUCCESS, which results in the SeqStart fact being replaced by a fact SeqDone, which records the name, start and end times of the sequence, along with the status OK, indicating that the sequence completed successfully. A sequence that terminates with failure results in the SeqStart fact being replaced by a fact SeqDone, which records the name, start and end times as before, along with the status FAIL. Finally, the print rule updates a CSV file containing a row for each sequence invocation, recording the start and end times and execution status.

This CSV file is useful for building various visualizations that track how ground commands are being performed by the rover. As an example, Fig. 7 shows a visualization used by the data management operations team to compare the

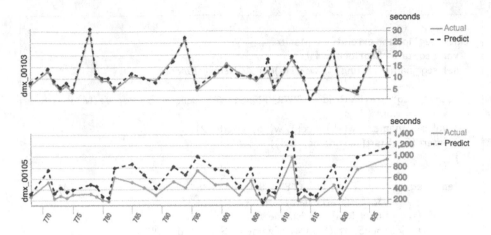

Fig. 7. Visualization showing actual vs predicted sequence run times

actual onboard execution times across multiple days (shown on the x-axis) for two sequences (dmx_00103 and dmx_00105) against the times predicted by ground tools. As the figure shows, such a visualization makes it easy to see that the predictions for the dmx_00103 sequence are much more accurate than the predictions for the dmx_00105 sequence. This observation can then be used to further refine the models used by the ground tools to improve prediction times.

3.2   Monitoring Communication Windows

Figure 8 shows the rules used for monitoring Curiosity's *communication windows* [30]. A communication window defines the periods when the spacecraft communicates either directly with Earth, or with one of several relay orbiting spacecraft. Due to the importance of communication, monitoring rover performance during a window is of great interest to the operations team. To aid this monitoring, we developed a set of rules that are used to generate summaries from rover telemetry; these summaries are in turn used to build useful visualizations that help the operational team monitor window performance.

A communication window consists of 3 phases – a *prep* phase, when on-board software configures the rover for the communication window (for instance, by turning on appropriate radios and retrieving from various cameras the images that will be sent to Earth); an *active* phase, during which the communication takes place; and a *cleanup* phase, for performing any cleanup actions (for instance, turning the radios off). Figure 8 shows four rules for processing telemetry for a communication window. The prep rule is triggered by the event EVR_BEGINS_PREP that indicates the start of a communication window; it adds the fact Prep(w, p) to the fact memory. Here w is the (unique) integer identifier associated with the window (this identifier is reported in the event message, and is extracted by the helper *wid* function shown in the example), and p is

```
class CommWindowMonitor extends EvrMonitor {
  def wid(s: String, k: Int=5) = { val w = words(s)(k) ; w. slice (1,w.length). toInt }

  "prep" —— EVR('id → "EVR_BEGIN_PREP", 'sclk → 'P, 'msg → 'M) ↦ {
    insert (' Prep(wid('M.s,4),  'P.d))
  }

  "active" —— EVR('id → "EVR_BEGIN_ACTIVE", 'sclk → 'A, 'msg → 'M)
            & 'Prep('W, 'P) ↦ {
    if  (wid('M.s,2) == 'W.i) {
      insert (' Active ('W.i,  'A.d))
    }
  }

  "cleanup" —— EVR('id → "EVR_CLEANUP", 'sclk → 'C, 'msg → 'M)
             & 'Active('W, 'A) ↦ {
    if  (wid('M.s,1) == 'W.i) {
      insert (' Cleanup('W.i,  'C.d)
    }
  }

  "print" —— 'Prep('W, 'P) & 'Active('W, 'A) & 'Cleanup('W, 'C) ↦ {
    updateCSV('W.i, 'P.d, 'A.d, 'C.d)
    remove('Prep)
    remove('Active)
    remove('Cleanup)
  }
}
```

Fig. 8. Rules for communication windows

the event timestamp (which indicates the time when prep started). Next, the `active` rule is used to detect when the active window begins; it is triggered by the EVR_BEGINS_ACTIVE event, and adds the fact Active(w, a) to the fact memory, where w is the window identifier and a is the event timestamp. In a similar fashion, the `cleanup` rule is triggered by the EVR_CLEANUP event, and adds the Cleanup fact to the memory. Finally, the `print` rule updates a CSV file that defines all windows that have been performed on the rover; each row of this CSV file contains the window identifier and times when the prep, active and cleanup phases started.

The CSV files are used to build the visualization shown in Fig. 9. This visualization uses the window definitions in the CSV file to provide context for assessing window performance. The top graph in the figure shows the percentage of CPU time taken up by various tasks, including the DMS and PDP tasks

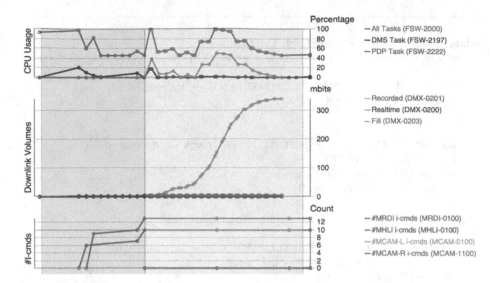

Fig. 9. Visualization showing communication window performance

which respectively read files from flash memory and generate data packets for downlink. The middle graph shows the volume of data sent through the radio to an overhead orbiter; as the figure shows, the downlink rate varies over time, reaching a maximum rate when the orbiter is directly overhead (approximately halfway into the active session). Finally, the bottom graph shows the number of images fetched from each of the four cameras during window prep; in the example shown, the software fetched 13 images from the MHLI camera and 10 images from the MRDI camera (and no images from the other two cameras). Such visualizations are useful to the operations team, which can use them to determine, for instance, that the PDP task needs 40 % of the CPU for packet generation when the radio is communicating at its highest rates. This knowledge helps guide decisions on whether or not to schedule other processor-intensive activities during communication windows.

4   Conclusion and Future Work

We have described the use of a rule-based engine, the LOGFIRE SCALA library, in building applications for processing telemetry. The applications are not limited to checking specific logical or temporal properties (as is common in runtime verification), but in addition generate summaries that are used to build effective visualizations supporting systems comprehension. We have described how these telemetry analysis applications are being deployed to process telemetry and build visualizations illustrating various aspects of the behavior of the Curiosity rover. The rule-based notation is shown to be sufficiently expressive and convenient for the task. The combination of a monitoring logic with a high-level programming language, in this case SCALA, has turned out to be a crucial advantage.

Future work includes studying alternatives for defining the internal LOGFIRE DSL. LOGFIRE is a *deep embedding*, meaning that we have defined the abstract syntax for rules in SCALA, in contrast to a *shallow embedding* as in [23], where we would have used SCALA's own language constructs for writing rules. This again means that as a default there is no type checking of rules beyond what we program it to be. Another consequence is that user-defined names must be either strings or symbols (of the SCALA class Symbol), and to get to their values, in case they represent event/fact parameters, the user has to apply get functions. A more elegant solution could potentially be achieved by defining the DSL as a syntactic extension of SCALA, for example using the SUGARSCALA tool available at [35] (part of SUGARJ). Finally, the intention is to deploy LOGFIRE more broadly, within MSL, as well as within other missions, as a general approach to log analysis and comprehension at JPL.

References

1. Allan, C., Avgustinov, P., Christensen, A.S., Hendren, L., Kuzins, S., Lhoták, O., de Moor, O., Sereni, D., Sittamplan, G., Tibble, J.: Adding trace matching with free variables to AspectJ. In: OOPSLA 2005. ACM Press (2005)
2. Barringer, H., Falcone, Y., Havelund, K., Reger, G., Rydeheard, D.: Quantified event automata: towards expressive and efficient runtime monitors. In: Giannakopoulou, D., Méry, D. (eds.) FM 2012. LNCS, vol. 7436, pp. 68–84. Springer, Heidelberg (2012)
3. Barringer, H., Goldberg, A., Havelund, K., Sen, K.: Program monitoring with LTL in eagle. In: Parallel and Distributed Systems: Testing and Debugging (PADTAD 2004), Santa Fee, New Mexico, USA, vol. 17. IEEE Computer Society, April 2004
4. Barringer, H., Goldberg, A., Havelund, K., Sen, K.: Rule-based runtime verification. In: Steffen, B., Levi, G. (eds.) VMCAI 2004. LNCS, vol. 2937, pp. 44–57. Springer, Heidelberg (2004)
5. Barringer, H., Havelund, K.: TRACECONTRACT: A scala dsl for trace analysis. In: Butler, M., Schulte, W. (eds.) FM 2011. LNCS, vol. 6664, pp. 57–72. Springer, Heidelberg (2011)
6. Barringer, H., Havelund, K., Kurklu, E., Morris, R.: Checking flight rules with TraceContract: application of a scala DSL for trace analysis. In: Scala Days 2011, Stanford University, California (2011)
7. Barringer, H., Rydeheard, D.E., Havelund, K.: Rule systems for run-time monitoring: from Eagle to RuleR. J. Log. Comput. **20**(3), 675–706 (2010)
8. Basin, D., Klaedtke, F., Müller, S.: Policy monitoring in first-order temporal logic. In: Touili, T., Cook, B., Jackson, P. (eds.) CAV 2010. LNCS, vol. 6174, pp. 1–18. Springer, Heidelberg (2010)
9. Bauer, A., Küster, J.-C., Vegliach, G.: From propositional to first-order monitoring. In: Legay, A., Bensalem, S. (eds.) RV 2013. LNCS, vol. 8174, pp. 59–75. Springer, Heidelberg (2013)
10. Bensalem, S., Havelund, K.: Dynamic deadlock analysis of multi-threaded programs. In: Ur, S., Bin, E., Wolfsthal, Y. (eds.) HVC 2005. LNCS, vol. 3875, pp. 208–223. Springer, Heidelberg (2006)
11. Bodden, E.: MOPBox: a library approach to runtime verification. In: Khurshid, S., Sen, K. (eds.) RV 2011. LNCS, vol. 7186, pp. 365–369. Springer, Heidelberg (2012)

12. Bostock, M., Ogievetsky, V., Heer, J.: D3: Data-driven documents. IEEE Trans. Vis. Comput. Graph. **17**, 2301–2309 (2011)
13. Clips website. http://clipsrules.sourceforge.net
14. D3 website. http://d3js.org
15. Decker, N., Leucker, M., Thoma, D.: Monitoring modulo theories. In: Ábrahám, E., Havelund, K. (eds.) TACAS 2014. LNCS, vol. 8413, pp. 341–356. Springer, Heidelberg (2014)
16. Doorenbos, R.B.: Production matching for large learning systems, Ph.D. thesis, Carnegie Mellon University, Pittsburgh, PA (1995)
17. Drools website. http://www.jboss.org/drools
18. Drools functional programming extensions website. https://community.jboss.org/wiki/FunctionalProgrammingInDrools
19. Forgy, C.: Rete: a fast algorithm for the many pattern/many object pattern match problem. Artif. Intell. **19**, 17–37 (1982)
20. Fusco, M.: Hammurabi - a Scala rule engine. In: Scala Days 2011, Stanford University, California (2011)
21. Goubault-Larrecq, J., Olivain, J.: A smell of ORCHIDS. In: Leucker, M. (ed.) RV 2008. LNCS, vol. 5289, pp. 1–20. Springer, Heidelberg (2008)
22. Hallé, S., Villemaire, R.: Runtime enforcement of web service message contracts with data. IEEE Trans. Serv. Comput. **5**(2), 192–206 (2012)
23. Havelund, K.: Data automata in Scala. In: Leucker, M., Wang, J., (eds.) Proceedings of the 8th International Symposium on Theoretical Aspects of Software Engineering, TASE 2014, Changsha, China, 1–3 September. IEEE Computer Society Press (2014)
24. Havelund, K.: Monitoring with data automata. In: Margaria, T., Steffen, B. (eds.) ISoLA 2014, Part II. LNCS, vol. 8803, pp. 254–273. Springer, Heidelberg (2014)
25. Havelund, K.: Rule-based runtime verification revisited. Softw. Tools Technol. Transf. (STTT) **17**(2), 143–170 (2015)
26. Havelund, K., Joshi, R.: Comprehension of spacecraft telemetry using hierarchical specifications of behavior. In: Merz, S., Pang, J. (eds.) ICFEM 2014. LNCS, vol. 8829, pp. 187–202. Springer, Heidelberg (2014)
27. Jess website. http://www.jessrules.com/jess
28. Luckham, D. (ed.): The Power of Events: An Introduction to Complex Event Processing in Distributed Enterprise Systems. Addison-Wesley, Reading (2002)
29. Lunar Atmosphere Dust Environment Explorer (LADEE) mission website. http://www.nasa.gov/mission_pages/LADEE/main
30. Makovsky, A., Ilott, P., Taylor, J.: Mars science laboratory telecommunications system design. Descanso Design and Performance Summary Series, Article 14 (2009)
31. Mars Science Laboratory (MSL) mission website. http://mars.jpl.nasa.gov/msl
32. Meredith, P., Jin, D., Griffith, D., Chen, F., Rou, G.: An overview of the MOP runtime verification framework. Softw. Tools Technol. Transf. (STTT) **14**(3), 249–289 (2012)
33. Rooscaloo website. http://code.google.com/p/rooscaloo
34. Stolz, V., Bodden, E.: Temporal assertions using AspectJ. In: Proceedings of the 5th International Workshop on Runtime Verification (RV 2005), vol. 144, no. 4, ENTCS, pp. 109–124. Elsevier (2006)
35. SugarJ website. http://www.student.informatik.tu-darmstadt.de/~xx00seba/projects/sugarj

Safety, Dependability and Performance Analysis of Aerospace Systems

Thomas Noll[✉]

Software Modeling and Verification Group,
RWTH Aachen University, Aachen, Germany
noll@cs.rwth-aachen.de
http://moves.rwth-aachen.de/

Abstract. The size and complexity of software in spacecraft is increasing exponentially, and this trend complicates its validation within the context of the overall spacecraft system. Current validation methods are labour-intensive as they rely on manual analysis, review and inspection. In this paper we give an overview of an integrated system-software co-engineering approach focusing on a coherent set of specification and analysis techniques for evaluation of system-level correctness, safety, dependability and performability of on-board computer-based aerospace systems. It features both a tailored modelling language and toolset for supporting (semi-)automated validation activities. Our modelling language is a dialect of the Architecture Analysis and Design Language, AADL, and enables engineers to specify the system, the software, and their reliability aspects. The COMPASS toolset employs state-of-the-art model checking techniques, both qualitative and probabilistic, for the analysis of requirements related to functional correctness, safety, dependability and performance.

1 Introduction

Building modern aerospace systems is highly demanding. They should be extremely dependable, offering service without interruption (i.e., without failure) for a very long time – typically years or decades. Whereas "five nines" dependability, i.e., a 99.999 % availability, is satisfactory for most safety-critical systems, for aerospace on-board systems it is not. Faults are costly and may severely damage reputations. Dramatic examples are known. Fatal defects in the control software of the Ariane-5 rocket and the Mars Pathfinder have led to headlines in newspapers all over the world. Rigorous design support and analysis techniques are called for. Bugs must be found as early as possible in the design process while performance and reliability guarantees need to be checked

We thank all co-workers in the COMPASS project for their contributions, including the groups of Alessandro Cimatti (FBK, Trento, IT), Xavier Olive (Thales Alenia Space, FR), David Lesens (Airbus Defence and Space, FR) and Yuri Yushtein (ESA/ESTEC, NL). This research has been funded by the European Space Agency via several grants.

© Springer International Publishing Switzerland 2015
C. Artho and P.C. Ölveczky (Eds.): FTSCS 2014, CCIS 476, pp. 17–31, 2015.
DOI: 10.1007/978-3-319-17581-2_2

whenever possible. The effect of fault diagnosis, isolation and recovery must be quantifiable.

Tailored effective techniques exist for specific system-level aspects. Peer reviewing and extensive testing detect most of the software bugs, performance is checked using queueing networks or simulation, and hardware safety levels are analysed using a profiled Failure Modes and Effects Analysis (FMEA) approach. Fine. But how is the consistency between the analysis results ensured? What is the relevance of a zero-bug confirmation if its analysis is based on a system view that ignores critical performance bottlenecks? There is a clear need for an integrated, coherent approach! This is easier said than done: the inherent heterogeneous character of on-board systems involving software, sensors, actuators, hydraulics, electrical components, etc., each with its own specific development approach, severely complicates this.

The COMPASS project [15] advances the system-software perspective by providing means for its validation in the early design phases, such that system architecture, software architecture, and their interfacing requirements are aligned with the overall functional intents and risk tolerances. Validation in the current practice is labour-intensive and consists mostly of manual analysis, review and inspection. We improve upon this by adopting a *model-based approach* using formal methods. In COMPASS, the system, the software and its reliability models are expressed in a single modelling language. This language originated from the need for a language with a rigorous formal semantics, and it is a dialect of the Architecture Analysis & Design Language (AADL). Models expressed in our AADL dialect are processed by the COMPASS toolset that automates analyses which are currently done manually. The automated analyses allow studying functional correctness of discrete, real-time and hybrid aspects under degraded modes of operation, generating safety & dependability validation artefacts, performing probabilistic risk assessments, and evaluating effectiveness of fault management. The analyses are mapped onto discrete, symbolic and probabilistic model checkers, but all of them are completely hidden away from the user by appropriate model-transformations. The COMPASS toolset is thus providing an easy-to-use push-button analysis technology.

The first ideas and concepts for the development of the COMPASS toolset emerged in 2007, due to a series of significant advances in model checking [2], and especially in its probabilistic counterpart [1]. These advances opened prospects for an integrated model-based approach towards system-software correctness validation, safety & dependability assessment and performance evaluation during the design phase. Its technology readiness level was estimated at level 1, i.e. basic principles were observed and reported. The European Space Agency (ESA) issued a statement of work to improve system-software co-engineering and this was commissioned to the COMPASS consortium consisting of RWTH Aachen University, Fondazione Bruno Kessler and Thales Alenia Space. Development started soon after, and in 2009 a COMPASS toolset prototype was delivered to the European space industry. Maturation was followed by subsystem-level case studies performed by Thales Alenia Space [10]. As of 2012, two large pilot projects took place in ESA for a spacecraft in development. This marked the maturation of the COMPASS toolset to early level 4, namely laboratory-tested. This paper summarises the background work. Altogether, it describes the current state of the art in system-software spacecraft co-engineering, ranging from the used techniques, to the tools and the conducted industrial projects.

The remainder is organised as follows. An introduction to the developed modelling language is given in Sect. 2, followed by an overview of the toolset and its supported analyses in Sect. 3. Section 4 draws a conclusion about the evaluation activities.

2   Modelling Using an AADL Dialect

The Architecture Analysis and Design Language (AADL) [24,35] is an industry standard for modelling safety-critical system architectures and it is developed and governed by the Society of Automotive Engineers (SAE). Although standardized by the SAE, it is backed by the aerospace community as well. AADL provides a cohesive and uniform approach to model heterogeneous systems, consisting of software (e.g., processes and threads) and hardware (e.g., processors and buses) components, and their interactions. Our variant of AADL was designed to meet the needs of the European space industry. It extends a core fragment of AADL 1.0 [32] by supporting the following essential features:

- Modelling both the system's *nominal and faulty behaviour*. To this aim, AADL provides primitives to describe software and hardware faults, error propagation (i.e., turning fault occurrences into failure events), sporadic (transient) and permanent faults, and degraded operation modes (by mapping failures from architectural to service level).
- Modelling (partial) *observability* and the associated observability requirements. These notions are essential to deal with diagnosability and Fault Detection, Isolation and Recovery (FDIR) analyses.
- Specifying *timed and hybrid behaviour*. In particular, to analyze continuous physical systems such as mechanics and hydraulics, our modelling language supports continuous real-valued variables with (linear) time-dependent dynamics.
- Modelling *probabilistic* aspects. These are important to specify random faults and systems repairs with stochastic timing.

In the following, we present the capabilities of our AADL dialect using a running example. A complete AADL specification consists of three parts, namely a description of the nominal behaviour, a description of the error behaviour and a fault injection specification that describes how the error behaviour influences the nominal behaviour. These three parts are discussed below. Due to space constraints, we refer the interested reader to [12] for a description of the formal semantics.

2.1   Nominal Behaviour

An AADL model is hierarchically organized into *components*, distinguished into software (processes, threads, data), hardware (processors, memories, devices, buses), and composite components (called *systems*). Components are defined by their *type* (specifying the functional interfaces as seen by the environment) and their *implementation* (representing the internal structure). An example of a component's type and implementation for a simple battery device [8] is shown in Fig. 1.

The component type describes the ports through which the component communicates. For example, the type interface of Fig. 1 features three ports, namely an outgoing event port `empty` which indicates that the battery is about to become discharged, an incoming data port `tryReset` which indicates that the battery device should (attempt to) reset, and an outgoing data port `voltage` which makes its current voltage level accessible to the environment.

A component implementation defines its subcomponents, their interaction through (event and data) port connections, the (physical) bindings at runtime, the operational behaviour via modes, the transitions between them, which are spontaneous or triggered by events arriving at the ports, and the timing and hybrid behaviour of the component. For example, the implementation of Fig. 1 specifies the battery to be in the `charged` mode whenever activated, with an `energy` level of 100 % as indicated by the `default` value of 1.0. This level is continuously decreased by 2 % (of the initial amount) per time unit (`energy'` denotes the first derivative of `energy`) until a threshold value of 20 % is reached, upon which the battery changes to the `depleted` mode. This mode transition triggers the `empty` output event, and the loss rate of energy is increased to 3 %. Moreover, the `voltage` value is regularly computed from the `energy` level (ranging between 6.0 and 4.0 [volts]) and made accessible to the environment via the corresponding outgoing data port. In addition, the battery reacts to the `tryReset` port to decide when a `reset` operation should be performed in reaction to faulty behaviour (see the description of error models below).

In general, the mode transition system—basically a finite-state automaton—describes how the component evolves from mode to mode while performing events. Invariants on the values of data components (such as "`energy >= 0.2`" in mode `charged`) restrict the residence time in a mode. Trajectory equations (such as those associated with `energy'`) specify how continuous variables evolve while residing in a mode. This is akin to timed and hybrid automata [28]. Here we assume that all invariants are linear. Moreover we constrain the derivatives occurring in trajectory equations to real constants, i.e., the evolution of continuous variables is described by simple linear functions.

A mode transition is given by $m - [e$ **when** g **then** $f] -> m'$. It asserts that the component can evolve from mode m to mode m' upon occurrence of event e (the trigger event) provided that guard g, a Boolean expression that may depend on the component's (discrete and continuous) data elements, holds. Here "data elements" refers to (both incoming and outgoing) data ports and

```
device Battery
  features
    empty: out event port;
    tryReset: in data port bool default false;
    voltage: out data port real default 6.0;
end Battery;
device implementation Battery.Imp
  subcomponents
    energy: data continuous default 1.0;
  modes
    charged: initial mode while energy' = -0.02 and energy >= 0.2;
    depleted: mode while energy' = -0.03 and energy >= 0.0;
  transitions
    charged -[then voltage := 2.0*energy+4.0]-> charged;
    charged -[reset when tryReset]-> charged;
    charged -[empty when energy = 0.2]-> depleted;
    depleted -[then voltage := 2.0*energy+4.0]-> depleted;
    depleted -[reset when tryReset]-> depleted;
end Battery.Imp;
```

Fig. 1. Specification of a battery component.

```
system Power
  features
    alert: out data port bool observable;
end Power;
system implementation Power.Imp
  subcomponents
    batt1: device Battery in modes (primary);
    batt2: device Battery in modes (backup);
    mon: device Monitor;
  connections
    data port batt1.voltage -> mon.voltage in modes (primary);
    data port batt2.voltage -> mon.voltage in modes (backup);
    data port mon.alert -> alert;
    data port mon.alert -> batt1.tryReset in modes (primary);
    data port mon.alert -> batt2.tryReset in modes (backup);
  modes
    primary: initial mode;
    backup: mode;
  transitions
    primary -[batt1.empty]-> backup;
    backup -[batt2.empty]-> primary;
end Power.Imp;
```

Fig. 2. The complete power system.

```
device Monitor
  features
    voltage: in data port real;
    alert: out data port bool;
end Monitor;
device implementation Monitor.Imp
  flows
    alert := (voltage < 4.5);
end Monitor.Imp;
```

Fig. 3. Specification of the monitor.

data subcomponents of the respective component. On transiting, the effect f which may update data subcomponents or outgoing data ports (like voltage) is applied. The presence of event e, guard when g and effect then f is optional. If absent, e defaults to an internal event, g to true, and f to the empty effect.

Mode transitions may give rise to modifications of a component's configuration: subcomponents can become (de-)activated and port connections can be (de-)established. This depends on the in modes clause, which can be declared along with port connections and subcomponents. This is demonstrated by the specification in Fig. 2, which shows the usage of the battery component in the context of a redundant power system. It contains two instances of the battery device, namely batt1 and batt2, being respectively active in the primary and the backup mode. The mode switch that initiates reconfiguration is triggered by an empty event arriving from the battery that is currently active. The data ports are reconfigured too in this example. The voltage port of batt2 is connected to the overall power system once switched to the backup mode.

A similar reconfiguration is also performed for the alerts from the monitor component, which checks the current voltage level and raises an alarm if it falls below a critical threshold of 4.5 [volts]. Its specification is shown in Fig. 3; it employs another modelling concept, a so-called *flow*. A flow establishes a direct dependency between an outgoing data port of a component and (some of) its incoming data ports, meaning that a value update of one of the given incoming data ports immediately causes a corresponding update of the outgoing data port.

2.2 Error Behaviour

Error models are an extension to the specification of nominal models [34] and are used to conduct safety and dependability analyses. For modularity, they are defined separately from nominal specifications. Akin to nominal models, an error model is defined by its type and its associated implementation.

An error model *type* defines an interface in terms of error states and (incoming and outgoing) error propagations. Error *states* are employed to represent the current configuration of the component with respect to the occurrence of errors. Error *propagations* are used to exchange error information between components. They are similar to input and output event ports, but differ in that error events

```
error model BatteryFailure
  features
    ok: initial state;
    dead: error state;
    resetting: error state;
    batteryDied: out error propagation;
  end BatteryFailure;
error model implementation BatteryFailure.Imp
  events
    fault: error event occurrence poisson 0.001;
    works: error event occurrence poisson 0.2;
    fails: error event occurrence poisson 0.8;
  transitions
    ok -[fault]-> dead;
    dead -[batteryDied]-> dead;
    dead -[reset]-> resetting;
    resetting -[works]-> ok;
    resetting -[fails]-> dead;
  end BatteryFailure.Imp;
```

Fig. 4. Specification of the battery error model.

are matched by identifier rather than by an explicit declaration of an event port connection.

An error model *implementation* provides the structural details of the error model. It is defined by a (probabilistic) machine over the error states declared in the error model type. Transitions between states can be triggered by error events, reset events, and error propagations.

Figure 4 presents a basic error model for the battery device. It defines a probabilistic error event, fault, which occurs once every 1000 time units on average. Whenever this happens, the error model changes into the dead state. In the latter, the battery failure is signalled to the environment by means of the outgoing error propagation batteryDied. Moreover, the battery is enabled to receive a reset event from the nominal model to which the error behaviour is attached. It causes a transition to the resetting state, from which the battery recovers with a probability of 20 %, and returns to the dead state otherwise.

2.3 Fault Injection

As error models bear no relation with nominal models, an error model does not influence the nominal model unless they are linked through *fault injection*.

A fault injection describes the effect of the occurrence of an error on the nominal behaviour of the system. More concretely, it specifies the value update that a data element of a component implementation undergoes when its associated error model enters a specific error state. To this aim, each fault injection has to be given by the user by specifying three parts: a state s in the error model (such as `dead` in Fig. 4), an outgoing data port or subcomponent d in the nominal model (such as `voltage` in Fig. 1), and the fault effect given by the expression a (such as the value 0, indicating the collapse of power). Multiple fault injections between error models and nominal models are possible.

The automatic procedure that integrates both models and the given fault injections, the so-called *model extension*, works as follows. The principal idea is that the nominal and error models are running concurrently. That is, the state space of the extended model consists of pairs of nominal modes and error states, and each transition in the extended model is due to a nominal mode transition, an error state transition, or a combination of both (in case of a reset operation). The aforementioned fault injection becomes enabled whenever the error model enters state s. In this case the assignment $d := a$ is carried out, i.e., the data subcomponent d is assigned with the fault effect a. This error effect is maintained as long as the error model stays in state s, overriding possible assignments to d in the nominal model. When s is left, the fault injection is disabled (though another one may be enabled). An example of an extended model can be found in [12].

3   The COMPASS Toolset

The COMPASS toolset is the result of a significant implementation effort carried out by the COMPASS Consortium. The GUI and most subcomponents are implemented in Python, using the PyGTK library. Pre-existing components, such as the NuSMV and MRMC model checker, are instead written in C. Overall, the core of the toolset consists of about 100,000 lines of Python code. Figure 5 shows the functionality of the toolset.

COMPASS takes as input one or more AADL models, and a set of properties. The latter are provided in the form of instantiated property *patterns* [17,25], which are templates containing placeholders that have to be filled in by the user. The COMPASS toolset provides templates for the most frequently used patterns, that ease property specifications by non-experts through hiding the details of the underlying temporal logic. The tool generates several outputs, such as traces, fault trees and FMEA tables, diagnosability and performability measures.

The toolset builds upon the following main components. NuSMV [14,23] (New Symbolic Model Verifier) is a symbolic model checker that supports state-of-the-art verification techniques such as BDD-based and SAT-based verification for CTL and LTL [2]. MRMC [30,31] (Markov Reward Model Checker) is a probabilistic model checker that supports the analysis of discrete-time and continuous-time Markov reward models. Specifications are written in PCTL (Probabilistic Computation Tree Logic) and CSL (Continuous Stochastic Logic [1], a probabilistic real-time version of CTL). SigRef [37] is used to minimize, amongst others, Interactive Markov Chains (IMC) [29] based on various notions of bisimulation. It is a symbolic tool using multi-terminal BDD representations of IMCs and applies signature-based minimization algorithms. A walkthrough of the toolset in terms of its screenshots in shown in Fig. 6.

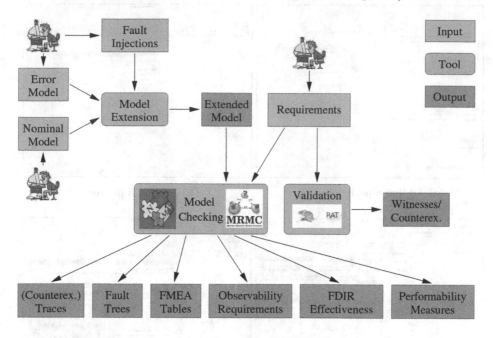

Fig. 5. Functional view of the COMPASS platform.

The tool also supports a graphical notation of our AADL dialect, that is a derivation of the AADL graphical notation [33]. We developed a graphical drawing editor enabling engineers to construct models visually using the adopted graphical notation. The editor is called the COMPASS Graphical Modeller and is part of the COMPASS toolset.

3.1 Functional Correctness

COMPASS supports random and guided *model-based simulation* of AADL models. Guided simulation can be performed by choosing either the next transition to be taken, or a target value for one or more variables. The generated traces can be inspected using a trace manager that displays the values of the model variables of interest (filtering is possible) for each step.

Property verification is based on model checking [2], an automated technique that verifies whether a property expressed in temporal logic, holds for a given model. Symbolic techniques [3,4,27] are used to tackle the problem of state space explosion. COMPASS relies on the NuSMV model checker, which supports both BDD-based and SAT-based verification for finite-state systems, and SMT-based verification techniques for timed and hybrid systems, based on the MathSAT solver [7,22]. On refutation of a property, a counterexample is generated, showing an execution trace of the model violating the property. An example of this is shown in Fig. 6(d). Finally, it is possible to run *deadlock checking*, in order to pinpoint deadlocks (i.e., states with no outgoing transitions) in the model.

26   T. Noll

(a) Adding a fault injection.   (b) Adding a property.

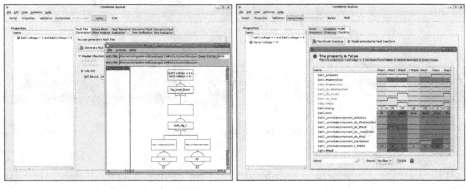

(c) A generated fault tree.   (d) A model-checking counterexample.

Fig. 6. Walkthrough of the COMPASS toolset.

3.2 Safety Assessment

COMPASS implements model-based safety assessment techniques, based on symbolic model checking [9,21], and supports traditional techniques such as *Failure Mode and Effects Analysis* (FMEA) [19] and *Fault Tree Analysis* (FTA) [18]. FMEA is an inductive technique that starts by identifying a set of (combinations of) failure modes and, using forward reasoning, assesses their impact on a set of system properties. The results are summarised in an *FMEA table*. It is also possible to generate *dynamic* FMEA tables, namely to enforce an order of occurrence between failure modes. FTA is a deductive technique, which, given a *top-level event* (TLE), i.e., the specification of an undesired condition, constructs all possible chains of basic faults that contribute to its occurrence. Pictorially, these chains are organized in a *fault tree* with a two-layer logical structure, corresponding to the disjunction of its minimal cut sets [9] (MCSs), where each MCS is a conjunction of basic faults. COMPASS also supports the generation of dynamic fault trees [6], where ordering constraints between basic faults are represented using priority AND (PAND) gates. Figure 6c depicts a simple fault tree for the power system model of Sect. 2, where the top level event is "batt1.voltage < 4.0 and batt2.voltage < 4.0". The tree shows that the only cause that can lead to the occurrence of TLE is when both batteries die.

3.3 Diagnosability and FDIR Analysis

The COMPASS toolset supports diagnosability and FDIR (Fault Detection, Isolation and Recovery) effectiveness analysis. These analyses work under the hypothesis of *partial observability*. Variables and ports in our AADL dialect can be declared to be observable (see, e.g., the data port alert in Fig. 2).

Diagnosability analysis investigates the possibility for an ideal diagnosis system to infer accurate and sufficient run-time information on the behaviour of the observed system. The COMPASS toolset follows the approach described in [13], where the violation of a diagnosability condition is reduced to the search of *critical pairs* in the so-called *twin plant* model, i.e., a pair of executions that are observationally indistinguishable but hide conditions that should be distinguished. As an example, property "batt1.voltage < 4.0 and batt2.voltage < 4.0" is not diagnosable, as the alert observable does not allow to distinguish the case where the batteries' voltages are low from the case where they are depleted through use. If we add the observable "alert2 := (voltage < 4.0)", then the property becomes diagnosable. Using techniques similar to those used for computing MCSs, it is also possible to automatically synthesize a set of observables that ensure diagnosability of a given model [5].

FDIR effectiveness analysis is a set of analyses carried out on an existing fault management subsystem. Fault detection is concerned with detecting whether a given system is malfunctioning, namely searching for observable signals such that every occurrence of the fault will eventually make them true. As an example, observable alert is a detection means for property "batt1.voltage< 4.0 and batt2.voltage < 4.0". Fault isolation analysis aims at identifying the specific cause of malfunctioning. It generates a fault tree that contains the minimal explanations that are compatible with the observable being true. As an example, observable alert has two possible failure explanations: either batt1 has died, or batt2 has died. The latter failure, that batt2 has died, is not dependent on the death of batt1, since the switch-over to the second battery can also occur by natural depletion of the first battery. Finally, fault recovery analysis is used to check whether a user-specified recoverability property holds. For instance, property "always (batt1.voltage < 4.4 implies eventually batt1.voltage > 5.5)" is true in the nominal model, but it is false when error behaviour is taken into account, as a battery may die.

3.4 Performability Analysis

We use probabilistic model checking techniques [2, Ch. 10] for analyzing a model on its performance. The COMPASS toolset in particular supports performance properties expressed in the probabilistic pattern system by [25]. It allows for the formal specification of steady-state, transient probabilities, timed reachability probabilities and more intricate performance measures such as combinations thereof. Examples of typical performance parameters are "the probability that the first battery dies within 100 h" or "the probability that both batteries die within the mission duration". These properties have a direct mapping to Continuous Stochastic Logic (CSL) [1] and are input to the underlying probabilistic model checker.

The probabilistic model checker furthermore requires a Markov model as input. This is obtained from the extended model through several steps. First, the extended model's reachable state space is generated through an exhaustive symbolic exploration. Second, the probabilistic rates as specified in the error models (cf. Sect. 2.2) are interwoven through the state space by replacing the transition label with the associated probabilistic rate. The resulting state space is a symbolic representation of an Interactive Markov Chain, i.e., a Continuous-Time Markov Chain (CTMC) that may exhibit non-determinism [29]. This IMC is passed through the third phase, in which its size is reduced using weak bisimulation minimization [16,36]. In this last step, the IMC may turn into a CTMC. In the final phase the CSL formulae are extracted from the performance requirements and then together with the CTMC are fed to the MRMC probabilistic model checker, to compute the desired probabilities. The result is a graph showing the cumulative distribution function over the time horizon specified in the performance requirement. In case the resulting IMC from the model does not yield a CTMC after bisimulation minimization, new analysis techniques using real-time stochastic games can be used [26]. These techniques are planned to be integrated into the toolset. Similar techniques are also used for fault tree evaluation, i.e., computing the probability of the top-level event in dynamic fault trees [6].

4   Industrial Evaluation

The COMPASS approach and toolset was intensively tested on serious industrial cases by Thales Alenia Space in Cannes (France). These cases include thermal regulation in satellites and satellite mode management with its associated FDIR strategy. It was concluded that the modelling approach based on AADL provides sufficient expressiveness to model all hardware and software subsystems in satellite avionics. The hierarchical structure of specifications and the component-based paradigm enables the reuse of models. Also incremental modelling is very well supported. The Reliability, Availability, Maintainability and Safety (RAMS) analyses as provided by the toolset were found to be mature enough to be adopted by industry, indicating that the integrated COMPASS approach significantly reduces the time and cost for safety analysis compared to traditional on-board design processes [38]. Those findings were confirmed by applying our formal modelling and analysis techniques on a regular industrial-size design of a modern satellite platform in parallel with the conventional software development of the platform [11,20].

References

1. Baier, C., Haverkort, B., Hermanns, H., Katoen, J.P.: Model-checking algorithms for continuous-time Markov chains. IEEE Trans. Softw. Eng. **29**(6), 524–541 (2003)
2. Baier, C., Katoen, J.P.: Principles of Model Checking. MIT Press, Cambridge (2008)
3. Biere, A., Cimatti, A., Clarke, E., Zhu, Y.: Symbolic model checking without BDDs. In: Cleaveland, W.R. (ed.) TACAS 1999. LNCS, vol. 1579, pp. 193–207. Springer, Heidelberg (1999)
4. Biere, A., Heljanko, K., Junttila, T.A., Latvala, T., Schuppan, V.: Linear encodings of bounded LTL model checking. Log. Methods Comput. Sci. **2**(5), 1–64 (2006)
5. Bittner, B., Bozzano, M., Cimatti, A., Olive, X.: Symbolic synthesis of observability requirements for diagnosability. In: Proceedings of 11th Symposium on Advanced Space Technologies in Robotics and Automation (ASTRA 2011), ESA/ESTEC (2011) http://robotics.estec.esa.int/ASTRA/Astra2011/Astra2011_Proceedings.zip
6. Boudali, H., Crouzen, P., Stoelinga, M.: A rigorous, compositional and extensible framework for dynamic fault tree analysis. In: Dependable and Secure Computing, pp. 128–143. IEEE (2010)
7. Bozzano, M., Bruttomesso, R., Cimatti, A., Junttila, T., van Rossum, P., Schulz, S., Sebastiani, R.: Mathsat: tight integration of SAT and mathematical decision procedures. J. Autom. Reasoning **35**, 265–293 (2005)
8. Bozzano, M., Cimatti, A., Katoen, J.-P., Nguyen, V.Y., Noll, T., Roveri, M.: The COMPASS approach: correctness, modelling and performability of aerospace systems. In: Buth, B., Rabe, G., Seyfarth, T. (eds.) SAFECOMP 2009. LNCS, vol. 5775, pp. 173–186. Springer, Heidelberg (2009)
9. Bozzano, M., Cimatti, A., Tapparo, F.: Symbolic fault tree analysis for reactive systems. In: Namjoshi, K.S., Yoneda, T., Higashino, T., Okamura, Y. (eds.) ATVA 2007. LNCS, vol. 4762, pp. 162–176. Springer, Heidelberg (2007)
10. Bozzano, M., Cavada, R., Cimatti, A., Katoen, J.P., Nguyen, V.Y., Noll, T., Olive, X.: Formal verification and validation of aadl models. In: Embedded Real Time Software and Systems Conference, AAAF & SEE (2010)
11. Bozzano, M., Cimatti, A., Katoen, J.P., Katsaros, P., Mokos, K., Nguyen, V.Y., Noll, T., Postma, B., Roveri, M.: Spacecraft early design validation using formal methods. Reliab. Eng. Syst. Saf. **132**, 20–35 (2014)
12. Bozzano, M., Cimatti, A., Katoen, J.P., Nguyen, V.Y., Noll, T., Roveri, M.: Safety, dependability, and performance analysis of extended AADL models. Comput. J. **54**(5), 754–775 (2011)
13. Cimatti, A., Pecheur, C., Cavada, R.: Formal verification of diagnosability via symbolic model checking. In: International Joint Conference on Artificial Intelligence (IJCAI), pp. 363–369. Morgan Kaufmann (2003)
14. Cimatti, A., Clarke, E., Giunchiglia, E., Giunchiglia, F., Pistore, M., Roveri, M., Sebastiani, R., Tacchella, A.: NuSMV 2: an opensource tool for symbolic model checking. In: Brinksma, E., Larsen, K.G. (eds.) CAV 2002. LNCS, vol. 2404, pp. 359–364. Springer, Heidelberg (2002)
15. COMPASS Consortium: The COMPASS project web site. http://compass.informatik.rwth-aachen.de/
16. Derisavi, S., Hermanns, H., Sanders, W.H.: Optimal state-space lumping in Markov chains. Inf. Process. Lett. **87**(6), 309–315 (2003)

17. Dwyer, M., Avrunin, G., Corbett, J.: Patterns in property specifications for finite-state verification. In: International Conference on Software Engineering (ICSE), pp. 411–420. IEEE CS Press (1999)
18. ECSS: Space product assurance: Fault tree analysis - adoption notice ECSS/IEC 61025. ECSS Standard Q-ST-40-12C, European Cooperation for Space Standardization, July 2008
19. ECSS: Space product assurance: Failure modes, effects (and criticality) analysis (FMEA/FMECA). ECSS Standard Q-ST-30-02C, European Cooperation for Space Standardization, March 2009
20. Esteve, M.A., Katoen, J.P., Nguyen, V.Y., Postma, B., Yushtein, Y.: Formal correctness, safety, dependability and performance analysis of a satellite. In: 34th International Conference on Software Engineering (ICSE 2012), pp. 1022–1031. ACM and IEEE CS Press (2012)
21. FBK: FSAP: The formal safety analysis platform. http://fsap.fbk.eu/
22. FBK: MathSAT. http://mathsat.fbk.eu
23. FBK: NuSMV: A new symbolic model checker. http://nusmv.fbk.eu
24. Feiler, P.H., Gluch, D.P.: Model-Based Engineering with AADL: an introduction to the sae architecture analysis & design language. Addison-Wesley Professional, Boston (2012)
25. Grunske, L.: Specification patterns for probabilistic quality properties. In: International Conference on Software Engineering (ICSE), pp. 31–40. ACM (2008)
26. Guck, D., Han, T., Katoen, J.-P., Neuhäußer, M.R.: Quantitative timed analysis of interactive Markov chains. In: Goodloe, A.E., Person, S. (eds.) NFM 2012. LNCS, vol. 7226, pp. 8–23. Springer, Heidelberg (2012)
27. Heljanko, K., Junttila, T.A., Latvala, T.: Incremental and complete bounded model checking for full PLTL. In: Etessami, K., Rajamani, S.K. (eds.) CAV 2005. LNCS, vol. 3576, pp. 98–111. Springer, Heidelberg (2005)
28. Henzinger, T.: The theory of hybrid automata. In: IEEE Symposium on Logic in Computer Science (LICS), pp. 278–292. IEEE CS Press (1996)
29. Hermanns, H.: Interactive Markov chains in practice. In: Hermanns, H. (ed.) Interactive Markov Chains. LNCS, vol. 2428, p. 129. Springer, Heidelberg (2002)
30. Katoen, J.P., Zapreev, I.S., Hahn, E.M., Hermanns, H., Jansen, D.N.: The ins and outs of the probabilistic model checker MRMC. Perform. Eval. 68(2), 90–104 (2011)
31. MRMC Consortium: MRMC – The Markov Reward Model Checker. http://www.mrmc-tool.org/
32. SAE: Architecture Analysis and Design Language (AADL). SAE Standard AS5506, International Society of Automotive Engineers, May 2004
33. SAE: Architecture Analysis and Design Language (AADL) Annex, Volume 1, Annex A: Graphical AADL Notation. SAE Standard AS5506/1, International Society of Automotive Engineers, June 2006
34. SAE: Architecture Analysis and Design Language Annex (AADL), Volume 1, Annex E: Error Model Annex. SAE Standard AS5506/1, International Society of Automotive Engineers, June 2006
35. SAE: Architecture Analysis and Design Language (AADL) Rev. B. SAE Standard AS5506B, International Society of Automotive Engineers, September 2012
36. Valmari, A., Franceschinis, G.: Simple $O(m \log n)$ time Markov chain lumping. In: Esparza, J., Majumdar, R. (eds.) TACAS 2010. LNCS, vol. 6015, pp. 38–52. Springer, Heidelberg (2010)

37. Wimmer, R., Herbstritt, M., Hermanns, H., Strampp, K., Becker, B.: Sigref – a symbolic bisimulation tool box. In: Graf, S., Zhang, W. (eds.) ATVA 2006. LNCS, vol. 4218, pp. 477–492. Springer, Heidelberg (2006)

38. Yushtein, Y., Bozzano, M., Cimatti, A., Katoen, J.P., Nguyen, V., Noll, T., Olive, X., Roveri, M.: System-software co-engineering: dependability and safety perspective. In: Proceedings of the 4th IEEE International Conference on Space Mission Challenges for Information Technology (SMC-IT 2011), pp. 18–25. IEEE CS Press (2011)

Formal Verification of Distributed Task Migration for Thermal Management in On-Chip Multi-core Systems Using nuXmv

Syed Ali Asadullah Bukhari[1], Faiq Khalid Lodhi[1]([⊠]), Osman Hasan[1], Muhammad Shafique[2], and Jörg Henkel[2]

[1] School of Electrical Engineering and Computer Science (SEECS),
National University of Sciences and Technology (NUST), Islamabad, Pakistan
{ali.asadullah,faiq.khalid,osman.hasan}@seecs.nust.edu.pk
[2] Chair for Embedded Systems (CES), Karlsruhe Institute of Technology (KIT),
Karlsruhe, Germany
{muhammad.shafique,henkel}@kit.edu

Abstract. With the growing interest in using distributed task migration algorithms for dynamic thermal management (DTM) in multi-core chips comes the challenge of their rigorous verification. Traditional analysis techniques, like simulation and emulation, cannot cope with the design complexity and distributed nature of such algorithms and thus compromise on the rigor and accuracy of the analysis results. Formal methods, especially model checking, can play a vital role in alleviating these issues. Due to the presence of continuous elements, such as temperatures, and the large number of cores running the distributed algorithms in this analysis, we propose to use the nuXmv model checker to analyze distributed task migration algorithms for DTM. The main motivations behind this choice include the ability to handle the *real* numbers and the scalable SMT-based bounded model checking capabilities in nuXmv that perfectly fit the stability and deadlock analysis requirements of the distributed DTM algorithms. The paper presents the detailed analysis of a state-of-the-art task migration algorithm of distributed DTM for many-core systems. The functional and timing verification is done on a larger grid size of 9×9 cores, which is thermally managed by the selected DTM approach. The results indicate the usefulness of the proposed approach, as we have been able to catch a couple of discrepancies in the original model and gain many new insights about the behavior of the algorithm.

Keywords: Model checking · Thermal management · Task migration · Multi-core architectures

1 Introduction

The ever-increasing need of the computing power and technological advances have led to many cores on a chip [33,39]. This accelerated increase, accompanied by higher power densities, has opened up the challenge of coping with

© Springer International Publishing Switzerland 2015
C. Artho and P.C. Ölveczky (Eds.): FTSCS 2014, CCIS 476, pp. 32–46, 2015.
DOI: 10.1007/978-3-319-17581-2_3

the elevated chip temperatures, which pose serious threats to the reliability of the computing systems. Various Thermal Management (TM) techniques [1, 8, 21] have recently been proposed to overcome these issues. In particular, the Dynamic Thermal management (DTM) [27, 40] for multi-core systems via the task migration mechanism has been identified as a very promising solution to the heating problems in many-core systems with high core integration by the ITRS roadmap of 2013 [18].

The DTM techniques can be broadly classified into two categories: central and distributed [19]. Central DTM (cDTM) is done by a central controller, which is responsible for the overall thermal management of the chip and thus, has the visibility of all the global parameters, such as the core temperatures, of the system [7]. This approach has the inherent issue of scalability as the cDTM often encounters performance degradation while dealing with many-core systems [12, 34, 36]. On the other hand, Distributed DTM (dDTM) manages the heating issues of the chip by employing several thermal management agents as opposed to a single controller [19, 34]. An agent in a distributed system perceives the environment through communication with other agents and can take decisions on its own to a certain extent [37]. The obvious gain in this method is that the need of global knowledge is no longer necessary and thus it resolves the above-mentioned scalability issue of cDTM. Since the dDTM agents are not aware of the overall thermal scenario of the complete chip, it is customary to approximate the required data by information exchange among the neighboring agents only. Based on this information, some dDTM techniques develop an overall thermal model of the system for predicting the core temperatures [28, 32, 41]. If this estimate is above a certain threshold then the task migration is activated. Other dDTM techniques, like [11, 13, 23], make the task migration decisions based on certain algorithms that manipulate the temperature values obtained from the neighboring cores only. For example, a recent task migration technique [23], estimates the average temperature of the complete chip by taking the inputs of the neighboring cores using the distributed signal average tracking algorithm [4, 5].

The need for a thorough analysis of these thermal management techniques is of vital importance as an inefficient task migration decision may lead to the creation of hot spots (regions with excessive temperatures within the chip) and thus endanger the reliability of the chip. Traditionally, the dDTM techniques are analyzed using either simulations or by running on real hardware systems. Both of these methods compromise on the accuracy of the analysis results by analyzing a subset of the possible scenarios only due to their large design-space, which is in turn caused by the distributed nature of DTM techniques and the presence of 100 s of cores in the present-age systems where the distrusted DTM techniques are employed. Moreover, choosing the sample set is another major issue while analyzing the dDTM techniques due to the enormous amount of possible options, like the possible temperature values for all the cores are actually infinite due to the continuous nature of temperature. This non-exhaustiveness and incompleteness of the analysis may lead to unwanted scenarios, like the delayed release of the Montecito chip using the Foxton DTM algorithm [10].

Formal verification [9] can overcome the above-mentioned inaccuracy limitations of simulation-based verification due to its inherent soundness and completeness. Given the reactive nature of DTM techniques, model checking has been used for their analysis [25,29,35]. Moreover, the SPIN model checker [16] has been recently used in conjunction with Lamport timestamps [22] to analyze the functional and timing properties of the Thermal-aware Agent-based Power Economy (TAPE) [17], which is a state-of-the-art agent-based dDTM scheme. However, this analysis is only done for a 9 core, i.e., 3×3, core system and the continuous values of algorithm parameters and the temperature have been abstracted by discrete values in order to cope with the state-space explosion problem of model checking [6]. These abstractions limit the usefulness of applying model checking for analyzing dDTM techniques as the exhaustiveness of the analysis is compromised to a certain degree.

The main focus of the current paper is to alleviate the above-mentioned issues encountered in [17]. For this purpose, we propose to use the recently released nuXmv model checker [3] to analyze dDTM systems. The distinguishing features of the nuXmv model checker include the ability to handle *real* numbers and implicit handling of state counters. Thus, the continuous values in dDTM approaches can be modeled more appropriately and the timing properties of the DTM approached can be analyzed without using the Lamport timestamps explicitly. Moreover, the SAT and SMT based engines of the nuXmv model checker facilitate analyzing larger models and we can thus analyze large grids of multi-core systems.

In order to illustrate the usefulness of the proposed approach, this paper presents the formal analysis of a recently proposed task migration algorithm for hot spot reduction in many-core systems [23]. The algorithm executes the task migration based on a simple criterion of comparing the temperature of the core(s) with the neighboring cores and the average temperature of the chip. The average temperature of the chip in turn is computed using the recently proposed technique of distributed average estimation for time-varying signals [4]. Besides the generic and simplistic nature of this algorithm (as it just manipulates the temperature values from its neighbor to make decision for task migration), another main motivation for choosing this as our case study is its close relationship with other advanced task migration algorithms, such as [24]. Moreover, model checking is not suitable for dDTM techniques like [28,32,41], due to their predictive nature.

2   Preliminaries

In this section, we give a brief introduction to the nuXmv model checker and the task migration algorithm for many-core systems [23], which we have formally verified in this paper. The intent is to facilitate the understanding of the rest of the paper for both the dDTM technique design and the formal methods communities.

2.1 nuXmv Model Checker

The nuXmv symbolic model checker [3,31] is a very recent formal verification tool that extends the NuSMV model checker [30], which in turn is a finite state transitions model checker. nuXmv extends the capabilities of the NuSMV by complementing NuSMV's verification techniques by SAT algorithms for finite state systems. For infinite state systems, it introduces new data types of *Integers* and *Reals* and also provides the support of Satisfiability Modulo Theories (SMT), using MathSAT [26], for verification.

The system that needs to be modeled is expressed in the nuXmv language, which supports the modular programming approach where the overall system is divided into several modules that interact with one another in the MAIN module. The properties to be verified can be specified in nuXmv using the Linear Temporal Logic (LTL) and Computation Tree Logic (CTL). The LTL specifications are written in nuXmv with the help of logical operations like, AND (&), OR (|), Exclusive OR (xor), Exclusive NOR (xnor), implication (->) and equality (<->), and temporal operators, like Globally (G), Finally (F), next (X) and until (U). Similarly, the CTL specifications can be written by combining logical operations with quantified temporal operators, like exists globally (EG), exists next state (EX) and forall finally (AF). In case a property turns out to be false, a counterexample in the execution trace of the FSM is provided.

2.2 Task Migration Algorithm for Hot Spot Reduction

The main goal of any dynamic DTM technique is to maintain an acceptable average temperature across all the cores. This reduction in the temperature does not always guarantee a balanced distribution that is actually required for the reduction of thermal hot spots. The algorithm proposed in [23], which is under consideration in this paper, overcomes this limitation by performing distributed task migration with the primary goal of achieving thermal reliability and reduced temperature variance across the chip. The algorithm makes use of the recently proposed distributed average signal tracking algorithm [4,5], which shows that the states of all the distributed agents converge to the average value of the time-varying reference signals. The following equation is used to estimate the average:

$$\dot{z}_i(t) = \alpha \sum_{j \in N_i} sgn[x_j(t) - x_i(t)]$$

$$x_i(t) = z_i(t) + r_i(t) \tag{1}$$

where $sgn(x)$ is the signum function defined as:

$$sgn(x) = \begin{cases} -1 & \text{if } x < 0 \\ 0 & \text{if } x = 0 \\ 1 & \text{if } x > 0 \end{cases} \tag{2}$$

and $z_i(t)$ is the estimated average signal, $x_i(t)$ and N_i are the states of the distributed agent i and its neighborhood, respectively, $r_i(t)$ is the reference signal with bounded derivatives in a finite time and α is a constant value greater than 0. The task migration algorithm makes use of this fact to estimate the average temperature of a core, without the need of global knowledge of the temperature of every core. The task migration policy is then executed only on the cores having a temperature greater than the estimated average temperature T_{avg}. As a result, a considerable amount of data exchange is avoided among the cores and only necessary task migration is done for effectively reducing the temperature. If a core has a temperature greater than the estimated T_{avg}, then the following task migration criterion is used to check if the task can be migrated from the *current* core to some *destination* core among the neighbors:

1. $T_{destination} < T_{current}$, where $T_{destination}$ and $T_{current}$ are the temperatures of the *destination* and *current* cores, respectively.
2. $P_{destination} < P_{current}$, where $P_{destination}$ is the task load of the destined core and $P_{current}$ is the counterpart of the *current* core.
3. $TNP_{destination} < TNP_{current}$, where $TNP_{destination}$ and $TNP_{current}$ are the workloads of the *destination* and *current* cores, respectively.

If the temperature T of the core is less than the T_{avg}, then the task migration policy is not activated and the core retains its temperature, otherwise the above mentioned conditions are checked to decide if the task migration is done for a core or not. All the 4 neighbors are passed through the criterion and tasks are exchanged if the conditions are met and then checked with the next neighbor. By the end of the algorithm execution, the most appropriate core is found for task exchange. The pseudo-code for this algorithm is given in Algorithm 1 [23], and Fig. 1 presents a typical execution of the algorithm to illustrate the above-mentioned behavior. The node 0, in Fig. 1, represents the current core and the neighboring cores are denoted by 1, 2, 3 and 4. Each core is checked for the satisfiability of the task migration conditions and the right core (shown black) is chosen. The results from MATLAB implementation of this DTM technique on a 6×6 grid show a 30 percent hot spot reduction and smaller temperature variance [23].

3   Modeling the DTM Algorithm in nuXmv

In this section, we explain the FSM for Algorithm 1 and its modeling in the language of the nuXmv model checker.

3.1   Our Refinements to the Original Task Migration Algorithm

While modeling Algorithm 1 in the nuXmv language, we had to handle some of the scenarios that were not mentioned in the paper [23] where the original algorithm was published. Before going into the implementation details of the model, we find it appropriate to point out the discrepancies in the existing algorithm and our proposed solutions.

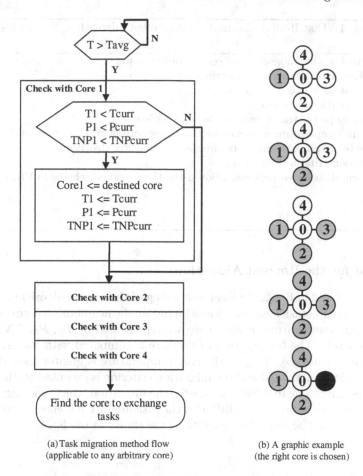

(a) Task migration method flow
(applicable to any arbitrary core)

(b) A graphic example
(the right core is chosen)

Fig. 1. A typical execution of the selected algorithm [23].

1. Since the migration algorithm executes concurrently on all the nodes, it may happen that two different nodes node A and B want to migrate their task to the same name node C at the same time. The algorithm proposed in [23] does not resolve this conflict. In our model, we have resolved this conflict by giving priority to the node that has a lower value of estimated T_{avg}. This means that all the nodes not only need to know the temperatures of their neighboring nodes, but also of the nodes that could possibly migrate tasks with their neighbors. This revision caters for the conflict resolution but increases the complexity of the algorithm.

2. Another conflict of a similar nature arises when any node A desires to retain its value, because its current temperature is lesser than the estimated T_{avg}, while one of its neighboring nodes wants to exchange the tasks, based on the execution of its task migration policy. This situation is also resolved by priority assignment based on T_{avg} in our refinement.

Algorithm 1. Distributed thermal management algorithm for avoiding hot spots [23]

Require: Task loads, many-core processor configuration
Ensure: Optimized temperature distribution
  Start simulation at room temperature
  for each execution cycle **do**
    1. Simulate power traces under different task loads
    2. Obtain temperature responses of the many-core microprocessor, and estimate average temperature using distributed state tracking algorithm
    if migration criteria is met **then**
      Perform distributed task migration using the proposed scheme in Fig. 1 core by core.
    end if
  end for

3.2 FSM for the Revised Algorithm

The FSM, depicted in Fig. 2, details the working of the refined algorithm for core 0. The temperature, task load, workloads including the neighboring cores and estimated average temperature by each core are represented by Ts, Ps, $TNPs$ and T_{avg}, respectively. The temperature of the core is compared with the estimated average temperature, i.e., T_{avg}. If the core temperature is greater then the task migration policy is activated and the migration criterion is executed on the neighboring cores one by one to select the core for the migration. Once, the destination core is selected, the improved condition for the task migration is checked to finalize the core selection. The respective conditions are shown in the FSM.

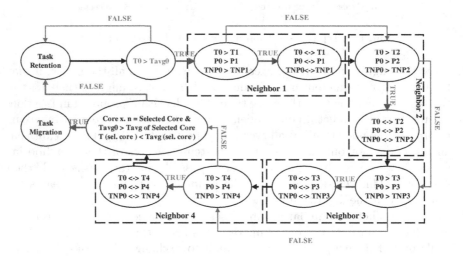

Fig. 2. Finite state machine showing the working of the algorithm for core 0.

3.3   Modeling the Average Estimation Algorithm

In order to model Eq. 1, we have to first take the integral of the $\dot{z}_i(t)$, The integral of a signum function is given as [38]:

$$\int sign(x)\, dx = |x| \tag{3}$$

and

$$\int \dot{z}_i(t)\, dt = \int \alpha \sum_{j \in N_i} sgn[x_j(t) - x_i(t)]\, dt$$

Thus, the equation for $z_i(t)$ becomes

$$z_i(t) = \alpha \sum_{j \in N_i} |x_j(t) - x_i(t)|$$

and we have

$$x_i(t) = \alpha \sum_{j \in N_i} |x_j(t) - x_i(t)| + r_i(t) \tag{4}$$

In our modeling, $x_i(t)$ becomes equivalent to T_{avg} that a core i estimates, and r_i becomes the core i's temperature.

3.4   Model for the 9 × 9 Grid

The algorithm under verification allows its nodes to exchange information with a maximum of four neighbors, i.e., north, south, east and west. Information exchange with the diagonal neighboring nodes is not allowed. In order to construct the model of any arbitrary $n \times n$ grid, which supports the originally proposed algorithm of [23], we need three distinct types of nodes, i.e., nodes that can communicate with 2, 3 and 4 neighbors, depending on their location in the grid. However, our refinement of the original algorithm requires 6 different types of nodes, as a node with 3 neighbors may need information of 4 or 5 second-level neighboring nodes depending on its location in the grid. We have defined second level neighbors of a core x as the cores that can communicate with the neighbors of that core x. Similarly, a four-neighbor node may require information of 4, 5 or 6 second level neighboring nodes depending on its location in the grid. Therefore, we have modeled the 9×9 grid using six different modules: n2_3, n3_4, n3_5, n4_6, n4_7 and n4_8 as shown in Fig. 3. The name of these modules nx_y show that the cores modeled by this module have x immediate neighbors and y other second-level neighbors that can exchange tasks with this core or its neighbors. The MAIN module calls the instances of these six distinct modules to complete the overall model of a 9 × 9 grid. This model is then used forverifying both functional and timing properties of the given algorithm in the

n4_8

0	1	2	3	4
9	10	11	12	13
18	19	20	21	22
27	28	29	30	31
36	37	38	39	40

np_q:
p: number of direct neighbors
q: number of in direct neighbors

0	1	2	3	4	5	6	7	8	n2_3
9	10	11	12	13	14	15	16	17	n3_4
18	19	20	21	22	23	24	25	26	n3_5
27	28	29	30	31	32	33	34	35	n4_6
36	37	38	39	40	41	42	43	44	n4_7
45	46	47	48	49	50	51	52	53	n4_8
54	55	56	57	58	59	60	61	62	
63	64	65	66	67	68	69	70	71	
72	73	74	75	76	77	78	79	80	

(a) Neighbors of a sample core   (b) Cores arrangement in the grid

Fig. 3. Categorization of cores based on the amount of information exchange.

next section. The code listing for the these modules and more implementation details are available at [2].

4   Verification of the DTM Algorithm

4.1   Experimental Setup

We used the version 1.0 of the nuXmv model checker along with the Windows 8.1 Professional OS running on a i3 processor, 2.93 GHz(4 CPUs), with 4 GB memory for our experiments. In order to assume realistic values of temperatures for our experimentation, we used the temperature range between 41 °C and 56 °C for a single core as has been reported in [14]. The verification is done for a 9×9 grid of nodes (cores) with all of them running processes as described in the previous section. The complete model contains 81 processes.

4.2   Functional Verification

We have done the functional verification of the DTM algorithm by verifying the following properties using the nuXmv's bounded model checking (BMC) support for *real* numbers:

Deadlock. A deadlock state in a system leads to an undesired cyclic behavior. In case of DTM, deadlock happens if the temperature of some core x is greater than the estimated temperature and it is unable to exchange its load with some other core. This behavior could result in the creation of thermal hot spots across the chip. In order to make sure that the DTM algorithm is free of deadlocks, the following property needs to be satisfied:

$$G(core_x.T_0 > core_x.T_{avg} \rightarrow F(core_x.T_0 <= core_k.T_0))$$

This property checks that any core having temperature greater than the average temperature will eventually get a reduction in temperature.

Liveliness. The liveliness property in a system makes sure that the system returns to its good working or desired state. In our verification, we have defined liveliness using the following specification:

$$G(core_x.T_0 < core_x.T_{avg} \rightarrow X(core_x.n = x))$$

This property states that if the temperature of a core is less than the estimated average temperature of the core, then in the very next state, the core does not need to migrate tasks to its neighbors.

Stability. Stability is one of the most important properties for any DTM algorithm. In the given algorithm, stability is attained when the temperature of all the cores will eventually be less than or equal to the estimated average temperature of the chip.

$$GF((core_0.T_0 <= core_0.T_{avg}) \& (core_1.T_0 <= core_1.T_{avg}) \ldots \ldots \& (core_{80}.T_0 <= core_{80}.T_{avg}))$$

The stability condition, $core_n.T_0 <= core_n.T_{avg}$, for a core n is defined using the fact that the algorithm tries to achieve stability by executing the task migration until the core has a temperature equal to or less than the estimated average as shown in Fig. 1. Also, the GF operator is used to ensure that our stability property holds true (some where in future or eventually) across any execution path (globally) of the algorithm. For our 9×9 grid, it means that eventually, there would be a state where all the cores of the system have a temperature that does not exceed the estimated average temperature.

Verification of Temperature Estimation Algorithm. An interesting observation is the estimation of the average chip temperature using Eq. 1. The graphs in Fig. 4 show the average chip temperature estimation behavior of six cores, each corresponding to one of the six different neighbor configurations in our grid.

Initially, each core sees the initial value of the T_{avg} as the average temperature of the core. The cores then estimate the temperature of the chip with

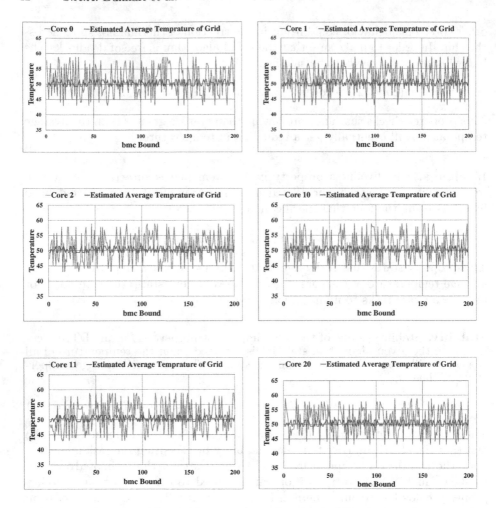

Fig. 4. Temperature estimation in °C

the help of underlying average tracking algorithm in the DTM. For illustration purposes, we have shown the actual average temperature of the grid, and the estimated temperature of the selected cores on the same plot. It shows that the average estimation algorithm making use of the temperature information form the neighboring node gives a good average estimate of the overall chip temperature, confirming the functionality of the average estimation algorithm. Moreover the estimated average by different cores is also following a similar pattern.

The verification times and the memory consumption for some of the functional properties, verified in this work, are given in Table 1. The time measurements in Table 1 is done by using nuXmv function `time`.

Table 1. Timing and memory resources for some of the properties verified.

Properties	Core	Module	Memory usage (MBs)	Time (s)
Liveliness property	0	n2_3	1015.69	745.67
Liveliness property	1	n3_4	1051.71	751.25
Liveliness property	2	n3_5	1025.64	749.65
Liveliness property	10	n4_6	1041.52	758.75
Liveliness property	11	n4_7	1031.74	781.85
Liveliness property	20	n4_8	1033.85	790.65
Deadlock property	0	n2_3	1351.41	1245.59
Deadlock property	1	n3_4	1325.35	1235.61
Deadlock property	2	n3_5	1315.63	1241.91
Deadlock property	10	n4_6	1359.54	1249.71
Deadlock property	11	n4_7	1359.54	1239.41
Deadlock property	20	n4_8	1343.51	1251.11
Stability property	-		2051.51	2253.56

Table 2. Number of transitions required to achieve stability.

Scenarios	Experimental Setup					n2_3	n3_4	n3_5	n4_6	n4_7	n4_8
	T0	T1	T2	T3	T4	0	1	2	10	11	20
nb0	56					49	52	51	63	67	62
nb1	56	56				53	53	54	61	63	61
nb2	56		56			61	57	55	71	73	69
nb3	56			56		-	20	57	72	79	80
nb4	56				56	-	-	-	89	87	91
nb12	56	56	56			63	59	53	94	92	85
nb13	56	56		56		62	61	54	91	98	96
nb14	56	56			56	-	57	51	107	114	113
nb23	56		56	56		62	62	59	117	112	105
nb24	56		56		56	-	58	57	103	109	112
nb34	56			56	56	-	60	65	100	105	102
nb123	56	56	56	56		-	-	-	115	120	117
nb124	56	56	56		56	-	-	-	119	124	118
nb134	56	56		56	56	-	-	-	121	125	131
nb234	56		56	56	56	-	-	-	132	129	141
nb1234	56	56	56	56	56	-	-	-	129	131	137

4.3 Timing Verification

The functional properties, presented in the previous section, have been verified for the initial temperature values taken randomly from the allowable range given in [14]. In this section, we verified various timing related properties for specific scenarios, with particular initial temperatures. In order to measure the time stamps between the states transition, we have used built-in nuXmv commands `execute_trace` and `execute_partial_trace`. Table 2 shows the time to stability for different selected cores (one from each module) under 16 possible conditions. Here, n2_3, n3_4, n3_5, n4_6, n4_7 and n4_8 represents different modules. T_0 represents the temperature of the tested core and T_1, T_2, T_3 and T_4 represent the temperature of neighbors of the tested core. The first case nb0 in Table 2, represents the case when the temperature of all the neighbor cores is less than the threshold. Similarly, the nb1234 represents the case when the temperature of all neighbor cores, i.e., 1, 2, 3 and 4, exceed the threshold. Whereas, the other cases represent the intermediate possibilities between these extreme scenarios. It can be seen from Table 2 that a maximum of 141 state transitions are required to reach stability when the given core, of type n4_8, and three of its neighbors are at a temperature of 56 °C.

5 Conclusion

This paper presents the formal verification of both functional and timing properties of a recent dDTM technique [23] for on-chip many-core systems using the nuXmv model checker. Due to the ability to handle *real* numbers and the powerful verification methods, based on SAT and SMT solvers, in nuXmv, we have been able to gain many new insights into the given algorithm. While modeling the selected task migration algorithm [23] in nuXmv, we identified a couple of ambiguities in the original algorithm [23] that have been fixed in our implementation of the algorithm using the nuXmv language. The analyzed model has 81 cores and the analysis is done within the range of 41 to 56 °C. To the best of our knowledge, such a big model cannot be handled rigorously by simulation-based testing. We plan to extend this work by proposing a common ground to analyze and compare dDTM schemes, such as [11,15,20,34], both in terms of functional and timing properties.

Acknowledgement. This work is supported in parts by the DAAD "Deutsch-Pakistanische Forschungskooperationen" project.

References

1. Brooks, D., Martonosi, M.: Dynamic thermal management for high-performance microprocessors. In: High-Performance Computer Architecture, pp. 171–182. IEEE (2001)
2. Bukhari, S.A.A., Lodhi, F.K.: Formal verification of distributed task migration for thermal management in on-chip multi-core systems using nuXmv, National University of Sciences and Technology (2014). http://save.seecs.nust.edu.pk/projects/fdDTM/fdDTM.html
3. Cavada, R., Cimatti, A., Dorigatti, M., Griggio, A., Mariotti, A., Micheli, A., Mover, S., Roveri, M., Tonetta, S.: The NUXMV Symbolic model checker. In: Biere, A., Bloem, R. (eds.) CAV 2014. LNCS, vol. 8559, pp. 334–342. Springer, Heidelberg (2014)

4. Chen, F., Cao, Y., Ren, W.: Distributed computation of the average of multiple time-varying reference signals. In: American Control Conference, pp. 1650–1655 (2011)
5. Chen, F., Cao, Y., Ren, W.: Distributed average tracking of multiple time-varying reference signals with bounded derivatives. IEEE Trans. Autom. Control $57(12)$, 3169–3174 (2012)
6. Clarke Jr., E.M., Grumberg, O., Peled, D.A.: Model Checking. MIT Press, Cambridge (1999)
7. Donald, J., Martonosi, M.: Techniques for multicore thermal management: classification and new exploration. In: Computer Architecture, pp. 78–88 (2006)
8. Donald, J., Martonosi, M.: Techniques for multicore thermal management: Classification and new exploration. In: ACM SIGARCH Computer Architecture News. vol. 34, pp. 78–88. IEEE Computer Society (2006)
9. Drechsler, R.: Advanced Formal Verification. Falk Symposium Series. Springer, Boston (2004)
10. Dunn, D.: Intel delays Montecito in roadmap shakeup. EE Times, Manufacturing/ Packaging, October 2005
11. Ebi, T., Faruque, M., Henkel, J.: Tape: thermal-aware agent-based power econom multi/many-core architectures. In: Computer-Aided Design. pp. 302–309 (2009)
12. Ebi, T., Kramer, D., Karl, W., Henkel, J.: Economic learning for thermal-aware power budgeting in many-core architectures. In: Hardware/Software Codesign and System Synthesis.pp. 189–196, ACM (2011)
13. Ge, Y., Malani, P., Qiu, Q.: Distributed task migration for thermal management in many-core systems. In: Design Automation Conference, pp. 579–584. ACM (2010)
14. Glocker, E., Schmitt-Landsiedel, D.: Modeling of temperature scenarios in a multicore processor system. Adv. Radio Sci. **11**, 219–225 (2013)
15. Henkel, J., Ebi, T., Amrouch, H., Khdr, H.: Thermal management for dependable on-chip systems. In: Asia and South Pacific Design Automation Conference, pp. 113–118 (2013)
16. Holzmann, G.J.: The model checker SPIN. IEEE Trans. softw. eng. **23**(5), 279–295 (1997)
17. Ismail, M., Hasan, O., Ebi, T., Shafique, M., Henkel, J.: Formal verification of distributed dynamic thermal management. In: Computer-Aided Design, pp. 248–255. IEEE (2013)
18. ITRS: (2014). http://www.itrs.net/Links/2013ITRS/2013Chapters/2013Overview. pdf
19. Kadin, M., Reda, S., Uht, A.: Central vs. distributed dynamic thermal management for multi-core processors: which one is better? In: Great Lakes Symposium on VLSI, pp. 137–140. ACM (2009)
20. Khdr, H., Ebi, T., Shafique, M., Amrouch, H., Henkel, J.: mDTM: multi-objective dynamic thermal management for on-chip systems. In: Design, Automation Test in Europe, p. 330 (2014)
21. Kong, J., Chung, S.W., Skadron, K.: Recent thermal management techniques for microprocessors. ACM Comput. Surv. **44**(3), 13:1–13:42 (2012)
22. Lamport, L.: Time, clocks, and the ordering of events in a distributed system. Commun. ACM **21**(7), 558–565 (1978)
23. Liu, Z., Huang, X., Tan, S.D., Wang, H., Tang, H.: Distributed task migration for thermal hot spot reduction in many-core microprocessors. In: ASIC, pp. 1–4 (2013)
24. Liu, Z., Xu, T., Tan, S.D., Wang, H.: Dynamic thermal management for multicore microprocessors considering transient thermal effects. In: Design Automation Conference, pp. 473–478 (2013)

25. Lungu, A., Bose, P., Sorin, D.J., German, S., Janssen, G.: Multicore power management: Ensuring robustness via early-stage formal verification. In: Formal Methods and Models for Codesign, pp. 78–87. IEEE (2009)
26. MathSAT 5: (2014). http://mathsat.fbk.eu/
27. Mukherjee, R., Memik, S.O.: Physical aware frequency selection for dynamic thermal management in multi-core systems. In: Computer-aided Design, pp. 547–552. ACM (2006)
28. Nath, R., Carmean, D., Rosing, T.S.: Power modeling and thermal management techniques for manycores. In: Computers and Communications. pp. 740–746. IEEE (2013)
29. Norman, G., Parker, D., Kwiatkowska, M., Shukla, E., Gupta, R.: Using probabilistic model checking for dynamic power management. Formal Aspects Comput. **17**, 202–215 (2003)
30. nuSMV: (2014). http://nusmv.fbk.eu/
31. nuXmv: (2014). https://nuxmv.fbk.eu/
32. Salami, B., Baharani, M., Noori, H.: An adaptive temperature threshold schema for dynamic thermal management of multi-core processors. In: Computer Architecture and Digital Systems, pp. 119–120 (2013)
33. Schauer, B.: Multicore processors-a necessity. In: ProQuest discovery guides, pp. 1–14 (2008)
34. Shafique, M., Henkel, J.: Agent-based distributed power management for kilo-core processors. In: Computer-Aided Design, pp. 153–160. IEEE (2013)
35. Shukla, S., Gupta, R.: A model checking approach to evaluating system level dynamic power management policies for embedded systems. In: High-Level Design Validation and Test Workshop, pp. 53–57. IEEE (2001)
36. Singh, A., Shafique, M., Kumar, A., Henkel, J.: Mapping on multi/many-core systems: Survey of current and emerging trends. In: Design Automation Conference (DAC), ACM/EDAC/IEEE.pp. 1–10 (2013)
37. Weiss, G.: Multiagent Systems: A Modern Approach to Distributed Artificial Intelligence. MIT Press, Cambridge (1999)
38. Wolfram: (2014). http://functions.wolfram.com/ComplexComponents/Sign/21/01/01/
39. Wyngaard, J., Inggs, M., Collins, J., Farrimond, B.: Towards a many-core architecture for HPC. In: Field Programmable Logic and Applications, pp. 1–4 (2013)
40. Yang, J., Zhou, X., Chrobak, M., Zhang, Y., Jin, L.: Dynamic thermal management through task scheduling. In: Performance Analysis of Systems and software, pp. 191–201 (2008)
41. Yun, B., Shin, K.G., Wang, S.: Predicting thermal behavior for temperature management in time-critical multicore systems. In: IEEE Real-Time and Embedded Technology and Applications Symposium, pp. 185–194 (2013)

Expression-Based Aliasing for OO–languages

Georgiana Caltais(✉)

Department of Computer Science, ETH Zürich, Zürich, Switzerland
georgiana.caltais@inf.ethz.ch

Abstract. Alias analysis has been an interesting research topic in verification and optimization of programs. The undecidability of determining whether two expressions in a program may reference to the same object is the main source of the challenges raised in alias analysis. In this paper we propose an extension of a previously introduced alias calculus based on program expressions, to the setting of unbounded program executions such as infinite loops and recursive calls. Moreover, we devise a corresponding executable specification in the $\mathbb{K}$-framework. An important property of our extension is that, in a non-concurrent setting, the corresponding alias expressions can be over-approximated in terms of a notion of regular expressions. This further enables us to show that the associated $\mathbb{K}$-machinery implements an algorithm that always stops and provides a sound over-approximation of the "may aliasing" information, where soundness stands for the lack of false negatives. As a case study, we analyze the integration and further applications of the alias calculus in SCOOP. The latter is an object-oriented programming model for concurrency, recently formalized in Maude; $\mathbb{K}$ definitions can be compiled into Maude for execution.

1 Introduction

A research direction of interest in Computer Science is the application of *alias analysis* in verification and optimization of programs. One of the challenges along this line of research has been the undecidability of determining whether two expressions in a program *may* reference the same object. A rich suite of approaches aiming at providing a satisfactory balance between scalability and precision has already been developed in this regard. Examples include: (i) intra-procedural frameworks [16,17] that handle isolated functions only, and their inter-procedural counterparts [12,16,23] that consider the interactions between function calls; (ii) type-based techniques [9]; (iii) flow-based techniques [4,7] that establish aliases depending on the control-flow information of a procedure; (iv) context-(in)sensitive approaches [10,30] that depend on whether the calling context of a function is taken into account or not; (v) field-(in)sensitive approaches [1,21] that depend on whether the individual fields of objects in a program are traced or not. More details on such classifications can be found in [26], for instance. For a comprehensive survey on alias analyses for object-oriented programs, corresponding issues and remaining open problems, we refer the interested reader to the works in [11,29].

© Springer International Publishing Switzerland 2015
C. Artho and P.C. Ölveczky (Eds.): FTSCS 2014, CCIS 476, pp. 47–61, 2015.
DOI: 10.1007/978-3-319-17581-2_4

Of particular interest for the work in this paper is the untyped, flow-sensitive, field sensitive, inter-procedural and context-sensitive calculus for *may aliasing*, introduced in [15]. The aforementioned calculus covers most of the aspects of a modern object-oriented language, namely: object creation and deletion, conditionals, assignments, loops and (possibly recursive) function calls. The approach in [15] abstracts the aliasing information in terms of explicit access paths [18] referred to as *alias expressions*. Consider, for an example, the code

$$x := y;$$
$$\textbf{loop } x := x.next \textbf{ end} \tag{1}$$

The corresponding execution causes x to become aliased to $y.next.next. \ldots$, with a possibly infinite number of occurrences of the field *next*. The set of associated alias expressions can be equivalently written as:

$$\{[x, y.next^k] \mid k \geq 0\}. \tag{2}$$

The sources of imprecision introduced by the calculus in [15] are limited to ignoring tests in conditionals, and to "cutting at length L", for the case of possibly infinite alias relation as in (2). Intuitively, the cutting technique considers sequences longer than a given length L as aliased to all expressions.

There is a huge literature on heap analysis for aliasing [11], but hardly any paper that presents a calculus as in [15] allowing the derivation of alias relations as the result of applying various instructions of a programming language.

Our focus is two folded. First, we want extend the framework in [15] to the setting of unbounded program executions such as infinite loops and recursive calls. In accordance, the goal is to provide a way to shift from "finite" to "infinite behaviours". This can be achieved in a rather straightforward manner, by redefining the construct **loop** p **end** in [15] according to the informal semantics: "execute p repeatedly any number of times, including zero". However, developing a corresponding mechanism for reasoning on "may aliasing" in a finite number of steps is not trivial. The key observation that paves the way to a possible (finite state-based) modeling in a non-concurrent setting is that the alias expressions and a back-tracking stack corresponding to loops and recursive calls grow in a regular fashion. Hence, they are finitely representable, as it is easy to see in (2), for instance. Such regularities cannot be exploited in concurrent contexts, due to the "non-determinism" of process interaction.

A similar technique exploiting regular behaviour of (non-concurrent) programs, in order to reason on "may aliasing", was previously introduced in [2]. In short, the results in [2] utilize abstract representations of programs in terms of finite pushdown systems, for which infinite execution paths have a regular structure (or are "lasso shaped") [3]. Then, in the style of abstract interpretation [8], the collecting semantics is applied over the (finite state) pushdown systems to obtain the alias analysis itself. In short, the main difference with the results in [2] consists in how the abstract memory addresses corresponding to pointer variables are represented. In [2] these range over a finite set of natural numbers. In this paper we consider alias expressions build according to the calculus in [15].

The work in [2] also proposes an implementation of pushdown systems in the K-framework [27]. The latter is an executable semantic framework based on Rewriting Logic (RL) [19], and has successfully been used for defining programming languages and corresponding formal analysis tools. Moreover, K definitions have a direct implementation in K-Maude [28].

We agree that it could be worth presenting our analysis as an abstract interpretation (AI) [8]. A modelling exploiting the machinery of AI (based on abstract domains, abstraction and concretization functions, Galois connections, fixedpoints, *etc.*) is an interesting, but different research topic per se.

Our second interest w.r.t. may aliasing is its integration in SCOOP [22] – a simple object oriented programming model for concurrency; thus an operational based approach on handling the alias calculus is more appropriate. The basis of a RL-based framework for the design and analysis of the SCOOP model was recently set in [22]. The reference implementation of SCOOP is Eiffel [20]. The integration of alias analysis belongs to a more ambitious goal, namely, the construction of a RL-based toolbox for the analysis of SCOOP programs (examples include a deadlock detector and a type checker).

Our Contribution. By drawing inspiration from, and building on top of the results in [2,15], in this paper we propose:

- an extension of the (finite) alias calculus in [15] to the setting of unbounded program executions, and a sound over-approximation technique based on "regular alias expressions", for non-concurrent settings;
- a RL-based specification of the extended calculus;
- an algorithm that always terminates and provides a sound over-approximation of "may aliasing" by exploiting a notion of regular (finitely representable) aliases, for non-concurrent settings.

Moreover, we analyze the integration, implementation and further applications of the alias calculus in SCOOP.

We refer the interested reader to [5] for the extended version of the current paper including: the full specification of the RL-based machinery, two examples emphasizing the naturalness of applying the executable aliasing framework and a case study exploiting the corresponding implementation in SCOOP, respectively, together with the detailed proofs of the formal results.

Paper Structure. The paper is organized as follows. In Sect. 2 we introduce the extension of the alias calculus in [15] to unbounded executions. In Sect. 3 we provide the RL-based executable specification of the calculus in the K semantic framework. The implementation in SCOOP, and further applications are discussed in Sect. 4. In Sect. 5 we draw the conclusions and provide pointers to future work.

2   The Alias Calculus

In this section we define an extension of the calculus in [15], to unbounded program executions. Moreover, based on the idea behind the *pumping lemma for regular languages* [25], we devise a corresponding sound over-approximation of "may aliasing" in terms of regular expressions, applicable in sequential contexts. This paves the way to developing an algorithm for the aliasing problem, as presented in Sect. 3, in the formal setting of the $\mathbb{K}$ semantic framework [27].

Preliminaries. We proceed by briefly recalling the notion of *alias relation* and a series of associated notations and basic operations, as introduced in [15].

We call an *expression* a (possibly infinite) path of shape $x.y.z.\ldots$, where x is a local variable, class attribute or *Current*, and $y, z, \ldots$ are attributes. Here, *Current*, also known as *this* or *self*, stands for the current object. For an arbitrary alias expression e, it holds that $e.Current = Current.e = e$. Let E represent the set of all expressions of a program. An *alias relation* is a symmetric and irreflexive binary relation over $E \times E$.

Given an alias relation r and an expression e, we define

$$r/e = \{e\} \cup \{x : E \mid [x, e] \in r\}$$

denoting the set consisting of all elements in r which are aliased to e, plus e itself.

Let x be an expression; we write $r - x$ to represent r without the pairs with one element of shape $x.e$.

We say that an alias relation is *dot complete* whenever for any t, u, v and a it holds that if $[t, u]$ and $[t.a, v]$ are alias pairs, then $[u.a, v]$ is an alias pair and, moreover, if a is in the domain of t, then $[t.a, u.a]$ is an alias pair. By the "domain of t" we refer to a method or a field in the class corresponding to the object referred by the expression associated to t. For instance, given a class NODE with a field *next* of type NODE, and a NODE object x, we say that *next* is in the domain of $t = x.next.next$. For the sake of brevity, we write *dot-complete*(r) for the closure under dot-completeness of a relation r.

The notation $r[x = u]$ represents the relation r augmented with pairs $[x, y]$ and made dot complete, where y is an element of u.

2.1   Extension to Unbounded Executions

We further introduce an extension of the alias calculus in [15] to infinite alias relations corresponding to unbounded executions such as infinite loops or recursive calls. The main difference in our approach is reflected by the definition of loops, which now complies to the usual fixed-point denotational semantics.

The alias calculus is defined by a set of axioms "describing" how the execution a program affects the aliasing between expressions. As in [15], the calculus ignores tests in conditionals and loops. The *program instructions* are defined as follows:

$$p ::= p;\, p \mid \textbf{then } p \textbf{ else } p \textbf{ end} \mid$$
$$\textbf{create } x \mid \textbf{forget } x \mid t := s \mid$$
$$\textbf{loop } p \textbf{ end} \mid \textbf{call } f(l) \mid x.\textbf{call } f(l). \tag{3}$$

In short, we write $r \gg p$ to represent the alias information obtained by executing p when starting with the initial alias relation r.

The axiom for sequential composition is defined in the obvious way:

$$r \gg (p\,;\,q) = (r \gg p) \gg q. \tag{4}$$

Conditionals are handled by considering the union of the alias pairs resulted from the execution of the instructions corresponding to each of the two branches, when starting with the same initial relation:

$$r \gg (\textbf{then }p\textbf{ else }q\textbf{ end}) = r \gg p \ \cup\ r \gg q. \tag{5}$$

As previously mentioned, we define $r \gg \textbf{loop }p\textbf{ end}$ according to its informal semantics: "execute p repeatedly any number of times, including zero". The corresponding rule is:

$$r \gg (\textbf{loop }p\textbf{ end}) = \bigcup_{n \in \mathbb{N}} (r \gg p^n) \tag{6}$$

where $\cup$ stands for the union of alias relations, as above. This way, our calculus is extended to infinite alias relations. This is the main difference with the approach in [15] that proposes a "cutting" technique restricting the model to a maximum length L. In [15], sequences longer than L are considered as aliased to all expressions. Orthogonally, for sequential settings, we provide finite representations of infinite alias relations based on over-approximating regular expressions, as we shall see in Sect. 2.2.

Both the creation and the deletion of an object x eliminate from the current alias relation all the pairs having one element prefixed by x:

$$r \gg (\textbf{create }x) = r - x$$
$$r \gg (\textbf{forget }x) = r - x. \tag{7}$$

The (qualified) function calls comply to their initial definitions in [15]:

$$r \gg (\textbf{call }f(l)) = (r[f^\bullet : l]) \gg \mid f \mid$$
$$r \gg (x.\textbf{call }f(l)) = x.((x'.r) \gg \textbf{call }f(x'.l)). \tag{8}$$

Here $f^\bullet$ and $\mid f \mid$ stand for the formal argument list and the body of f, respectively, whereas $r[u : v]$ is the relation r in which every element of the list v is replaced by its counterpart in u. Intuitively, the negative variable x' is meant to transpose the context of the qualified call to the context of the caller. Note that "." (*i.e.*, the constructor for alias expressions) is generalized to distribute over lists and relations: $x.[a, b, \ldots] = [x.a, x.b, \ldots]$.

For an example, consider a class C in an OO-language, and an associated procedure f that assigns a local variable y, defined as: $f(x)\,\{\ y := x\ \}$. Then, for instance, the aliasing for $a.\textbf{call }f(a)$ computes as follows:

$$\emptyset \gg a.\textbf{call }f(a) =$$
$$a.(a'.\emptyset \gg y := a'.a) =$$
$$a.(\emptyset \gg y := \textit{Current}) =$$
$$\textit{dot-complete}(\{[a.y, a]\}).$$

Recursive function calls can lead to infinite alias relations. In sequential settings, as for the case of loops, the mechanism exploiting sound regular over-approximations in order to derive finite representations of such relations is presented in the subsequent sections.

The axiom for assignment is as well in accordance with its original counterpart in [15]:

$$r » (t := s) = \textbf{given } r_1 = r[ot = t]$$
$$\textbf{then } (r_1 - t)[t = (r_1/s - t)] - ot \textbf{ end} \tag{9}$$

where ot is a fresh variable (that stands for "old t"). Intuitively, the aliasing information w.r.t. the initial value of t is "saved" by associating t and ot in r and closing the new relation under dot-completeness, in r_1. Then, the initial t is "forgotten" by computing $r_1 - t$ and the new aliasing information is added in a consistent way. Namely, we add all pairs (t, s'), where s' ranges over $r_1/s - t$ representing all expressions already aliased with s in r_1, including s itself, but without t. Recall that alias relations are not reflexive, thus by eliminating t we make sure we do not include pairs of shape $[t, t]$. Then, we consider again the closure under dot-completeness and forget the aliasing information w.r.t. the initial value of t, by removing ot.

Remark 1. It is worth discussing the reason behind *not* considering transitive alias relations. Assume the following program:

$$\textbf{then } x := y \textbf{ else } y := z \textbf{ end}$$

Based on the Eqs. (5) and (9) handling conditionals and assignments, respectively, the calculus correctly identifies the alias set: $\{[x, y], [y, z]\}$. Including $[x, z]$ would be semantically equivalent to the execution of the two branches in the conditional at the same time, which is not what we want.

2.2   A Sound Over-Approximation

In a sequential setting, the challenge of computing the alias information in the context of (infinite) loops and recursive calls reduces to evaluating their corresponding "unfoldings", captured by expressions of shape

$$r » p^{\omega},$$

with ω ranging over naturals plus infinity, r an (initial) alias relation ($r = \emptyset$), and p a *basic control block* defined by:

$$p :: = p;\, p \mid \textbf{then } p \textbf{ else } p \textbf{ end} \mid$$
$$\textbf{create } x \mid \textbf{forget } x \mid$$
$$t := s. \tag{10}$$

The value $r \gg p^\omega$ refers to the alias relation obtained by recursively executing the control block p, and it is calculated in the expected way:

$$r \gg p^0 = r$$
$$r \gg p^{k+1} = (r \gg p^k) \gg p.$$

Consider again the code in (1):

$$x := y;$$
$$\textbf{loop } x := x.next \textbf{ end}.$$

Its execution generates the alias relation

$$(((\emptyset \gg (x := y)) \gg (x := x.next)) \gg (x := x.next) \ldots$$

including an infinite number of pairs of shape:

$$[x, y.next], [x, y.next.next], [x, y.next.next.next] \ldots . \tag{11}$$

A similar reasoning does not hold for concurrent applications, where process interaction is not "regular".

In what follows we provide a way to compute finite representations of infinite alias relations in sequential settings. The key observation is that alias expressions corresponding to unbounded program executions grow in a regular fashion. See, for instance, the aliases in (11), which are pairs of type $[x, y.next^{k \geq 1}]$.

Regular expressions are defined similarly to the regular languages over an alphabet. We say that an expression is *regular* if it is a local variable, class attribute or *Current*. Moreover, the concatenation $e_1 . e_2$ of two regular expressions e_1 and e_2 is also regular. Given a regular alias expression e, the expression e^* is also regular; here $(-)^*$ denotes the Kleene star [14]. We call an alias relation *regular* if it consists of pairs of regular expressions.

Lemma 1. *Assume p a program built according to the rules in (3). Then, in a sequential setting, the relation $\emptyset \gg p$ is regular.*

Proof. The result follows by induction on the structure of p.

Inspired by the idea behind the *pumping lemma for regular languages* [25], we define a *lasso* property for alias relations, which identifies the repetitive patterns within the structure of the corresponding alias expressions. The intuition is that such patterns will occur for an infinite number of times due to the execution of loops or recursive function calls. Then, we supply sound over-approximations of "lasso" relations, based on regular alias expressions.

In the context of alias relations, we say that the lasso property is satisfied by r and r' whenever the following two conditions hold: (1) r behaves like a *lasso base* of r'. Namely, all the pairs $[e_1, e_2] \in r$ are used to generate elements $[e'_1, e'_2] \in r'$, by repeating tails of prefixes of e_1 and e_2, respectively, and (2) r' is a *lasso extension* of r. Namely, all the pairs in r' are generated from elements of

r by repeating tails of their prefixes. For example, if e_1 above is an expression of shape $x.y.z.w$, then e_1' can be $x.y.y.z.w$ if we consider the tail y of the prefix $x.y$, or $x.y.z.y.z.w$ if we take the tail $y.z$ of the prefix $x.y.z$.

Formally, consider r and r' two alias relations, and x_i, y_i and z_i a set of (possibly empty) expressions, for $i \in \{1, 2\}$. Then:

$$\text{lasso}(r, r') = ([x_1 y_1 z_1, x_2 y_2 z_2] \in r \quad \text{iff} \quad [x_1 y_1 y_1 z_1, x_2 y_2 y_2 z_2] \in r'). \tag{12}$$

For the simplicity of notation we sometimes omit the dot-separators between expressions. For instance, we write $x\,y\,z$ in lieu of $x.y.z$.

Assuming a lasso over r and r', we compute a relation consisting of regular expressions over-approximating r and r' as:

$$\begin{aligned} \text{reg}(r, r') = \{ & [x_1 y_1^* z_1, x_2 y_2^* z_2] \mid \\ & [x_1 y_1 z_1, x_2 y_2 z_2] \in r \wedge \\ & [x_1 y_1 y_1 z_1, x_2 y_2 y_2 z_2] \in r' \} \end{aligned} \tag{13}$$

where x_i, y_i and z_i are possibly empty expressions, for $i \in \{1, 2\}$. As previously indicated, the over-approximation is sound w.r.t. the repeated application of a basic control block as in (10), in the way that it does not introduce any false negatives:

Lemma 2. *Consider r and r' two alias relations, and p a basic control block in a sequential setting. If $r \gg p = r'$ and $\text{lasso}(r, r') = true$, then the following holds for all $n \geq 1$:*

$$r \gg p^n \in \text{reg}(r, r').$$

Proof. The reasoning is by induction on n. The base case follows immediately, whereas the induction step is proved by "reductio ad absurdum".   □

3   A $\mathbb{K}$-Machinery for Collecting Aliases

In this section we provide the specification of a RL-based mechanism collecting the alias information in the $\mathbb{K}$ semantic framework [27]. We choose $\mathbb{K}$ more as a notational convention to enable compact and modular definitions. In reality, the $\mathbb{K}$-rules in this section are implemented in Maude, as rewriting theories, on top of the formalization of SCOOP [22] (we refer to Sect. 4 for more details on our approach).

In short, our strategy is to start with a program built on top of the control structures in (3), then to apply the corresponding $\mathbb{K}$-rules in order to get the "may aliasing" information in a designated $\mathbb{K}$-cell ($\langle\, - \,\rangle_{\text{al}}$). Independently of the setting (sequential or concurrent) one can exploit this approach in order to evaluate the aliases of a given finite length L. We also show that for sequential contexts, the application of the $\mathbb{K}$-rules is finite and the aliases in the final configuration soundly over-approximate the (infinite) "may alias" relations of the calculus.

Brief Overview of $\mathbb{K}$. $\mathbb{K}$ [27] is an executable semantic framework based on Rewriting Logic [19]. It is suitable for defining (concurrent) languages and corresponding formal analysis tools, with straightforward implementation in $\mathbb{K}$-Maude [28]. $\mathbb{K}$-definitions make use of the so-called *cells*, which are labelled and can be nested, and (rewriting) *rules* describing the intended (operational) semantics.

A *cell* is denoted by $\langle\ -\ \rangle_{[name]}$, where [name] stands for the *name of the cell*. A construction $\langle\ .\ \rangle_n$ stands for an *empty cell* named n. We use "pattern matching" and write $\langle\ c\ ...\rangle_n$ for a cell with content c at the top, followed by an arbitrary content $(...)$. Orthogonally, we can utilize cells of shape $\langle...\ c\ \rangle_n$ and $\langle\ ...c...\ \rangle_n$, defined in the obvious way.

Of particular interest is $\langle\ -\ \rangle_k$ – the *continuation cell*, or the *k-cell*, holding the stack of program instructions (associated to one processor), in the context of a programming language formalization. We write

$$\langle\ i_1 \curvearrowright i_2\ ...\rangle_k$$

for a set of instructions to be "executed", starting with instruction i_1, followed by i_2. The associative operation $\curvearrowright$ is the instruction sequencing.

A $\mathbb{K}$-rewrite rule

$$\langle\ c\ ...\rangle_{n_1}\langle\ c'\ \rangle_{n_2} \Rightarrow \langle\ c'\ ...\rangle_{n_1}\langle...\ c'\ \rangle_{n_3} \tag{14}$$

reads as: if cell n_1 has c at the top and cell n_2 contains value c', then c is replaced by c' in n_1 and c' is added at the end of the cell n_3. The content of n_2 remains unchanged. In short, (14) is written in a $\mathbb{K}$-like syntax as:

$$\langle\ \frac{c}{c'}\ ...\rangle_{n_1}\ \langle\ c'\ \rangle_{n_2}\ \langle...\ \frac{\cdot}{c'}\ \rangle_{n_3}.$$

We further provide the details behind the $\mathbb{K}$-specification of the alias calculus. As expected, the k-cell retains the instruction stack of the object-oriented program. We utilize cells $\langle-\rangle_{al}$ to enclose the current alias information, and the so-called *back-tracking cells* $\langle-\rangle_{bkt-...}$ enabling the sound computation of aliases for the case of **then** − **else** − **end** and, in non-concurrent contexts, for loops and (possibly recursive) function calls. As a convention, we mark with (♣) the rules that are sound only for non-concurrent applications, based on Lemma 2. Due to space limitations, in what follows we introduce only the $\mathbb{K}$-rules for handling assignments and loops. The entire specification can be found in [5].

As expected, the assignment rule simply restores the current alias relation according to its axiom in (9), and removes the assignment instruction from the top of the k-cell:

$$\left\langle\ \frac{r}{(r_1 - t)[t = (r_1/s\ -\ t)] - ot}\ \right\rangle_{al}\ \langle\ \frac{t := s}{\cdot}\ ...\rangle_k\ \ \text{with}\ r_1 = r[ot = t] \tag{15}$$

For **loop** p **end**, we utilize a meta-construction $p\ \boxed{1}\ $**loop** p **end** simulating the unfolding corresponding to (6), and a back-tracking stack $\langle-\rangle_{bkt-1}$ collecting the alias information obtained after each execution of p. Moreover, the

$\mathbb{K}$-implementation exploits the result in Lemma 2. Whenever a "lasso" is reached, the infinite rewriting is prevented by resuming the infinite application of p in terms of a sound over-approximating alias relation. The $\mathbb{K}$-rules are as follows.

First, the aforementioned unfolding is performed, and the alias relation before p is stored in the back-tracking cell as $\langle r \rangle_{\text{al-o}} \langle p \rangle_{\text{l}}$:

$$\langle\, r\, \rangle_{\text{al}} \left\langle \frac{\textbf{loop } p \textbf{ end}}{p\,\boxed{1}\,\textbf{loop } p \textbf{ end}} \cdots \right\rangle_{\text{k}} \left\langle \frac{\cdot}{\langle\, r\, \rangle_{\text{al-o}} \langle\, p\, \rangle_{\text{l}}} \cdots \right\rangle_{\text{bkt-l}} \tag{16}$$

If the alias relation r' obtained after the successful execution of p (marked by $\boxed{1}$ at the top of the continuation) is not a lasso of the aliasing r before p (previously stored in $\langle - \rangle_{\text{bkt-l}}$) then p is constrained to a new execution by becoming the top of the k-cell, and r' is memorized for back-tracking:

$$\langle\, r'\, \rangle_{\text{al}} \left\langle \frac{\boxed{1}\,\textbf{loop } p \textbf{ end}}{p\,\boxed{1}\,\textbf{loop } p \textbf{ end}} \cdots \right\rangle_{\text{k}} \left\langle \frac{\langle\, r\, \rangle_{\text{al-o}} \langle\, p\, \rangle_{\text{l}}}{\langle\, r'\, \rangle_{\text{al-o}} \langle\, p\, \rangle_{\text{l}}} \cdots \right\rangle_{\text{bkt-l}} \text{ if not } \text{lasso}(r, r') \; (\clubsuit) \tag{17}$$

Last, if a lasso is reached after the execution of p, then the current aliasing is soundly replaced by a "regular" over-approximation $\text{reg}(r, r')$, the corresponding back-tracking information is removed from $\langle - \rangle_{\text{bkt-l}}$ and the **loop** instruction is eliminated from the k-cell:

$$\left\langle \frac{r'}{\text{reg}(r, r')} \right\rangle_{\text{al}} \left\langle \frac{\boxed{1}\,\textbf{loop } p \textbf{ end}}{\cdot} \cdots \right\rangle_{\text{k}} \left\langle \frac{\langle\, r\, \rangle_{\text{al-o}} \langle\, p\, \rangle_{\text{l}}}{\cdot} \cdots \right\rangle_{\text{bkt-l}} \text{ if } \text{lasso}(r, r') \; (\clubsuit) \tag{18}$$

In a non-concurrent setting, the machinery orchestrating the $\mathbb{K}$-rules introduced in this section implements an algorithm that always terminates and provides a sound over-approximation of "may aliasing".

Theorem 1. *Consider p a program built on top of the control structures in (3), that executes in a sequential setting. Then, the application of the corresponding $\mathbb{K}$-rules when starting with p and an empty alias relation, is a finite rewriting of shape*

$$\langle\, \emptyset\, \rangle_{\text{al}} \langle\, p\, \rangle_{\text{k}} \stackrel{(*)}{\Longrightarrow} \langle\, r\, \rangle_{\text{al}} \langle\, \cdot\, \rangle_{\text{k}},$$

with r a sound over-approximation of the aliasing information corresponding to the execution of p.

Proof. The key observation is that, due to the execution of loops and/or recursive calls, expressions can infinitely grow in a *regular* fashion. Hence, a lasso is always reached. Consequently, the control structure generating the infinite behaviour is removed from the k-cell, according to the associated $\mathbb{K}$-specification for loops and/or recursive calls. This guarantees termination. Moreover, recall that the regular expressions replacing the current alias information are a sound over-approximation, according to Lemma 2. □

Observe that the RL-based machinery can simulate precisely the "cutting at length L" technique in [15]. It suffices to disable the rules ($\clubsuit$) and stop the rewriting after L steps.

4   Integration in SCOOP

In this section we provide a brief overview on the integration and applicability of the alias calculus in SCOOP [22] – a simple object-oriented programming model for concurrency. Two main characteristics make SCOOP simple: (1) just one keyword programmers have to learn and use in order to enable concurrent executions, namely, *separate* and (2) the burden of orchestrating concurrent executions is handled within the model, therefore reducing the risk of correctness issues.

In short, the key idea of SCOOP is to associate to each object a processor, or *handler* (that can be a CPU, or it can also be implemented in software, as a process or thread). Assume a processor p that performs a call $o.f()$ on an object o. If o is declared as "separate", then p sends a request for executing $f()$ to q – the handler of o (note that p and q can coincide). Meanwhile, p can continue. Processors communicate via *channels*.

The Maude semantics of SCOOP in [22] is defined over tuples of shape

$$\langle p_1 :: St_1 \mid \ldots \mid p_n :: St_n, \sigma \rangle$$

where, p_i denotes a processor (for $i \in \{1, \ldots, n\}$), St_i is the call stack of p_i and σ is the *state* of the system. States hold the information about the *heap* (which is a mapping of references to objects) and the *store* (which includes formal arguments, local variables, *etc.*.).

The assignment instruction, for instance, is formally specified as the transition rule:

$$\frac{a \text{ is fresh}}{\Gamma \vdash \langle p :: t := s; St, \sigma \rangle \rightarrow \langle p :: \text{eval}(a, s); \text{wait}(a); \text{write}(t, a.data); St, \sigma \rangle} \quad (19)$$

where, intuitively, "eval(a, s)" evaluates s and puts the result on channel a, "wait(a)" enables processor p to use the evaluation result, "write$(t, a.data)$" sets the value of t to $a.data$, St is a call stack, and Γ is a typing environment [24] containing the class hierarchy of a program and all the type definitions.

At this point it is easy to understand that the K-rule for assignments

$$\langle \frac{r}{(r_1 - t)[t = (r_1/s - t)] - ot} \rangle_{\text{al}} \langle \frac{t := s \ldots}{.} \rangle_{\text{k}} \text{ with } r_1 = r[ot = t] \quad (15)$$

can be straightforwardly integrated in (19) by enriching the state structure with a new field encapsulating the alias information, and considering instead the transition $\Gamma \vdash \langle p :: t := s; St, \sigma \rangle \rightarrow \langle p :: \text{eval}(a, s); \text{wait}(a); \text{write}(t, a.data); St, \sigma' \rangle$ where

$$\sigma.aliases = r \qquad \sigma'.aliases = (r_1 - t)[t = (r_1/s - t)] - ot$$

with r and r_1 as in [20]. The integration of all the K-rules of the alias calculus on top of the Maude formalization of SCOOP can be achieved by following a similar approach.

For a case study, one can download the SCOOP formalization at: https://dl.dropboxusercontent.com/u/1356725/SCOOP.zip and run. The command > `maude SCOOP.maude ..\examples\aliasing-linked_list.maude` corresponding to the code in (1):

$$x := y; \ \textbf{loop} \ x := x.next \ \textbf{end}.$$

The console outputs the aliased expressions for a rewriting of depth 100 which include, as expected, pairs of shape $[x, y.next^k]$. (The over-approximating mechanism for sequential settings is still to be implemented.)

As can be observed based on the code in `aliasing-linked_list.maude`, in order to implement our applications in Maude, we use intermediate (still intuitive) representations. For instance, the class structure defining a node in a simple linked list, with filed *next* is declared as:

```
class 'NODE
    create {'make}
    ( attribute { 'ANY } 'next : [?, . , 'NODE] ; )
    [...]
end ;
```

where `'next : [?, . , 'NODE]` stands for an object of type NODE, that is handled by the current processor (.) and that can be Void (?), and `'make` plays the role of a constructor. The intermediate representation of the instruction block in (1) is:

```
assign ('x, 'y);
until False loop ( assign ('x, 'x . 'next(nil)) ; ) end ;
```

For a detailed description of SCOOP and its Maude formalization we refer the interested reader to the work in [22].

4.1 Further Applications of the Alias Calculus

Apart from providing an alias analysis tool, the alias calculus can be exploited in order to build an abstract semantics of SCOOP. For example, an abstraction of the assignment rule (15) would omit the evaluation of the right-hand side of the assignment $t := s$ and the associated message passing between channels:

$$\overline{\Gamma \vdash \langle p :: t := s; St, \sigma \rangle \rightarrow \langle p :: St, \sigma' \rangle}$$

where

$$\sigma.aliases = r \qquad \sigma'.aliases = (r_1 - t)[t = (r_1/s - t)] - ot$$

with r and r_1 as in (15). This way one derives a simplified, reduced semantics of SCOOP, more appropriate for model checking, for instance; the current SCOOP formalization in Maude is often too large for this purpose. A survey on abstracting techniques on top of Maude executable semantics is provided in [19].

Furthermore, the aliasing information could be used for the so-called "deadlocking" problem, where two or more executing threads are each waiting for the other to finish. In the context of SCOOP, this is equivalent to identifying whether a set of processors reserve each other circularly (*i.e.*, there is a Coffman deadlock). This situation might occur, for instance, in a Dinning Philosophers scenario, where both philosophers and forks are objects residing on their own processors. The difficulty of identifying such deadlocks stems from the fact that SCOOP processors are known from object references, which *may be aliased*.

5   Conclusions

In this paper we provide an extension of the alias calculus in [15] from finite alias relations to infinite ones corresponding to loops and recursive calls. Moreover, we devise an associated executable specification in the $\mathbb{K}$ semantic framework [27]. In Theorem 1 we show that the RL-based machinery implements an algorithm that always terminates with a sound over-approximation of "may aliasing", in non-concurrent settings. This is achieved based on the sound (finitely representable) over-approximation of ("lasso shaped") alias expressions in terms of regular expressions, as in Lemma 2. We also discuss the integration and applicability of the alias calculus on top of the Maude formalization of SCOOP [22].

An immediate direction for future work is to identify interesting (industrial) case studies to be analyzed using the framework developed in this paper. We are also interested in devising heuristics comparing the efficiency and the precision (*e.g.*, the number of false positives introduced by the alias approximations) between our approach and other aliasing techniques. In this respect, we anticipate that the rewriting modulo associativity, together with the pattern matching capabilities of Maude will accelerate the identification of the "lasso" properties and the corresponding over-approximating regular alias expressions. This could eventually provide an effective reasoning apparatus for the "may aliasing" problem.

Another research direction is to derive alias-based abstractions for analyzing concurrent programs. We foresee possible connections with the work in [13] on *concurrent Kleene algebra* formalizing choice, iteration, sequential and concurrent composition of programs. The corresponding definitions exploit abstractions of programs in terms of traces of events that can depend on each other. Thus, obvious challenges in this respect include: (i) defining notions of dependence for all the program constructs in this paper, (ii) relating the concurrent Kleene operators to the semantics of the SCOOP concurrency model and (iii) checking whether fixed-points approximating the aliasing information can be identified via fixed-point theorems.

Furthermore, it would be worth investigating whether the graph-based model of alias relations introduced in [15] can be exploited in order to derive finite $\mathbb{K}$ specifications of the extended alias calculus. In case of a positive answer, the general aim is to study whether this type of representation increases the speed of the reasoning mechanism, and why not – its accuracy. With the same purpose, we refer to a possible integration with the technique in [6] that handles point-to graphs via a stack-based algorithm for fixed-point computations.

We are also interested to what extent an abstract semantics based on aliases for SCOOP can be exploited for building more efficient analysis tools such as deadlock detectors, for instance. A survey on similar techniques that abstract away from possibly irrelevant information w.r.t. the problem under consideration is provided in [19].

Acknowledgements. We are grateful for valuable comments to the anonymous reviewers, Măriuca Asăvoae, Alexander Kogtenkov, José Meseguer, Bertrand Meyer, Benjamin Morandi and Sergey Velder. The research leading to these results has received funding from the European Research Council under the European Union's Seventh Framework Programme (FP7/2007–2013) / ERC Grant agreement no. 291389.

References

1. Albert, E., Arenas, P., Genaim, S., Puebla, G.: Field-sensitive value analysis by field-insensitive analysis. In: Cavalcanti, A., Dams, D.R. (eds.) FM 2009. LNCS, vol. 5850, pp. 370–386. Springer, Heidelberg (2009)
2. Asavoae, I.M.: Abstract semantics for alias analysis in K. Electr. Notes Theor. Comput. Sci. **304**, 97–110 (2014)
3. Bouajjani, A., Esparza, J., Maler, O.: Reachability analysis of pushdown automata: application to model-checking. In: Mazurkiewicz, A., Winkowski, J. (eds.) CONCUR 1997. LNCS, vol. 1243, pp. 135–150. Springer, Heidelberg (1997)
4. Burke, M., Carini, P., Choi, J.-D., Hind, M.: Flow-insensitive interprocedural alias analysis in the presence of pointers. In: Pingali, K., Banerjee, U., Gelernter, D., Nicolau, A., Padua, D. (eds.) Languages and Compilers for Parallel Computing. LNCS, vol. 892, pp. 234–250. Springer, Berlin Heidelberg (1995)
5. Caltais, G.: Expression-based aliasing for OO-languages. CoRR, abs/1409.7509 (2014)
6. Chase, D.R.., Wegman, M.N., Zadeck, F.K.: Analysis of pointers and structures. In: PLDI, pp. 296–310 (1990)
7. Choi, J.-D., Burke, M., Carini, P.: Efficient flow-sensitive interprocedural computation of pointer-induced aliases and side effects. In: Proceedings of the 20th ACM SIGPLAN-SIGACT Symposium on Principles of Programming Languages, POPL 1993, pp. 232–245. ACM, New York, NY, USA (1993)
8. Cousot, P., Cousot, R.: Abstract interpretation and application to logic programs. J. Log. Program. **13**(2&3), 103–179 (1992)
9. Diwan, A., McKinley, K.S., Moss, J.E.B.: Type-based alias analysis. SIGPLAN Not. **33**(5), 106–117 (1998)
10. Emami, M., Ghiya, R., Hendren, L.J.: Context-sensitive interprocedural points-to analysis in the presence of function pointers. In: Proceedings of the ACM SIGPLAN 1994 Conference on Programming Language Design and Implementation, PLDI 1994, pp. 242–256. ACM, New York, NY, USA (1994)
11. Hind, M.: Pointer analysis: haven't we solved this problem yet? In: PASTE, pp. 54–61 (2001)
12. Hind, M., Burke, M., Carini, P., Choi, J.-D.: Interprocedural pointer alias analysis. ACM Trans. Program. Lang. Syst. **21**(4), 848–894 (1999)

13. Hoare, C.A.R.T., Möller, B., Struth, G., Wehrman, I.: Concurrent Kleene algebra. In: Bravetti, M., Zavattaro, G. (eds.) CONCUR 2009. LNCS, vol. 5710, pp. 399–414. Springer, Heidelberg (2009)
14. Kleene, S.C.: Representation of events in nerve nets and finite automata. In: Shannon, C., McCarthy, J. (eds.) Automata Studies, pp. 3–41. Princeton University Press, Princeton (1956)
15. Kogtenkov, A., Meyer, B., Velder, S.: Alias and change calculi, applied to frame inference. CoRR, abs/1307.3189 (2013)
16. Landi, W.: Undecidability of static analysis. ACM Lett. Program. Lang. Syst. $1(4)$, 323–337 (1992)
17. Landi, W., Ryder, B.G:. Pointer-induced aliasing: a problem classification. In: Proceedings of the 18th ACM SIGPLAN-SIGACT Symposium on Principles of Programming Languages, POPL 1991, pp. 93–103. ACM, New York, NY, USA (1991)
18. Larus, J.R., Hilfinger, P.N.: Detecting conflicts between structure accesses. In: PLDI, pp. 21–34. ACM, New York (1988)
19. Meseguer, J., Roşu, G.: The rewriting logic semantics project: a progress report. In: Owe, O., Steffen, M., Telle, J.A. (eds.) FCT 2011. LNCS, vol. 6914, pp. 1–37. Springer, Heidelberg (2011)
20. Meyer, B.: Eiffel: The Language. Prentice-Hall, Englewood Cliffs (1991)
21. Miné, A.: Field-sensitive value analysis of embedded C programs with union types and pointer arithmetics. In: Proceedings of the 2006 ACM SIGPLAN/SIGBED Conference on Language, Compilers, and Tool Support for Embedded Systems, LCTES 2006, pp. 54–63. ACM, New York, NY, USA (2006)
22. Morandi, B., Schill, M., Nanz, S., Meyer, B.: Prototyping a concurrency model. In: ACSD, pp. 170–179 (2013)
23. Myers. E.M.: A precise inter-procedural data flow algorithm. In: Proceedings of the 8th ACM SIGPLAN-SIGACT Symposium on Principles of Programming Languages, POPL 1981, pp. 219–230. ACM, New York, NY, USA (1981)
24. Nienaltowski, P.: Practical Framework for Contract-based Concurrent Object-oriented Programming, ETH (2007)
25. Rabin, M.O., Scott, D.: Finite automata and their decision problems. IBM J. Res. Dev. $3(2)$, 114–125 (1959)
26. Robert, V., Leroy, X.: A formally-verified alias analysis. In: Hawblitzel, C., Miller, D. (eds.) CPP 2012. LNCS, vol. 7679, pp. 11–26. Springer, Heidelberg (2012)
27. Rosu, G., Serbanuta, T.F.: K overview and SIMPLE case study. In Proceedings of International K Workshop (K 2011), ENTCS. Elsevier (2013) (to appear)
28. Şerbănuţă, T.F., Roşu, G.: K-Maude: a rewriting based tool for semantics of programming languages. In: Ölveczky, P.C. (ed.) WRLA 2010. LNCS, vol. 6381, pp. 104–122. Springer, Heidelberg (2010)
29. Sridharan, M., Chandra, S., Dolby, J., Fink, S.J., Yahav, E.: Alias analysis for object-oriented programs. In: Clarke, D., Noble, J., Wrigstad, T. (eds.) Aliasing in Object-Oriented Programming. LNCS, vol. 7850, pp. 196–232. Springer, Heidelberg (2013)
30. Wilson, R.P., Lam, M.S.: Efficient context-sensitive pointer analysis for C programs. In: Proceedings of the ACM SIGPLAN 1995 Conference on Programming Language Design and Implementation, PLDI 1995, pp. 1–12. ACM, New York, NY, USA (1995)

Checking Integral Real-Time Automata for Extended Linear Duration Invariants

Changil Choe[1]([⊠]), Univan Ahn[2], and Song Han[1]

[1] Faculty of Mathematics, Kim Il Sung University, Pyongyang,
Democratic People's Republic of Korea
{mathcci,mathsonghan}@yahoo.com
[2] Faculty of Physics, Kim Il Sung University, Pyongyang,
Democratic People's Republic of Korea
univan.ahn@gmail.com

Abstract. Linear duration invariants are important safety properties of real-time systems. They are represented as linear inequalities of integrated durations of system states and form a decidable subclass of Duration Calculus formulas. The problem of whether a real-time automaton satisfies a linear duration invariant can be transformed into a finite number of linear programming problems. In this paper, extended linear duration invariants, which are linear inequalities of integrals of physical quantities that characterize real-time systems, are introduced. The semantics of extended linear duration invariants is defined by introducing integral real-time automata whose states are labeled with a finite number of integrable functions. The problem of checking an integral real-time automaton for an extended linear duration invariant is transformed into a finite number of nonlinear programming problems which can be solved easily. A case study of a reaction tank is discussed to demonstrate the effectiveness of the technique introduced in the paper.

Keywords: Real-time system · Real-time automaton · Linear duration invariant · Integral real-time automaton · Extended linear duration invariant

1 Introduction

Duration Calculus (abbreviated to DC) represents a logical approach to the formal design of real-time systems [1]. DC uses durations of states over time intervals to specify and reason about real-time behavior of embedded systems. The duration of a state in a time interval is the total presence time of the state in the interval. Linear constraints on the durations of system states form a class of important properties of real-time systems. This class was given the name *linear duration invariants* and was first introduced in [2].

A linear duration invariant is a DC formula of the form

$$c_{min} \leq \ell \leq c_{max} \rightarrow \sum_{i=1}^{n} c_i \int s_i \leq C,$$

© Springer International Publishing Switzerland 2015
C. Artho and P.C. Ölveczky (Eds.): FTSCS 2014, CCIS 476, pp. 62–75, 2015.
DOI: 10.1007/978-3-319-17581-2_5

where c_{min}, c_{max}, c_i $(1 \leq i \leq n)$ and C are real numbers, and s_i $(1 \leq i \leq n)$ are states of the system. A linear duration invariant means that for any observation time intervals, if the length ℓ of the interval satisfies the constraint $c_{min} \leq \ell \leq c_{max}$ then the durations of the system states over that interval should satisfy the constraint $\sum_{i=1}^{n} c_i \int s_i \leq C$. Many desired properties of real-time systems can be represented as linear duration invariants.

In [2], Zhou also defined a satisfaction problem of a linear duration invariant for a *real-time automaton* and proved that the problem of checking satisfaction of a linear duration invariant by a real-time automaton can be transformed into a finite number of linear programming problems. After the publication of [2], much work has been devoted to extending this satisfaction problem to timed automata and checking timed automata for linear duration invariants, e.g. [3–7].

In this paper, we introduce *extended linear duration invariants* that are represented as linear constraints on the accumulated physical quantities in the observation intervals. An extended linear duration invariant has the form

$$c_{min} \leq \ell \leq c_{max} \rightarrow \sum_{i=1}^{m} c_i \int f_i \leq C.$$

Here, c_{min}, c_{max}, c_i $(1 \leq i \leq m)$ and C are real numbers, and f_i $(1 \leq i \leq m)$ are integrable functions assigned to the states of the system. $\int f_i$ $(1 \leq i \leq m)$ stand for the integrals of f_i $(1 \leq i \leq m)$ in the observation intervals. The formal definition of $\int f$ is given in Sect. 2.

To define the semantics of extended linear duration invariants, we introduce a variant of real-time automata called *integral real-time automata*. An integral real-time automaton is a real-time automaton whose states are labeled with a finite number of integrable functions. The semantics of extended linear duration invariants with respect to integral real-time automata is defined as a conservative extension of the semantics of linear duration invariants with respect to real-time automata.

Then we prove that the problem of checking an integral real-time automaton for an extended linear duration invariant can be reduced to a finite number of nonlinear programming problems. (In [2], the problem of checking a real-time automaton for a linear duration invariant was reduced to a finite number of linear programming problems.) The constraints of these nonlinear programming problems constitute convex polyhedra in Euclidean spaces and the objective functions are separable. Nonlinear programming problems of this type have already been well studied and any algorithm for solving these problems can be used for deciding our satisfaction problem.

As a case study, we represent a reaction tank as an integral real-time automaton, specify its safety requirement using an extended linear duration invariant, and prove that the model satisfies the specification. The reaction tank is a very small two-state system which seems to be considered for the first time in this paper. It motivated us to extend the real-time automata approach for systems verificationto nonlinear programming. It will be useful if we have a verification technique for dealing with nonlinear accumulations of physical quantities using DC, since rough linearization of nonlinear behaviors may weaken confidence in the verification.

The paper is organized as follows. In the next section we introduce integral real-time automata and extended linear duration invariants. In Sect. 3 we define the semantics of extended linear duration invariants with respect to integral real-time automata. In Sect. 4 we present a technique for checking integral real-time automata against extended linear duration invariants. The reaction tank is discussed throughout the paper to validate the technique introduced in the paper.

2   Integral Real-Time Automata and Extended Linear Duration Invariants

In this section, we introduce integral real-time automata and extended linear duration invariants, and define the semantics of extended linear duration invariants with respect to integral real-time automata.

2.1   Integral Real-Time Automata

Before introducing integral real-time automata, we recall the definition of real-time automata and consider a real-time automaton for a gas burner [2,8,9].

Definition 1. *A real-time automaton A is a tuple $< S, T, \text{low}, \text{up} >$ which satisfies the following conditions [2]:*

- *S is a finite set of states $\{s_1, s_2, \ldots, s_n\}$.*
- *$T \subseteq S \times S$ is a finite set of transitions.*
- *The functions $\text{low} : T \to R$ and $\text{up} : T \to (R \cup \{\infty\})$ denote the lower- and upper-bound timing constraints on the transitions, where $0 \leq \text{low}(\rho) \leq \text{up}(\rho)$ and $\text{low}(\rho) = 0 \to \text{up}(\rho) > 0$ for any $\rho \in T$.*

Every state of a real-time automaton is both an initial and an accepting state. The set of real-time automata is a subclass of the timed automata of [10], where each automaton has one clock that is reset after every transition.

Let us consider an example of real-time system that is represented as a real-time automaton, a gas burner first investigated in [11]. A gas burner works by repeating heating and idling. When it moves from idling to heating, gas flows for a little time before it is ignited. And when it fails to ignite the gas, gas still flows until the flame failure is detected and the gas valve is closed. To prevent a dangerous accumulation of gas, the time intervals where gas is leaking should not become too long.

The real-time requirement of the gas burner is that in any observation interval not smaller than one minute, the proportion of total time of gas leaks should not be more than one-twentieth of the interval. This requirement can be refined into the following two design decisions.

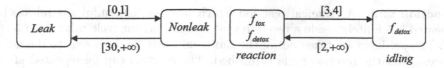

Fig. 1. Left: A real-time automaton for the gas burner. Right: An integral real-time automation for the reaction tank.

Des1 : Any gas leak should be stoppable within one second.
Des2 : The time between two gas leaks should not be less than thirty seconds.

Des1 and *Des2* can be represented by the real-time automaton in Fig. 1, which has two states of *Leak* and *Nonleak*.

The timing constraint on transition (*Leak*, *Nonleak*) is a bounded and closed interval $[0, 1]$. This denotes that the automaton can stay in the *Leak* state for at most one time unit before a transition to the *Nonleak* state takes place. The timing constraint on transition (*Nonleak*, *Leak*) is a left closed, unbounded interval $[30, \infty)$. This denotes that the automaton must stay in the *Nonleak* state for at least 30 time units before a transition to the *Leak* state can take place, and it can even stay in the *Nonleak* state forever.

We now introduce integral real-time automata and consider an integral real-time automaton model of a safety critical system. $\mathbb{R}^+$ denotes the set of nonnegative real numbers. $Intg(\mathbb{R}^+)$ denotes the set of integrable functions over $\mathbb{R}^+$.

Definition 2. *An integral real-time automaton D is a tuple $< S, T, \text{low}, \text{up}, L >$ which satisfies the following conditions:*

- $< S, T, \text{low}, \text{up} >$ *is a real-time automaton.*
- $L : S \longrightarrow 2^{Intg(\mathbb{R}^+)}$ *assigns a finite set of integrable functions to each state $s \in S$.*

A function which is assigned to a state represents the generation process of a certain physical quantity, which progresses during the continuous presence of that state. What we are interested in this paper is an inequality which is related to the integrals of such generation processes. So no other conditions are given to the functions which are assigned to the states other than the integrability condition. Integrability is needed to make the model checking decidable. Every state of an integral real-time automaton is both an initial and an accepting state.

The reason for defining integral real-time automata might be questioned because there is a possibility that integral real-time automata can be transformed into the hybrid automata of [12]. Such a question will be solved after we introduce extended linear duration invariants and define their semantics using integral real-time automata in Sect. 3. It is enough to represent the system as a simple integral real-time automaton for the model checking of an extended linear duration invariant. If necessary, we can consider the model checking of hybrid automata for extended linear duration invariants.

Let us consider an example of a safety critical system which can be represented as an integral real-time automaton.

Reaction tank. A chemical reaction which involves a harmful gas release is repeated indefinitely inside a reaction tank. Each reaction cycle takes from 3 to 4 h. The products are taken out of the tank and waste liquid is sent to the next process after the reaction cycle is finished. The reaction can be repeated after 2 h from the end of the preceding reaction, or it may never be resumed. An air cleaner is installed and works constantly to neutralize the released harmful gas.

The left function of Fig. 2, denoted by f_{tox}, shows the variation of the amount of harmful gas which is released during the reaction. The right function of Fig. 2, denoted by f_{detox}, shows the neutralization ability of the air cleaner.

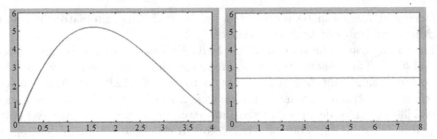

Fig. 2. Left: The harmful gas release characteristic during the reaction. Right: The neutralization ability of the air cleaner.

The analytic expressions of f_{tox} and f_{detox} are as follows.

$$f_{tox}(x) = 0.35x^3 - 3.23x^2 + 7.53x \qquad 0 \le x \le 4$$
$$f_{detox}(x) = 2.4 \qquad x \ge 0$$

Air pollution of the working environment will be caused if the air cleaner fails to neutralize harmful gas in real time. This imposes a safety requirement on the reaction tank; in any observation interval not smaller than 12 h, the air cleaner should be completely capable of neutralizing the released harmful gas.

Figure 1 shows an integral real-time automaton model of the reaction tank. The automaton has two states of *reaction* and *idling*. Two functions f_{tox} and f_{detox} are assigned to the *reaction* state. This denotes that harmful gas release and its neutralization occur together in the *reaction* state. A function f_{detox} is assigned to the *idling* state. This denotes that already released harmful gas is neutralized in the *idling* state without extra release of harmful gas.

A real-time automaton can be considered as an integral real-time automaton whose states are labeled with one constant function $f(x) = 1$. In that sense, the notion of integral real-time automata is an extension of the notion of real-time automata. It is possible to represent an integral real-time automaton as a weighted timed automaton [17,18], if the functions which are assigned to the states of the integral real-time automaton are constant or piecewise constant.

Remark 1. We assumed that the domains of the functions which are assigned to the states are $\mathbb{R}^+$ when we defined integral real-time automata. However, readers may notice that the domain of the function f_{tox} assigned to the *reaction* state in Fig. 1 is $[0,4]$. The reason we confine the domain of f_{tox} to $[0,4]$ is that the system can stay in the *reaction* state at most 4 h. We can easily extend the domain of f_{tox} to $\mathbb{R}^+$ by assigning 0 to every x greater than 4.

2.2   Extended Linear Duration Invariants

Before defining extended linear duration invariants, we recall the definition of
linear duration invariants and consider an example of linear duration invariant specifications of real-time requirements. Linear duration invariants form a
decidable subclass of DC. The syntax, semantics and proof system of DC were
summarized in the monograph [13].

DC is effective in expressing various patterns of real-time requirements, but
its formulas are highly undecidable. Only a very small class of chop free formulas
including linear duration invariants is decidable [14]. Because linear duration
invariants are important properties of real-time systems, model checking of linear
duration invariants has attracted great deal of attention since the introduction
of DC.

Definition 3. *A linear duration invariant for the real-time automaton A is a
DC formula of the form*

$$c_{min} \leq \ell \leq c_{max} \rightarrow \sum_{i=1}^{n} c_i \int s_i \leq C.$$

Here, c_{min}, c_{max}, c_i $(1 \leq i \leq n)$ and C are real numbers, and s_i $(1 \leq i \leq n)$
are states of A. ℓ is a term which takes the length of the interval for each
observation interval. $\int s$ is a term which takes the integrated duration of s for
each observation interval. The real-time requirement of the gas burner mentioned
in Sect. 2.1 is represented as $\ell \geq 60 \rightarrow (19 \int Leak - \int Nonleak) \leq 0$ [11]. If it is
obvious from the context, we call the linear duration invariants for a real-time
automaton simply the linear duration invariants. *LDI* will be used to denote a
linear duration invariant.

Now we define extended linear duration invariants and consider an example
of extended linear duration invariant specifications.

Definition 4. *An extended linear duration invariant for the integral real-time
automaton D is a formula of the form*

$$c_{min} \leq \ell \leq c_{max} \rightarrow \sum_{i=1}^{m} c_i \int f_i \leq C.$$

Here, c_{min}, c_{max}, c_i $(1 \leq i \leq m)$ and C are real numbers, and f_i $(1 \leq i \leq m)$
are functions assigned to the states of D. ℓ is a term which takes the length of
the interval for each observation interval. $\int f_i$ is a term which takes the integral
of f_i for each observation interval. If it is obvious from the context, we call the
extended linear duration invariants for an integral real-time automaton simply
the extended linear duration invariants. *ELDI* will be used to denote an extended
linear duration invariant.

An essential difference between linear duration invariants and extended linear
duration invariants comes from the difference of the calculations of $\int s$ and $\int f$.
We use an example to show this.

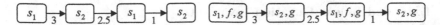

The left side of the above diagram is a behavior of a real-time automaton. For this behavior, $\int s_1$ and $\int s_2$ are calculated as $\int s_1 = 3+1 = 4$ and $\int s_2 = 2.5$. The right side of the above diagram is a behavior of an integral real-time automaton. For this behavior, $\int f$ and $\int g$ are calculated as $\int f = \int_0^3 f(x)dx + \int_0^1 f(x)dx$ and $\int g = \int_0^3 g(x)dx + \int_0^{2.5} g(x)dx + \int_0^1 g(x)dx$.

The linear duration invariants and the extended linear duration invariants also have a difference in the structures of their linear terms. The linear term $\sum_{i=1}^n c_i \int s_i$ of a linear duration invariant for the real-time automaton A consists of subterms $c_1 \int s_1, \ldots, c_{n-1} \int s_{n-1}$ and $c_n \int s_n$, whose number is equal to the number of states of A. (Note that some c_i could be 0.) But the linear term $\sum_{i=1}^m c_i \int f_i$ of an extended linear duration invariant for the integral real-time automaton D consists of subterms $c_1 \int f_1, \ldots, c_{m-1} \int f_{m-1}$ and $c_m \int f_m$, whose number is equal to the number of different functions assigned to the states of D. (Note that some c_i could also be 0.)

For example, the number of different functions assigned to the states of the integral real-time automaton in Fig. 1 is 2. Hence, the linear term of any extended linear duration invariant for this integral real-time automaton consists of two subterms $c_1 \int f_{tox}$ and $c_2 \int f_{detox}$.

Readers who are familiar with DC can easily find that extended linear duration invariants are not formulas of DC, because there is no term $\int f$ in the syntax of DC. To define extended linear duration invariants strictly, we first should extend DC by adding the term $\int f$ to the syntax of DC and then define extended linear duration invariants as the formulas of the extended DC. In this paper, we do not consider the extension of DC and define extended linear duration invariants by directly extending linear duration invariants. That is why we called extended linear duration invariants in Definition 4 simply formulas rather than DC formulas.

It is possible to extend the syntax of DC to be allowed to include the real valued term $\int f$. The early paper of Zhou Chaochen et al. [15] would be helpful for this work, where the authors extended DC by introducing real valued term dt to capture properties of piecewise continuous states. The semantics of the term dt in [15] is different from the one of the term $\int f$ in this paper, however. And the main concern of the authors in [15] was to introduce a proof theory for the extended DC, rather than developing a model checking technique. Nevertheless, [15] provides a good approach for extending DC by introducing the real valued term $\int f$.

Returning to the reaction tank, the safety requirement which was already considered in Sect. 2.1 can be specified as the extended linear duration invariant

$$12 \le \ell \to \int f_{tox} - \int f_{detox} \le 0.$$

Here, $\int f_{tox}$ represents the total amount of gas released in each observation interval and $\int f_{detox}$ represents the total amount of gas which can be neutralized in that interval. It is impossible to specify this real-time requirement as a linear duration invariant.

From the above discussion, readers will understand the motivation of introducing integral real-time automata and extended linear duration invariants. In the next section, we define the semantics of extended linear duration invariants with respect to integral real-time automata.

3   Semantics of Extended Linear Duration Invariants

We define the semantics of extended linear duration invariants with respect to integral real-time automata by conservatively extending the semantics of linear duration invariants with respect to real-time automata.

Given an integral real-time automaton $D =< S, T, \text{low}, \text{up}, L >$, ρ is used to denote a transition of D, i.e. an element of T. For a transition $\rho = (s, s')$, the notations $\overleftarrow{\rho} = s$ and $\overrightarrow{\rho} = s'$ are used.

$\rho_1\rho_2\ldots\rho_n$ is called a behavior if $\overrightarrow{\rho_i} = \overleftarrow{\rho_{i+1}}$ for every $i\,(1 \leq i \leq n-1)$. Beh is used to denote a behavior. $TBeh = (\rho_1, t_1)(\rho_2, t_2)\ldots(\rho_n, t_n)$ is called a time-stamped behavior obtained from $Beh = \rho_1\rho_2\ldots\rho_n$, where $\text{low}(\rho_i) \leq t_i \leq \text{up}(\rho_i)$ for every $i\,(1 \leq i \leq n)$. For example, $Beh = \rho_1\rho_2\rho_1$ is a behavior of the integral real-time automaton in Fig. 1, where $\rho_1 = (reaction, idling)$ and $\rho_2 = (idling, reaction)$. $TBeh = (\rho_1, 3.5)(\rho_2, 3)(\rho_1, 4)$ is a time-stamped behavior obtained from $Beh = \rho_1\rho_2\rho_1$.

$\rho_1\rho_2\ldots\rho_n$ is called a sequence. A sequence may violate transition consecutivity of the automaton. Seq is used to denote a sequence. Given a sequence $Seq = \rho_1\rho_2\ldots\rho_n$, $TSeq = (\rho_1, t_1)(\rho_2, t_2)\ldots(\rho_n, t_n)$ is called a time-stamped sequence obtained from $Seq = \rho_1\rho_2\ldots\rho_n$, where $\overrightarrow{\rho_i} = \overleftarrow{\rho_{i+1}}$ for every $i\,(1 \leq i \leq n-1)$. For example, $Seq = \rho_1\rho_1\rho_2$ is a sequence of the integral real-time automaton in Fig. 1. $TSeq = (\rho_1, 3.5)(\rho_1, 4)(\rho_2, 3)$ is a time-stamped sequence obtained from $Seq = \rho_1\rho_1\rho_2$. $\rho_1\rho_1\rho_2$ is a sequence, but it is not a behavior. A behavior is a sequence and a time-stamped behavior is a time-stamped sequence.

L_D denotes the set of behaviors of the integral real-time automaton D. L_D is a regular language over the alphabet T, as it is accepted by a finite automaton where every state is both an initial and an accepting state.

For a time-stamped sequence $TSeq = (\rho_1, t_1)(\rho_2, t_2)\ldots(\rho_n, t_n)$ of D, $\ell(TSeq)$ is defined as

$$\ell(TSeq) = \sum_{i=1}^{n} t_i.$$

For example, the value of ℓ for $TSeq = (\rho_1, 3.5)(\rho_1, 4)(\rho_2, 3)$ is $\ell(TSeq) = 3.5 + 4 + 3 = 10.5$.

Let f be a function assigned to a state of D. For the time-stamped sequence $TSeq = (\rho_1, t_1)(\rho_2, t_2)\ldots(\rho_n, t_n)$ of D, $\int f(TSeq)$ is defined as

$$\int f(TSeq) = \sum_{i=1}^{n} \left\{ \begin{array}{ll} \int_0^{t_i} f(x)dx & f \in L(\overleftarrow{\rho_i}) \\ 0 & otherwise \end{array} \right\}.$$

For example, the value of $\int f_{tox}$ for the time-stamped sequence $TSeq = (\rho_1, 3.5)(\rho_2, 3)(\rho_1, 4)$ in Fig. 1 is $\int f_{tox}(TSeq) = \int_0^{3.5} f_{tox}(x)dx + \int_0^4 f_{tox}(x)dx$, since f_{tox} is only assigned to $\overleftarrow{\rho_1}$.

We denote the linear term $\sum_{i=1}^m c_i \int f_i$ of $ELDI$ by LF. For a time-stamped sequence $TSeq = (\rho_1, t_1)(\rho_2, t_2) \ldots (\rho_n, t_n)$ of D, $LF(TSeq)$ is defined as

$$LF(TSeq) = \sum_{i=1}^m c_i \int f_i(TSeq).$$

Lemma 1. $LF(TSeq_1 \cdot TSeq_2) = LF(TSeq_2 \cdot TSeq_1) = LF(TSeq_1) + LF(TSeq_2)$ for any time-stamped sequences $TSeq_1$ and $TSeq_2$.

Here, $TSeq_1 \cdot TSeq_2$ is the concatenation of $TSeq_1$ and $TSeq_2$. The proof of the lemma is a straightforward from the definition of $LF(TSeq)$.

We can now move to the semantics of extended linear duration invariants using the functions defined above.

Definition 5. *The satisfaction of* $ELDI$ *by* D *is definied as follows.*

- *$ELDI$ is satisfied by a time-stamped sequence $TSeq$ of D iff $c_{min} \leq \ell(TSeq) \leq c_{max}$ implies $LF(TSeq) \leq C$. Otherwise $ELDI$ is said to be violated by $TSeq$.*
- *$ELDI$ is satisfied by a sequence Seq, denoted by $Seq \models ELDI$, iff $ELDI$ is satisfied by every time-stamped sequence obtained from Seq. Otherwise $ELDI$ is said to be violated by Seq.*
- *Let L be a language over T. $ELDI$ is satisfied by L, denoted by $L \models ELDI$, iff $Seq \models ELDI$ for every $Seq \in L$. Otherwise $ELDI$ is said to be violated by L.*
- *$ELDI$ is satisfied by D, denoted by $D \models ELDI$, iff $L_D \models ELDI$. Otherwise $ELDI$ is said to be violated by D.*

Remark 2. In [2], the meaning of the term $\int s$ of a linear duration invariant was defined as

$$\int s(TSeq) = \sum_{i=1}^n \left\{ \begin{array}{ll} t_i & \overleftarrow{\rho_i} = s \\ 0 & otherwise \end{array} \right\}.$$

That is, $\int s(TSeq)$ calculates the total duration of the state s. However, $\int f(TSeq)$ calculates the total accumulation of the physical quantity f for the duration of the states labeled with f.

4   Checking Algorithm

In this section, we present an algorithm for checking whether an integral real-time automaton satisfies an extended linear duration invariant. Our algorithm is an extension of the technique developed in [2] to check if a real-time automaton satisfies a linear duration invariant. We first show the main idea of the algorithm through an example of checking the reaction tank for its safety requirement. We then formalize our algorithm which reduces the checking task to a finite set of nonlinear programming problems which can be easily solved.

4.1 Verification of the Reaction Tank: Main Idea of the Checking Algorithm

We denote the integral real-time automaton of the reaction tank (Fig. 1) by D and its real-time requirement $12 \leq \ell \to \int f_{tox} - \int f_{detox} \leq 0$ by $ELDI_D$. The problem $L_D \models ELDI_D$ must be solved for the verification of the reaction tank.

D has two transitions $\rho_1 = (reaction, idling)$ and $\rho_2 = (idling, reaction)$, but it can produce infinitely many behaviors. They (namely L_D) can be expressed in terms of regular language as $(\rho_1\rho_2)^* \cup (\rho_1\rho_2)^*\rho_1 \cup (\rho_2\rho_1)^* \cup (\rho_2\rho_1)^*\rho_2$, where $*$ stands for repetition and $\cup$ for union. Note that both *reaction* and *idling* are initial states of D. Then the problem $L_D \models ELDI_D$ can be divided into four problems $(\rho_1\rho_2)^* \models ELDI_D$, $(\rho_1\rho_2)^*\rho_1 \models ELDI_D$, $(\rho_2\rho_1)^* \models ELDI_D$ and $(\rho_2\rho_1)^*\rho_2 \models ELDI_D$ by considering $(\rho_1\rho_2)^*$, $(\rho_1\rho_2)^*\rho_1$, $(\rho_2\rho_1)^*$ and $(\rho_2\rho_1)^*\rho_2$ individually.

Recalling the definition of the extended linear duration invariants, we can easily deduce that the problem $(\rho_1\rho_2)^* \models ELDI_D$ and $(\rho_2\rho_1)^* \models ELDI_D$ are equivalent with respect to the satisfaction. Thus, three problems $(\rho_1\rho_2)^* \models ELDI_D$, $(\rho_1\rho_2)^*\rho_1 \models ELDI_D$ and $(\rho_2\rho_1)^*\rho_2 \models ELDI_D$ must be solved for the verification of the reaction tank.

Let us first consider the problem $(\rho_1\rho_2)^* \models ELDI_D$. For any time-stamped sequence $TSeq_1 = (\rho_1, t_1)(\rho_2, t_2)$ obtained from $Seq_1 = (\rho_1\rho_2)^1$, $LF(TSeq_1)$ is calculated as follows.

$$LF(TSeq_1) =$$
$$\int_0^{t_1} f_{tox}(x)dx - \int_0^{t_1} f_{detox}(x)dx - \int_0^{t_2} f_{detox}(x)dx =$$
$$\int_0^{t_1}(0.35x^3 - 3.23x^2 + 7.53x)dx - \int_0^{t_1} 2.4dx - \int_0^{t_2} 2.4dx =$$
$$0.09t_1^4 - 1.08t_1^3 + 3.76t_1^2 - 2.4t_1 - 2.4t_2.$$

The value of $0.09t_1^4 - 1.08t_1^3 + 3.76t_1^2 - 2.4t_1 - 2.4t_2$ is smaller than 0 for each (t_1, t_2) which ranges over $[3, 4] \times [2, \infty)$. From this fact and Lemma 1, the value of $LF(TSeq_k)$ is smaller than 0 for each time-stamped sequence $TSeq_k$ obtained from $Seq_k = (\rho_1\rho_2)^k$. Then, $ELDI_D$ is satisfied by $(\rho_1\rho_2)^*$ from the definition of the satisfaction.

Let us next consider the problem $(\rho_1\rho_2)^*\rho_1 \models ELDI_D$. $(\rho_1\rho_2)^*\rho_1$ can be unfolded as $\rho_1 \cup (\rho_1\rho_2)\rho_1 \cup (\rho_1\rho_2)^2\rho_1 \cup \dots$. Then, the problem $(\rho_1\rho_2)^*\rho_1 \models ELDI_D$ is divided into infinite number of problems: $(\rho_1\rho_2)^k\rho_1 \models ELDI_D$ ($k \geq 0$). For every time-stamped sequence $TSeq$ obtained from $(\rho_1\rho_2)^k\rho_1$ ($k \geq 2$), the value of $\ell(TSeq)$ is greater than 12 and the value of $LF(TSeq)$ is smaller than 0. This implies that $ELDI_D$ is satisfied by every $(\rho_1\rho_2)^k\rho_1$ ($k \geq 2$). Thus, it is enough to solve the problems $\rho_1 \models ELDI_D$ and $\rho_1\rho_2\rho_1 \models ELDI_D$ to decide the problem $(\rho_1\rho_2)^*\rho_1 \models ELDI_D$.

It is obvious that $ELDI_D$ is satisfied by ρ_1 because $\ell(TSeq)$ is smaller than 12 for every time-stamped sequence obtained from ρ_1. The problem $\rho_1\rho_2\rho_1 \models ELDI_D$ is transformed into a nonlinear programming problem as follows.

Every time-stamped sequence $(\rho_1, t_1)(\rho_2, t_2)(\rho_1, t_3)$ which is obtained from $\rho_1\rho_2\rho_1$ must satisfy the constraints $3 \le t_1 \le 4$, $t_2 \ge 2$ and $3 \le t_3 \le 4$. For this time-stamped sequence, the value of ℓ is $t_1 + t_2 + t_3$ and the value of LF is $\int_0^{t_1} f_{tox}(x)dx + \int_0^{t_3} f_{tox}(x)dx - \int_0^{t_1} f_{detox}(x)dx - \int_0^{t_2} f_{detox}(x)dx - \int_0^{t_3} f_{detox}(x)$ $dx = 0.09t_1^4 - 1.08t_1^3 + 3.76t_1^2 - 2.4t_1 - 2.4t_2 + 0.09t_3^4 - 1.08t_3^3 + 3.76t_3^2 - 2.4t_3$.

Therefore, we can decide the problem $\rho_1\rho_2\rho_1 \models ELDI_D$ by solving the following nonlinear programming problem.

Constraints:

$3 \le t_1 \le 4$, $t_2 \ge 2$, $3 \le t_3 \le 4$ and $t_1 + t_2 + t_3 \ge 12$.

Objective function:

$0.09t_1^4 - 1.08t_1^3 + 3.76t_1^2 - 2.4t_1 - 2.4t_2 + 0.09t_3^4 - 1.08t_3^3 + 3.76t_3^2 - 2.4t_3$.

If the maximal value of the objective function is less than or equal to 0, then $ELDI_D$ is satisfied by $\rho_1\rho_2\rho_1$. And if the maximal value of the objective function is greater than 0, then $ELDI_D$ is violated by $\rho_1\rho_2\rho_1$. By solving the problem, we can easily know that the maximal value of this objective function is -0.64. Therefore, $ELDI_D$ is satisfied by $\rho_1\rho_2\rho_1$.

The third problem $(\rho_2\rho_1)^*\rho_2 \models ELDI_D$ can also be solved in the way used above and we skip it.

4.2   Algorithm

In this subsection, we formalize the technique shown above. We confine ourselves to the subclass of integral real-time automata which satisfy $low(\rho) > 0$ for each transition ρ. Let $D = < S, T, low, up, L >$ be an integral real-time automaton which satisfies the above constraint.

We first consider the extended linear duration invariants which have the form

$$c_{min} \le \ell \to \sum_{i=1}^{m} c_i \int f_i \le C.$$

For convenience, we denote an extended linear duration invariant of this form by $ELDI$.

Definition 6. *Two languages L_1 and L_2 over T are called equivalent with respect to ELDI, denoted by $L_1 \equiv L_2$, if $L_1 \models ELDI$ iff $L_2 \models ELDI$.*

The equivalence of two languages in this paper is slightly different from the one in [2], but the two equivalences have the same meaning. We identify a regular expression with the language it denotes.

L_D can be transformed into an equivalent finite union of regular expressions of the form $\rho_1 \ldots \rho_m Seq_1^* \ldots Seq_k^*$. The procedure which was used in [2] to transform L_A (where A is a real-time automaton) into an equivalent finite union of regular expressions of the form $\rho_1 \ldots \rho_m Seq_1^* \ldots Seq_k^*$ can also be used in our case without any modification. We do not repeat it in this paper.

Thus, we can decide the problem $L_D \models ELDI$ if we have a technique for solving the problem $\rho_1 \ldots \rho_m Seq_1^* \ldots Seq_k^* \models ELDI$.

Given a sequence $Seq = \rho_1 \rho_2 \ldots \rho_m$, we let $\ell_{min} = \sum_{i=1}^{m} \text{low}(\rho_i)$ and $\rho_1 \rho_2 \ldots$ $\rho_m{}^{min} = (\rho_1, \text{low}(\rho_1))(\rho_2, \text{low}(\rho_2)) \ldots (\rho_m, \text{low}(\rho_m))$. And by solving the following nonlinear programming problem, we can obtain the time-stamped sequence $TSeq^{max} = (\rho_1, t_1^0)(\rho_2, t_2^0) \ldots (\rho_m, t_m^0)$ which has the maximal value of LF among all time-stamped sequences obtained from Seq, where we accept $x < \infty$ for $x \in \mathbb{R}$, and $\infty > 0$.

Constraints:

$$\text{low}(\rho_1) \le t_1 \le \text{up}(\rho_1), \ldots, \text{low}(\rho_m) \le t_m \le \text{up}(\rho_m) \text{ and } t_1 + \ldots + t_m \ge c_{min}.$$

Objective function:

$$LT(TSeq).$$

We formulate the following three theorems and give sketches of the constructive proofs which reduces the problem $\rho_1 \ldots \rho_m Seq_1{}^* \ldots Seq_k{}^* \models ELDI$ to a finite set of nonlinear programming problems.

Theorem 1. *ELDI is violated by* $\rho_1 \ldots \rho_m Seq_1{}^* \ldots Seq_k{}^*$ *if* $LF(TSeq_i{}^{max}) > 0$ *for some* i $(1 \le i \le k)$.

Proof. Let $t_0 = t_1^0 + \ldots t_m^0$. We set $n_1 = \lceil \frac{c_{min} - \ell_{min}}{t^0} \rceil$, $n_2 = \lceil \frac{C - LF(\rho_1 \rho_2 \ldots \rho_m{}^{min})}{LF(TSeq_i{}^{max})} \rceil$ and $n = \max\{n_1, n_2\}$. Then, *ELDI* is violated by $\rho_1 \ldots \rho_m{}^{min}(TSeq_i{}^{max})^n$ which is an element of $\rho_1 \ldots \rho_m Seq_1{}^* \ldots Seq_k{}^*$.

Theorem 2. $\rho_1 \ldots \rho_m Seq_1{}^* \ldots Seq_k{}^*$ *is equivalent to a finite union of sequences if* $LF(TSeq_i{}^{max}) \le 0$ *for every* i $(1 \le i \le k)$.

Proof. Seq^* is equivalent to $\bigcup_{i=1}^{n}(Seq)^i$ for some n (> 0), if $LF(TSeq^{max}) \le 0$. To prove it, we consider the case $C < LF(TSeq^{max}) < 0$. Other cases can be considered in a similar way. We set $n_1 = \lceil \frac{c_{min}}{\ell_{min}} \rceil$, $n_2 = \lceil \frac{C}{LF(TSeq^{max})} \rceil$ and $n = \max\{n_1, n_2\}$. For this n, $Seq^* \equiv \bigcup_{i=1}^{n}(Seq)^i$

Then, $\rho_1 \ldots \rho_m Seq_1{}^* \ldots Seq_k{}^* \equiv \rho_1 \ldots \rho_m \bigcup_{i=1}^{n_1}(Seq)^i \ldots \bigcup_{i=1}^{n_k}(Seq)^i$. Therefore, $\rho_1 \ldots \rho_m Seq_1{}^* \ldots Seq_k{}^*$ is equivalent to a finite union of sequences from the distribution law for the concatenation over the union.

Theorem 3. *For any* $Seq = \rho_1 \ldots \rho_n$, *the problem* $Seq \models ELDI$ *is solvable using nonlinear programming.*

Proof. Consider the timed sequence $TSeq = (\rho_1, t_1)(\rho_2, t_2) \ldots (\rho_n, t_n)$. The constraints of the nonlinear programming problem are obtained from the timing constraints of D and from the left-hand side of the implication in the definition of *ELDI*. That is,

$$\text{low}(\rho_1) \le t_1 \le \text{up}(\rho_1), \ldots, \text{low}(\rho_n) \le t_n \le \text{up}(\rho_n) \text{ and } c_{min} \le \ell(TSeq).$$

The objective function of the nonlinear programming problem is

$$LF(TSeq) \ (= \sum_{i=1}^{m} c_i \int f_i(TSeq)).$$

If the maximal value of the objective function is smaller than or equal to C, *ELDI* is satisfied by *Seq*. Otherwise, *ELDI* is violated by *Seq*.

The algorithm presented above can be easily generalized to the decision procedure for the satisfaction problem of extended linear duration invariants which have the form $c_{min} \leq \ell \leq c_{max} \rightarrow \sum_{i=1}^{m} c_i \int f_i \leq C$. We do not discuss this generalization further in this paper.

In this section, we have confined ourselves to the integral real-time automata whose lower-bound timing constraints on the transitions are not 0. The algorithm, however, can also be used in other cases of integral real-time automata by replacing each 0 with a sufficiently small positive number. For a better understanding of the algorithm presented in this section, readers are referred to [2].

4.3   Solvability of the Nonlinear Programming Problems

Fortunately, the nonlinear programming problems which are generated as a result of applying the above checking algorithm are solvable.

Let P be the nonlinear programming problem generated from the problem $Seq \models ELDI$, where $Seq = \rho_1 \rho_2 \dots \rho_n$. The feasible set of P is a simple convex polyhedron of $\mathbb{R}^n$. (See Theorem 3.) The objective function of P has the structure

$$F(t_1) + F(t_2) + \dots + F(t_n).$$

Here $t_i \in [\text{low}(\rho_i), \text{up}(\rho_i)]$ and $F(t_i) = \pm \int_0^{t_i} f_{i_1}(x)dx \pm \int_0^{t_i} f_{i_2}(x)dx + \dots + \pm \int_0^{t_i} f_{i_{n_i}}(x)dx$. $f_{i_1}, f_{i_2}, \dots, f_{i_{n_{i-1}}}$ and $f_{i_{n_i}}$ are functions assigned to $\overleftarrow{\rho_i}$. $\pm$ denotes $+$ or $-$. That is, the objective function of P is a separable function. The methods for solving nonlinear programming problems of this type have already been studied well, e.g. [16].

5   Conclusion

The case study of the reaction tank demonstrates that extended linear duration invariants introduced in the paper represent a practical pattern of safety properties of real-time systems. The semantics of extended linear duration invariants is defined using integral real-time automata. By introducing extended linear duration invariants and integral real-time automata, we could extend the real-time automata approach for systems verification to the nonlinear programming.

References

1. Chaochen, Z., Hoare, C.A.R., Ravn, A.P.: A calculus of durations. Inf. Process. Lett. **40**(5), 269–276 (1991)
2. Zhou, C.: Linear duration invariants. In: Langmaack, H., de Roever, W.-P., Vytopil, J. (eds.) FTRTFT 1994 and ProCoS 1994. LNCS, vol. 863, pp. 86–109. Springer, Heidelberg (1994)

3. Kesten, Y., Pnueli, A., Sifakis, J., Yovine, S.: Integration graphs: a class of decidable hybrid systems. In: Grossman, R.L., Ravn, A.P., Rischel, H., Nerode, A. (eds.) HS 1991 and HS 1992. LNCS, vol. 736, pp. 179–208. Springer, Heidelberg (1993)
4. Braberman, V.A., Van Hung, D.: On checking timed automata for linear duration invariants. In: Proceedings of the 19th Real-Time Systems Symposium RTSS 1998, pp. 264–273. IEEE Computer Society Press, Los Alamitos (1998)
5. Zhang, M., Van Hung, D., Liu, Z.: Verification of linear duration invariants by model checking CTL properties. In: Fitzgerald, J.S., Haxthausen, A.E., Yenigun, H. (eds.) ICTAC 2008. LNCS, vol. 5160, pp. 395–409. Springer, Heidelberg (2008)
6. Zhang, M., Liu, Z., Zhan, N.: Model checking linear duration invariants of networks of automata. In: Arbab, F., Sirjani, M. (eds.) FSEN 2009. LNCS, vol. 5961, pp. 244–259. Springer, Heidelberg (2010)
7. Thai, P.H., Van Hung, D.: Verifying linear duration constraints of timed automata. In: Liu, Z., Araki, K. (eds.) ICTAC 2004. LNCS, vol. 3407, pp. 295–309. Springer, Heidelberg (2005)
8. Ravn, A.P., Rischel, H., Hansen, K.M.: Specifying and verifying requirements of real-time systems. IEEE Trans. Softw. Eng. 19(1), 41–55 (1993)
9. Chaochen, Z., Xiaoshan, L.: A mean-value duration calculus. In: Roscoe, A.W. (ed.) A Classical Mind, Essays in Honour of C. A. R. Hoare, pp. 431–451. Prentice Hall International, Englewood Cliffs (1994)
10. Alur, R., Dill, D.L.: A theory of timed automata. Theor. Comput. Sci. 126(2), 183–235 (1994)
11. Sørensen, E.V., Ravn A.P., Rischel H.: Control Program for a Gas Burner: Part 1: Informal Requirements, ProCoS Case Study 1. ProCoS I, ESPRIT BRA 3104, Report No. ID/DTH EVS2, Department of Computer Science, Technical University of Denmark, Lyngby (1990)
12. Alur, R., Courcoubetis, C., Henzinger, T.A., Ho, P.-H.: Hybrid automata: an algorithmic approach to the specification and verification of hybrid systems. In: Grossman, R.L., Ravn, A.P., Rischel, H., Nerode, A. (eds.) HS 1991 and HS 1992. LNCS, vol. 736, pp. 209–229. Springer, Heidelberg (1993)
13. Chaochen, Z., Hansen, M.R.: Duration Calculus. A Formal Approach to Real-Time Systems. Springer, Heidelberg (2004)
14. Chaochen, Z., Hansen, M.R., Sestoft, P.: Decidability and undecidability results for duration calculus. In: Enjalbert, P., Finkel, A., Wagner, K.W. (eds.) (STACS 93). LNCS, vol. 665, pp. 58–68. Springer-Verlag, Heidelberg (1993)
15. Chaochen, Z., Ravn, A.P., Hansen, M.R.: An extended duration calculus for hybrid real-time systems. In: Grossman, R.L., Nerode, A., Ravn, A.P., Rischel, H. (eds.) Hybrid Systems. LNCS, vol. 736, pp. 36–59. Springer, Heidelberg (1993)
16. Zhang, H., Wang, S.: Global optimization of separable objective functions on convex polyhedra via piecewise-linear approximation. J. Comput. Appl. Math. 197, 212–217 (2006)
17. Behrmann, G., Larsen, K.G., Rasmussen, J.I.: Priced timed automata: algorithms and applications. In: de Boer, F.S., Bonsangue, M.M., Graf, S., de Roever, W.-P. (eds.) FMCO 2004. LNCS, vol. 3657, pp. 162–182. Springer, Heidelberg (2005)
18. Bouyer, P.: Weighted timed automata: model-checking and games. In: Brookes, S., Mislove (eds.) Proceedings of the 22nd Annual Conference on Mathematical Foundations of Programming Semantics, Electronic Notes in Theoretical Computer Science, vol. 158, pp. 3–17 (2006)

A Normalized Form for FIFO Protocols Traces, Application to the Replay of Mode-based Protocols

Mamoun Filali (✉), Meriem Ouederni, and Jean-Baptiste Raclet

IRIT CNRS, Université de Toulouse, Toulouse, France
{filali,Jean-Baptiste.Raclet}@irit.fr,
meriem.ouederni@enseeiht.fr

Abstract. The traditional concern of runtime verification is the ability to detect an incorrect system behavior and maybe to act on such systems whenever incorrect behavior of a software system is detected [20]. In this paper, our concern is to provide a system observation through which the system behavior could for instance be diagnosed, e.g., to resolve unexpected bugs. Such a system observation is elaborated from a partial observation. Our work is at the protocol level: given a distributed application relying on a FIFO protocol for message passing, our concern is to reconstruct a full execution given by its observable send events.

1 Introduction

The availability of a web-based infrastructure, e.g., internet, has popularized worldwide distributed applications. Nowadays, commercial transactions and several administrative procedures, e.g., eGovernment, are often executed in a distributed setting. The interpretation of data produced by such applications is very useful and of utmost importance. For instance, it enable programme diagnosis in order to understand the executed traces. In addition, if an unexpected bug occurs at execution time, the interpretation allows us to replay, i.e., reconstruct, the traces leading to the fault. Thus, one may be able to debug the program and find the root cause of the bug. In this paper, we address the following problem: how can we faithfully make an interpretation of data available at runtime? Runtime verification [20] can be identified as one domain addressing such a topic. Actually, the traditional concern of runtime verification is the ability to detect an incorrect system behavior and maybe to act on such systems whenever incorrect behavior of a software system is detected. In this paper, our aim is to provide a system observation through which the system behavior could for instance be diagnosed. Such a system observation is elaborated from a partial observation. Our work is at the protocol level: given a distributed application relying on a FIFO protocol for message passing, our concern is to reconstruct a full execution given by its observable send events. We motivate the use of send events as follows: first, the decision to receive is usually considered as an internal or private decision; moreover, sends are seen over the network while the receipts are not.

© Springer International Publishing Switzerland 2015
C. Artho and P.C. Ölveczky (Eds.): FTSCS 2014, CCIS 476, pp. 76–92, 2015.
DOI: 10.1007/978-3-319-17581-2_6

The rest of the paper is organized as follows. After the definition of basic semantics notions in Sect. 2, we illustrate and motivate the studied model in Sect. 3. Section 4 introduces a normal form of executions. A replay algorithm based upon this normal form is studied in Sect. 5. Before concluding, we review some related works in Sect. 6.

2 FIFO Protocols Semantics

In this section, we present the semantics of the studied model: FIFO protocols. After presenting the notations used throughout the paper, we recall the basic semantic notions used in the sequel. Transition systems [2] together with runs and traces, the basic notions for observing a transition system, are first defined. After defining syntactically send-receive protocols systems, their semantics is given as transition systems.

2.1 Notations

Finite Sequences (lists). Let S be a set, S^* is the set of finite sequences over S. An element $x_1 \ldots x_n$ of S is also denoted $x_{(i)}$. [] is the empty sequence, [e] is a one element (e) list, given a non empty sequence l: $x_1 \ldots x_n$, $hd(l)$ is the first element of l: x_1, $tl(l)$ is the sequence resulting from the suppression of x_1: $x_2 \ldots x_n$, $last(l)$ is the last element of l: x_n, $butlast(l)$ is the sequence resulting from the suppression of x_n: $x_1 \ldots x_{n-1}$. $\mathbf{set}(l)$ is the set of the elements of the list l: $\{x_1 \ldots x_n\}$. By abuse of notation, we write $\forall\, e \in l$. ... instead of $\forall\, e \in \mathbf{set}(l)$. ... . Given a set H, $l\backslash H$ is the sequence resulting from the suppression of the elements of H within l. The concatenation of two lists l, l' is denoted $l@l'$. Given a sequence L of sequences over S, $concat(L)$ is the sequence resulting from the concatenation of the elements of L.

Updates. Given a structured datatype, e.g., an array, a record, ..., := denotes its update. For instance, given an array A where s is a valid index, $A[s := v]$ is the array resulting from the update by v of the element of A at index s, given a record R with a field named f, $R[f := v]$ is the record resulting from the update by v of the field named f.

2.2 Transition Systems

Definition 1 (Labelled Transition Systems). *A labelled transition system defined over a set of states S and a set of labels Σ is a couple $Sys = (I, \rightarrow)$ where I: the set of initial states is a subset of S and $\rightarrow$: the labelled transition relation is a subset of $S \times \Sigma \times S$.*

In the following, given a transition $tr = (s, l, s')$, its label l, will be denoted $Lab(tr)$. s the initial state is denoted $Src(tr)$, s' the destination state is denoted $Dst(tr)$.

Definition 2 (Runs). *Given a labelled transition system* $Sys = (I, \rightarrow)$ *over* S *and* Σ, *a run is an element of* $(S \times \Sigma \times S)^*$: $s_0 l_0 s_0' \ldots s_n l_n s_n'$ *such that* $n \in \mathbb{N}$, $s_0 \in I$ *and* $\forall \, i \leq n$. $(s_i, l_i, s_i') \in \rightarrow \wedge \forall i < n$. $s_i' = s_{i+1}$. *Its set of runs is denoted* $\mathcal{R}_{Sys}$.

A run is a sequence of interleaved states and labels obtained through the execution of the algorithm or protocol modelled as a transition system.

Notations. Given an initital state s and a run r, $\mathcal{R}(s)$ is the set of runs starting at s. Given a non empty run $r = s_0 l_0 s_0' \ldots s_n l_n s_n'$, ends$(r)$ denotes the pair (s_0, s_n').

Definition 3 (Traces). *Given a labelled transition system* $Sys = (I, \rightarrow)$ *over* S *and* Σ, $\mathcal{E} \subseteq \Sigma$ *called the espilon set, a trace is an element of* Σ^* *obtained as a projection of a run where letters of the epsilon set* $\mathcal{E}$ *have been suppressed.*

$$\text{Traces}(Sys, \mathcal{E}) = \bigcup_{s_{(i)}, s_{(i)}'} \{l_0 \ldots l_n \backslash \mathcal{E}. \ (s_0, l_0, s_0') \ldots (s_n, l_n, s_n') \in \mathcal{R}_{Sys}\}$$

Intuitively, a trace is a sequence of labels that *can* be observed through the execution of the algorithm or protocol modelled as a transition system: $\text{Trace}((s_0, l_0, s_0') \ldots (s_n, l_n, s_n'), \mathcal{E}) = l_0 \ldots l_n \backslash \mathcal{E}$.[1]

2.3   FIFO Protocols Systems

Definition 4 (Send-receive protocols). *A Send receive protocol is defined as a tuple* (St, δ) *over a set* $\mathcal{P}$ *of peers, a set* $\mathcal{L}$ *of locations[2] and* $\mathcal{M}$ *a set of messages. To each peer* p *is assigned an automaton* (St_p, δ_p) *where* St_p, *a location of* $\mathcal{L}$, *is the initial state of the peer* p *and* δ_p *is the set of transitions of the peer* p. *A transition is one of:*

- *a send transition denoted* $(st, q!m, st')$: *in state* st, *the peer* p *sends the message* m *to the peer* q *through the input queue of peer* $q \in \mathcal{P}$ *and moves to state* st'.
- *a receive transition denoted* $(st, ?m, st')$: *in state* st, *the peer* p *receives (or consumes) the message* m *through its own input queue and moves to state* st'.
- (st, ϵ, st') *is an epsilon transition (internal transition).*

In the following, we consider deterministic send-receive protocols, that is, we omit ϵ transitions and consider only deterministic transitions; we then use δ transitions as partial functions: the state resulting when moving from state st through a δ transition is denoted $\delta(st)$.

Definition 5 (FIFO Send-Receive Systems). *Given a send-receive protocol* (St, δ) *defined over* $(\mathcal{P}, \mathcal{L}, \mathcal{M})$, *we define its FIFO labelled transition system* $\text{FIFO\_LTS}((\mathcal{P}, \mathcal{L}, \mathcal{M}, St, \delta))$ *as the following tuple:*

---

[1] We write Trace(r) when $\mathcal{E}$ is clear in the context.

[2] The location has to be understood here as the local, or internal state of a peer.

S *the set of global states is a mapping giving for each peer its local state and its FIFO queue:* $\mathcal{P} \to \mathcal{L} \times \mathcal{M}^*$. *We represent a global state as an array of records indexed by the set of peers:*

$$\textbf{array } \mathcal{P} \textbf{ of record } \text{state} : \mathcal{L}, \text{queue} : \text{list } \textbf{of } \mathcal{M} \textbf{ end}$$

Σ *its set of labels as the (disjoint) union of:*

- *its send labels:* $\mathcal{P} \times \mathcal{M} \times \mathcal{P}$, *where an element is denoted* $_sS_d^m$ *where s is the source peer, d the destination peer and m the sent message from s to d.*
- *its receive labels:* $\mathcal{P} \times \mathcal{M}$, *where an element is denoted* R_p^m *where p is the receiving peer and m the received message.*
  - *The set of initial states is the singleton* $\{p \mapsto \{\text{state} := \{St_p, \text{queue} := []\}\}$
- $\to$ *its transition relation as the union* $S \cup R$ *where:*
- S *is the set of send transitions:*[3]

$$S = \bigcup_s S_s$$
$$S_s = \bigcup_{r,m}\{(St, _sS_r^m, St').$$
$$s \neq r \wedge (St[s], r!m, St'[s]) \in \delta_s$$
$$\wedge St' = St[\, s := St[s][\text{state} := St'[s].\text{state}]$$
$$r := St[r][\text{queue} := St[r].\text{queue}@[m]]]\}$$

- $\mathcal{R}$ *is the set of receive transitions:*

$$\mathcal{R} = \bigcup_r \mathcal{R}_r$$
$$\mathcal{R}_r = \bigcup_m\{(St, R_r^m, St').$$
$$(St[r], ?m, St'[r]) \in \delta_r$$
$$\wedge St[r].\text{queue} \neq [] \wedge m = hd(St[r].\text{queue})$$
$$\wedge St' = St[r := St[r][\text{state} := St'[r].\text{state},$$
$$\text{queue} := tl(St[r].\text{queue})]]\}$$

Intuitively, each peer p has a FIFO queue that contains the sequence of data items that have been sent to peer p but not yet received by p. Each receive transition removes a data item from the queue of the receiving peer and each send transition adds a data item to the queue of the destination peer. Moreover, we note that FIFO queues are unbounded. It follows that our transition systems are infinite.

Notations. Given a label l (an element of Σ):

- The predicate isSend, resp. isReceive, denotes if l is a send label, resp. a receive label.
- The function On denotes its peer: $\text{On}(_sS_d^m) = s, \text{On}(R_r^m) = r$.

In the following, we consider a fixed FIFO protocol so we will omit the tuple $(\mathcal{P}, \mathcal{L}, \mathcal{M}, St, \delta)$.

---

[3] Note that the definition although circular, the state field of the structure is constrained through δ_s.

Definition 6 (FIFO Protocols Traces). *The traces of a FIFO protocol system are defined as the projection of the set of its runs over Send labels.*

$$\text{FIFO\_Traces}(\mathcal{P}, \mathcal{L}, \mathcal{M}, St, \delta) = \text{Traces}(\text{FIFO\_LTS}(\mathcal{P}, \mathcal{L}, \mathcal{M}, St, \delta), \bigcup_{r,m}\{R_r^m\},)$$

Remark. FIFO automata differ from what could be called a "Fifo *channel* automata" [21] where peers communicate through FIFO communication channels: FIFO automata define for every peer a *unique* FIFO on which the peer receives all the messages the other peers have sent to it. Operationally, such a protocol is similar to that of JMS [15].

The FIFO automata, considered in this paper, define the usual send-receive order over the basic send receive events of a distributed system computation but they *also* introduce a compatible total order over the sends to a given peer. In the domain of embedded systems, one can usually rely on such a semantics. Actually it is weaker than the instantaneous broadcast which is common in synchronous languages.

3   An Illustrative Example

As an illustrative example, we consider one of the folklore algorithms for the distributed spanning tree construction [12]. Given a network of peers PEERS knowing initially their respective local neighborhood as a set of peers, we have to construct a spanning tree where the root ROOT is a priori designated, e.g., peer 0. At the end, each peer (but peer 0) has to know its father and its sons with respect to the constructed spanning tree. As a working example, we shall consider the network topology illustrated in Fig. 1. Figure 2 suggests one spanning tree that would be possible to construct given the supposed underlying topology (Fig. 1).

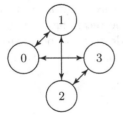   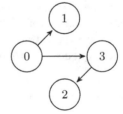

Fig. 1. Underlying network topology   **Fig. 2.** Spanning tree

3.1   A Distributed Spanning Tree Construction Algorithm

A so called diffusing computation [10] can be used for building a spanning tree. Peer 0 initiates the computation by sending the message BeMySon to each of its neighbours. When a peer receives its first BeMySon message, it takes the sender as its father and sends to each neighbor peer,[4] but its father, a BeMySon message. It then waits for an acknowledgement for each of the sent messages. Its set of sons consists of the peers that have acknowledged positively by an OK message. When a peer (but the root) has received all the acknowledgments, in turn, he acknowledges its father by an OK message. While waiting for an acknowledgment, a peer can receive a BeMySon message, in that case, it acknowledges it negatively by a NO message. The computation is terminated once the root has received all its awaited acknowledgments.

In the following, we suppose that communication is FIFO: each peer has a queue where it receives the messages sent to him. The Figs. 3 and 4 illustrate respectively the automaton of the root peer and a not root peer.[5] We have modeled the algorithm in the language PusCal [18](based on the semantics formalism: TLA+ [17]).

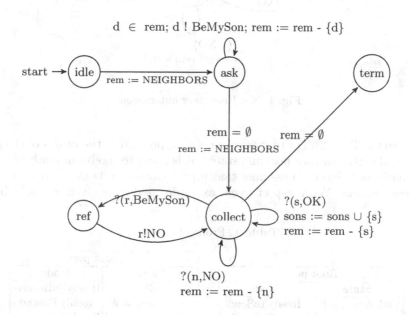

Fig. 3. Root peer automaton

3.2 Replaying a Trace

Replay consists in synthesizing a run where epsilon transitions, i.e., receive transitions have been guessed and interleaved with given send transitions of an actual

---

[4] We have supposed that each peers knows initially its local neighborhood.
[5] These automata differ with respect to the initial and terminal transitions (from the idle state and to the term state).

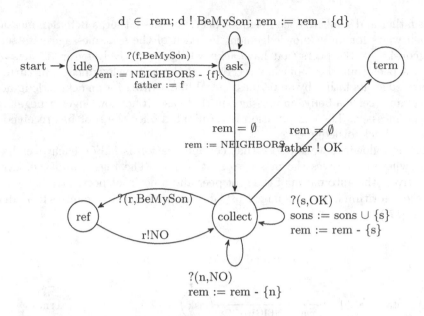

Fig. 4. Not Root peer automaton

trace (see the Table 2). For that purpose, we suppose given the *modes* of the protocol: modes give for each peer and state if it is ready to receive or ready to send. The considered algorithm assumes that a peer cannot be both ready to receive and ready to send. With respect to our example, modes are given by the Table 1.

Table 1. Protocol modes

Root peer			Not root peer	
State	Mode		State	Mode
$ask \wedge rem \neq \emptyset$	ReadyToSend		idle	ReadyToReceive
$collect \wedge rem \neq \emptyset$	ReadyToReceive		$ask \wedge rem \neq \emptyset$	ReadyToSend
ref	ReadyToSend		$collect \wedge rem \neq \emptyset$	ReadyToReceive
			ref	ReadyToSend
			$collect \wedge rem = \emptyset$	ReadyToSend

4   A Normal Form for FIFO Protocols Traces

In this section, we propose a normal form for FIFO protocol traces. Given a trace, a normal form is a run which can be seen as the representant of all the runs with the same trace. In fact, given a trace, we do not reconstruct the actual run which led to the trace in question *but* a run with the same trace. Such a run

Table 2. Replay of the protocol from an actual trace

Trace	Synthesized interleaved receives for the replay
$_0S_3^{[data:=\text{"}BeMySon\text{"},sender:=0]}$	
	$R_3^{[data:=\text{"}BeMySon\text{"},sender:=0]}$
$_3S_2^{[data:=\text{"}BeMySon\text{"},sender:=3]}$	
$_0S_1^{[data:=\text{"}BeMySon\text{"},sender:=0]}$	
	$R_2^{[data:=\text{"}BeMySon\text{"},sender:=3]}$
$_2S_1^{[data:=\text{"}BeMySon\text{"},sender:=2]}$	
	$R_1^{[data:=\text{"}BeMySon\text{"},sender:=0]}$
$_1S_2^{[data:=\text{"}BeMySon\text{"},sender:=1]}$	
	$R_2^{[data:=\text{"}BeMySon\text{"},sender:=1]}$
$_2S_1^{[data:=\text{"}NO\text{"},sender:=2]}$	
	$R_1^{[data:=\text{"}BeMySon\text{"},sender:=2]}$
$_1S_2^{[data:=\text{"}NO\text{"},sender:=1]}$	
	$R_2^{[data:=\text{"}NO\text{"},sender:=1]}$
$_2S_3^{[data:=\text{"}OK\text{"},sender:=2]}$	
	$R_3^{[data:=\text{"}OK\text{"},sender:=2]}$
$_3S_0^{[data:=\text{"}OK\text{"},sender:=3]}$	
	$R_1^{[data:=\text{"}BeMySon\text{"},sender:=0]}$
$_1S_0^{[data:=\text{"}OK\text{"},sender:=1]}$	

is called the normalized run. Should such a run be replayed, it would produce the same trace as the trace in question. In the following, we are concerned by the correctness of the normalized run (re)construction.

4.1 Basic Operations

We introduce two basic operations that will be used for normalization. These operations preserve runs and their semantics, i.e., traces.

- *Unrolling* consists in pushing to the front of a run, a given transition. Intuitively, we unroll the effect of such a transition from the end until the front is reached. Intuitively, unroll expresses that a transition at the end of a run can also occur at the beginning of such a run.
- *Partitioning* consists in splitting a run in two such that the first run contains only transitions from a given peer and the other run contains the remaining transitions issued by the other peers.

Unrolling. The parameters of the unroll operation are as follows: (sw_1, sw_2) swaps a pair (t_1, t_2) as the pair $(sw_1(t_1, t_2), sw_2(t_1, t_2))$. r is the run over which the unrolling occurs and e is the transition to be unrolled.

84 M. Filali et al.

unroll is described recursively by the following text:

$$\text{unroll}_{sw_1, sw_2}(r, e) \triangleq \textbf{if } r = [] \textbf{ then } [e]$$
$$\textbf{else} \quad \text{unroll}_{sw_1, sw_2}(\text{butlast}(r), sw_1(\text{last}(r), e)))$$
$$@[sw_2(\text{last}(r), e)]$$

Subsequently, we apply the unroll operation over runs. In order to preserve run properties, we consider the following local properties:[6] of the swap operation

– a swap preserves the adjacency of (run) elements.

$$\text{Dst}(tr) = \text{Src}(tr') \Rightarrow \text{Dst}(sw_1(tr, tr')) = \text{Src}(sw_2(tr, tr'))$$

– a swap preserves the ends of adjacent (run) elements.

$$\text{Dst}(tr) = \text{Src}(tr') \Rightarrow \begin{array}{l} \text{Src}(sw_1(tr, tr')) = \text{Src}(tr) \\ \wedge \text{Dst}(sw_2(tr, tr')) = \text{Dst}(tr') \end{array}$$

– a swap preserves the trace of runs of 2 elements.

$$\text{Dst}(tr) = \text{Src}(tr')$$
$$\Rightarrow \text{Trace}([sw_1(tr, tr')]@[sw_2(tr, tr')]) = \text{Trace}([tr]@[tr'])$$

Theorem 1 (Unrolling a Receive over Receives). *Unrolling a receive over a receive run yields a new receive run with the same ends.*

$$\forall \ r \ e. \ r@[e] \in \mathcal{R}(i) \wedge (\forall \ tr \in r@[e]. \ \text{isReceive}(\text{Lab}(tr)))$$
$$\Rightarrow \quad \text{unroll}_{sw_{R_1}, sw_{R_2}}(r, e) \in \mathcal{R}(i)$$
$$\wedge \text{Trace}(\text{unroll}_{sw_{R_1}, sw_{R_2}}(r, e)) = \text{Trace}(r@[e])$$
$$\wedge \text{ends}(\text{unroll}_{sw_{R_1}, sw_{R_2}}(r, e)) = \text{ends}(r@[e])$$

where sw_{R_1} and sw_{R_2} instantiate the generic swap:

$$sw_{R_1}((S_1, R_{p'}^{m'}, S_1'), (S_2, R_p^m, S_2')) =$$
$$\textbf{if } p = p' \textbf{ then } (S_1, R_{p'}^{m'}, S_1')$$
$$\textbf{else } (S_1,$$
$$R_p^m,$$
$$S_1[p := [\text{state} := S_2'[p].\text{state},$$
$$\text{queue} = tl(S_1[p].\text{queue})]])$$
$$| \ sw_{R_1}(e_1, e_2) = e_1$$

$$sw_{R_2}((S_1, R_{p'}^{m'}, S_1'), (S_2, R_p^m, S_2')) =$$
$$\textbf{if } p = p' \textbf{ then } (S_2, R_p^m, S_2')$$
$$\textbf{else } (S_1[p := [\text{state} := S_2'[p].\text{state}, \qquad ,$$
$$\text{queue} = tl(S_1[p].\text{queue})]]$$
$$R_{p'}^{m'},$$
$$S_2')$$
$$| \ sw_{R_2}(e_1, e_2) = e_2$$

---

[6] They are local since they apply to two elements: tr, tr' and not globally, e.g., to a list of elements.

Remark. Intuitively, such a global swap expresses that receives of different peers are independent: they can be swapped.

Theorem 2 (Unrolling a Send over Receives). *Unrolling a send issued by a node s over a receive run not issued by s yields a new run with the same initial and end state.*

$$\forall\, r\; e. \quad r@[e] \in \mathcal{R}(i)$$
$$\wedge\; (\forall\; tr \in r.\; \text{isReceive}(\text{Lab}(tr))) \wedge \text{On}(\text{Lab}(tr)) \neq \text{On}(\text{Lab}(e))$$
$$\wedge\; \text{isSend}(e)$$
$$\Rightarrow \quad \text{unroll}_{sw_{S_1},sw_{S_2}}(r,e) \in \mathcal{R}(i)$$
$$\wedge\; \text{Trace}(\text{unroll}_{sw_{S_1},sw_{S_2}}(r,e)) = \text{Trace}(r@[e])$$
$$\wedge\; \text{ends}(\text{unroll}_{sw_{S_1},sw_{S_2}}(r,e)) = \text{ends}(r@[e])$$
$$\wedge\; \text{isSend}(\text{Lab}(hd(\text{unroll}_{sw_{S_1},sw_{S_2}}(r,e))))$$
$$\wedge\; \forall\; tr \in tl(\text{unroll}_{sw_{S_1},sw_{S_2}}(r,e)).\; \text{isReceive}(\text{Lab}(tr))$$

where sw_{S_1}, sw_{S_2} instantiate the generic swap:

$$sw_{S_1}((S_1, R_{r_1}^{m_1}, S_1'), (S_{2,s_2}\, S_{r_2}^{m_2}, S_2')) =$$
$$\mathbf{if}\; s_2 \neq r_1\; \mathbf{then}$$
$$(S_1,$$
$$_{s_2}S_{r_2}^{m_2},$$
$$S_1(s_2 := ((S1's_2)\{state := state(S2'(s_2))\}),$$
$$r_2 := ((S1'r_2)\{queue := ((queue(S_1 r2))@[m2])\})))$$
$$\mathbf{else}\; (S_1, R_{r_1}^{m_1}, S_1')$$
$$\mid\, sw_{S_1}(e_1, e_2) = e_1$$

$$sw_{S_2}((S_1, R_{r_1}^{m_1}, S_1'), (S_{2,s_2}\, S_{r_2}^{m_2}, S_2'))$$
$$\mathbf{if}\; s_2 \neq r_1\; \mathbf{then}$$
$$(S_1(s_2 := ((S_1's_2)\{state := state(S2'(s_2))\}),$$
$$r_2 := ((S_1'r_2)\{queue := ((queue(S_1 r2))@[m2])\}))\, "$$
$$R_{r_1}^{m_1},$$
$$S_2')$$
$$\mathbf{else}\; (S_{2,s_2}\, S_{r_2}^{m_2}, S_2')$$
$$\mid\, sw_{S_2}(e_1, e_2) = e_2$$

Remark. Intuitively, if a send of a node s occurs in a run after a receive of node s' ($s' \neq s$), it can also occur before. Such sends can be swapped.

Partitioning. The `partition` operation has two parameters: a peer p and a run r. Partitioning divides a run into two complementary runs: the first contains only transitions of peer p and the second contains transitions that do not belong to p. In order to obtain runs, partitioning is done through the `unroll` operation:

all the transitions of **p** are successively unrolled; hence transitions of **p** are pushed to the front thus separating them from the transitions from peers other than **p**.

The **partition** operation is described recursively by the following text:

$$\text{partition}(p, r) \triangleq \textbf{if } r = [\,] \textbf{ then } ([\,], [\,])$$
$$\textbf{else let } (o, n) = \text{partition}(p, \text{butlast}(r)) \textbf{ in}$$
$$\textbf{if } \text{On}(\text{Lab}(\text{last}(r))) = p \textbf{ then}$$
$$\textbf{let } a' = \text{unroll}_{sw_{R_1}, sw_{R_2}}(\text{last}(r), n) \textbf{ in}$$
$$(n@[hd(a')], tl(a'))$$
$$\textbf{else } (o, n@[\text{last}(r)])$$

$$\text{on}(p, r) \quad \triangleq \text{fst}(\text{partition}(p, r))$$
$$\text{not\_on}(p, r) \quad \triangleq \text{snd}(\text{partition}(p, r))$$

Theorem 3 (Partitionning Receives). *For any peer p, a run over receive transitions is partitioned into two adjacent runs.*

$$\forall r.\ r \in \mathcal{R}(i) \wedge (\forall\ tr \in r.\ \text{isReceive}(\text{Lab}(tr)))$$
$$\Rightarrow \quad \text{on}(p, r)@\text{not\_on}(p, r) \in \mathcal{R}(i)$$
$$\wedge\ \text{Trace}(\text{on}(p, r)@\text{not\_on}(p, r)) = \text{Trace}(r)$$
$$\wedge\ \text{ends}(\text{on}(p, r)@\text{not\_on}(p, r)) = \text{ends}(r)$$

4.2 Normalization

Normalization splits a run into a sequence of *packed* runs and a **trail** run. Each packed run has one send transition and preceding receive transitions from the same peer. In the trail part, we have all the receive transitions that have not yet been followed by a send of the same peer. The Fig. 5 illustrates normalization. More precisely:

- the empty run is split into an empty sequence and an empty trail.
- Given a run split into a sequence packed runs and a trail run, adding a transition to this run yields the following: a receive transition (R_1^a in the Fig. 6) is added to the trail part leaving the packed runs unchanged. For a send transition ($_2S_3^d$ in the Fig. 7), we partition the trail part into the **on s** part and the **not_on s** part. The new packed part is the concatenation of the **on** part and the send transition, and the new trail part is the remaining **not_on** part.

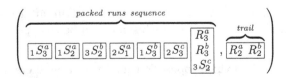

Fig. 5. Normalized run structure

$$\left(\underbrace{\boxed{_1S_3^a}\ \boxed{_1S_2^a}\ \boxed{_3S_2^b}\ \boxed{_2S_1^a}\ \boxed{_1S_3^b}\ \boxed{_2S_3^c}\ \boxed{\begin{array}{c}R_3^a\\R_3^b\\_3S_2^c\end{array}}}_{\text{packed runs sequence}},\ \overbrace{\boxed{R_2^a\ R_2^b\ R_1^a}}^{\text{trail}} \right)$$

Fig. 6. Normalized run structure (after a Receive wrt. Fig. 5)

Normalization is formalized as follows:

$$\text{normalize}(r) \triangleq \textbf{if } r = [] \textbf{ then } ([],[])$$

$$\textbf{else let } (p,t) = \text{normalize}(\text{butlast}(r)) \textbf{ in}$$

$$\textbf{if } \text{isReceive}(\text{Lab}(\text{last}(r))) \textbf{ then } (p, t@[\text{last}(r)])$$

$$\textbf{else}$$

$$\textbf{let } s = \text{On}(\text{Lab}(\text{last}(r))) \textbf{ in}$$

$$\textbf{let } u = \text{unroll}_{sw_{S_1},sw_{S_2}}(\text{not\_on}(s,t), \text{last}(r)) \textbf{ in}$$

$$(p@\text{on}(s,t)@[\text{hd}(u)], \text{tl}(u))$$

$$\text{packed}(r) \quad \triangleq \text{fst}(\text{normalize}(r))$$

$$\text{trail}(r) \quad \triangleq \text{snd}(\text{normalize}(r))$$

$$\left(\underbrace{\boxed{_1S_3^a}\ \boxed{_1S_2^a}\ \boxed{_3S_2^b}\ \boxed{_2S_1^a}\ \boxed{_1S_3^b}\ \boxed{_2S_3^c}\ \boxed{\begin{array}{c}R_3^a\\R_3^b\\_3S_2^c\end{array}}\ \boxed{\begin{array}{c}R_2^a\\R_2^b\\_2S_3^d\end{array}}}_{\text{packed runs sequence}},\ \overbrace{\boxed{R_1^a}}^{\text{trail}} \right)$$

Fig. 7. Normalized run structure (after a Send wrt. Fig. 5)

Theorem 4 (Normalization). *Normalization splits a run to two adjacent runs called the packed run and the trail run. A run and its packed run have the same trace.*

$$\forall\ r.r \in \mathcal{R}(i) \Rightarrow \begin{array}{l} \text{packed}(r)@\text{trail}(r) \in \mathcal{R}(i) \\ \wedge\ \text{Trace}(\text{packed}(r)) = \text{Trace}(r) \\ \wedge\ \forall\ tr \in \text{trail}(r).\ \text{isReceive}(\text{Lab}(tr)) \end{array}$$

Remark. We have $\text{packed}(r) \in \mathcal{R}(i)$. Moreover, since the trail contains only receive transitions, its trace is empty.

5   Application to Trace-based Replay

In this section, we give the formal specification of a replay through a given observation. Note that we are not concerned by the construction of the observation by itself *but* by the reconstruction of an execution from the observation of a run and its correctness.

5.1   Replay Definition

Intuitively, a replay function reconstructs a run which has a given trace supposed to be obtained through an actual execution.

Definition 7 (Replay). *Given a transition system* $Sys = (I, \rightarrow)$, *a replay function* rf *takes as parameter an initial state* $i \in I$ *and the trace* tr *of a run starting at* i *and returns a run of* Sys *starting at* I *with the same trace.*

$$
\text{replay}((I, \rightarrow), rf) \triangleq \\
\forall i \in I. \ \forall r \in \mathcal{R}_{(I, \rightarrow)}(i). \quad rf(i, \text{Trace}(r)) \in \mathcal{R}_{(I, \rightarrow)}(i) \\
\wedge \ \text{Trace}(rf(i, \text{Trace}(r))) = \text{Trace}(r)
$$

This definition deserves some comments:

- we do not reconstruct the actual execution that leads to the given trace *but* an execution with the same trace.
- As said in Sect. 2, the construction of the observation relies on a total order on the sends to a given peer. Such a total order can be established thanks to elaborated order mechanisms [16] or to highly precise network time protocols [19].

An interesting property of a replay function is to be incremental: runs can be reconstructed through trace suffixes and corresponding starting states. Such a property is formalized as follows:[7]

Property 1 (incremental replay).

$$
\text{replay}((I, \rightarrow), rf) \Rightarrow \\
\forall i \in I. \ \forall p \ s. \ p@s \in \mathcal{R}_{(I, \rightarrow)}(i) \Rightarrow \text{replay}((p(I), \rightarrow), rf)
$$

The incremental replay property is interesting with respect to space saving: provided that we do not have to reconstruct a run from the initial state, we can store only a suffix of the trace and its corresponding starting state. Such a property is also interesting with respect to the so called "right to be forgotten"; actually, it allows to forget a prefix of a run and make henceforth the replay starts after that prefix. Of course, it does not forbid to apply memoization. Without surprise, this fact tells us the "right to be forgotten" and the "right to store" are linked.

5.2   Mode Based FIFO Protocols

In mode based protocol, when ready to interact with the environment, a peer is ready either in the receiving mode : it is ready to receive messages *or* in the sending mode: it is ready to send messages. Such a mode can be represented through a function defined over the product of peers and states as follows:

$$
\text{mode : peer} \times \text{state} \rightarrow \{\text{Ready2Receive}, \text{Ready2Send}\}
$$

The Table 1 details such a function for our illustrative example.

---

[7] We use the functional overloading seen in Sect. 2: $p(I)$ is the state reached after the execution of the run prefix p.

5.3   A Replay Algorithm

The considered replay algorithm takes as input:

- a FIFO protocol recorded trace,
- the mode of the states of each peer through the function mode,
- and the automata of the peers through their respective δ transition function.

It reconstructs a run following the structure of a normalized run (see Fig. 5). Actually, it builds recursively a sequence of packed runs. Each packed run is built through the reconstruct_run function and proceeds as follows: for each $_sS_r^m$ label of the recorded trace, a pack of labels is reconstructed recursively through the reconstruct_pack function.

$$\text{reconstruct\_pack}(St, {}_sS_r^m) \triangleq$$
$$\textbf{if } \text{mode}(s, St[s]) = \text{Ready2Send } \textbf{then}$$
$$\textbf{let } St' = St\,[s := St[s][\text{state} := \delta_s(St[s])],$$
$$r := St[r][\text{queue} := St[r].\text{queue}@[m]]]$$
$$\textbf{in } [(St, {}_sS_r^m, St')]$$
$$\textbf{else if } St[s].\text{queue} \neq [\,] \textbf{ then}$$
$$\textbf{let } m = hd(St[s].\text{queue}) \textbf{ in}$$
$$\textbf{let } St' = St[s := [\text{state} := \delta_s(St[s]), \text{queue} := tl(St[s].\text{queue})]$$
$$\textbf{in } [(St, R_s^m, St')]@\text{reconstruct\_pack}(St', {}_sS_r^m)$$
$$\textbf{else } [\,]$$

$$\text{reconstruct\_run}(St, tr) \triangleq$$
$$\textbf{if } tr = [\,] \textbf{ then } [\,]$$
$$\textbf{else let } p = \text{reconstruct\_pack}(St, hd(tr)) \textbf{ in}$$
$$\textbf{if } p \neq [\,] \textbf{ then}$$
$$\textbf{let } (\_, \_, St') = last(p) \textbf{ in}$$
$$p@\text{reconstruct\_run}(St', tl(tr))$$
$$\textbf{else } [\,]$$

Remark. The reconstruct_pack function returns an empty run for an initial state.

Lemma 1 (reconstruct_run).

$$\forall r.\ r \in \mathcal{R}(i) \Rightarrow \text{reconstruct\_run}(i, \text{Trace}(r)) = \text{packed}(r)$$

from this lemma and Theorem 4, we deduce

Theorem 5 (Replay Algorithm). *The function* reconstruct_run *defines a replay algorithm.*

$$\text{replay}(\text{FIFO\_LTS}, \text{reconstruct\_run})$$

6   Related Works

The seminal work related to our concerns is probably that of Mazurkiewicz [9]. Let us recall that basic trace theory is defined over an alphabet of actions Σ. and a symmetric and reflexive relation I called the independence relation. Two elements of Σ^* are said to be equivalent if one can be obtained from the other by commuting independent actions:

$$x \simeq y \equiv \exists\, u\, v.\ \exists\, (a,b) \in I.\ x = uabv \wedge y = ubav$$

In fact, a trace is an equivalence class with respect to the transitive closure of the previous relation($\simeq$). With respect to our model, such a commutation does exist for receive transitions occurring on different nodes. Our normalization relies on such a property. In addition, with respect to our model, we also use semi-commutations [5, 8] (the independence relation is not symmetric). Actually, when a receive is followed by a send on a different node, we can swap these actions (but not the reverse, in general).This is the second property, our normalization relies on.To the best of our knowledge, the use of such tools for the reconstruction problem is new.

The basic references of FIFO protocols are [6, 22]. As remarked in Sect. 2.3, the model studied in this paper does not consider channels. First investigations show that our algorithm can be extended to some variants of the basic model. We are currently studying such extensions. With respect to recovery, our algorithm is *trace* based: we rely on the observation of send events in order to reconstruct of a full observation, while, for instance, the algorithm of [7, 14] is basically *state* based.

Last, we mention the work of [3] which deals with realizability and synchronizability properties. Indeed, their work has been the starting point of our study: we reuse the asynchronous communication model with fifo buffers as the semantics model. They show that such a model can be used for important application classes [1, 11].

In the work given by [4], logged messages are needed to allow us deduce the cause of failure (diagnosis) and recover by compensating the logged actions (atomicity). However, only some messages are logged due to security and privacy issues. This results in a partial log and the authors propose two heuristic-based methods for computing the smallest number of messages needed to replay an execution, starting from a partial log. This work considers transactional properties and leaves out of scope assumptions related to distributed systems in general, e.g., does not deal with asynchronous communication semantics.

7   Conclusion

In this paper, we have studied how to rebuild a full distributed computation from its partial observation. The study has been done at the semantic model level: first we have formalized the underlying distributed system protocol as a transition system, then we have proposed an algorithm for reconstructing a run given its trace. The correctness of the algorithm has been established with respect to a given definition of replay. Concerning the actual implementation context of the algorithm, we have suggested some basic ideas.

For our future work, we envision two directions: first, it would be interesting to study the replay problem in order to·take into account other models of distributed systems. We are especially interested in real-time distributed systems. Another direction that seems promising is to better understand the needs of high level applications relying on run-time data [13] in order to provide them an appropriate knowledge.

Acknowledgements. We thank the reviewers and the editors for enhancing the readability of the paper.

References

1. Armstrong, J.: Getting Erlang to talk to the outside world. In: Proceedings of the 2002 ACM SIGPLAN Workshop on Erlang, ERLANG 2002, pp. 64–72. ACM, New York (2002)
2. Arnold, A.: Finite Transition Systems - Semantics of Communicating Systems. Prentice Hall, Upper Saddle River (1994)
3. Basu, S., Bultan, T., Ouederni, M.: Deciding choreography realizability. In: Field, J., Hicks, M.(eds.) POPL, pp. 191–202. ACM (2012)
4. Biswas, D., Gazagnaire, T., Genest, B.: Small logs for transactional services: Distinction is much more accurate than (positive) discrimination. In: HASE, pp. 97–106. IEEE Computer Society (2008)
5. Bouajjani, A., Muscholl, A., Touili, T.: Permutation rewriting and algorithmic verification. Inf. Comput. **205**(2), 199–224 (2007)
6. Brand, D., Zafiropulo, P.: On communicating finite-state machines. J. ACM **30**(2), 323–342 (1983)
7. Chandy, K., Misra, J.: Parallel Program Design. Addison-Wesley, Reading (1988)
8. Clerbout, M., Latteux, M.: Semi-commutations. Inf. Comput. **73**(1), 59–74 (1987)
9. Diekert, V., Rozenberg, G. (eds.): The Book of Traces. World Scientific, Singapore (1995)
10. Dijkstra, E., Scholten, C.: Termination detection for diffusing computations. Inf. Process. Lett. **11**(1), 1–4 (1980)
11. Fähndrich, M., Aiken, M., Hawblitzel, C., Hodson, O., Hunt, G., Larus, J.R., Levi, S.: Language support for fast and reliable message-based communication in singularity OS. SIGOPS Oper. Syst. Rev. **40**(4), 177–190 (2006)
12. Fokkink, W.: Distributed Algorithms: An Intuitive Approach. MIT Press, Cambridge (2013)
13. Gößler, G., Le Métayer, D., Raclet, J.-B.: Causality analysis in contract violation. In: Barringer, H., Falcone, Y., Finkbeiner, B., Havelund, K., Lee, I., Pace, G., Roşu, G., Sokolsky, O., Tillmann, N. (eds.) RV 2010. LNCS, vol. 6418, pp. 270–284. Springer, Heidelberg (2010)
14. Hélary, J.-M., Mostéfaoui, A., Netzer, R.H.B., Raynal, M.: Communication-based prevention of useless checkpoints in fistributed computations. Distrib. Comput. **13**(1), 29–43 (2000)

15. Java message service. http://www.oracle.com/technetwork/java/index-jsp-142945. html
16. Lamport, L.: Time, clocks and the ordering of events in a distributed system. CACM **21**(7), 558–565 (1978)
17. Lamport, L.: Specifying Systems: The TLA+ Language and Tools for Hardware and Software Engineers. Addison-Wesley Longman Publishing Co. Inc, Boston (2002)
18. Lamport, L.: Euclid writes an algorithm: a fairytale. Int. J. Softw. Inf. **5**(1–2), 7–20 (2011)
19. Lee, E.A., Zhao, Y.: Reinventing computing for real time. In: Kordon, F., Sztipanovits, J. (eds.) Monterey Workshop 2005. LNCS, vol. 4322, pp. 1–25. Springer, Heidelberg (2007)
20. Leucker, M., Schallhart, C.: A brief account of runtime verification. J. Log. Algebr. Program. **78**(5), 293–303 (2009)
21. Lynch, N.A.: Distributed Algorithms. Morgan Kaufmann Publishers Inc., San Francisco (1996)
22. von Bochmann, G.: Finite state description of communication protocols. Comput. Netw. **2**, 361–372 (1978)

Dynamic State Machines for Formalizing Railway Control System Specifications

Roberto Nardone[1]([✉]), Ugo Gentile[1], Adriano Peron[1], Massimo Benerecetti[1], Valeria Vittorini[1], Stefano Marrone[3], Renato De Guglielmo[2], Nicola Mazzocca[1], and Luigi Velardi[2]

[1] Università di Napoli "Federico II", Napoli, Italy
{ugo.gentile,roberto.nardone,adrperon,massimo.benerecetti,
valeria.vittorini,nicola.mazzocca}@unina.it
[2] Ansaldo STS, Napoli, Italy
{renato.deguglielmo,luigi.velardi}@ansaldo-sts.com
[3] Seconda Università di Napoli, Caserta, Italy
stefano.marrone@unina2.it

Abstract. activities regulated by international standards which explicitly recommend the usage of Finite State Machines (FSMs) to model the specification of the system under test. Despite the great number of work addressing the usage of FSMs and their extensions, actual model-driven verification processes still lacks concise and expressive enough notations, able to easily capture characteristic features of specific domains. This paper introduces DSTM4Rail, a hierarchical state machines formalism to be used in verification contexts, whose peculiarity mainly resides in the semantics of fork-and-join which allows dynamic (bounded) instantiation of machines (processes). The formalism described in this paper is industry driven, as it raises from real industrial needs in the context of an European project. Hence, the proposed semantics is motivated by illustrating concrete issues in modeling specific functionalities of the Radio Block Centre, the vital core of the ERTMS/ETCS Control System.

Keywords: State machine · Dynamic instantiation · Railway control system · Metamodel · Model driven · System testing · CRYSTAL

1 Introduction

One of the most critical components installed in modern railways is the signaling system which aims at guaranteeing the complete control of the railway traffic with a high-level of safety, essentially to prevent trains from colliding. These systems shall be validated against system requirements, given by the client and by international standards, such as the CENELEC norms as for the European standards is concerned (i.e., EN50128 [6] and EN50126 [5]). The first step of the V&V process is to describe the system behaviour and requirements by using a state-based language (highly recommended by the standards during these phases of the life cycle). The work described in this paper is part of a wider research activity

© Springer International Publishing Switzerland 2015
C. Artho and P.C. Ölveczky (Eds.): FTSCS 2014, CCIS 476, pp. 93–109, 2015.
DOI: 10.1007/978-3-319-17581-2_7

carried out within the ongoing ARTEMIS Joint Undertaking project CRYSTAL (CRitical sYSTem engineering AcceLeration) [8] with the objective to alleviate the high effort (in terms of costs and time) required by the V&V activities [3]. CRYSTAL is strongly industry-oriented and will provide ready-to-use integrated *tool chains* having a mature technology-readiness level. To achieve technical innovation, CRYSTAL developed a user-driven approach [20] by applying engineering methods to industrially relevant *Use Cases* from the automotive, aerospace, rail and health sectors and aims at increasing the maturity of existing concepts developed in previous projects on European and national level (e.g., CESAR [7] and MBAT [17]). Our work is conducted in the railway domain, according to the needs expressed by Ansaldo STS (ASTS), an international transportation leader in the field of signaling and integrated transport systems for passenger traffic (Railway/Mass Transit) and freight operation. Our ultimate goal in CRYSTAL is to reduce the time needed for the definition of *system level* tests of railway control systems. To meet this objective a model-driven approach for the automated generation of test cases is being developed. The starting point is the definition of a domain specific formal state-based language (DSTM4Rail) to be used for modeling the system behavior and formalize the requirements (from which the test specifications are obtained). This paper specifically introduces DSTM4Rail (Dynamic STate Machine for Railway control systems). The name of the language says that its definition was driven by the specific needs expressed by ASTS. At the state, DSTM4Rail has been developed to model the behavior and the requirements of a *railway* control system for *system testing* purposes, but it could be applied to model different critical control systems. The motivation for a new language resides in the requirements expressed by the railway industry: a formal language to be integrated into a model-driven process *as simple as possible and as rich as needed* [10]. Consequently, the idea to extend existing languages has been discarded in order to open to the effective usage of the language in the industrial setting. The formalism metamodel we propose allows for modeling the dynamic (bounded) instantiation of machines (processes) as well as communications and timing constraints. The focus of the paper is on the control flow, hence here the semantics of fork-and-join is formally defined in order to model discrete behaviors through finite state-transition systems. The paper is organized as follows. Section 2 presents the application domain and states the language requirements. Section 3 describes DSTM4Rail through its metamodel and introduces its formal syntax and semantics. Section 4 gives some meaningful examples of language application to real examples. Section 5 provides a discussion about the related work and clarifies the motivation behind the introduction of DSTM4Rail. Finally, Sect. 6 contains some closing remarks.

2   RBC Use Case and Language Requirements

The CRYSTAL Use Case from ASTS is the Radio Block Centre (RBC) system, a computer-based system whose aim is to control the movement of the set of trains on the track area that is under its supervision, in order to guarantee a safe inter-train distance according to the ERTMS/ETCS specifications. ERTMS/ETCS

(European Rail Traffic Management System/European Train Control System) is a standard for the interoperability of the European railway signaling systems that ensures both technological compatibility among trans-European railway networks and integration of the new signalling systems with the existing national train interlocking systems. The RBC system is in charge of timely transmitting to the on-board system of each train its up-to-date Movement Authority (MA) and the related speed profile, in addition it is responsible for the management of the emergency situations within its own sub-track. The industrial needs regarding the specification language can be summarized as follows: (a) it must have formal syntax and formal semantics; (b) it must be easy to understand and use; (c) it must suit for modeling domain specific behavior and requirements. In other words, the language must provide *primitives* able to cope in a non-ambiguous and simple way with specific modeling issues, and specifically:

R1 *concurrent execution flows*: concurrency shall be allowed as RBC manages concurrent execution flows (e.g., it handles simultaneously several communications with other systems).

R2 *instantiation/termination* of machine: fork and join of control flows shall be allowed as well as the possibility to instantiate synchronously and asynchronously new machines. In addition, the *preemption* property should be considered on joins, in order to force the termination of a machine.

R3 *trigger and condition*: a special trigger (say "any") shall be defined in order to help modelers when specifying a transition which is triggered by the occurrence of an event *not* belonging to a given set; similarly a special "any" condition shall be allowed.

R4 *broadcast communication*: broadcasting communication between machines shall be allowed in order to manage situations in which different machines need to be triggered by the same event (e.g. in case of watchdog timers).

R5 *timers*: timers shall be considered as well as the trigger corresponding to their expiration; activation/deactivation of timers shall be introduced as actions.

R6 *variables*: variables are necessary in order to store information and to enable a concise representation of machines.

In order to contextualize DSTM4Rail we provide a general picture of the model-driven test case generation approach we are currently developing within the CRYSTAL project. Fig 1(b) shows the system level testing process adopted by ASTS (instantiated on the RBC).

A set of Test Specifications is derived from the requirements. Then, Test Cases are obtained from the Test Specifications and translated into executable tests. These activities shall be conducted by the V&V team, which is independent from the development team and should not know any information about the development (mandatory, since CENELEC standards are applicable). Fig 1(a) depicts the proposed test case generation approach: it has impact on the part of the testing process enclosed in the dashed box in Fig. 1(b). Chains of model transformations yield Test Cases by applying model checking techniques from a state-based specification of the system behavior and the Test Specifications [2,18]. These models should be independent from the specific model

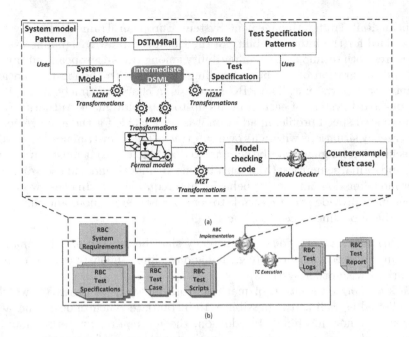

Fig. 1. Test case generation approach.

checker. Hence, besides the definition of a proper formal state-based language (DSTM4Rail), the approach will require the development of a domain specific modeling language (Intermediate DSML) both as the target language of model transformation engines from the state-based models and as the source language to different model checkers. The Test Specification Patterns will provide general reusable models for recurrent classes of requirements [9].

3   DSTM4Rail

DSTM4Rail extends Hierarchical State Machines [1] by adding concepts of fork, join and recursive execution of machines inside a box, allowing for the *dynamic instantiation* of machines. The main advantages are: (1) each state machine may be parametric over a finite set of dynamically evaluated parameters, and (2) the same machine may be instantiated many times without explicitly replicating its entire structure. From now on we refer to an *executing* state machine as a *process*.

3.1   Metamodel

An excerpt of the DSTM4Rail metamodel is shown in Fig. 2. An Ecore diagram is used, according to the technology adopted to generate the model editor and graphical interface [21]. As the focus of the paper is on the representation and evolution of the control flow, the described portion of the metamodel introduces

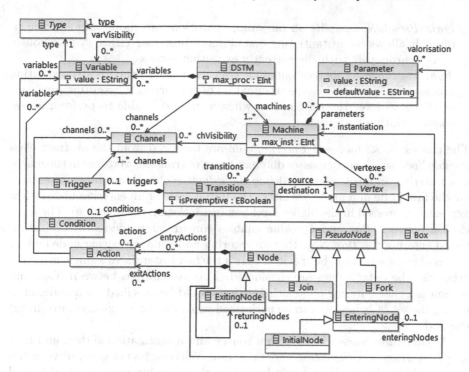

Fig. 2. DSTM4Rail metamodel.

the syntactical elements aiming at covering the requirements *R1*, *R2*, *R4* and *R6* of Sect. 2. Concepts and relationships pertaining to data flow are just outlined.

The main class is Dynamic State Machine *(DSTM)*, which represents the entire specification model. It is characterized by the attribute *max_proc*, which indicates the maximum number of processes active in each instant of time (to bound a DSTM being a FSM). A DSTM is composed of different *Machines*, *Channels* and *Variables*. For the sake of simplicity, in this paper we consider *Channels* and *Variables* with a global scope; they allow for communication between machines. A single *Machine* is composed of *Vertexes*, *Transitions* and *Parameters*.

The class *Vertex* is abstract since different kinds of vertexes (with different features and constraints) may be present in a machine. The vertex types are:

- *Node*: node of a machine;
- *Entering Node*: *PseudoNode*, entry point of a machine;
- *Initial Node*: default entering node of a machine (at most one for each machine);
- *Exiting Node*: exit (or final) point of a machine (more than one if return conditions are required);
- *Box*: encloses one or more state machines which are concurrently instantiated when the box is entered;

- *Fork*: *PseudoNode*, splits an incoming transition into more outgoing transitions; it allows for instantiating one or more processes either synchronously or asynchronously with the currently executing process;
- *Join*: *PseudoNode*, merges outgoing transition from concurrently executing processes; it synchronizes the termination of concurrently executing processes or allows to force the termination when a process is able to perform a *preemptive* exiting transition.

The classes *Fork*, *Join* and *EnteringNode* are inherited from the abstract class *PseudoNode* which encompasses different types of transient vertexes in the machine. Entering and exiting nodes define the *interface* of each machine, in particular the first node of a process is either the initial node or an entering node (when explicitly expressed in the higher level box instantiating the machine). The association between *Box* and *Machine* enables concurrent processes to be instantiated entering the *Box*. Note that an entering node and/or exiting node and/or values of parameters can be specified only if the box instantiates a single machine, otherwise the default ones are considered. Two associations between *Node* and *Action* say that entering and exiting actions could be specified for a node, indicating the set of behaviours to be performed when entering (exiting) into (from) the node.

A *Transition* is associated with a source and a destination vertex, and may specify a *Trigger*, a *Condition* and an *Action*. Without loss of generality we can assume that a *Trigger* is a freely built logical expression over standard logical connectors on a suitable set of elementary triggers (basic *events*); Similarly a *Condition* is a freely built logical expression over standard logical connectors on a suitable set of atomic *propositions* which provides a fine-grained control over the firing of the transition; finally the *Action* is a sequence of elementary actions (*operations*), induced by the application domain, to be performed when the transition fires. Triggers are related to the reception of messages on channels, hence an association with *Channel* is present. Similarly conditions may be expressed on a set of variables (an association is present between *Condition* and *Variable*). An action may cause the update of a variable or the transmission of messages on channels, hence two associations with *Channel* and *Variable* have been inserted. A *Transition* can specify also an entering node, if different from the default one, of an activated machine (when entering a box), hence an association with *EnteringNode* is present. Similarly it can specify a precise exit node, when returning from a box, hence another association with *ExitingNode* is also present.

A set of constraints are defined in order to forbid the definition of transitions between any kind of vertexes, the introduction of triggers when exiting the *PseudoNode*s, the truth of the attribute *isPreemptive* (of *Transition*) when the destination of a transition is not a *Join*, the specification of entering or exiting nodes for the set of transitions which not connect boxes. These constraints are formally defined in the next Subsection.

3.2　Formal Syntax

In this Subsection we formally provide the fragment of the abstract syntax of DSTM4Rail needed to represent the control flow (with respect to the metamodel elements previously described).

Let $\mathcal{T}$, $\mathcal{C}$ and $\mathcal{A}$ be the syntactical categories of *triggers*, *conditions* and *actions*, respectively. An element of $\mathcal{T}$ (resp. $\mathcal{C}$, $\mathcal{A}$) is a trigger (resp. condition, action) expression. Assume that the symbol $\overline{\tau} \in \mathcal{T}$ represents the trigger "always_available" and the symbol $\overline{\alpha} \in \mathcal{A}$ represents the action "no_action". Let X be a set of *variables* and let C a set of *channels*.

Definition 1 (Dynamic State Machine). *A DSTM D over $\mathcal{T}$, $\mathcal{C}$ and $\mathcal{A}$ is a tuple $\langle M_1, \ldots, M_n, X, C, max\_proc, max\_inst \rangle$ where:*

- *a machine M_i is a tuple $\langle N_i, En_i, df_i, Ex_i, Bx_i, Y_i, Fk_i, Jn_i, T_i, \mathrm{Src}_i, \mathrm{Dec}_i, \mathrm{Trg}_i \rangle$, with $i \in \{1, ..., n\}$, where:*
  - N_i *is a (finite) set of nodes and $Ex_i \subseteq N_i$ is a set of exiting nodes;*
  - En_i *is a (finite) set of entering PseudoNodes;*
  - $df_i \in En_i$ *is the initial node (default);*
  - Bx_i *is a (finite) set of boxes;*
  - $Y_i : Bx_i \to \{1, \ldots, n\}^\star$ *assigns to every box a sequence (list) of machine indexes;*
  - Fk_i *is a (finite) set of fork PseudoNodes;*
  - Jn_i *is a (finite) set of join PseudoNodes;*
  - T_i *is a (finite) set of transition labels, where:*
    $Source_i = (N_i \setminus Ex_i) \cup En_i \cup Bx_i \cup (Bx_i \times Ex(D)) \cup Fk_i \cup (Fk_i \times \{\downarrow\}) \cup Jn_i$
    and $Target_i = N_i \cup Bx_i \cup (Bx_i \times En(D)) \cup Fk_i \cup Jn_i \cup (Jn_i \times \{\otimes\})$ are the sets collecting all the possible sources and targets for the transitions of machine M_i, respectively;
    $\mathrm{Src}_i : T_i \to Source_i$ *maps each transition label into a sequence of source (pseudo)nodes and boxes of M_i;*
    $\mathrm{Dec}_i : T_i \to \mathcal{T} \times \mathcal{C} \times \mathcal{A}$ *associates each transition with its decoration, namely the trigger, condition and action of t;*
    $\mathrm{Trg}_i : T_i \to Target_i$ *maps each transition into a sequence of target (pseudo) nodes and boxes of M_i;*

  A transition $t \in T_i$ must match one of the following cases (constraints):
    - * *"implicit transition" whenever the $\mathrm{Src}_i(t) \in En_i$, $\mathrm{Trg}_i(t) \in N_i$ and the decoration $\mathrm{Dec}_i(t) = \langle \overline{\tau}, true, \alpha \rangle$ with $\alpha \in \mathcal{A}$, moreover for every $en \in En_i$ only one implicit transition exists;*
    - * *"internal transition" whenever both $\mathrm{Src}_i(t) \in N_i$ and $\mathrm{Trg}_i(t) \in N_i$;*
    - * *"entering fork transition" whenever $\mathrm{Src}_i(t) \cap (Fk_i \cup (Fk_i \times \{\downarrow\}) \cup Jn_i \cup (Jn_i \times \{\otimes\})) = \emptyset$ and the target $\mathrm{Trg}_i(t) \in Fk_i$;*
    - * *"asynchronous fork" whenever the source $\mathrm{Src}_i(t) \in (Fk_i \times \{\downarrow\})$ and the target $\mathrm{Trg}_i(t) \in N_i$ and decoration is $\mathrm{Dec}_i(t) = (\overline{\tau}, true, \alpha)$ with $\alpha \in \mathcal{A}$;*

* "*entering join*" *whenever the source* $\mathrm{Src}_i(t) \in N_i$ *and the target* $\mathrm{Trg}_i(t) \in Jn_i \cup (Jn_i \times \{\otimes\})$;
* "*exiting join transition*" *whenever the source* $\mathrm{Src}_i(t) \in Jn_i$, $\mathrm{Trg}_i(t) \cap (Fk_i \cup (Fk_i \times \{\downarrow\}) \cup Jn_i \cup (Jn_i \times \{\otimes\})) = \emptyset$ *and decoration* $\mathrm{Dec}_i(t) = (\overline{\tau}, true, \alpha)$ *with* $\alpha \in \mathcal{A}$;
* "*call by default*" *whenever the target* $\mathrm{Trg}_i(t) \in Bx_i$; *moreover if* $\mathrm{Src}_i(t) \in Fk_i$, *then* $\mathrm{Y}(\mathrm{Trg}_i(t)) = j$ *for some* $j \in \{1,...,n\}$, *the decoration is* $\mathrm{Dec}_i(t) = (\overline{\tau}, true, \alpha)$ *with* $\alpha \in \mathcal{A}$;
* "*call by entering*" *whenever the target* $\mathrm{Trg}_i(t)$ *is of the form* (bx, en) *where* $bx \in Bx_i$ *and* $en \in En_j$ *with* $j = \mathrm{Y}_i(bx)$[1]; *if, in addition,* $\mathrm{Src}_i(t) \in Fk_i$ *decoration is* $\mathrm{Dec}_i(t) = (\overline{\tau}, true, \alpha)$ *with* $\alpha \in \mathcal{A}$;
* "*return by default*" *whenever* $\mathrm{Src}_i(t) \in Bx_i$ *and decoration* $\mathrm{Dec}_i(t) = (\overline{\tau}, true, \alpha)$ *with* $\alpha \in \mathcal{A}$;
* "*return by exiting*" *whenever* $\mathrm{Src}_i(t)$ *is of the form* (bx, ex), *where* $bx \in Bx_i$ *and* $ex \in Ex_j$ *with* $j = \mathrm{Y}_i(bx)$ *and decoration is* $\mathrm{Dec}_i(t) = (\overline{\tau}, true, \alpha)$ *with* $\alpha \in \mathcal{A}$;
* "*return by interrupt*" *whenever* $\mathrm{Src}_i(t) \in Bx_i$ *and decoration is* $\mathrm{Dec}_i(t) = (\tau, true, \alpha)$ *with* $\tau \in \mathcal{T} \setminus \{\overline{\tau}\}$ *and* $\alpha \in \mathcal{A}$.

– X *(resp. C) is a (finite) set of variables (resp. channels);*
– max_proc *is the maximum number of processes concurrently active in each instant of time;*
– $max\_inst : \{M_1, ..., M_n\} \to \{1, ..., max\_proc\}$ *assigns to each machine the maximum number of instantiations.*

Note that this definition constrains transitions to belong to a predefined set of kinds, avoiding the possibility to freely connect vertexes of a machine; furthermore the decoration of transitions shall not have triggers or conditions in specific cases.

3.3   Sketch of the Formal Semantics

In this Subsection we provide the formal semantics of DSTM. In order to improve the paper readability, we give the definitions regarding the control flow evolution. Other definitions, regarding data flow evolution, are hence not reported in this paper.

The evolution of a DSTM is a sequence of instantaneous reactions (*steps*). A step is a maximal set of transitions which are triggered by the current set of available events, under the following constraints:

1. A node/box cannot be entered and exited simultaneously in a step (this is instead possible for PseudoNodes); as a consequence, if a transition t_i enters into a node n (resp. box b) in a step, and a transition t_j exits from n (resp. b), then t_j cannot fire in the same step;

---

[1] In this case the box must contain a single machine.

2. The events generated by the firing of a transition (exit actions of the exited node, actions of the transition and entry actions of the entered node) cannot trigger other transitions in the same step but only in the next one.

As usual, formal semantics can be provided by means of a Labeled Transition System (LTS) which is a 4-tuple $L = \langle S, \Sigma, \Delta, S_0 \rangle$, where:

- S is a non-empty set of states;
- Σ is a non-empty alphabet of labels;
- Δ is a transition relation, i.e., a subset of $S \times \Sigma \times S$;
- $S_0 \subseteq S$ is a set of initial states.

With reference to a DSTM D (see Definition 1), $s \in S$ represents the *current* state of D including: (a) the current control locations, (b) the values of variables, (c) the content of channels, (d) the set of events produced by actions.

In the following, some abbreviations are used: $M(D) = \{M_1, \ldots, M_n\}$, $N(D) = \bigcup_1^n N_i$ and $Bx(D) = \bigcup_1^n Bx_i$.

A labelled tree T is a pair $\langle T, \lambda \rangle$, where $T \subseteq \mathbb{N}^*$ is a prefix closed set of vertices (i.e. if $n \in T$ and $n' \prec n$ then $n' \in T$ with $\prec$ the usual prefix relation between strings) and λ is a function labelling vertices over a suitable alphabet. We denote Leaves(T) the set of leaves of T. A control tree is a tree labelled over the set of machines, boxes and nodes.

Definition 2 (Control Tree). *A Control Tree CT over a DSTM D is a pair $\langle T_{ct}, \lambda \rangle$, where*

- T_{ct} *is a tree;*
- λ *is a labeling function* $\lambda : T_{ct} \to M(D) \cup N(D) \cup Bx(D)$

satisfying the following constraints for every $n \in T_{ct}$:

1. $\lambda(\epsilon) = M_1$;
2. $n \in Leaves(T_{ct}) \Leftrightarrow \lambda(n) \in N(D)$;
3. $n \notin Leaves(T_{ct}) \Leftrightarrow \lambda(n) \in M(D) \cup B(D)$;
4. *if* $n = n'.i$ *(i.e., n' is the parent of n) with $i \in \mathbb{N}$:*
   - $n \in Leaves(T_{ct}) \Rightarrow \lambda(n) \in N_j$ *and* $\lambda(n') = M_j$, *for some* $j \in \{1, \ldots, n\}$;
   - $n \notin Leaves(T_{ct})$ *and* $\lambda(n) = bx$ *with* $bx \in Bx_j \Rightarrow \lambda(n') = M_j$;
   - $n \notin Leaves(T_{ct})$ *and* $\lambda(n) = M_j \Rightarrow \lambda(n') = bx \in Bx_k$ *and j occurs in* $Y_k(bx)$, *for some* $k \in \{1, \ldots, n\}$.

This formalization defines the structure of a Control Tree: the root represents the highest level process, the leaves represent specific nodes in which each process is waiting, while internal vertices represent callers and callee processes. If a vertex represents a node or a box of a machine, then its parent shall necessarily represent that machine; if a vertex represents a machine, then its parent shall necessarily represent the box used to instantiate that machine. Notice that a vertex of a control tree cannot be labelled by a pseudostate in accordance with the intuition that control cannot permanently stay in a pseudostate.

Definition 3 (DSTM State). *The state of a DTSM is a tuple*

$$\langle CT, Fr, \rho, \eta, \eta', \chi \rangle, \quad where:$$

1. *CT is a Control Tree of the DTSM, which describes the current state of the control flow;*
2. *Fr, the* frontier *of CT, contains the vertices of CT that can be source of transitions in the current step;*
3. $\rho : X \rightarrow D_X$ *is the valuation function of the variables in X;*
4. $\eta : E \rightarrow \{0, 1\}$ *is a boolean valuation function of the events available in the current step (i.e. tha characteristic function of the set of available events);*
5. $\eta' : E \rightarrow \{0, 1\}$ *is a boolean valuation function (characteristic function) of the set of events generated in the current step and available in the next one;*
6. $\chi : \mathcal{C} \rightarrow D_C$ *is the valuation function of the channels content.*

CT is a tree representing processes, (instances of) boxes and nodes of D currently active in the DSTM. The frontier Fr is the subset of CT vertices, which can be updated due to a transition firing in the LTS. The frontier is used to avoid the firing of sequences of transitions in a step. In fact, in order to fire, a transition has to exit only from vertices belonging to Fr. When a transition of the DSTM fires, CT is updated and the vertices corresponding to the sources of the transition are removed from Fr, in order to keep track of the portion of CT that has been already updated.

   Fig 3 exemplifies the Control Tree in the simplest case of transition firing between vertices. Let us suppose that the process, instance of M_i in Fig. 3(a), is in the node a; after the firing of the transition the Control Tree evolves as indicated in Fig. 3(b): the root represents M_i. Its child is a before the firing, and b after the firing. Fig 4 and 5 show the evolution of the Control Tree in case of fork and join. The fork implies that other two branches are added to the process M_i reporting the boxes bx_1 and bx_2 which have instantiated the processes M_j (which is in a state a') and M_k (which is in a state a'') respectively. After the firing, the processes M_i, M_j and M_k concurrently evolve. Similarly the join in Fig. 5(a) merges the control flow into a single one when the flowing processes are terminated (including the internal one): in fact, when processes M_j and M_k reach their exit nodes (resp. ex_j and ex_k) and M_i is in the node a, the Control Tree evolves removing the branches representing instantiated processes; the process M_i resumes from the node b.

4   Application to the RBC Use Case

This Section describes the application of DSTM4Rail to the modeling of some RBC functionalities, chosen with the aim to highlight how this language solves easily (natively with state machines) some key modeling issues of the railway control systems. Specifically requirements *R1* and *R2* in Sect. 2 are covered with these use cases.

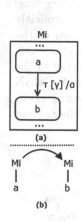

(a)

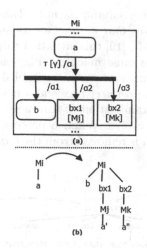

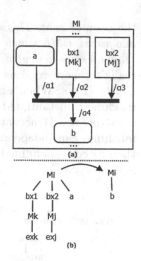

Fig. 3. Transition between nodes.

Fig. 4. *fork* PseudoNode.

Fig. 5. *join* Pseudo-Node.

Communication establishment. When a train is going to establish a safe connection with an RBC, it sends a proper "initiation of communication session" (CONN_REQ) message to it. RBC may accept only connection requests from a limited number of trains: this number is defined by the P_MAX_TRAIN parameter and depends on physical features. Over this value, RBC refuses a new connection sending to the train a proper message (CONN_REF). *This case recalls the need of having variables and parameters inside a machine, as well as a flexible mechanisms for dynamic instantiation and join of processes.* Hence, we have to model the process which accepts or refuses the requests by checking the number of already accepted connections, stored in the *cont* variable, as well as the dynamic instantiation of the processes in charge of managing the communication with the specific train. *Another difference with existing modeling languages is that the first process remains active to manage other communication requests after the instantiation of a lower level machine.* Fig 7 shows the modeling solution of this problem in DSTM4Rail where the main process is called COMM_EST and the lower level process are called TRAIN_CONN. A transition exits from the node *idle*, triggered by the CONN_REQ reception event and, if the number of already accepted connections *cont* is less than the value of the parameter P_MAX_TRAIN, *cont* is incremented and the fork instantiates a new process entering in the box *connect*. The state of the main process proceeds to the node *idle* in order to manage other communication requests. Note that the dynamic instantiation of this machine is constrained (by construction) to be at maximum P_MAX_TRAIN. When a process TRAIN_CONN terminates, the control flow exiting from the box *connect* is joined with the control flow coming from the *idle* node in order to capture this termination and decrement the counter *cont*. *This modeling solution is not allowed by widespread used languages as UML which requires that a machine is suspended when lower level machines are activated.* In UML [19] this situation can be managed by explicitly realizing more replicas of the same machine. Fig 6 shows the evolution of the *ControlTree*. When a new communication is established, a new TRAIN_CONN machine is instantiated by the *connect* box and a new branch is inserted in the *ControlTree*. Hence, at a certain instant of time a set of parallel TRAIN_CONN machines can independently evolve. When a process reaches the *exiting* node, then its corresponding branch is removed from the *ControlTree* and the process is deallocated.

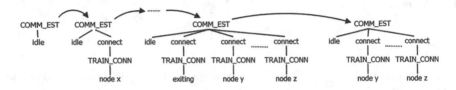

Fig. 6. Evolution of the *ControlTree*.

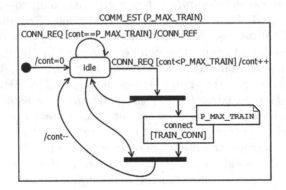

Fig. 7. Train registration management.

Establishment of communication session. Once the CONN_REQ request is accepted, the communication session between the train and RBC must be established. If the procedure succeeds RBC authorizes the train to move (Start-of-Mission, SoM). The Euroradio defines a protocol for safe communication establishment. Ultimately, RBC sends the SYSTEM_VERSION message to the train; the train answers with an ACK and a SESSION_ESTABLISHED message. If the SESSION_ESTABLISHED message is received by RBC before the ACK, RBC sends the SYSTEM_VERSION message again. After three attempts or if other messages are received in the meanwhile, the procedure is aborted and the SoM procedure cannot be performed. This scenario may be easily modeled by providing a machine with multiple exit points: Fig. 8(a) shows how the SOM_PROCEDURE machine is instantiated only after the termination of the SESSION_ESTABLISHMENT process (whose model is depicted in Fig. 8(b)) through the *ok* exiting node.

Management of the train movement. During the movement of the train, the RBC periodically sends the Movement Authority (MA) to the train (Sect. 2); concurrently, RBC has to monitor the commands that come from the Centralized Traffic Control (CTC) where a human operator may raise an alarm which require the train to brake: in these case an Unconditional Emergency Stop (UES) message is sent to the train. On the other hand, when the train successfully ends its trip, RBC performs the "End of Mission" (EoM) procedure. This scenario needs for representing concurrently executing machines one of whom may force the termination of the others. DSTM4Rail models this situstion by a preemptive join, as shown in Fig. 9 where the processes CENTRAL_CONTROL and PERIODIC_MA are executed concurrently but, when the first machine reaches the *UES* exiting node, the join on the left preemptively forces the process PERIODIC_MA to terminate. In this case the machine EMERGENCY_MANAGEMENT is instantiated. On the contrary, if the process PERIODIC_MA terminates in the *EoM* exiting node, the join on the right preemptively forces the CENTRAL_CONTROL to terminate, and the END_OF_MISSION machine is instantiated.

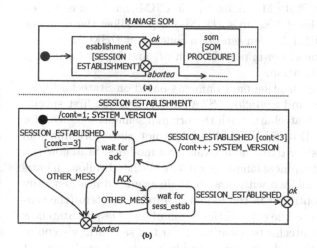
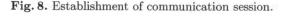
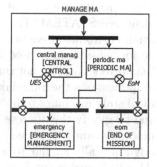

Fig. 8. Establishment of communication session.

Fig. 9. Management of the train movement.

5 Discussion and Related Work

A number of formal methods and techniques have been developed by the scientific community in the past decades and applied to the development of critical systems, including railway applications [4]. Thought their usage is not largely common in industrial settings, Finite State Machines (FSMs) are widely used in modeling systems where control handling aspects are predominant. State-charts [13] extend FSMs with hierarchy, concurrency and communication among concurrent components. Hierarchy is achieved by injecting FSMs into states of other FSMs. Concurrency is achieved by composing FSMs in parallel and by letting them run synchronously.

Among different variants of Statecharts, those integrated in UML 2.0 [19] are widespread used. UML State Machines admit parallel execution through the usage of composite states and regions. In this formalism, the fork (and join) is used in order to split (and merge) an incoming transition into two or more transitions terminating on orthogonal target vertices (i.e., vertices in different regions of a composite state). Recursive activation and dynamic instantiation is not natively admitted. Communicating Hierarchical Machines (CHMs) are a variant of Statecharts introduced for succinctness reasons. They introduced the idea to have a collection of finite state machines (modules) having nodes and boxes. A transition entering a box represents a call to one or more instances of another module. In a Statechart there is no notion of module and instance. If multiple instances of the same module are required by the specification, each instance has to be explicitly defined. On the other way the introduction of modules allows to define Recursive State Machines (RSMs) where a module can recursively call itself [1]. Notice that, in the case of Recursive State Machines, we are not anymore in the category of Finite State Machines. In [15] CHMs has been extended introducing Dynamic Hierarchical Machines (DHMs) which allow the dynamic activation of machines: any DHM M_1 can send to a concurrent DHM M_2 a third DHM M_3, which starts running either in parallel with M_1 and M_2, or inside M_2, depending on contextual information.

Among the commercial specification environments based on Statecharts, we considered STATEMATE [14] and Stateflow. STATEMATE is the first specification environment adopting Statecharts with the original semantics defined for the formalism and revised in [14]. STATEMATE does not allow fork and join PseudoNodes and do not consider dynamic activation of modules. Stateflow is a component of a the Simulink graphical language used in Matlab. It allows hierarchical state machines to be combined with flow chart diagrams ad it is generally used to specify the discrete controller in the model of a hybrid system (the continuous dynamics are specified by the capabilities of Simulink). Despite Stateflow is syntactically similar to a Statecharts notation, from the semantic viewpoint ([11,12]) it avoids any form of non determinism and it imposes an explicit strict scheduling in presence of concurrency, thus being in truth a graphical notation for a sequential imperative language.

Differently from Statecharts we adopt, in the proposed formalism, the possibility of dynamically instantiate modules. The dynamic (possibly recursive) activation of modules is obtained by the structural elements of fork and join PseudoNodes (and not by message passing as in DHMs). Moreover, the non-finiteness of RSMs and DHMs is cut off by bounding the number of simultaneous possible instances of a module. Our work moves from the cited language, mainly allowing for the dynamic instantiation of machines and removing the assumptions, implicitly intended in many languages, that control flows, exiting from a fork, must be merged thorough a join operator. DSTM4Rail, in fact, allows for recursive activation of the same machine by specifying a novel semantics for fork and join operators. Moreover, the computational power of RSMs and DHMs is cut off by bounding the number of simultaneous possible instances of a module. In doing this we follow the approach adopted in many works; e.g., see [16], where the proposed specification language is syntactically inspired by Statecharts (Requirements State Machines), but the semantics is revised and adapted to cope with the needs of the specific application domain (avionic systems).

Specifically, with respect to the UML 2.0, the syntactical elements are similar with the exception of the introduction of the box concept, the asynchronous characterization of the fork and the additional notion of preemptive join. Some other concepts have been removed, since considered redundant and easily realizable in different ways: for example, regions inside composite states can be obtained with the parallel instantiation of machines. The semantics of DSTM4Rail, instead, is completely different for what concerning parallel execution. With respect to the Hierarchical Machines, we assume a similar idea of hierarchy between machines but we enrich this notion with recursive instantiation and parallel execution of machines, through the introduction of syntactical concepts of fork and join, muted from UML. Hence this formalism is substantially different, in syntax and semantics, from Hierarchical Machine (which not permit recursion), from Recursive Machine (which not permit parallelism) and from Communicating Machine (which not permit recursion and dynamic instantiation).

6   Conclusions

This paper presented DSTM4Rail, a formal language for the specification of the behavior of critical control systems extending the approach of Hierarchical State Machine. The critical nature of the systems to model and the high level of usability required by the application domain suggested: (1) a strong formalization of the language; (2) the synthesis and the extension of some of the features of existing FSM-based languages, and (3) the capability to be integrated into modern model-driven processes. The language has its main strengths in the extended semantics of fork and join which allows for the dynamic instantiation and the preemptive termination of machines. The modeling approach has been applied to a modern railway control system in order to demonstrate its potentialities.

Acknowledgments. This paper is partially supported by research project CRYS-TAL (Critical System Engineering Acceleration), funded from the ARTEMIS Joint Undertaking under grant agreement n. 332830 and from ARTEMIS member states Austria, Belgium, Czech Republic, France, Germany, Italy, Netherlands, Spain, Sweden, United Kingdom. The work of Dr. Nardone has been supported by MIUR under

108   R. Nardone et al.

project SVEVIA (PON02_00485_3487758) of the public-private laboratory COSMIC (PON02 00669).

References

1. Alur, R., Kannan, S., Yannakakis, M.: Communicating hierarchical state machines. In: Wiedermann, J., Van Emde Boas, P., Nielsen, M. (eds.) ICALP 1999. LNCS, vol. 1644, pp. 169–178. Springer, Heidelberg (1999)
2. Ammann, P., Black, P., Majurski, W.: Using model checking to generate tests from specifications. In: Proceedings of the 2nd IEEE Internernational Conference on Formal Engineering Methods (ICFEM 1998), pp. 46–54. IEEE Computer Society (1998)
3. Barberio, G., Di Martino, B., Mazzocca, N., Velardi, L., Amato, A., De Guglielmo, R., Gentile, U., Marrone, S., Nardone, R., Peron, A., Vittorini, V.: An interoperable testing environment for ERTMS/ETCS control systems. In: Bondavalli, A., Ceccarelli, A., Ortmeier, F. (eds.) SAFECOMP 2014. LNCS, vol. 8696, pp. 147–156. Springer, Heidelberg (2014)
4. Bjorner, D.: New results and trends in formal techniques and tools for the development of software for transportation systems - A review. In: Tarnai, G. and Schnieder, E. (eds.) Symposium on Formal Methods for Railway Operation and Control Systems (FORMS 2003), L'Harmattan Hongrie, Budapest/Hungary, Germany, May 2003
5. CENELEC, EN 50126:2012: Railway applications - Demonstration of Reliability, Availability, Maintainability and Safety (RAMS) - Part 1: Generic RAMS process
6. CENELEC, EN 50128:2011: Railway applications - Communication, signalling and processing systems - Software for railway control and protection systems
7. CESAR: Cost-Efficient methods and proceses for SAfety Relevant embedded systems. http://www.cesarproject.eu/
8. CRYSTAL: CRitical sYSTem engineering AcceLeration. http://www.crystal-artemis.eu/
9. Gentile, U., Marrone, S., Mele, G., Nardone, R., Peron, A.: Test specification patterns for automatic generation of test sequences. In: Lang, F., Flammini, F. (eds.) FMICS 2014. LNCS, vol. 8718, pp. 170–184. Springer, Heidelberg (2014)
10. Glinz, M.: Statecharts for requirements specification - as simple as possible, as rich as needed. In: International Workshop on Scenarios and State Machines: Models Algorithms and Tools (2002)
11. Hamon, G.: A denotational semantics for Stateflow. In: The Fifth ACM International Conference on Embedded Software, pp. 164–172. ACM Press (2005)
12. Hamon, G., Rushby, J.: An operational semantics for stateflow. In: Wermelinger, M., Margaria-Steffen, T. (eds.) FASE 2004. LNCS, vol. 2984, pp. 229–243. Springer, Heidelberg (2004)
13. Harel, D.: Statecharts: a visual formalism for complex systems. Sci. Comput. Program. 8, 231–274 (1987)
14. Harel, D., Naamad, A.: The STATEMATE semantics of statecharts. ACM Trans. Softw. Eng. Methodol. 5(4), 333 (1996)
15. Lanotte, R., Maggiolo-Schettini, A., Peron, A., Tini, S.: Dynamical hierachical machines. Fundamenta Informaticae 54, 237–252 (2003)
16. Leveson, N.G., Heimdahl, M.P.E., Hildreth, H., Reese, J.D.: Requirements specification for process-control systems. IEEE Trans. Softw. Eng. 20(9), 684–707 (1994)

17. MBAT: Combined Model-based Analysis and Testing of Embedded Systems. http://www.mbat-artemis.eu/
18. Mohalik, S., Gadkari, A.A., Yeolekar, A., Shashidhar, K.C., Ramesh, S.: Automatic test case generation from simulink/stateflow models using model checking. Softw. Test. Verif. Reliab. **24**(2), 155–180 (2014)
19. OMG. Unified Modeling Language (UML), v2.4.1, Superstructure Specification
20. Pflügl, H., El-Salloum, C., Kundner, I.: CRYSTAL, CRitical sYSTem engineering AcceLeration, a Truly European Dimension. ARTEMIS Magazine **14**, 12–15 (2013)
21. Steinberg, D., Budinsky, F., Paternostro, M., Merks, E.: EMF: Eclipse Modeling Framework. Addison-Wesley Professional (2009)

Checking the Conformance of a Promela Design to its Formal Specification in Event-B

Dieu-Huong Vu$^{(\boxtimes)}$, Yuki Chiba, Kenro Yatake, and Toshiaki Aoki

School of Information Science, Japan Advanced Institute of Science and Technology,
Kanazawa, Japan
{huongvd,chiba,k-yatake,toshiaki}@jaist.ac.jp

Abstract. Verification of a design with respect to its requirement specification is important to prevent errors before constructing an actual implementation. Existing works focus on verification tasks where specifications are described using temporal logics or using the same languages as that used to describe designs. In this paper, we consider cases where specifications and designs are described using different languages. For verifying such cases, we propose a framework to check if a design conforms to its specification based on their simulation relation. Specifically, we define the semantics of specifications and designs commonly as labelled transition systems (LTS), and check if a design conforms to its specification based on the simulation relation of their LTS. In this paper, we present our framework for the verification of reactive systems, and we present the case where specifications and the designs are described in Event-B and Promela/Spin, respectively. As a case study, we show an experiment of applying our framework to the conformance check of the specification and the design of OSEK/VDX OS.

Keywords: Formal verification · Model checking · Formal specification · Design · Simulation relation

1 Introduction

A software development process begins with informal requirements which the target software is expected to meet. The informal requirements are translated into formal specifications to ensure their consistency. Then, system designs are developed as models for implementation. Finally, the implementation is done according to the designs using programming languages. In this development process, we should verify the fact that the designs satisfy the requirements described by formal specifications since incorrect designs likely lead to significant costs caused by back tracking of development steps.

We focus on the development of reactive systems. Most of them are considered as safety-critical because their failure may result in loss of lives and assets (e.g., operating systems for mobile vehicles). Reactive systems do not execute by themselves but in combination with their environments. Environments are the external systems which invoke the services of the target systems, e.g., software

© Springer International Publishing Switzerland 2015
C. Artho and P.C. Ölveczky (Eds.): FTSCS 2014, CCIS 476, pp. 110–126, 2015.
DOI: 10.1007/978-3-319-17581-2_8

applications running on the operating systems. The specification of such a reactive system represents its externally visible behavior. That is, the specification represents what the system does in response to the invocations of its environments. Formal specification languages such as VDM [14], Z [16] and Event-B [1] allow us to formally describe the specification. For example, it is straightforward to describe the effect of adding an item into a container using notions such as sets, relations and functions in the formal specification languages. Generally, important properties of the reactive systems, e.g., the properties regarding to pre-conditions and post-conditions of the system services, could be straightforwardly described in the formal specification languages. On the other hand, the design represents the collaboration of internal components to realize observable behaviors described in the specification. It usually contains implementable data structures such as record types, flags, and hash tables. We consider that imperative specification languages like Promela/Spin are appropriate to describe the design since the data structures and behaviors based on them can be straightforwardly described. For example, an algorithm to search and retrieve a certain item from the container could be straightforwardly described in Promela using various control structures based on the data structures such as arrays, record types, or hash tables. The problem is how to verify the designs with respect to their specifications when they are described in different specification languages.

To verify the designs with respect to their specifications, existing works focus on cases where the specifications are described using temporal logics [6,7] or using the same languages as that used to describe the designs [5]. This paper proposes a method to verify the designs against their formal specifications where the specifications and the designs are described in different specification languages. We adopt Event-B for the specification and Promela/Spin for the design. One may say that some of the formal specification languages provide refinement and automatic generation of codes. We can describe the specification in an appropriate specification language; then, we derive the behaviors of the design from the higher-level specification. However, deriving highly optimized behaviors of the design from the highly abstracted specification is generally very hard. Therefore, this approach is not appropriate to verify the systems with complex data structures and highly optimized behaviors like the operating systems. Our idea is to describe the design in the specification language which is easy to represent the design. Then, we verify the design against the specification. Our approach provides another way to ensure that the design is consistent with the specification. Another question may arise here. The specification can be described in temporal logic if we describe the design in Promela/Spin. However, it is well-known that correctly describing properties in temporal logic is difficult [8]. Whereas, by using the rich notions (e.g., sets and relations) in the formal specification languages like Event-B, one could easily describe the properties to be checked against the design. In addition, the tool of the formal specification languages provides a function to verify the consistency and the correctness of the properties. Thus, we think that dealing with the specification and the design based on the different specification languages is appropriate for systems in which there exist a big gap between the specification and the design like the operating systems.

Our approach to check the design against the specification is based on a simulation relation [11,13,18] between them. Firstly, we formally describe specification in Event-B [20] to remove ambiguity and inconsistency in the specification which is written in a natural language. Then, we generate an LTS from this formal specification; and, from each state, verification conditions which must be met by the corresponding state of the design are generated. Finally, we apply model checking [3] to the design to check the verification conditions. In this way, we can check the correspondence of state transitions, or the simulation relation, between the specification and the design. This ensures that the design conforms to the specification.

This paper presents a framework for the verification of reactive systems. We present the formal definition of our framework, and as a case study, we show an experiment of applying our framework to the conformance check of the specification and the design of OSEK/VDX OS [17] (OSEK OS, for short). Verification of OSEK OS is important because it is widely used in automotive control softwares; its bugs may has devastating effects to the human life. The paper is organized as follows: In Sects. 2 and 3, we present the definitions of specifications and designs, respectively. In Sect. 4, we present the definition of our verification framework. In Sects. 5 and 6, we present the case study with the results of several experiments and discuss the effectiveness of our framework. In Sect. 7, we cite the related works. In Sect. 8, we conclude this paper.

2 Specifications

In this section, we present notations of Event-B used in the specification and formal model of the specification.

Specification in Event-B. A reactive system is a system that operates by reacting to stimuli from its environment. Typically, operating systems are reactive, because they react to the invocations from the software applications. A reactive system is captured as a collection of services, which are triggered by the invocations from the environment. We regard the specifications of the reactive systems in Event-B as highly abstracted level descriptions: data structures are represented using notion of sets, relations and functions; and system services are represented in terms of events with guards and substitutions. When the guard of an event is true, the event is fired and its substitution is executed atomically. Figure 1 demonstrates the specification of OSEK OS in Event-B. The **VARIABLES** enumerates the state variables; for example, tasks and res represent all the created tasks and the managed hardware resources. The **INVARIANTS** defines constraints on values of the state variables: it defines data types, e.g., TASK is an abstract data structure and tasks is a subset of TASK; and conditions for the correctness of the behaviors, e.g., at any time only one task is in running state. The **EVENTS** describes system services, e.g., ActivateTask activates a task. The events modify values of the variables and make the corresponding state transitions. The events must preserve the invariants to guarantee the consistency of the specification.

```
VARIABLES  tasks,res,inr,evt,tstate,rdyQu,pri
INVARIANTS
tasks⊆TASK
∀ta,tb·ta∈tasks∧tb∈tasks∧tstate(ta)=run∧ tstate(tb)=run⇒ta=tb
EVENTS
ActivateTask=
any t
where grd1:t∈ tasks,grd2:tstate(t)=sus
then   act1:tstate(t):=rdy,act2:rdyQu:=rdyQu∪{t}

ChainTask=
any t1,t2
where grd1:t1,t2 ∈ tasks,grd2:tstate(t1)=run,grd2:tstate(t2)=sus
then   act1:tstate(t1):=sus,act2:tstate(t2):=rdy,
       act3:rdyQu:=rdyQu∪{t2}
```

Fig. 1. Specification of OSEK OS in Event-B

Formal Semantics. $\mathcal{V}$ is the set of *variables*. $\mathcal{D}$ is the *domain*, which is the set of values. Exp is the set of expressions in the specifications. An *expression* may contain variables in $\mathcal{V}$, values in $\mathcal{D}$, arithmetic operators, logical operators, and set operators. BExp is the set of boolean expressions (BExp $\subset$ Exp). A *substitution* $a : \mathcal{V} \to$ Exp is a mapping from $\mathcal{V}$ to Exp. We note that value assignments are also substitutions because $\mathcal{D} \subseteq$ Exp. ACT is the set of substitutions for specifications. A *guard* is a boolean expression. GRD is the set of guards. An *event* is a pair $\langle g, a \rangle$ of a guard g and a substitution a. $\mathcal{E}$ is the set of events. If $e = \langle g, a \rangle$ then we write $grd(e) = g$ and $act(e) = a$. A *state* is a value assignment. $[exp]_\sigma$ denotes the interpretation of the value of an expression exp in a state σ. We say a guard g holds in a state σ iff $[g]_\sigma = tt$. Init is the set of special initialization events that have no guard. We denote $\sigma \xrightarrow{e} \sigma'$ for an event $e = \langle g, a \rangle$ and states σ and σ' if $[g]_\sigma = tt$ and $\sigma' = \{v \mapsto [a(v)]_\sigma \mid v \in V\}$.

Definition 1 *(Specification Models). A specification model is a tuple $S = \langle \mathcal{V}_S, \mathcal{D}_S, \Sigma_S, \text{Init}_S, Inv \rangle$ where $\mathcal{V}_S \subseteq \mathcal{V}$ is the set of variables used in S, $\mathcal{D}_S \subseteq \mathcal{D}$ is the domain, $\Sigma_S \subseteq \mathcal{E}$ is the set of events, $\text{Init}_S \in$ Init is the initialization of S, and $Inv \in$ BExp is the invariant of S. An LTS derived from the specification model S is defined as $M_S = \langle Q_S, \Sigma_S, \delta_S, I_S \rangle$ where $Q_S = \{\sigma \mid \sigma : \mathcal{V}_S \to \mathcal{D}_S\}$ is a non-empty set of states, $\delta_S = \{\sigma \xrightarrow{e} \sigma' \mid \sigma, \sigma' \in Q_S, e \in \Sigma_S\}$ is a transition relation, and $I_S = \{act(e) \mid e \in \text{Init}_S\}$ is a set of initial states.*

In Event-B, a substitution can be deterministic or non-deterministic. We regard a non-deterministic substitution as multiple deterministic substitutions. Therefore, we assume that the LTS is deterministic.

3 Designs and Environments of the Target System

In this section, we present the design model of reactive systems described in Promela. We assume that the design only defines a set of service functions, it cannot operate by itself. To operate it, we need an environment which calls functions of the reactive system. Therefore, the design needs to be verified in the combination with their environments. We also present the environment model and the combination model.

```
typedef TCB {int id, pr, dpr, ... }        typedef Taskinfor { ... }
typedef RCB {int id, pr, tid, ... }        Taskinfor tsk1, tsk2, tsk3;
TCB tsk[5];                                _DeclareTask(tsk1.id, tsk1.pr1);
RCB res[5];                                _DeclareTask(tsk2.id, tsk2.pr2);
int ready[25];                             _DeclareTask(tsk3.id, tsk3.pr3);
inline _schedule() { ... }                 _ActivateTask(tsk1.id);
inline _DeclareTask(tid, pr) { ... }       _ChainTask(tsk1.id, tsk2.id);
inline _ActivateTask(tid) { ... }          _ChainTask(tsk2.id, tsk3.id);
inline _ChainTask(tid, id) { ... }         _ActivateTask(tsk2.id);
inline _TerminateTask(tid) { ... }         _TerminateTask(tsk3.id);
inline _GetTaskState(tid) { ... }          _TerminateTask(tsk2.id);
                                           _ActivateTask(tsk3.id);
```

Fig. 2. Design model and environment model in Promela

Design in Promela. Promela allows us to describe the design with highly optimized behaviors in an imperative manner. The abstract data structures in Event-B are replaced by the implementable data structures. Design decisions to realize the external behaviors are explicitly described using various control structures. Service functions of reactive systems can be described by using inline functions. Figure 2 (left) illustrates a design of OSEK OS. We call this model a *design model*. It is described in about 2800 lines of Promela code, according to the approach in [2]. It first defines data structures such as `tsk` and `ready` which represent an array of tasks and ready queues, respectively. They replace the abstract data structures `task` and `rdyQu` in Event-B. Following these data structures, a set of functions is defined. For example, `_ActivateTask` and `_TerminateTask` are the functions to perform activation and termination of tasks, respectively. The function signature contains a function name and some parameters (function arguments). The functions are called from the environment. When a function is invoked, its parameters are instantiated by values specified from the environment. The body of the function consists of substitutions.

Environment of Target System. Figure 2 (right) shows an example of an environment for the OSEK OS. We call this model an *environment model*. It first defines entities in the environment such as tasks and resources. Then, it defines sequences of function calls to the OSEK OS. By combining the design and the environment, we can make a closed system which can operate by itself. We call this a *combination model*. In terms of Promela, a combination model can be obtained by including the Promela code of the design into that of the environment model. As we explain later, an environment model is constructed from the specification model, and input to Spin to check the simulation relation.

Formal Semantics. $\mathcal{P}$ is the set of *parameters* (function arguments). In the design, an expression may contain constants, variables, parameters and arithmetic operators, therefore, a so-called *parameterized expression*. The set of parameterized expressions is denoted as PExp. A function body is defined as a substitution. The substitution may contain the parameterized expressions. We use *p-substitution* to denote the substitution in the design. *p-substitution* is a mapping from $\mathcal{V}$ to PExp. The set of p-substitutions is denoted as PSubst. Id is the set of *identifiers* (used as function names). For the simplicity, we assume that functions have only one parameter. The design also includes an initialization function which assigns the initial values for the variables. Design models are defined as follows.

Definition 2 *(Design Model).* *A design model is a tuple* $D = \langle \mathcal{V}_D, \mathcal{D}_D, \mathcal{P}_D, F, \Sigma_D, I_D \rangle$ *where* $\mathcal{V}_D \subseteq \mathcal{V}$ *is the set of variables used in* D, $\mathcal{D}_D \subseteq \mathcal{D}$ *is the domain of* D, $\mathcal{P}_D \subseteq \mathcal{P}$ *is a finite set of parameters for* D, F *is a set of function signatures defined as* $F = \{id(p) \mid id \in \mathrm{Id}, p \in \mathcal{P}_D\}$, Σ_D *is a relation such that* $\Sigma_D \subseteq F \times \mathrm{PSubst}$, *and* I_D *is a set of value assignments of the initialization function such that* $I_D \subseteq \{\sigma \mid \sigma : \mathcal{V}_D \to \mathcal{D}_D\}$.

We assume that the functions in the design are deterministic to have a unique successor state for each current state and each called function. This assumption is realistic for the implementation of the reactive systems like the automotive operating systems. On the other hand, it is generally non-deterministic to select a function applicable in each state. This is described in environment models. Environment models are defined as follows.

Definition 3 *(Environment Model).* *An* environment model for a design model D *is a tuple* $E = \langle \mathcal{V}_E, \mathcal{D}_E, \Sigma_E, I_E \rangle$ *where* $\mathcal{V}_E \subseteq \mathcal{V}$ *is a set of variables used in* E, $\mathcal{D}_E = \mathcal{D}_D$ *is the domain of* E, Σ_E *is a set of* invocations *to* D *such that* $\Sigma_E \subseteq \{id(v) \mid id \in \mathrm{Id}, v \in \mathcal{V}_E\}$, *and* I_E *is a set of value assignments from* $\mathcal{V}_E$ *to* $\mathcal{D}_D$.

A combination of a design and an environment describes the execution of the design according to the environment. An expression in the combination contains constants from $\mathcal{D}$, variables in $\mathcal{V}$, and arithmetic operators. The set of expressions in combinations is denoted as Exp'. A substitution for combinations is a mapping from $\mathcal{V}$ to Exp'. The set of substitutions for combinations is denoted as $\mathrm{SubstDE}$. For a mapping π from $\mathcal{P}$ to $\mathcal{V}$ and a parameterized expression $pexp \in \mathrm{PExp}$, $pexp_\pi$ is the result of replacing each parameter p appearing in $pexp$ by $\pi(p)$. In other words, if $a(v)$ is an expression in D then $a(v)_\pi$ is an expression in the combination obtained by replacing each parameter p appearing in $a(v)$ by $\pi(p)$. Combination models are defined as LTSs as follows.

Definition 4 *(Combination Model).* *Let* $D = \langle \mathcal{V}_D, \mathcal{D}_D, \mathcal{P}_D, F, \Sigma_D, I_D \rangle$ *be a design model and* $E = \langle \mathcal{V}_E, \mathcal{D}_E, \Sigma_E, I_E \rangle$ *an environment model.*

1. *We denote* $\sigma \xrightarrow{id(v)} \sigma'$ *for an invocation* $id(v) \in \Sigma_E$ *and states* σ *and* σ' *if there exist* $(id(p), a) \in \Sigma_D$ *and a mapping* $\pi : \mathcal{P}_D \to \mathcal{V}_E$ *such that* $\pi(p) = v$ *and* $\sigma' = \{v \mapsto [a(v)_\pi]_\sigma \mid v \in \mathcal{V}_D \cup \mathcal{V}_E\}$.
2. *The* combination model *of* D *and* E *(denoted as* $D{\cdot}E$*) is an LTS* $\langle Q_{D{\cdot}E}, \Sigma_{D{\cdot}E}, \delta_{D{\cdot}E}, I_{D{\cdot}E} \rangle$ *where* $Q_{D{\cdot}E} = \{\sigma \mid \sigma : \mathcal{V}_D \cup \mathcal{V}_E \to \mathcal{D}_D\}$ *is a set of states,* $\Sigma_{D{\cdot}E} = \Sigma_E$, $\delta_{D{\cdot}E} = \{\sigma \xrightarrow{id(v)} \sigma' \mid \sigma, \sigma' \in Q_{D{\cdot}E}, id(v) \in \Sigma_E\}$ *is a transition relation, and* $I_{D{\cdot}E} = I_D \cup I_E$ *is a set of initial states of* D *and* E.

4   Checking the Design Against its Formal Specification

In this section, we present a framework for checking a design against its formal specification based on a simulation relation. We first present an overview, then, we present formal definitions.

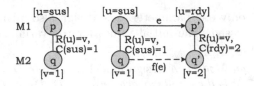

Fig. 3. Simulation relation

4.1   Overview

Suppose that M1 and M2 are two LTSs. We define M2 simulating M1 based on semantics of LTSs by extending the given relation on the states. The states are value assignments which are mappings from the variables to the values. Therefore, the relation on states of M1 and those of M2 are established based on mappings R and C where R is the mapping from variables of M1 to those in M2, C is the mapping from values in M1 to those in M2. Figure 3 (left) shows a relation between state p of M1 and state q of M2. p relates to q based on R and C because $u = sus$ in state p corresponds to $v = 1$ in state q with mappings $R(u) = v$ and $C(sus) = 1$. M2 simulates M1 if for each transition in M1 from state p to state p' and p relates to state q of M2, there exists state q' and a corresponding transition in M2 from q to q' such that p' relates to q'. In Fig. 3 (right), a line arrow connecting p to p' represents a one-step transition from p to p', and a dashed arrow connecting q to q' represents an n-step transition from q to q'. To check whether M2 simulates M1, we check whether there exists a reachable state q' from q such that $v = 2$ corresponds to $u = rdy$ in p' with mappings $R(u) = v$ and $C(rdy) = 2$.

Figure 4 shows the steps to verify the simulation between a specification and a design using the Spin model checker. Firstly, bounds for the verification are given and an LTS is generated from the Event-B specification within the bounds. Next, the LTS is in turn used to generate the environment, which exercises service functions described in the design. The verification then amounts to checking the validity of certain relations between variables of the Promela design and variables of the Event-B specification in every reachable state. This is done using Spin assertions which are generated from states of the LTS and the given relations represented as mappings. In the end, the verification of the assertions ensures that the design conforms to the specification.

Giving Bounds. As specified in Event-B, there may be infinitely many states and transitions of target system because variables in Event-B obtain values in unbounded domains. Model checking does an exhaustive check of the system. It needs a representation of the system as a finite set of all possible states. So, abstract types in Event-B must be replaced by concrete types, e.g., tasks$\subseteq$ $TASK$ where $TASK = \{a, b, c, d\}$. Also, types having infinite ranges of values like Int and Nat must be restricted as finite ranges by giving a minimum value and a maximum value for the ranges. By such restriction, the state space and the set of transitions explored from Event-B specification become finite sets. This

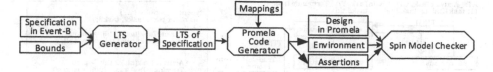

Fig. 4. Checking simulation relation of the design and its formal specification (steps)

makes the LTS explored from the specification finite. We define such restrictions as bounds of the verification.

Generating an LTS from the Specification. In order to generate the LTS from the specification and bounds, the LTS Generator computes all possible transitions and reachable states. Every value used in the computation must be within the bounds. Starting at the initialization, the generator enumerates all possible values for the constants and variables of the specification that satisfy the initialization and the invariant to compute the set of initial states. To compute all possible transitions from a state, the generator finds all possible values for event parameters of an individual event to evaluate the guard of that event. If the guard holds in the given state, the generator computes the effect of the event based on substitution of that event. When new states are generated, we repeat this process to these states until no new state is generated.

Generating the Environment. In order to verify that designs satisfy their formal specifications, environments of the target systems are constructed and combined with the designs. Environments trigger the specific behaviors of the designs by calling functions of the designs; we construct such comprehensive environments that they represent all possible behavior described in their specifications. In the previous step, we generated the LTS of the specification. In this step, we generate the environment by translating the LTS into Promela such that the enabled events in LTS are translated to the corresponding function calls in Promela. This is performed by the Promela Code Generator.

Figure 5(a) demonstrates an LTS, which is generated from the specification of OSEK OS. The LTS represents possible sequences of state transitions within the bounds. Here, the rectangles represent the states and the labeled arrows represent the events that are enabled in each state. For example, two events AT(t1), AT(t2) are enabled in state $s0$, and two events TT(t1), AT(t2) are enabled in state $s1$. In our framework, the states are defined as the value assignments; however, we show them here as values, e.g., (sus, sus, sus), for readability. The LTS is translated into Promela to generate the environment, e.g., from (a) to (b) of Fig. 5. For this generation, we give a mapping from the events in the LTS to the function calls in the environment. It could be one-to-one or one-to-many mapping. Figure 5 shows a sample case of one-to-one mapping. Here, event AT(t1) in the LTS is mapped to function call _ActivateTask(task1.tid) in the environment; also, event TT(t1) is mapped to function call _TerminateTask(task1.tid). The states and transitions in the

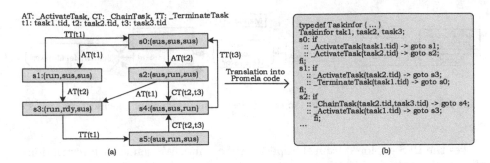

Fig. 5. Generation of environment from LTS

LTS are represented by labels and if-statements in the environment. There may be more than one function call applicable in each state. For example, _ActivateTask(task2.tid) and _TerminateTask(task1.tid) are applicable in state $s1$; which function call actually applied is non-deterministic. By combining the design model and the environment model, we obtain the combination model, which will be input to the model checker in the last step of the framework.

Generating the Assertions. Verification conditions, which represent constraints on the simulation relation between the specification and the design, are encoded as assertions. They will be checked by Spin. From each reachable state of the LTS, we generate an assertion that must be met by the corresponding state of the design. This generation is based on the mappings R and C from the variables, the values in the specification to those in the design. This is also performed by the Promela Code Generator. In sample case of Fig. 3 (right), for example, from state p' where $u = rdy$ at the top with mappings $R(u) = v$ and $C(rdy) = 2$, the generator outputs an assertion $v = 2$ to check whether there exists corresponding state q' at the bottom.

4.2 Formal Definitions

We now give formal definitions of the relation between states, the bounds, the simulation relation of two LTSs within the bounds, and steps in the framework.

Definition 5 *(Relation Between States). Let $S = \langle \mathcal{V}_S, \mathcal{D}_S, \Sigma_S, \mathrm{Init}_S, Inv \rangle$ be a specification model, $M_S = \langle Q_S, \Sigma_S, \delta_S, I_S \rangle$ the LTS derived from S, $D = \langle \mathcal{V}_D, \mathcal{D}_D, \mathcal{P}_D, F, \Sigma_D, I_D \rangle$ a design model, $E = \langle \mathcal{V}_E, \mathcal{D}_E, \Sigma_E, I_E \rangle$ an environment model for D, and $D{\cdot}E = \langle Q_{D{\cdot}E}, \Sigma_{D{\cdot}E}, \delta_{D{\cdot}E}, I_{D{\cdot}E} \rangle$ the combination model of D and E. We say a state $\sigma_{D{\cdot}E} \in Q_{D{\cdot}E}$ relates to a state $\sigma_S \in Q_S$ based on mappings $R : \mathcal{V}_S \to \mathcal{V}_D$ and $C : \mathcal{D}_S \to \mathcal{D}_D$ (denoted $\sigma_S \preceq_{R,C} \sigma_{D{\cdot}E}$), if for any $x \in \mathcal{V}_S$ and $y \in \mathcal{V}_D$, $R(x) = y$ implies $C(\sigma_S(x)) = \sigma_{D{\cdot}E}(y)$.*

We omit R, C from $\preceq_{R,C}$ if they are clear from the context.

As mentioned earlier, the bounds are introduced to obtain a finite LTS from the Event-B specification. A finite LTS is obtained from an infinite LTS when we restrict the state space and the set of actions that trigger the state transitions. The bounds are defined as follows:

Definition 6 *(Bounds).* Bounds for LTS $\langle Q, \Sigma, \delta, I \rangle$ are defined as a pair $B = \langle G, H \rangle$ of mappings G and H where $G : 2^Q \to 2^Q$, $G(Q) \subseteq Q$, and $Q' \subseteq Q''$ implies $G(Q') \subseteq G(Q'')$ and $H : Q \times \Sigma \to \{tt, ff\}$ and for any state $p \in Q$, there exist finitely many actions $a \in \Sigma$ such that $H(p, a) = tt$.

Definition 7 *(Bounded LTS).* An LTS obtained by restricting an LTS $M = \langle Q, \Sigma, \delta, I \rangle$ within bounds $B = \langle G, H \rangle$ is defined as $M{\downarrow}_B = \langle \widehat{Q}, \widehat{\Sigma}, \widehat{\delta}, \widehat{I} \rangle$, where $\widehat{Q} = G(Q)$, $\widehat{\Sigma} = \{a \mid \forall p \in Q, a \in \Sigma, H(p, a) = tt\}$, $\widehat{\delta} = \{p \xrightarrow{a} p' \in \delta \mid H(p, a) = tt\}$, and $\widehat{I} = G(I)$.

To implement the bounds for LTS associated to the Event-B specification, we restrict the range of the variable values. When every range of the variable values has been restricted, the state space and set of actions of the LTS become finite sets. We give a mapping X for implementing such bounds to generate the LTS. X is a mapping from variables to finite sets of values that the variables may obtain. We use $\mathrm{ES}_X(\sigma)$ to denote the set of all events which are applicable to state σ and satisfy restrictions defined by X.

Suppose $S = \langle \mathcal{V}_S, \mathcal{D}_S, \Sigma_S, \mathrm{Init}_S, Inv \rangle$ be a specification model and $\langle Q_S, \Sigma_S, \delta_S, I_S \rangle$ an LTS derived from S. With the mapping X, we define mappings G and H as follows: $G(Q_S) = \{\sigma \in Q_S \mid \forall v \in \mathcal{V}_S.\sigma(v) \in X(v))\}$, $G(I_S) \subset G(Q_S)$, and $H(\sigma, e) = tt$ iff $e \in \mathrm{ES}_X(\sigma)$.

We now define a simulation relation between two LTSs. In general, a one-step transition in the specification is followed by an n-step transition in the design. In the definition, Σ^+ denotes the set of non-empty strings of Σ, δ^+ denotes an n-step transition relation, and $p \xrightarrow{a_1 a_2 \ldots a_n} p' \in \delta^+$ denotes an n-step transition from state p to state p'.

Definition 8 *(Simulation Relation).* Let $M_1 = \langle Q_1, \Sigma_1, \delta_1, I_1 \rangle$ and $M_2 = \langle Q_2, \Sigma_2, \delta_2, I_2 \rangle$ be LTSs, and $f : \Sigma_1 \to \Sigma_2^+$ a function from Σ_1 to Σ_2^+. Suppose a relation $\preceq \subseteq Q_1 \times Q_2$ is given. M2 simulates M1 with respect to $\preceq$ if for all $q_1, q_1' \in Q_1$, $q_2 \in Q_2$, $a \in \Sigma_1$ such that $q_1 \preceq q_2$ and $q_1 \xrightarrow{a} q_1' \in \delta_1$, there exist $q_2' \in Q_2$ such that $q_1' \preceq q_2'$ and $q_2 \xrightarrow{f(a)} q_2' \in \delta_2^+$. If M2 simulates M1 with respect to $\preceq$, we denote $M1 \preceq M2$.

Definition 9 *(Simulation Relation of Two LTSs Within Bounds).* Let M_1 and M_2 be two LTSs, and B be bounds. The simulation relation of M_1 and M_2 within bounds B is defined as $M_1 \preceq_B M_2$ if $M_1{\downarrow}_B \preceq M_2$. If $M_1 \preceq_B M_2$ holds, we say M_2 simulates M_1 within B.

If an error is found when applying our framework to verify the design against the bounded specification, there actually exists a state transition in the bounded specification that is not followed by the design. It is obvious that this state transition is also included in the original specification; thus, the design does not conform to the original specification. Formally, $M_1 \npreceq_B M_2 \Rightarrow M_1 \npreceq M_2$.

Generating the Environments. An environment is generated from the LTS of the specification model. Let $S = \langle \mathcal{V}_S, \mathcal{D}_S, \Sigma_S, \text{Init}_S, Inv \rangle$ be a specification model and $M_S = \langle Q_S, \Sigma_S, \delta_S, I_S \rangle$ be the LTS derived from S. Based on the given mapping $f : \Sigma_S \to \Sigma_{D.E}^+$ from the events in the LTS to the function calls in the environment, mapping $R' : \mathcal{V}_S \to \mathcal{V}_E$ and mapping $C : \mathcal{D}_S \to \mathcal{D}_D$, the environment model $E = \langle \mathcal{V}_E, \mathcal{D}_E, \Sigma_E, I_E \rangle$ with $\mathcal{D}_E = \mathcal{D}_D$ is generated such that $\Sigma_E = \{ f(e) \mid e \in \Sigma_S \}$ and $I_E = \{ f(e) \mid e \in I_S \}$.

Generating the Assertions. The relation on states of the specification and the combination is given based on the mappings $R : \mathcal{V}_S \to \mathcal{V}_D$ and $C : \mathcal{D}_S \to \mathcal{D}_D$; verification conditions are generated as follows:

- For initial state, to check whether $\sigma_S^0 \preceq \sigma_{D.E}^0$, an assertion is generated:
$$\bigwedge_{x \in \mathcal{V}_S, y \in \mathcal{V}_D, y = R(x)} (\sigma_{D.E}^0(y) = C(\sigma_S^0(x))),$$

- For all (reachable) states $\sigma_S, \sigma_S' \in Q_S$ and $\sigma_{D.E} \in Q_{D.E}$ such that $\sigma_S \xrightarrow{e} \sigma_S' \in \delta_{S\downarrow_B}$, and $\sigma_S \preceq \sigma_{D.E}$, in order to verify whether there exists state $\sigma_{D.E}' \in Q_{D.E}$ and transition $\sigma_{D.E} \xrightarrow{f(e)} \sigma_{D.E}' \in \delta_{D.E}^+$ such that $\sigma_S' \preceq \sigma_{D.E}'$, an assertion is generated: $\bigwedge_{x \in \mathcal{V}_S, y \in \mathcal{V}_D, y = R(x)} (\sigma_{D.E}'(y) = C(\sigma_S'(x)))$

In the last step, we input the combination model and the assertions to Spin to check the simulation relation of the specification and the design. The assertions will be verified in every reachable state of the combination. This ensures that for each state transition in the specification, there exists a corresponding transition in the combination. Such kind of correspondence shows the consistency of the functions in the design with the events in the specification. This is useful to check properties relevant to the pre-conditions and the post-conditions of the service functions of the reactive systems. The typical bugs caused by the computational statements of the functions can be found by checking the relations between data elements of the design and the specification in every reachable state. In the end, the verification of simulation between the design and the specification has been completed within the bounds.

5   Case Study

We implemented a generator that produces: the LTS of the bounded specification; the environment in Promela; and the assertions. As an application of our framework to a practical system, we conducted several experiments to verify that a design of OSEK OS in Promela conforms to its formal specification in Event-B. These two models are partially illustrated in Figs. 1 and 2.

In this framework, bounds are set for the verification to make sure that every variable in the Event-B specification obtains values in finite ranges. As shown in Fig. 1, variables `tasks`, `res`, `evt`, and `inr` define entities managed by OSEK OS such as tasks, resources, events, and interrupt routines; variable `pri` defines the priority assigned to tasks, resources, and interrupt routines; and variable `tstate` defines the task state. The finite ranges of values for them must be introduced in the experiments as bounds for the verification. By using various bounds, we can separate the cases that deal with distinct groups of system services from which check the relation between different groups. This helps us to avoid the state explosion and keep important behaviors of the target system we want to verify in the cases.

All experiments are conducted on an Intel(R) Core(TM) i7 Processor at 2.67 GHz running Linux. Verification results outputted by Spin are shown in Table 1. Here, the first column ("No.") represents experiment numbers. The next column presents size of ranges for variables tasks, pri, res, evt, and inr. Values in this column express bounds of the verification. Column "LTS Generation" shows statistics of the LTS generator. Here, columns "#State", and "#Trans" present the number of distinct states and that of transitions appearing in the LTS; column "Time" presents the time taken (s) for the generation. Column "Model Checking" presents statistics of the model checker including total actual memory usage, the time taken (s), and the verification result in which "√" indicates the verification has been completed. Groups of system services of OSEK OS consist of task management, resource management, event mechanism, and interruption management. In the table, experiments No.1-No.9 are performed to check the task management independently from the other groups of system services. In these cases, we show ranges for tasks and pri. Experiments No.10-No.14 are performed to check relation between task management, resource management, event mechanism, and interruption management; therefore, we show ranges for tasks, pri, res, evt, and inr.

From the experiment results, we can see that the time taken and the total actual memory usage for the generation of the LTS from Event-B specification and the verification of the simulation relation are reasonable. For the model checking result, no errors were returned in all cases of experiments. Several safety properties of OSEK OS have been confirmed by these experiments such as "tasks and interrupt routines shall not terminate while occupying resources" and "high-priority tasks such as life saving units must always be executed before all low priority tasks". This is because the design of OSEK OS has already been reviewed carefully by many researchers and engineers. Still, this result offers a confidence on the conformance of the OSEK OS design with respect to its specification within input bounds.

6   Discussion

Generality of the Framework. OSEK OS is the operating system which is widely used in the automotive systems. Our framework is applied to verify the design of a practical system, that is, OSEK OS design. The framework directly checks the design against its formal specification. Although we show the experiments, when our framework is applied to the operating system, it is not limited to this application. In the framework, the simulation relation is defined based on semantic of LTS. In models, the states are interpreted as value assignments. The

Table 1. Experiment outputs

No	Size of ranges					LTS generation			Model checking			
	tasks	pri	res	evt	inr	#State	#Trans	Time(s)	Memory(Mb)	Time(s)	Result
1	1	1	0	0	0	2	2	1.0	129.2	3	√
2	2	2	0	0	0	4	10	1.0	129.2	3.5	√
3	3	3	0	0	0	8	36	1.0	129.2	3.5	√
4	4	3	0	0	0	16	112	1.2	129.2	4.2	√
5	5	3	0	0	0	32	320	1.2	130.6	4.9	√
6	6	3	0	0	0	64	864	1.3	132.6	10.3	√
7	7	3	0	0	0	128	2240	1.3	324.5	26.1	√
8	8	3	0	0	0	256	5632	2.1	382.8	99.2	√
9	9	3	0	0	0	512	13824	3.0	430.8	362.1	√
10	5	7	0	0	2	128	1536	2.0	133.1	17.5	√
11	2	1	1	0	0	8	22	1.1	130.1	7.6	√
12	2	1	0	1	0	10	27	1.1	129.2	4.7	√
13	3	6	1	0	2	80	520	1.2	129.2	8.3	√
14	3	6	1	1	2	152	1036	2.0	132.3	14.1	√

design is described as a collection of functions which update the value assignments. The environment is described as a collection of invocations. This style of models is adopted not only for operating systems but also other reactive systems.

In our case study, Promela is used as a specification language to describe the design and the environment; however, our framework can be applied for the designs described in not only Promela but also other languages as long as they can deal with a collection of functions for the design and sequences of invocations for the environment.

Notion of Bounds. We introduce a formalization of the bounds for verifying the simulation relation of the design and the formal specification with Event-B. The bounds are used to obtain a finite LTS associated to Event-B model. This bound can be applied generally to any design and its formal specification as long as the formal models of the inputs are defined as LTSs. In Sect. 4, we present the interpretation of the bound in a concrete model, that is, Event-B model. In the first step of interpreting the bounds in the specification, we introduce finite ranges of variable values in the specification. Next, we regard the typical bugs that can be found in the verification with a large value domain. For finding such bugs of the target system, in addition to restrict the range of values, one can restrict system services of the target system. The intention of such additional restriction is to exclude transitions not relevant to the bugs and to reduce size of model for which model checking is feasible. It is important to give the appropriate restrictions or the proper bounds for the model. We could do this by studying behavior scenarios for each property to be checked. Based on the behavior scenarios, we could estimate the appropriate range of values for the variables and determine what system services must be included in the bounded model. Also, we could make sure that the critical scenarios are actually contained in the bounded model by traversing the execution sequences of the LTS accordingly with the scenarios. Consequently, the bounds need to be decided depending on the properties to be checked.

Comprehensiveness of Environment. The behaviors of the target systems depend on patterns of function calls from their environments. For the comprehensive verification of reactive systems, we need to use the environments that cover all possible patterns of invocations. Accordingly, an advantage of our framework is that it is able to systematically generate all possible patterns of invocations from the LTS of the specification in Event-B. This is essential to generate the environments for the comprehensiveness of verification with respect to the specification.

7   Related Works

Verification of Systems Using Model Checking. Reference [6] presents a case study on checking the operating systems compliant with OSEK/VDX. The authors describe the specification in temporal logic formulas. Separately, we describe the specification in Event-B. This improves the consistency of properties extracted from the specification and provides general environments for comprehensive verifications.

Verification of Systems Based on Simulation Relations. FDR [5] is a refinement checker for the process algebra CSP. Inputs of FDR are the specifications and the implementations written in the same language. Our framework accepts the inputs written in different languages. References [19] and [9] present approaches to verify the OS kernels based on theorem proving. Theorem proving can be used to verify the infinite systems; however, it generally requires a lot of interactive proofs. In our framework, we use model checking combining with tools of Event-B. Although, ranges are bounded due to the limitation of model checking; however, we are able to improve quality of the properties checked and get completely automatic verification. Therefore, we have a high degree of confidence in the verification results.

Generation of LTS from Event-B Model. Reference [10] presents the ProB tool which supports interactively animating B models. Using ProB, users can see the current state and set an upper limit on the number of ways that the same operation can be executed. In our works, we firstly set finite ranges for types in Event-B specification, then, explore all possible sequences of state transitions within defined ranges. Reference [4] defines the semantic of Event-B model as labeled transition systems to reason about behavioral aspects of specifications in Event-B. We formally define the framework from scratch. We precisely define finite ranges of variable values in Event-B specification as bounds of our verification; then, we generate all possible behaviors from Event-B specification within defined ranges.

Construction of the Environment of the Operating System. In previous works, we verified the OSEK OS by constructing a general model of the environment from scratch [21]: it includes a class diagram and state diagrams of objects in the environment. These diagrams are composed to generate the environment scripts. In current work, the environment is generated from the Event-B specification. Hence, by construction, it is comprehensive with respect to the specification. The environment is used to exercise the design and check the given relation between variables of the Promela design and variables of the Event-B specification in every reachable state. This guarantees that the design conforms to the specification. Also, the correctness of the specification is guaranteed by tools of Event-B; the quality of the environment is improved.

Combination of Event-B Model and Model Checking. For combination of Event-B and model checking, tools like ProB [10] and Eboc [12] work as model checkers for Event-B. As another approach, [15] translates Event-B model into Promela model and use Spin to check the model. We consider that we could obtain a skeleton of the design in Promela if we apply the mappings to the Event-B specification; however, we still need to add design decisions into the target model. We used Promela to describe the design. Our work has not directly translated Event-B code into Promela but translate LTS of the Event-B specification and assertions into Promela. Then, we use Spin to check the simulation relation between the design model and LTS of the specification in Promela.

8   Conclusion

We proposed an approach to verify designs against their formal specifications which are described in different specification languages respectively. A primary achievement of the approach is to make it possible to describe the specification and the design in appropriate languages for a verification of the design. Formal specification languages are intended to facilitate describing the specifications. Promela is intended to analyze the designs. Our approach follows these intentions faithfully. In fact, as mentioned in Sect. 1, it is natural for reactive systems like operating systems to describe the designs in the imperative specification languages. On the other hand, describing their detailed properties in temporal logic is generally hard. It is easy to imagine that the temporal logic formulas representing the specification shown in the case study become very complex and prone to mistakes. Instead of the temporal logic, we provide a way to represent the specification in formal specification language Event-B and check the design against it with the Spin model checker. Event-B is appropriate to represent the specification because it has rich notions such as sets and relations. In addition, Event-B allows us to ensure the consistency and the correctness of the specification by its verification facilities such as discharging proof obligations and refinement. That is, we can check the design against such consistent and correct specification. This would drastically improve the reliability of model checking results because the specification is reliable. There is a possibility that our approach is applicable not only for Event-B and Promela but also the other specification languages. We plan to extend the verification framework to accept the additional choice of the specification languages.

References

1. Abrial, J.R.: Modeling in Event-B: System and Software Engineering. Cambridge University Press, New York (2010)
2. Aoki, T.: Model checking multi-task software on real-time operating systems. In: The 11th IEEE International Symposium on Object Oriented Real-Time Distributed Computing, pp. 551–555 (2008)
3. Baier, C., Katoen, J.P.: Principles of Model Checking. Representation and Mind Series. The MIT Press, Cambridge (2008)
4. Bert, D., Potet, M.L., Stouls, N.: Genesyst: a tool to reason about behavioralaspects of B event specifications. Application to security properties (2010)
5. Broadfoot, P., Roscoe, B.: Tutorial on FDR and its applications. In: Havelund, K., Penix, J., Visser, W. (eds.) SPIN 2000. LNCS, vol. 1885, p. 322. Springer, Heidelberg (2000)
6. Choi, Y.: Model checking trampoline OS: a case study on safety analysis for automotive software. Softw. Test. Verif. Reliab. 24(1), 38–60 (2014)
7. Clarke, E.M., Grumberg, O., Long, D.E.: Model checking and abstraction. ACM Trans. Program. Lang. Syst. 16(5), 1512–1542 (1994)
8. Dwyer, M.B., Avrunin, G.S., Corbett, J.C.: Patterns in property specifications for finite-state verification. In: Proceedings of the 21st International Conference on Software Engineering, ICSE 1999, pp. 411–420. ACM, New York (1999)
9. Klein, G., Andronick, J., Elphinstone, K., Heiser, G., Cock, D., Derrin, P., Elkaduwe, D., Engelhardt, K., Kolanski, R., Norrish, M., Sewell, T., Tuch, H., Winwood, S.: seL4: formal verification of an operating-system kernel. Commun. ACM 53(6), 107–115 (2010)
10. Leuschel, M., Butler, M.: ProB: An automated analysis toolset for the B method. Int. J. Softw. Tools Technol. Transfer 10(2), 185–203 (2008)
11. Lynch, N., Vaandrager, F.: Forward and backward simulations I.: Untimed systems. Inf. Comput. 121(2), 214–233 (1995)
12. Matos, P.J., Fischer, B., Marques-Silva, J.: A Lazy Unbounded Model Checker for EVENT-B. In: Breitman, K., Cavalcanti, A. (eds.) ICFEM 2009. LNCS, vol. 5885, pp. 485–503. Springer, Heidelberg (2009)
13. Milner, R.: Communication and concurrency. PHI Series in computer science. Prentice Hall, Upper Saddle River (1989)
14. Muller, A.: VDM the Vienna development method (2009)
15. Muller, T.: Formal methods, model-cheking and Rodin plugin development to link Event-B and Spin (2009)
16. O'Regan, G.: Z formal specification language. In: O'Regan, G. (ed.) Mathematics in Computing, pp. 109–122. Springer, London (2013)
17. OSEK/VDX Group: OSEK/VDX operating system specification 2.2.3. http://portal.osek-vdx.org/
18. Reeves, S., Streader, D.: Guarded operations, refinement and simulation. Electron. Notes Theor. Comput. Sci. 259, 177–191 (2009)
19. In der Rieden, T., Knapp, S.: An approach to the pervasive formal specification and verification of an automotive system. In: Proceedings of the 10th International Workshop on Formal Methods for Industrial Critical Systems, pp. 115–124 (2005)

20. Vu, D.H., Aoki, T.: Faithfully formalizing OSEK/VDX operating system specification. In: Proceedings of the 3rd Symposium on Information and Communication Technology, pp. 13–20 (2012)
21. Yatake, K., Aoki, T.: Model checking of OSEK/VDX OS design model based on environment modeling. In: Roychoudhury, A., D'Souza, M. (eds.) ICTAC 2012. LNCS, vol. 7521, pp. 183–197. Springer, Heidelberg (2012)

A Formal Model of SysML Blocks Using CSP for Assured Systems Engineering

Jaco Jacobs$^{(\boxtimes)}$ and Andrew Simpson

Department of Computer Science, University of Oxford, Wolfson Building,
Parks Road, Oxford OX1 3QD, UK
{jaco.jacobs,andrew.simpson}@cs.ox.ac.uk

Abstract. The Systems Modeling Language (SysML) is a semi-formal, visual modelling language used in the specification and design of systems. In this paper, we describe how Communicating Sequential Processes (CSP) and its associated refinement checker, Failures Divergences Refinement (FDR), gives rise to an approach that facilitates the refinement checking of the behavioural consistency of SysML diagrams. We formalise the conjoined behaviour of key behavioural constructs — state machines and activities — within the context of SysML. Furthermore, blocks, the fundamental modelling construct of the SysML language, can be combined in a compositional approach to system specification. The use of a process-algebraic formalism enables us to explore the behaviour of the resulting composition more rigorously. We demonstrate how CSP, in conjunction with SysML, can be used in a formal top-down approach to systems engineering. A small case study validates the contribution.

1 Introduction

Accidents associated with complex systems are frequently the result of unforeseen interactions amongst components that all satisfy their individual requirements [1]. These *component interaction accidents* are increasingly common: state of the art systems are more interdependent on other technologically advanced systems and interact in ways not foreseen or intended by the original designer. The *Mars Polar Lander* accident is one example of such a failure: both the landing legs and the control software of the descent engines functioned as specified by their respective behavioural specifications. The systems engineers, however, did not consider all the potential interactions between the landing legs and the control software of the descent engines [1].

The OMG's *Systems Modeling Language* (SysML) [2] is a graphical modelling notation used in the specification and integration of complex, large-scale systems. A keystone of this activity is ensuring that requirements, as imposed by the various stakeholders, are adequately captured and subsequently addressed when specifying a potential solution. The intention of SysML, thus, is to accurately specify intended component behaviour with the expectation to minimise interaction accidents. However, SysML is a semi-formal notation. If we are to

© Springer International Publishing Switzerland 2015
C. Artho and P.C. Ölveczky (Eds.): FTSCS 2014, CCIS 476, pp. 127–141, 2015.
DOI: 10.1007/978-3-319-17581-2_9

carry out an extensive analysis of component interactions, more mathematical rigour is indispensable.

Reasoning about behaviour — in particular, the myriad of interactions between components — is a rather cumbersome activity for the human mind. In addition, our cognitive ability to cope with multiple, separate descriptions of behaviour, and ultimately fuse these into a unified interpretation, is rather limited. We need to augment our faculties with appropriate notations in order to effectively reason about such behaviours. Moreover, if we are going to utilise these notations in a meaningful fashion, we require mechanised tool support. *Communicating Sequential Processes* (CSP) [3] is one such notation, backed up by *Failures Divergences Refinement* (FDR) in the form of a refinement checker.

Activities and state machines are the core behavioural constructs used to ascribe behaviour to SysML blocks. The aforementioned constructs are frequently used in combination: activities are used to assign behavioural features that ought to execute in a particular state, or on a given transition [2]. In this paper, we provide a behavioural semantics for the conjoined behaviour of state machines and activities. In the past, there have been several contributions where the sole focus lied either with the formalisation of state machines, or activities. To the best of our knowledge, this paper is the first contribution where the intention is on the provision of a behavioural semantics that encompasses both these formalisms.

At the structural level, SysML takes a compositional stance with regards to systems specification: a block can be comprised of other blocks, which, in turn, might themselves consist of blocks. However, for the approach to be effective and useful, the behavioural conduct of these blocks need to be specified in a consistent manner. Moreover, the approach needs to enable the modeller to sufficiently abstract away details irrelevant to a particular level of abstraction.

This paper is a companion of sorts to the work presented in [4]: it extends the formalisation of state machines to encompass entry, exit, and do behaviours modelled via activities. In doing so, a formal behavioural semantics is provided for activities, in terms of CSP.

The structure of the remainder of this paper is as follows. In Sect. 2, we provide a brief introduction to SysML. Section 3 outlines our process-algebraic approach to formalise SysML activities, state machines, and blocks. We show how CSP can be employed to analyse expositions composed of multiple, communicating state machine and activity constructs. In Sect. 4, we employ a small case study to illuminate and validate the contribution. Section 5 summarises the contributions of this paper, and places it in context with respect to other research.

2   Background

In this section, we give a necessarily brief introduction to SysML. We assume familiarity with CSP.

Blocks. Blocks are the fundamental modelling constructs of SysML and provide the context in which behaviours execute. A *block* is often composed of other blocks, termed *parts*, each of which has its own associated behaviour. The classifier behaviour of a block can serve as an abstraction of the behaviours of its parts. Thus, the abstraction serves as a specification that the parts must realise: the parts must interact in such a way that their combined behaviour conforms to the abstraction. This interpretation also sits well with the concept of refinement and abstraction in CSP.

The *classifier behaviour* is the main behaviour of a block, and executes from the instant the instance is created until the point of destruction. The modelling construct most frequently used to represent the classifier behaviour is a state machine. In most systems engineering methodologies, activities are typically used as a complementary modelling notation to state machines: it is the behavioural formalism normally associated with the effect component of a transition; alternatively, it is used to model behaviours related to a particular state.

Typically, two block instances communicate using signal events. The initiating block sends a signal event to a target block. This signal event is defined as part of the supplementary behaviours — described using activities — associated with the initiating state machine: the entry or exit behaviours of the active state; or the effect component of the enabled transition. The receipt of the signal event in the target block may subsequently trigger a transition in its state machine. The approach described above is popular when modelling event-based systems.

A *signal* is a classifier that types the asynchronous messages that are communicated between blocks. Each signal optionally has an associated set of attributes which correspond to the parameters that make up the content of the message. A *connector* connects two or more parts or references. The connection formally allows the connected components to interact, although the connector does not characterise the nature of the interaction. Instead, the interaction is stipulated by the behaviours of the connected blocks.

Activities. *Activities* allow the modeller to describe complex routes along which actions execute. These routes are termed *flows*. In SysML activities there are two types of flows: control flows and object flows.

Actions are the fundamental building blocks of *activities* and always execute within the context of an activity. An action accepts inputs and produces outputs. The flow of input and output items between actions are described using *object flows*. *Control flows*, on the other hand, impose additional constraints on the execution of actions. When a control flow connects one action to another, the target action cannot start until the source action has completed. *Control nodes* are used in the specification of control flow: they are used to impose control logic on the execution of actions. The control nodes are the fork, join, decision, merge, initial and final nodes.

Several types of actions exist: the *send signal event action* sends a signal event; the *receive signal event action* waits on the receipt of a particular signal event; and the *value specification action* allows the specification of a particular value to an input of an action. *Opaque actions* allow the specification of actions in a language external to SysML.

State Machines. *State machines* graphically depict state-dependent behaviour in terms of nodes and labelled edges: nodes represent states, whereas the edges correspond to transitions between states.

In SysML, a *state* is an abstraction of the mode that the owning block finds itself in. A change of state is effected by the arrival of a triggering event, causing an appropriate transition to fire. A *transition* consists of a trigger, a guard and an effect. The *trigger* denotes the event that serves as stimulus for the transition to fire; the *guard* is a conditional expression used to decide whether the transition is to fire at all; and the *effect* is a supplementary behaviour that executes on the transition.

3   A CSP View of SysML Blocks

This section outlines an approach to integrate the semi-formal SysML notation with the process algebra CSP. In order to define a formal semantics for blocks, parts and state machines, we need a precise description of their syntax. To this end, we define simple mathematical constructs that are closely related to the syntactical structure of their corresponding SysML counterparts.

Activities. Broadly speaking, our approach maps every node and every edge in an activity diagram to a CSP process. We restrict actions to either have either a single outgoing control or object flow, but not both; our semantics allows for simple forks and joins in the sense that a fork node splits control into multiple flows that eventually all end in a corresponding join node. We present the formalisation as it relates to a single activity A; $\mathcal{A}$ denotes the set containing all activities in our universe of discourse.

An *activity* $A \in \mathcal{A}$ consists of a finite collection of *nodes*, denoted N_A, and *edges* between those nodes, denoted E_A. We partition N_A such that N_A^I represents the set of *initial nodes*, N_A^F the set of *final nodes*, N_A^{FK} the set of *fork nodes*, N_A^{JN} the set of *join nodes*, N_A^{SS} the *send signal event actions*, N_A^{RS} the *receive signal event actions*, N_A^O the *opaque actions*, and N_A^{PN} the set of activity parameter nodes. The edges are partitioned such that E_A^{OF} represents the object flows, and E_A^{CF} represents the set of control flows.

We define the following functions, to return for a particular flow $f \in E_A$: the source node, $source : E_A \to N_A$; and the target node, $target : E_A \to N_A$. Additionally, we define functions to return for a particular node $n \in N_A$: the set of outgoing control flows, $outgoing_{cf} : N_A \nrightarrow \mathbb{P} E_A^{CF}$; and the outgoing object flow, $outgoing_{of} : N_A \nrightarrow E_A^{OF}$. Assume that the construction $name(n)$ returns the name of the send or receive signal event, or opaque action for $n \in N_A^{SS} \cup N_A^{RS} \cup N_A^O$.

The formalisation makes use of a mapping function $\mathcal{F}$. In particular, $\mathcal{F}(A, c)$ is the process modelling the construct c, either an edge or a node, of activity A.

Activity Parameter Node. An activity parameter node $n \in N_A^{PN}$, models a para-meter, p, that can be used within the context of the activity. In CSP, the node is modelled as an argument to the process modelling the activity. Diagrammat-ically, an object flow $of \in E_A^{OF}$ connects the parameter node with other nodes that use this as a parameter. For the purpose of this paper we assume that a single argument is represented by each activity parameter node that serve as input to the activity. The activity's behaviour starts as the process modelling the initial node $n_0 \in N_A^I$

$$A(p) =$$
$$\text{let}$$
$$\mathcal{F}(A, n_0) = \ldots$$
$$\text{within}$$
$$\mathcal{F}(A, n_0)$$

An activity without a parameter is modelled similarly, but the process parameter p is elided.

Control Flow Edge. A control flow $cf \in E_A^{CF}$ can be thought of as a CSP process. The behaviour of this process is dependent on the target node of the control flow, given by $target(cf)$. If the target is not a join node, i.e. $target(cf) \notin N_A^{JN}$, the process simply designates its behaviour to be that of the target node.

$$\mathcal{F}(A, cf) =$$
$$\quad \mathcal{F}(A, target(cf)) \qquad \text{if } target(cf) \notin N_A^{JN}$$
$$\quad Join(cf) \qquad\qquad\quad \text{otherwise}$$

In the case where $target(cf) \in N_A^{JN}$, there will be, based on our assumption of activities above, $k-1$ other control flows which terminate in the same join node. Let the control flows be $cf_0 .. cf_{k-1}$. Exactly one of the control flows, cf_0, will exhibit the behaviour of the join node.

$$Join(e) =$$
$$\quad join \rightarrow Skip \qquad\qquad\quad \text{if } e \neq cf_0$$
$$\quad join \rightarrow \mathcal{F}(A, target(e)) \quad \text{otherwise}$$

The above construction ensures that exactly one of the previously forked flows continues after the join. Many interpretations of activity diagrams assume con-trol flows to have associated guards, typically expressed in natural language. Due to obvious reasons natural language guards are not suitable for a precise behavioural semantics and are thus excluded.

Object Flow Edge. An object flow $of \in E_A^{OF}$ is used to model the passing of parameters[1] between activity parameter nodes, call behaviour actions or send

---

[1] We restrict ourselves to signal parameters here, although in SysML these can be any classifier that can serve as an input to an activity.

and receive signal events. The behaviour of an object flow edge is a parametrised process that takes as input the value of the argument, say p, passed along the object flow. Throughout, process arguments are placed within square brackets to denote them as such.

$$\mathcal{F}(A, of)[p] = \mathcal{F}(A, target(of))[p]$$

Initial Node. An initial node $n \in N_A^I$ has a single outgoing edge, a control flow $cf \in outgoing_{cf}(n)$. The process behaves like the control flow edge emanating from the initial node.

$$\mathcal{F}(A, n) = \mathcal{F}(A, cf)$$

Send Signal Event Action. A send signal event action $n_1 \in N_A^{SS}$ has a single outgoing control flow $cf \in outgoing_{cf}(n_1)$.

$$\mathcal{F}(A, n_1) = name(n_1) \rightarrow \mathcal{F}(A, cf)$$

Optionally, an incoming object flow *of* is possible, which serves as input to the send signal event action, and models the parameters send as part of the send signal event. In our semantics, the object flow *of*, if present, emanates from an activity parameter node $n_2 \in N_A^{PN}$ and terminates on send signal event[2] node n_1[3]. The construction $par(n_2)$ is the parameter available within the context of the owing activity (defined within the let within construct).

$$\mathcal{F}(A, n_1) = name(n_1).par(n_2) \rightarrow \mathcal{F}(A, cf)$$

Alternatively, the send signal event has a single incoming object flow, but no incoming control flow. In this case the process modelling the send signal event action would have an input argument, p, passed from the process modelling the object flow. The outgoing control flow is given by $cf \in outgoing_{cf}(n_1)$. The formalisation follows.

$$\mathcal{F}(A, n_1)[p] = name(n_1).p \rightarrow \mathcal{F}(A, cf)$$

The above models the case where the parameter comes from: an object flow emanating from a value specification action; the output of an opaque action; or the output of a receive signal event action.

Receive Signal Event Action. A receive signal event action $n \in N_A^{RS}$ has a single outgoing control flow $cf \in outgoing_{cf}(n)$. Note that it is not possible to have an outgoing object flow if an outgoing control flow is present.

$$\mathcal{F}(A, n) = name(n) \rightarrow \mathcal{F}(A, cf)$$

---

[2] A *value specification action*, rather than an activity parameter node, connected via an object flow, can be used for constants.

[3] Note that an incoming control flow is still present and also terminates on n_1.

Alternatively, the receive signal event may be passed a parameter as part of the event. In this case it is conceivable that an object flow will exit the action. The formalisation follows.

$$\mathcal{F}(A, n) = name(n)?p \rightarrow \mathcal{F}(A, outgoing_{of}(n))[p]$$

The input p on the CSP channel corresponds to the parameter passed as part of the receive signal event.

Final Node. A final node $n \in N_A^F$ has no outgoing edges. It is trivially modelled as the CSP *Skip* process.

$$\mathcal{F}(A, n) = Skip$$

Fork Node. A fork node $n \in N_A^{FK}$ splits the control flow in k parallel flows $cf_0 \ldots cf_{k-1}$.

$$\mathcal{F}(A, n) = [\![join]\!] \, j : outgoing_{cf}(n) \bullet \mathcal{F}(A, j)$$

The above alphabetised indexed parallel construction ensures that all the different threads of control only synchronise on the *join* event; all other events are interleaved.

Join Node. A join node $n \in N_A^{JN}$ synchronises k parallel control flows and has a single outgoing control flow $cf = outgoing_c f(n)$.

$$\mathcal{F}(A, n) = \mathcal{F}(A, cf)$$

State Machines. This paper is a companion of sorts to the work presented in [4]: it extends the formalisation of state machines to encompass entry, exit, and do behaviours modelled via activities. This hybrid approach is typical of most systems engineering methodologies used in practice today. In addition, as the activities execute within the context of an owing state machine, the run to completion execution semantics of state machines are applicable. We briefly reprise the necessary mathematical structures and CSP descriptions of [4] to ensure this paper is self-contained. We restrict ourselves to non-hierarchical state machines and ignore guard conditions on transitions in order to simplify the presentation here. The interested reader can refer to [4] for an account of more complex state machines.

A *state machine* $M \in \mathcal{M}$ consists of a finite set of *states*, denoted S_M, and *transitions* between those states, denoted T_M. We partition S_M such that S_M^I represents the set of *initial states*, S_M^F the set of *final states*, S_M^S the set of *simple states*. A function $outgoing : S_M \rightarrow \mathbb{P}T_M$ returns the set of outgoing transitions for a given state.

We define the following functions, to return for a transition $t \in T_M$: the source state, $source : T_M \rightarrow S_M$; the target state, $target : T_M \rightarrow S_M$; the trigger, $trigger : T_M \rightarrow \mathcal{S}$; and the effect, given by $effect : T_M \rightarrow \mathcal{A}$. $\mathcal{S}$ is the set of signals.

The entry and exit behaviours of a particular state are given by the following functions: $entry : S_M \to \mathcal{A}$; and $exit : S_M \to \mathcal{A}$. In each case, an activity modelling the behaviour is returned.

A mapping function $\mathcal{F}$ is used to formalise the behaviour; $\mathcal{F}(M, s)$ is a process that describes the behaviour of M in state s.

Initial State. An initial state $s \in S_M^I$ has a single outgoing transition t that defines its unique starting point. Optionally, an effect component can be specified for the transition using an activity $A \in \mathcal{A}$. In the following: $effect(t)$ returns a behaviour specified via an activity; similarly, $entry(target(t))$ returns the entry behaviour of the target state specified via an activity.

$$\mathcal{F}(M, s) = effect(t) \,\mathring{,}\, entry(target(t)) \,\mathring{,}\, \mathcal{F}(M, target(t))$$

Simple State. The CSP channel *local* is used for communicating with the event queue of the state machine M. The arrival of a SysML signal event serves as the trigger; consequently this is made available as a CSP event. If the signal signature has a data component associated with it, this is made available as an input along with the channel modelling the event[4].

We need to consider the eventuality where the state machine receives a signal event not expected in the current state s. Here, the state machine discards the unexpected event. In the following, assume that $unexpected(s)$ returns the set of unexpected events for state s (receive signal events that are valid in other states of S_M but not in s). The components *proc* and *disc* denote the event being processed and discarded, respectively. In both cases, it is removed from the event queue.

$$
\begin{aligned}
\mathcal{F}(M, s) = \\
\square\, t : outgoing(s) \bullet local.proc.trigger(t) \to \\
\quad exit(s) \,\mathring{,}\, effect(t) \,\mathring{,}\, entry(target(t)) \,\mathring{,}\, \mathcal{F}(M, target(t)) \\
\square \\
\square\, t : unexpected(s) \bullet local.disc.trigger(t) \to \mathcal{F}(M, s)
\end{aligned}
$$

Final State. Consider a final state $s \in S_M^F$. A final state has no outgoing transitions and is trivially modelled as the deadlocked process.

$$\mathcal{F}(M, s) = Skip$$

Event Queue. The state machine as a whole is modelled with a single process that contains all the localised process descriptions defined above. The overall structure is similar to that given by Davies and Crichton [5]. The state machine receives all communications through an event queue, modelled as a CSP buffer of size 1. It communicates with this buffer on a CSP channel, *local*. Each of the

---

[4] Next, the guard (if it exists) is evaluated and if false the event is discarded without effect. Conversely, if the guard evaluates to true the behavioural construct specified for the effect are executed before behaving as the process associated with the destination state. Guards are omitted in this paper due to space restrictions.

localised processes has access to this channel in order to receive communications from the event queue. The overall process $M(queue, local)$ initially behaves as the process associated with the initial state $\mathcal{F}(M, s_0)$. Throughout, the state machine behaves like the various processes until it possibly reaches a final state, after which it behaves as $\mathcal{F}(M, s_f)$. The local process EQ models the event queue. Here, we assume a queue with a maximum capacity of 1; the queue blocks when full. The datatype $Dispatcthed$, communicated along with the event on channel $local$, models the dispatching of an event: an event can either be processed, $proc$ or, if the state machine is in a state where the dispatched event is not expected, discarded, $disc$.

$$
\begin{aligned}
&M(queue, local) = \\
&\quad \text{let} \\
&\qquad \mathcal{F}(M, s_0) = \ldots \\
&\qquad \ldots \\
&\qquad \mathcal{F}(M, s_f) = Stop \\
&\qquad EQ = queue?e \rightarrow local?p!e \rightarrow EQ \\
&\quad \text{within} \\
&\qquad \mathcal{F}(M, s_0) \; [| \; \{| \; in \; |\} \; |] \; EQ
\end{aligned}
$$

The state machine of a block B_i only receives (through its event queue) the provided receptions. The required features are communicated across the connectors linking parts. In our formalisation, the name of the part is used as the channel name.

Blocks. The formalisation above additionally allows us to showcase how CSP can be used in a compositional approach to specification and refinement within the context of systems engineering.

Assume a block $B_i \in \mathcal{B}$ composed of K constituent blocks $B_0 .. B_{K-1}$, where $i \geq K$. We known that the aggregate behaviour exhibited by blocks $B_0 .. B_{K-1}$ must adhere to that of the composite block B_i; B_i is an abstract specification block that the more concrete implementation blocks $B_0 .. B_{K-1}$ must implement. Stated in terms of CSP: the characteristic process of B_i serves as the specification process and $B_0 .. B_{K-1}$, suitably combined using parallel composition, form the implementation process.

Assume that $classifier(B)$ represents the classifier behaviour of a SysML block. Using CSP the conformance of the implementation process to that of the specification can be stated thus.

$$
classifier(B_i) \sqsubseteq \; \| \, P : \{B_0 .. B_{K-1}\} \bullet classifier(P)
$$

Events introduced at the lower level of implementation are excluded from the above observation; the hiding operator of CSP can be used to conceal such events.

Using this approach, and assuming the refinement holds, B_i can be safely substituted for the concrete composition $B_0 .. B_{K-1}$. This stepwise, compositional approach to systems specification and design sits well with CSP's approach to refinement. This statement is not necessarily true for conventional model checkers that rely on temporal logics to assert safety or liveness properties. In a *system of systems*, B_i, previously our *system of interest*, is now just a component block representing one of the subsystems.

4   A Robotic Arm

In this section we apply the concepts central to our methodology to an illustrative case study. We study a single component, a robotic arm, of a fully fledged case study that is well known in the formal methods community. The production cell is an industrial installation of a metal processing plant located in Karlsruhe, Germany [6]. However, in the interest of brevity and clarity, we consider the arm as our system of interest. The arm is one subsystem of the travelling crane, which is yet another component of the much bigger system — the production cell.

A *bidirectional motor* can operate in two opposing directions. An *electromagnet* can activate or deactivate a magnetic field using an electric current. A *potentiometer* provides a value within certain limits so as to indicate the range of extension.

The arm is equipped with a bidirectional motor responsible for vertical extension. An electromagnet is placed at the front of the arm for handling metal objects; a potentiometer is present to indicate the range of extension of the arm.

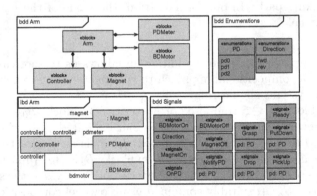

Fig. 1. The block definition and internal block diagrams of the arm system.

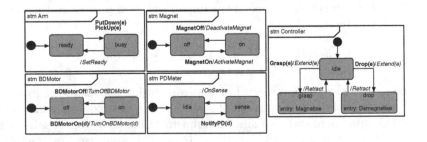

Fig. 2. The state machine diagrams of the arm system.

Refer to Fig. 1. The structural aspects of the system are modelled using blocks for the controller, bidirectional motor, electromagnet, and the potentiometer; signals and enumeration definitions further illuminate the design by introducing the messages and associated parameters communicated between state machines and activities.

Figures 2 and 3 show the state machines and activities of the arm system.

The channels used by the state machine of the bidirectional motor can be defined thus. The Direction enumeration of Fig. 1 can be represented with a CSP datatype. Channel and datatype definitions for other state machines are similar.

datatype $Dispatched = proc \mid disc$
datatype $Direction = fwd \mid rev$
datatype $BDMotorSignal =$
    $BDMotorOn.Direction \mid BDMotorOff$
channel $bdmotor : BDMotorSignal$
channel $bdmotorlocal : Dispatched.BDMotorSignal$

In the above, the channel $bdmotor$ is used by other state machines to communicate with the state machine of the bidirectional motor via its associated event queue; the channel $bdmotorlocal$ is used by the event queue of the bidirectional motor to dispatch events (to the bidirectional motor's state machine) for processing.

The CSP process modelling the characteristic behaviour of the Controller follows. The activity Extend is associated with the effect component of the transitions emanating from the idle state; the activity Magnetise represents the entry behaviour of the grasp state. CSP datatype definitions are used to type the provided receptions of the Controller block; these serve as triggers for the classifying state machine. The name of the instance is used as the channel name when communicating with a state machine; a channel with the same name and the suffix local is used to model the internal event queue of the corresponding state machine.

$Controller(queue, local) =$
  let
    $I_0 = IDLE$
    $IDLE =$
      $local.proc.Grasp?e \rightarrow$
        $Extend(local, e) \; _9^9 \; Magnetise \; _9^9 \; GRASP$
        $\Box$
      $local.proc.Drop?e \rightarrow$
        $Extend(local, e) \; _9^9 \; Demagnetise \; _9^9 \; DROP$
        $\Box$
      $local.disc?e : \{\mid OnPD \mid\} \rightarrow IDLE$
    $GRASP =$
      $Retract(local) \; _9^9 \; IDLE$
      $\Box$
      $local.disc?e : \{\mid Grasp, Drop, OnPD \mid\} \rightarrow GRASP$
    $DROP = \ldots$

$$EQ = queue?e \rightarrow local?p!e \rightarrow EQ$$
within
$$I_0 \, [| \, \{| \, local \, |\} \, |] \, EQ$$
$$CONTROLLER = Controller(controller, controllerlocal)$$
$$\alpha CONTROLLER =$$
$$\quad Union(\{\{| \, controller, controllerlocal \, |\},$$
$$\quad\quad \alpha Magnetise, \alpha Demagnetise, \alpha Extend, \alpha Retract\})$$

The processes *Magnetise* and *Extend*, modelling the activities used in the *CONTROLLER* process, follows. The event queue is passed in as the activity executes within the context of its owing state machine.

$$Magnetise =$$
   let
$$\quad I_0 = SS_0$$
$$\quad SS_0 = magnet.magnetOn \rightarrow F_0$$
$$\quad F_0 = Skip$$
   within
$$\quad I_0$$
$$\alpha Magnetise = \{| \, magnet.MagnetOn \, |\}$$

$$Extend(local, pd) =$$
   let
$$\quad I_0 = VS_0$$
$$\quad VS_0 = SS_0(fwd)$$
$$\quad SS_0(o) = bdmotor.BDMotorOn.o \rightarrow SS_1$$
$$\quad SS_1 = pdmeter.NotifyPD.pd \rightarrow RS_0$$
$$\quad RS_0 =$$
$$\quad\quad local.proc.OnPD \rightarrow SS_2$$
$$\quad\quad \square$$
$$\quad\quad local.disc?ev : \{| \, Grasp, Drop \, |\} \rightarrow RS_0$$
$$\quad SS_2 = bdmotor.BDMotorOff \rightarrow F_0$$
$$F_0 = Skip$$
   within
$$\quad I_0$$
$$\alpha Extend =$$
$$\quad \{| \, bdmotor.BDMotorOn.fwd, bdmotor.BDMotorOff,$$
$$\quad pdmeter.NotifyPD \, |\}$$

The processes, along with their respective alphabets, denoting concrete parts for the magnet, bidirectional motor and potentiometer can be similarly defined, but are excluded here due to space constraints. Activities and alphabets used within these state machines can also be similarly defined.

$$MAGNET = Magnet(magnet, magnetlocal)$$
$$BDMOTOR = BDMotor(bdmotor, bdmotorlocal)$$
$$PDMETER = PDMeter(pdmeter, pdmeterlocal)$$

The definition of the process ARM, modelling the abstract block that serves as the specification that the parts must realise, follows.

$$Arm(queue, local) =$$
$$\text{let}$$
$$\quad I_0 = READY$$
$$\quad READY = \ldots$$
$$\quad BUSY =$$
$$\quad\quad SetReady \,\S\, READY$$
$$\quad\quad \square$$
$$\quad\quad local.disc?e : \{|\; PickUp, PutDown \;|\} \rightarrow BUSY$$
$$\quad EQ = queue?e \rightarrow local?p!e \rightarrow EQ$$
$$\text{within}$$
$$\quad I_0 \;[|\; \{|\; local \;|\} \;|]\; EQ$$
$$ARM = Arm(arm, armlocal)$$
$$\alpha ARM =$$
$$\quad Union(\{\{|\; arm, armlocal \;|\}, \alpha SetReady\})$$

Assuming that $P = \{CONTROLLER, MAGNET, BDMOTOR, PDMETER\}$ we then have $CONCRETE = \|p : P \bullet [\alpha p]p$. In the aforementioned, αp denotes the set of events communicable by P. The set of processes P represent the concrete implementation blocks whose conjoined behaviour must be that of the block arm that serves as its specification. The similarity with CSP here is striking: refinement in CSP is expressed between specification and implementation processes.

$CONCRETE^R$ is the process with events suitably renamed to ensure compatible alphabets.

$$CONCRETE^R =$$
$$\quad CONCRETE[\, controller.Grasp.pd_0 \leftarrow arm.PickUp.pd_0,$$
$$\quad\quad\quad\quad\quad\quad controller.Drop.pd_0 \leftarrow arm.PutDown.pd_0,$$
$$\quad\quad\quad\quad\quad\quad controller.Grasp.pd_1 \leftarrow arm.PickUp.pd_1 \ldots]$$

The set *Hidden* are those events not present in the alphabet of the abstract specification process ARM; Σ denotes the set of all CSP events within the context of the specification. Thus

$$Hidden = \Sigma \setminus \{|\; arm.PickUp, arm.PutDown,$$
$$\quad\quad\quad\quad\quad armlocal.proc.PickUp, armlocal.proc.PutDown,$$
$$\quad\quad\quad\quad\quad armlocal.disc.PickUp, armlocal.disc.PutDown,$$
$$\quad\quad\quad\quad\quad client \;|\}$$

FDR verifies the assertion

$$ARM \sqsubseteq CONCRETE^R \setminus Hidden \quad\quad\quad\quad [\sqsubseteq holds]$$

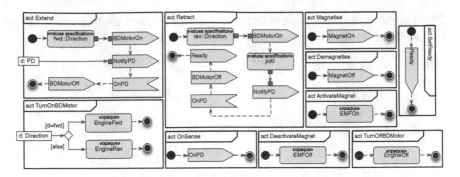

Fig. 3. The activity diagrams of the arm system.

Given that the refinement holds, *ARM* can be substituted for its parts in the complete system: the behaviour of the concrete implementation processes, denoted by *CONCRETE*, can neither refuse nor accept an event that *ARM* can. Stated another way, the characteristic behaviour of *CONCRETE* is completely contained within that of *ARM*. The compositional approach presented above is effective in alleviating the state space explosion problem: subsystems can be developed and formally verified in isolation and subsequently combined to form an integrated system description.

5 Conclusions

There is a wealth of literature on the formalisation of activity and state machine diagrams, primarily within the context of UML. In order to limit the scope we only report on approaches that utilise CSP.

Ng and Butler [7] proposed the formalisation of UML state machine diagrams using CSP as the semantic domain [7]. They define the translation in terms of a mapping function from structural diagrammatic constructs to their CSP counterparts. The work of Yeung and colleagues [8] built on that of Ng and Butler by generalising inter-level transitions.

Xu et al. [9] formalised activity diagrams in CSP. A transformation function is defined that maps the mathematical representation of an activity to the semantic domain of CSP. The goal in [9] is on providing a formal semantics for activities in terms of CSP, rather than checking behavioural conformance. Only a limited number of diagrammatic constructs are considered and object flows are omitted. Constructs such as send and receive event actions are not addressed.

Our work is different than the aforementioned contributions in a number of ways. This paper presents a compositional approach to refinement and speci-fication, evaluated within the context of SysML. In addition, we consider the behaviour of several interacting state machines, supplemented with behaviours described via activities. In contrast, previous approaches placed emphasis on the formalisation of a single state machine (or activity); considering the execution semantics in terms of interaction with other state machines (or activities) was not their primary focus.

The choice of CSP is due to a number of factors. The behavioural aspects of SysML can be modelled naturally by a process-algebraic formalism such as CSP, resulting in a formal framework where assertions about requirements can be proved or refuted with relative ease [4]. CSP's approach to process composition, combined with the fact that refinement is preserved within context, would allow us to decompose a complex design of a system (or system of systems) in such a way that the automated analysis is computationally feasible. In particular, the decompositional approach to specification, as illuminated by the case study in Sect. 4, allows us to substitute a collection of blocks with a single block that depicts the intended behaviour of the whole. Furthermore, CSP's approach to establish refinement — by comparing the behaviour of a characteristic specification process to that of a concrete implementation process — coincides with SysML's compositional outlook to specification and the notion that a block can act as a specification of constituent blocks. In contrast, in conventional model checking approaches where there is no concept of refinement, this distinction is less clear. The above approach is mechanisable via a model-to-model (SysML meta- model to CSP meta-model) and subsequent model-to-text (machine-readable CSP) transformation. Details of an implementation have been omitted due to space constraints.

References

1. Leveson, N.G.: Engineering a Safer World: Systems Thinking Applied to Safety. MIT Press, Cambridge (2012)
2. Object Management Group: Systems Modeling Language Specification, version 1.3 (2012). http://www.omg.org/spec/SysML/1.3, March 2014
3. Hoare, C.A.R.: Communicating Sequential Processes. Prentice Hall, London (1985)
4. Jacobs, J., Simpson, A.: Towards a process algebra framework for supporting behavioural consistency and requirements traceability in SysML. In: Groves, Lindsay, Sun, Jing (eds.) ICFEM 2013. LNCS, vol. 8144, pp. 265–280. Springer, Heidelberg (2013)
5. Davies, J.W.M., Crichton, C.R.: Concurrency and refinement in the unified modeling language. Electron. Notes in Theoret. Comput. Sci. **70**(3), 217–243 (2002)
6. Lewerentz, Claus, Lindner, Thomas (eds.): Formal Development of Reactive Systems. LNCS, vol. 891. Springer, Heidelberg (1995)
7. Ng, M.Y., Butler, M.: Towards formalizing UML state diagrams in CSP. In: Proceedings of the 1st International Conference on Software Engineering and Formal Methods (SEFM 2003), pp. 138–147. IEEE (2003)
8. Yeung, W.L., Leung, K.R.P.H., Dong, W., Wang, J.: Improvements towards formalizing UML state diagrams in CSP. In: Proceedings of the 12th Asia-Pacific Software Engineering Conference (APSEC 2005), pp. 176–182. IEEE (2005)
9. Xu, D., Philbert, N., Liu, Z., Liu, W.: Towards formalizing UML activity diagrams in CSP. In: Proceedings of the 2008 International Symposium on Computer Science and Computational Technology (ISCSCT 2008), pp. 450–453. IEEE (2008)

Parallelism Analysis: Precise WCET Values for Complex Multi-Core Systems

Timon Kelter$^{(\boxtimes)}$ and Peter Marwedel

Department of Computer Science, TU Dortmund, Otto-Hahn-Straße 16,
44227 Dortmund, Germany
{timon.kelter,peter.marwedel}@tu-dortmund.de

Abstract. In the verification of safety-critical real-time systems, the problem of determining the *worst-case execution time* (WCET) of a task is of utmost importance. Safe formal methods have been established for solving the single-task, single-core WCET problem. The de-facto standard approach uses abstract interpretation to derive basic block execution times and a combinatorial path analysis which derives the longest path through the program. WCET analyses for multi-core computers have extended this methodology by assuming that shared resources are partitioned in either time or space and that therefore each core can still be analyzed separately. For real-world multi-cores this assumption is often not true, making the classic WCET analysis approach either inapplicable or highly pessimistic. To overcome this, we present a new *technique to explore the interleavings of a parallel task system* as well as an *exclusion criterion* to prove that certain interleavings can never occur. We show how this technique can be integrated into existing WCET analysis approaches and finally provide results for the application of this new analysis type to a collection of real-time benchmarks, where average WCET reductions of 32 % were observed.

Keywords: WCET · Multi-core · Parallelism · Shared resources

1 Introduction

WCET analysis is an important prerequisite for schedulability analysis and for overall system validation of safety-critical real-time systems, i.e. systems in which tasks must complete within a given deadline. The runtime of any task τ depends on its inputs, on the system state at the start of τ and on the interference imposed on τ by preempting tasks on the same core or by parallel tasks running on other cores. To compute the WCET, first an abstract interpretation on the domain of abstract system hardware states is run. With the resulting hardware state overestimations a safe bound on the runtime of each basic block can be derived. This procedure is called *microarchitectural analysis* (MA). As the last step, the *path analysis* determines the longest path through the program with the help of the basic block runtimes determined by the MA [19]. In this paper we propose

© Springer International Publishing Switzerland 2015
C. Artho and P.C. Ölveczky (Eds.): FTSCS 2014, CCIS 476, pp. 142–158, 2015.
DOI: 10.1007/978-3-319-17581-2_10

an abstract interpretation of the system hardware state that is able to efficiently explore all possible interactions between multiple concurrently running tasks.

As soon as multiple cores may access a shared hardware resource in parallel, the runtimes of parallel tasks are no longer independent but they depend on

1. The order in which the requests arrive at the shared resource and
2. The policy with which requests to the shared resource are arbitrated.

Previous work has eliminated the first dependency by choosing a *state-partitioned* arbitration strategy which guarantees that the actions of any core C cannot modify the state of the shared resource as seen by cores $C_o \neq C$. This implies, that the delay for any access from C is independent of the potential concurrent accesses from all $C_o \neq C$. Therefore, we can still perform a per-core analysis and the state space does not become much bigger than for the single-core case. An example for such a state-partitioned strategy is *time-division multiple access* (TDMA) [5]. However, state-partitioned arbitration increases the average access delay compared to *state-permeable* strategies like *fair arbitration* (FAIR) and *fixed-priority arbitration* (PRIO) [6]. WCET analysis for these types of arbitration has been nonexistent or pessimistic at best. Therefore our main goal in this paper is to make a first step towards a precise WCET analysis for shared state-permeable resources, since they are often found in real-world systems.

2 Related Work

WCET Analysis. There is an extensive body of work on single-core WCET analysis as summarized in [19], which led to the standard approach of separating the microarchitectural analysis from the path analysis. Our techniques also build upon this concept by extending the former analysis to multi-cores.

The first known approach to multi-core WCET analysis is based on the *Real-Time Calculus* (RTC) [14,15]. It uses "access curves" to strongly abstract from the concrete system, which introduces strong pessimism in the results and is restricted to timing-compositional architectures [4]. The only known, non-RTC-based approach to the analysis of shared state-permeable resources is based on parallel summaries [10]. For a shared cache, it precomputes worst-case interference summaries for each core which contain the effects that *all* program points in *all* possibly concurrently running tasks can have on the state of the shared resource, which also introduces considerable pessimism. The authors of [1] combined the summary-based shared cache approach from [10] with a safe abstraction for the analysis of TDMA buses [5], which results in a scalable but pessimistic WCET analysis for multi-core WCET estimation. Finally, model-checkers have been used to determine multi-core WCETs [3] and these could potentially also handle state-permeable resources. Unfortunately the approach does not scale to bigger programs or realistic systems, since the generic model checker has few possibilities of pruning the huge search space.

Parallel Program Analysis. Static analysis of the synchronization structure of concurrent programs was first considered by [17] where the analysis of the "concurrency state" of the system and the notion of a parallel execution graph was first established. We build our work on this, though the analysis in [17] worked at a far more coarse-grained level. A reference approach to bit-vector-based abstract interpretation on programs with explicit fork-join parallelism is given in [9]. Unfortunately, the microarchitectural analysis that we are examining here is not a bit-vector problem. In reachability analysis for parallel programs "stubborn sets" [18] can be used to prune the search space, but again the microarchitectural analysis differs significantly from reachability analysis. Finally, a recent publication [12] examines the computation of feasible synchronization-aware parallel interleavings. Their approach focuses on path analysis and is thus orthogonal to ours.

3   System and Task Model

We assume a task set T containing only strictly periodic tasks, as often found in hard real-time systems. In the following sections, we will need a common reference point in time for all running tasks, where times are measured in multiples of the shortest clock cycle. Therefore we first require that all $\tau_i \in T$ are sharing the same period $p_i = p_T$ and that each task is executed non-preemptively on a separate core. We will discuss how to lift these restrictions in Sect. 5. Each task τ_i may have a different release time r_i within the common period.

The analysis can be adapted to any topology, but for our experiments we will use an example architecture with $n = |T|$ ARM7TDMI cores,[1] each having a private cache and a scratchpad. The cores are connected to a shared bus which is arbitrated under either TDMA, FAIR round-robin or fixed core priorities. Behind the bus, shared instruction and data caches are located as well as non-cached memories.

4   Parallelism Analysis

Before starting with the formal part of the framework, we briefly sketch the intuition behind the analysis procedure. Our goal will be to efficiently explore all feasible interleavings of multiple tasks running in parallel. As an example, consider the execution of the tasks from Fig. 1 under the assumption that both tasks start concurrently at time 0. For this assumption we can find all valid parallel execution scenarios from the *parallel execution graph* (PEG) shown in Fig. 2. The construction of this graph starts with nodes corresponding to the initial system states, in this case with only the node AE (the δ-values will be explained below). From these start nodes, we iteratively simulate cycle steps of the system. To keep our example PEG from Fig. 2 sufficiently small, we assume that every block will take one cycle to complete. Therefore, our initial block AE is terminated after the first cycle and the execution must continue in one of the nodes AE, BE, BF and AF. To generate these successors we simply follow all

---

[1] The choice of ARM7TDMI cores is motivated by the fact that we already have an implementation of the abstract pipeline model for these cores (compare Sect. 4.4).

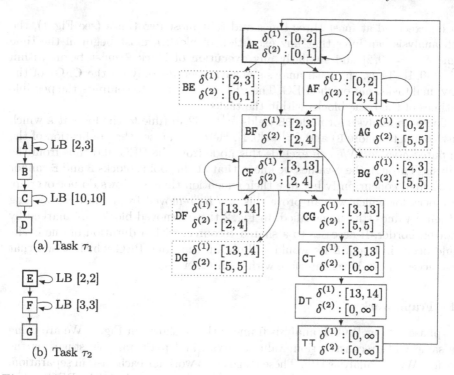

Fig. 1. Two example tasks with given loop bounds.

Fig. 2. The final parallel execution graph for tasks τ_1 and τ_2 from Fig. 1, starting synchronously at time 0.

combinations of successor blocks in the task CFGs. The loop bounds are not used here. If we continue the graph construction in this manner, we will end up with a full product graph of the task CFGs. When every core has reached the end of its task, indicated by the "⊤" sign in Fig. 2, we add a back-edge from ⊤⊤ to AE to account for the repeated execution of the tasks in the cyclic schedule. The purpose of this final PEG is, that it contains each basic block of each task in all possible parallel execution scenarios. Thus we can derive the WCET of each basic block from the PEG and use these to compute the task WCETs.

As visible, the PEG in Fig. 2 is *not* a full product graph of the graphs from Fig. 1. The construction of the graph has been stopped at nodes BE, AG, BG, DF and DG. To explain why this was done, and why it is correct, we need the δ-values and the loop bounds. We define $\delta^{(i)}$ as an interval containing all points in time, measured from the beginning of the common period p_T, at which a node may be entered on core i. Initially we set $\delta^{(1)} = \delta^{(2)} = [0,0]$ for node AE, since core 1 (2) enters node A (E) at time 0. From here on, every time we visit a node X in the analysis, we recompute its δ intervals with the help of a path analysis which computes the length of the shortest and longest paths to the basic blocks in X. As an example, when we visit node AE the second time, we have already seen, that both block A and E complete within one cycle. Therefore, since A can be executed at most three times and E at most two times (see Fig. 1), the path analysis can infer that any execution of block A must begin in the time frame $\delta^{(1)} = [0, 2]$ and similarly any execution of block E must begin within $\delta^{(2)} = [0, 1]$. Thus, the path analysis always operates only on the CFGs of the individual tasks, *not* on the PEG. The PEG is only used to compute the possible runtimes of the basic blocks within the tasks.

The path analysis for node BE yields $\delta^{(1)} = [2, 3]$ (due to the loop at A which must complete before B) and $\delta^{(2)} = [0, 1]$. Here we can see the application of the computed δ-values: We can exclude this node from the PEG and thus from the analysis. Through the δ-values we know, that at this point blocks B and E cannot be executed concurrently because their execution time windows do not overlap. All blocks for which we can prove this can be removed from the PEG as long as their δ-values stay unmodified. In Fig. 2 these removed blocks are marked by a dotted border. If accesses to a shared resource, with a duration of one cycle, would occur in B and E we would still obtain the same PEG which shows that these accesses can never interfere with each other.

4.1 Framework

The phases of our WCET analysis framework are shown in Fig. 3. We are using the same CFG reconstruction, value analysis and path analysis stages as the classical WCET analysis [19]. These stages also work for each task in separation. Only for the microarchitectural analysis, we first construct the initial PEG states, based on the system schedule. Then we conduct a data-flow analysis on the PEG until the PEG itself as well as the associated system states have reached a fixpoint. From this converged PEG we extract the basic block runtimes that are finally used to compute the WCET and BCET in an IPET-based path analysis.

4.2 Prerequisites

To precisely define our analysis procedure we will need some terminology which is introduced in the following.

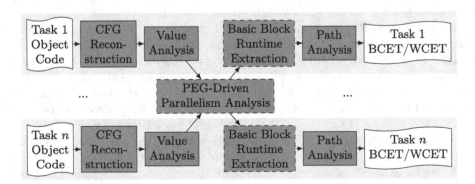

Fig. 3. The analysis framework. The dashed parts are new contributions compared to [19] and will be discussed in the next sections.

Given a set of tasks T together with CFGs $G_\tau = (V_\tau, E_\tau)$ for all $\tau \in T$, a *task execution position* ψ_τ is a tuple (v, i, c, d), where $v \in V_\tau$ is a basic block, $i \in v$ is an instruction within that basic block and c is the number of cycles that were already spent on the processing of this instruction. Finally, d is the number of cycles that the task must wait until its execution will begin. A *system execution position* (SEP) Ψ on n cores is an n-tuple with $\Psi \in \hat{\Psi} = \times_{i=1}^{n} \hat{\psi}_{\tau_i} \cup \{\top\}$, τ_i being the task mapped to core i. The special token $\top$ indicates that the respective core is currently running idle. Here and in the following we use $\hat{A}$ to denote the set of all tuples of type A. The motivation for this definition is, that other than in our introductory example from Fig. 2, real basic blocks will contain more than one instruction[2] each of which may take multiple cycles to complete. Still we need to be able to split the execution of each basic block into chunks which may be as small as a single CPU cycle, as we will see in the following. We will use SEPs to specify the point at which the execution is resumed in a PEG block, therefore SEPs correspond to the block labels from Fig. 2 (e.g. AE, BE, AF, etc.).

An *abstract parallel system state* (APSS) $\Sigma \in \hat{\Sigma}$ is a structure which models a set of concrete states of an entire parallel system, including all cores and memory hierarchy elements. Again, $\hat{\Sigma}$ is the set of all possible APSSs. We give more detail on how to form proper APSSs at a later point, for now we only require a *cycle step function* $\xi_\Sigma : \hat{\Sigma} \times \hat{\Psi} \times 2^{\{1,\ldots,n\}} \to (\{0,1\}^n \times \hat{\Sigma})$. The invocation of $\xi_\Sigma(\Sigma, \Psi, \alpha)$ must simulate all possible state transfers that may happen when a single clock cycle is executed at position Ψ in system state Σ. However, only the cores in the set $\alpha \subseteq \{1, \ldots, |T|\}$ may perform a cycle step, to be able to account for different release times. For any *instruction completion vector* $c \in \{0,1\}^n$ which may occur in this cycle, it must specify the result state, where c defines for each core, whether it has completed the execution of its current instruction (1) or not (0). The "current instruction" is always given by the "program counter" register value.

The APSSs will be subject to a data-flow analysis, therefore we also require a partial order $\sqsubseteq$ on $\hat{\Sigma}$ such that $(\hat{\Sigma}, \sqsubseteq)$ is a lattice [7], with a *supremum* or *join* function $\sqcup : \hat{\Sigma} \times \hat{\Sigma} \to \hat{\Sigma}$. Intuitively, since APSSs represent sets of concrete states, $\Sigma_1 \sqsubseteq \Sigma_2$ specifies whether Σ_2 completely contains Σ_1. To ensure the termination of the data-flow framework ξ_Σ must also be monotonic with respect to $\sqsubseteq$.

A *Parallel Execution Graph* $G_P = (V_P, E_P)$ is a directed graph with node set $V_P \subseteq \hat{\Psi} \cup \{\bot\}$ and edge set $E_P \subseteq V_P \times V_P$. $\bot$ is a special PEG node which is exclusively used to model the situation that the execution of the parallel system has not yet started. For any PEG we define a *block time window* function $\delta : V_P \to \hat{I}^n$, an *edge state function* $\lambda : E_P \to \hat{\Sigma}$ and a *block length function* $\omega_P : V_P \to \mathbb{N}$. $\hat{I} = \{[x, y] \subset 2^\mathbb{N} | x \leq y\}$ is the set of all execution time intervals, measured in cycles from the last point where all cores were synchronized. The time window function will be used to rule out infeasible SEPs as indicated in Fig. 2, the edge state function is used to propagate the possible hardware states from one PEG node to the other and the block length function specifies how many cycles were spend on the execution of a PEG node. The three functions are not defined a priori. They will be computed by the algorithms presented in the following.

---

[2] In the example we have not even differentiated between basic blocks and instructions.

Algorithm 1. PEG-driven parallelism analysis

1: **function** PARALLELISMANALYSIS($\Sigma_{\text{start}}, G_{\tau_1}, ..., G_{\tau_n}$)
2: $\quad \forall \tau : \forall v \in V_\tau : \omega_C(v) = \emptyset$ $\qquad\qquad$ ▷ Initialize all context block runtimes to $\emptyset$
3: $\quad Q \leftarrow (v_{\tau_1}^{\text{start}}, 0, 0, r_1) \times \cdots \times (v_{\tau_n}^{\text{start}}, 0, 0, r_n)$ $\qquad\qquad$ ▷ Initialize start block
4: $\quad G_P \leftarrow (Q \cup \{\bot\}, \emptyset)$
5: $\quad \delta(\bot) \leftarrow [0,0]^n, \omega_P(\bot) \leftarrow \infty$ $\qquad\qquad$ ▷ Initialize pre-execution state $\bot$
6: $\quad \forall v \in Q : \delta(v) \leftarrow \emptyset^n, \lambda((\bot, v)) \leftarrow \Sigma_{\text{start}}, \omega_P(v) = \infty$ $\qquad$ ▷ Initialize start state
7: $\quad$ **while** $Q \neq \emptyset$ **do**
8: $\qquad v = \text{POPFRONT}(Q)$ $\qquad\qquad\qquad\qquad\qquad$ ▷ Analyze next block
9: $\qquad \omega_C \leftarrow \text{GATHERNEWBBTRACES}(\psi, G_P, \omega_P, \omega_C)$ $\qquad\qquad$ ▷ Update ω_C
10: $\qquad$ **for** $i \in \{1, ..., n\}$ **do** $\qquad\qquad$ ▷ Update δ-window for all cores
11: $\qquad\qquad \delta(v)^{(i)} \leftarrow \bigcup_{(u,v) \in E_P} \delta(u)^{(i)} + \omega(u)$
12: $\qquad\qquad$ **if** IsLOOPHEADOREXIT($v^{(i)}$) **then**
13: $\qquad\qquad\qquad \delta(v)^{(i)} = r_i + \text{PATHANALYSIS}(v^{(i)}, G_{\tau_i}, \omega_C)$
14: $\qquad$ **if** $\forall_{i \in \{1, ..., n\}} \delta(v)^{(i)} \neq \emptyset \wedge \bigcap_{i=1}^n \delta(v)^{(i)} = \emptyset$ **then** $\qquad$ ▷ If BEC holds ...
15: $\qquad\qquad$ **continue** $\qquad\qquad\qquad\qquad$ ▷ ... skip the current block v ...
16: $\qquad$ **else** $\qquad\qquad\qquad\qquad\qquad\qquad$ ▷ ... else analyze v
17: $\qquad\qquad \lambda_{\text{prev}} \leftarrow \lambda, G_{P,\text{prev}} \leftarrow G_P$
18: $\qquad\qquad (G_P, \lambda, \omega_P) \leftarrow \text{ANALYZEBLOCK}(v, G_P, \lambda, \omega_P)$
19: $\qquad\qquad$ **if** $\lambda_{\text{prev}} \neq \lambda \vee G_{P,\text{prev}} \neq G_P$ **then** ▷ If graph or states were altered ...
20: $\qquad\qquad\qquad \forall (v, z) \in E_P : \text{PUSHBACK}(Q, z)$ $\qquad$ ▷ ... propagate the changes.
21: $\qquad\qquad\qquad$ **if** $E_{P,\text{prev}} \neq E_P$ **then** $\qquad\qquad$ ▷ If edges were added ...
22: $\qquad\qquad\qquad\qquad \forall v \rightsquigarrow_{G_P} z : \text{PUSHBACK}(Q, z)$ $\qquad$ ▷ ... propagate δ-changes
23: $\quad$ **return** ω_C

We denote by $v_1 \rightsquigarrow_G v_2$ that there is a path in the directed graph $G = (V, E)$ from $v_1 \in V$ to $v_2 \in V$, i.e. that v_2 is *reachable* from v_1.

Our goal in the parallelism analysis is to compute the *CFG block lengths* $\omega_C : V_\tau \to \hat{I}$, which are then used by the path analysis. Note this these are *not* identical to ω_P. The block lengths in Fig. 1 are given by ω_C, whereas the block lengths in Fig. 2 are given by ω_P.

4.3 Analysis Algorithm

The outline of the main analysis is shown in Algorithm 1. It starts with an initialization of the initial context block runtimes ω_C in line 2 and of the work-list Q in line 3. According to the system schedule, the SEP consists of the begin of the start block of each task ($v_{\tau_i}^{\text{start}}$) with a delay of r_i cycles. This SEP is assigned a time window of $[0, 0]$. We also create a virtual edge $(\bot, v)$ pointing to it, which is assigned the initial APSS Σ_{start}. The start block $\bot$ itself has a runtime of zero cycles and executes in the start window $[0, 0]$ to mark that the schedule starts here. Then we process items from the queue Q until it gets empty (line 7). In the main loop, we extract the first block v from the queue and check whether v models the end of a basic block v_τ on any core in the call to GATHERNEWBBTRACES in line 9. For any such context block v_τ, its runtime $\omega_C(v_\tau)$ is updated in GATHERNEWBBTRACES as shown in Algorithm 2.

In line 11 we infer the block time window for all task positions $v^{(i)} \in v$ from the windows and runtimes of its predecessors.[3]

If v is part of a sequential block chain, the δ-update in line 11 is sufficient. On the other hand, if v is a loop head (like A in Fig. 1) or a loop exit (like B in Fig. 1), then we have to take the loop bounds into account to determine the block time window, like we have done in the computation of $\delta^{(1)}$ in e.g. AE and BE in Fig. 2. This is done in line 13, where the existing path analysis of our framework is used to compute the shortest and the longest path from $v_{\tau_i}^{start}$ to $v^{(i)}$. We currently use an adapted IPET analysis based on Integer Linear Programming [11] here, but advanced single-source all-sinks analyses would be even better suited [8]. It follows the given loop bounds and uses ω_C as the runtime of individual basic blocks in G_{τ_i}. If any block $u \in G_{\tau_i}$ with $u \rightsquigarrow_{G_{\tau_i}} v^{(i)}$ and $\omega_C(u) = \emptyset$ exists, the path analysis will return $\emptyset$ for the path length to $v^{(i)}$, thus keeping $\delta(\psi)^{(i)} = \emptyset$.

The δ values are used in line 14, where we try to apply the *block exclusion criterion* by intersecting all block time windows. However, this test can only be applied if the time windows for each task could already be determined, i.e., if they are not empty. If the intersection is empty, this SEP cannot be reached from its current predecessors and we its analysis in line 15. This is exactly what we have done with BE in Fig. 2. Still, we may need to analyze v in the future when it becomes accessible via new edges. Then we will re-check whether our exclusion criterion still holds. Thus, this skipping is effectively either postponing or avoiding the graph growth at v.

If the exclusion criterion does not hold (line 16), we analyze the *parallel execution block* (PEB) beginning at node v (line 18). This analysis will determine a block runtime $\omega_P(v)$, an output APPS for all out-edges of v and possibly alter G_P. If the output states or the graph are changed, we push the successors of v into the work-list at line 20. By doing this, all changes to the block time windows δ, edge states λ and block runtimes ω_P will be propagated through the graph. Finally, if we have added edges to the PEG, we also push all blocks z which are reachable from v into Q (line 22), to ensure that a new attempt to compute $\delta(z)$ is started, if z is a loop head or exit. The algorithm terminates when no more edges are added and all edge states have converged.

All in all Algorithm 1 is a standard data-flow analysis work-list algorithm, with the difference that we are dynamically expanding (line 18) the underlying graph. When PARALLELISMANALYSIS has finished, all reachable blocks of all tasks will have been visited in one or more parallel execution blocks and BBRUNTIME will therefore yield valid runtimes for all basic blocks.

To complete the view on the analysis, Algorithm 3 shows the function ANALYZEBLOCK which is tightly coupled with Algorithm 1. First, the incoming APSSs are joined in line 2. The current system execution position Ψ_{run} is initialized to v (remember that $V_P \subseteq \hat{\Psi}$) and the block duration $\omega_P(v)$ is set to zero. Then we simulate the effect of successive system cycle steps on Ψ_{run} and Σ_{run}, until on any core, either (a) the end of a basic block is reached or (b) the successor SEP is ambiguous. The latter happens, when it is uncertain in APSS

---

[3] Here and in the following we use $()^{(i)}$ to access the i-th element of a tuple.

Algorithm 2. Update of basic block runtimes

1: **function** GATHERNEWBBTRACES($v, G_P, \omega_P, \omega_C$)
2:     **for** $i \in \{1, \ldots, n\}, (u, v) \in E_P$ **do**
3:         **if** $v^{(i)(1)} \neq u^{(i)(1)}$ **then**   ▷ If v is context block start on core k, ...
4:             $u_{\tau,\text{pred}} = u^{(i)(1)}$ ▷ ... collect the length of all paths to starts of $u_{\tau,\text{pred}} \in V_\tau$.
5:             $\omega_C(u_{\tau,\text{pred}}) \leftarrow \omega_C(u_{\tau,\text{pred}}) \cup$ TRACETOSTARTS($u_{\tau,\text{pred}}, u, i, G_P, \omega_P$)

6:     **return** ω_C
7: **function** TRACETOSTARTS($v_\tau, v, i, G_P, \omega_P$)
8:     **if** $v^{(i)} = (v_\tau, i_0, 0, 0)$ **then**   ▷ If $v^{(i)}$ is a begin of v_τ, ...
9:         **return** $\omega_P(v)$ ▷ ... finish this trace.
10:    **else**   ▷ Else continue with the recursion.
11:        **return** $\bigcup_{(u,v)\in E_P} \{\omega_P(v) + \text{TRACETOSTARTS}(v_\tau, u, i, G_P, \omega_P)\}$

Σ_{run} whether the current instruction of at least one core will complete or not. In this case we track all completion combinations in separate successor blocks.

The first step in each cycle is to invoke the APSS cycle step function ξ_Σ, which is done in line 5, but only for those cores with zero delay cycles (set α). The APSS cycle step function ξ_Σ returns a mapping $\kappa \subseteq \hat{I} \times \hat{\Sigma}$, i.e. it associates instruction completion vectors to successor APSSs. Line 6 checks the two block termination conditions (a) and (b) mentioned above. The helper function $\phi_c^\alpha : \hat{\Psi} \to \hat{\Psi}$ generates the successor SEP for a given SEP Ψ, instruction completion vector c and active core set α. If neither a basic block end is reached, nor the successor SEP is ambiguous, we take over the results of the cycle step as our new working SEP Ψ_{run} and APSS Σ_{run} in line 7 and increment the cycle counter for this block in line 8. Here, $\Psi_{\text{run}}^{(i)(1)}$ is the basic block executed by core i, $\kappa^{(1)(1)}$ is the first instruction completion vector and $\kappa^{(1)(2)}$ is its associated successor APSS.

If the block end is detected, we terminate the current block as shown from line 9 on. It will be one invariant of our analysis that the length of a block can only stay the same or be reduced in successive analyses of the same block. Therefore we only check in line 10, whether the block has been shortened. This may happen due to a newly joined-in APSS, that triggers an earlier ambiguous successor SEP. In this case, we remove all previous out-edges of the current block v (line 11). In any case, we add for each instruction completion vector c an out-edge to $\phi_c^\alpha(\Sigma_{\text{run}})$ which gets annotated with the respective out-state Σ_c (lines 13–16). In the end, the modified graph, edge states and block lengths are returned in line 18.

With Algorithm 3 we completed the macroscopic side of the analysis. In the next subsection we will examine the microscopic perspective, namely how to efficiently represent abstract parallel system states.

4.4 Parallel System State Models

An APSS must model the *state* of all microarchitectural components which are relevant to the timing of the system, i.e. all cores and their pipelines and all *memory hierarchy elements* (MHEs) like private and/or shared caches, buses and

Algorithm 3. PEG block analysis

1: **function** ANALYZEBLOCK$(v, G_P, \lambda, \omega_P)$
2:    $\Sigma_{\text{run}} \leftarrow \bigsqcup_{\forall e=(u,v)\in E_P} \lambda(e)$ ▷ Join incoming states
3:    $\Psi_{\text{run}} \leftarrow v, \omega_{P,\text{prev}} \leftarrow \omega_P, \omega_P(v) \leftarrow 0$
4:    **while** true **do**
5:        $\kappa \leftarrow \xi_\Sigma(\Sigma_{\text{run}}, \Psi_{\text{run}}, \alpha = \{i|\Psi_{\text{run}}^{(i)} = (\cdot, \cdot, \cdot, 0)\})$ ▷ Simulate next cycle in block
6:        **if** $|\kappa| = 1 \wedge \nexists i : (\phi^\alpha_{\kappa^{(1)(1)}}(\Psi_{\text{run}}))^{(i)(1)} \neq \Psi_{\text{run}}^{(i)(1)}$ **then**   ▷ Split/Basic block end?
7:            $\Sigma_{\text{run}} \leftarrow \kappa^{(1)(2)}, \Psi_{\text{run}} \leftarrow \phi^\alpha_{\kappa^{(1)(1)}}(\Psi_{\text{run}})$ ▷ If not, prepare next cycle
8:            $\omega_P(v) \leftarrow \omega_P(v) + 1$
9:        **else**   ▷ Else terminate the current block
10:           **if** $\omega_P(v) < \omega_{P,\text{prev}}(v)$ **then**   ▷ Remove old edges on block shrinking
11:               $E_P \leftarrow E_P \setminus \{(v, w) \in E_P\}$
12:           **for** $(c \rightarrow \Sigma_c) \in \kappa$ **do**   ▷ Add new successors and out-states
13:               $V_P \leftarrow V_P \cup \{v_{\text{new}} = \phi^\alpha_c(\Sigma_{\text{run}})\}$
14:               $\delta(v_{\text{new}}) \leftarrow \emptyset^n, \omega_P(v_{\text{new}}) \leftarrow \infty$
15:               $E_P \leftarrow E_P \cup \{e_{\text{new}} = (v, v_{\text{new}})\}$
16:               $\lambda(e_{\text{new}}) \leftarrow \Sigma_c$
17:           **break**
18:    **return** (G_P, λ, ω_P) ▷ Return all modifications

memories. Here, *state* denotes an approximation of the relevant content of the component as well as the operation that the component is currently performing.

Therefore we define an APSS Σ as a set of tuples, where each tuple contains abstract states for each pipeline and memory hierarchy element in the system. The rationale behind Σ being a set of tuples is, that we may have to split the state, e.g. when two different paths in the pipeline must be considered. These different execution paths may have identical instruction completion vectors, but still we need to maintain them separately in a common Σ set, to trace the different microarchitectural behaviors.

The driving force behind the microarchitectural simulation are the cores' pipelines, which are modeled as non-deterministic finite-state machines [19]. In each cycle, the abstract pipeline states follow all transitions which are enabled according to their current state which includes the currently executing instructions. Multiple transitions may be enabled due to uncertainty in the analysis, e.g. due to statically unknown memory access targets and register values. In such a case, one successor state is generated for every possible transition. During the abstract cycle step, the pipeline models issue memory transactions as dictated by the machine specification. Completion of such transactions is signaled back from the abstract MHE states to the affected pipeline state. Finally, the completion of instructions, known as the *commit* of an instruction, is communicated to our framework via an entry in the instruction completion vector as introduced in Sect. 4.2.

In every cycle step, i.e. every invocation of ξ_Σ, we perform the cycle step independently on each tuple $\sigma \in \Sigma$. The results are then sorted by completion vector and returned to returned to the PEG block analysis (Algorithm 3). Inside the individual σ tuples we use established abstract domains, namely *abstract finite state machines* for pipelines [19], *cache block age maps* for caches [19] and

TDMA offset sets for TDMA busses [5]. For FAIR and PRIO arbitration no suitable abstractions were found in the per-core analysis. Since we explicitly track parallel interleavings in the PEG, we can analyze these protocols for the first time by providing *abstract arbitration functions* as shown in the following.

Arbitration Functions. A simplified version of the bus state is illustrated in Fig. 4, where a PEG block Ψ is shown. The state Σ_{run} for this block (see Algorithm 3) holds two sub-states, of which σ_2 is presented in more detail. In this sub-state the two cores in this example are currently performing a multiplication and an instruction fetch. Bus B1 is a TDMA bus, from its state we know that we currently are either at cycle 0 or 4 in the fixed-length, cyclic TDMA schedule. The state for FAIR-arbitrated buses like B2 holds an overapproximation of the cores which may have last accessed the bus. In the case of B2 this reveals that the last access has definitely been carried out by core 2.

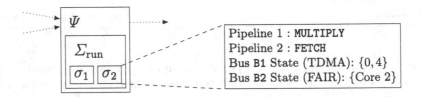

Fig. 4. An example PEG block Ψ with attached APSS Σ_{run}.

With these state definitions we can easily define the abstract arbitration functions which determine possible arbitration winners:

- **TDMA**: All cores whose *grant window* has a non-empty intersection with the current TDMA offsets *may* be granted. If we assume a schedule of length 10 cycles, in which cycles [0–4] are assigned to core 1 (grant window of core 1) and cycles [5–9] are assigned to core 2 (grant window of core 2), then in the state from Fig. 4 a request to B1 would only be granted for core 1.
- **FAIR**: All cores which are the next in the core list for at least one previously accessing core c_p *may* be granted. In Fig. 4 if both cores request access to B2, only the request from core 1 will be granted.
- **PRIO**: All requests with the highest priority *may* be granted. Thus for PRIO we do not need to maintain any kind of state, since the arbitration can be done solely based on the fixed priorities.

Different arbitration outcomes are then distributed to different result tuples σ. Since the PEG already carries the burden of constructing all possible interleaving scenarios, we can formulate the arbitration analysis in a rather simple manner, here. By construction, this has not been possible for the standard per-core WCET analysis approach.

4.5 Correctness

Formally complete proofs cannot be given here due to space constraints, but we try to provide some intuition on why the analysis is correct. In the following, we use G_P^i, λ^i, ω_P^i and δ^i to denote the PEG and the values of the three functions *after* i-th iteration of the main loop of Algorithm 1. Also, we denote the PEG node v that is analyzed in iteration i as v^i. The special iteration number 0 is used to denote the state *before* the first iteration of the main loop. First of all, through the monotonicity of ξ_Σ, we can prove Lemma 1, which states that with rising analysis iteration count, for each $v \in V_P$ the block runtime will only shrink, the incoming APSS will only get more imprecise and the execution time intervals for each task execution position will only become wider.

Lemma 1. *For any iteration j of the main loop of the parallelism analysis (line 7 in Algorithm 1), any iteration $i < j$ and any SEP v, the following invariants hold:*

1. $\forall u \in V_P^i : u \rightsquigarrow_{G_P^i} v \implies u \rightsquigarrow_{G_P^j} v,$
2. $\lambda_{in}^i(v) \sqsubseteq \lambda_{in}^j(v)$ *where* $\lambda_{in}^i(v) = \bigsqcup_{e=(u,v)\in E_P^i} \lambda^i(e),$
3. $\omega_P^i(v) \geq \omega_P^j(v),$ *and*
4. $\forall k \in \{1,\ldots,n\} : \delta^i(v)^{(k)} \sqsubseteq \delta^j(v)^{(k)}.$

For any possible task set execution, which we model as a sequence S of SEPs, we can prove with Lemma 1, that the APSSs attached to the converged PEG are safe over-approximations of the concrete system states with which S is traversed. This yields Theorem 1.

Theorem 1. *The basic block runtimes ω_C as returned by Algorithm 1 are safe over-approximations of the concrete block runtimes in any possible parallel execution scenario.*

5 Analysis Extensions

If the underlying architecture is guaranteed to be free of *timing anomalies* [4], then in each block analysis (Algorithm 3, line 5) we can skip all instruction completion vectors $c \in \kappa$ which are dominated by another vector, i.e. $c_1 \prec_c c_2 \Leftrightarrow \forall i \in \{1,\ldots,n\} : c_2^{(i)} \Rightarrow c_1^{(i)}$. The dominated vectors correspond to an earlier termination of an instruction and since in a timing-anomaly-free architecture every local worst-case action is always also the global worst-case action, we can assume that they are never part of the worst-case path. This can drastically reduce the state space and the PEG size.

In task sets with explicit synchronization points we have to consider these points in the path analysis as shown in [13]. In addition we can also use them to prune the PEG as we have done in Sect. 4, since a task which is waiting for synchronization cannot progress until a partner has arrived to complete the rendez-vous. This idea has already been used in [17] and similar to there, it can be used on top of the timing information to further prune the PEG.

The extension of our framework to task sets with non-uniform periods is also possible. With non-uniform task periods we can still compute the global hyperperiod, i.e. the smallest common multiple of all task periods and build a PEG for this hyperperiod. The problem that we face here is, that with the current framework we cannot determine the absolute point in time at which we are when a task instance has finished executing, since then we can no longer compute the block time window on the basis of the local CFG and a task release time. This means we would have to assume in every successive cycle step, that the next task instance might start or not, which would drastically increase the PEG size. However this can be limited if we take into account synchronization structures or if timing-based approximations of the task instance spawn behavior can be found.

6   Evaluation

We implemented the analysis algorithms inside the WCC compiler framework [2], which was also used in [6]. We ran our evaluations on single-core tasks from the MRTC and DSPStone real-time benchmark suites. Out of these single-core tasks we formed packages of 2 to 4 tasks, all of which were assigned a release time of 0. We analyzed the system topology from Sect. 3 with 2 or 4 cores, depending on the task set. In the evaluation, we focus on analyzing state-permeable bus arbitration methods (PRIO and FAIR) which were not analyzable (PRIO) or not precisely analyzable (FAIR) without the presented parallelism analysis. The bus which is arbitrated by these methods is the shared memory bus introduced in Sect. 3.

In Fig. 5 the results of our block exclusion criterion (BEC) from Algorithm 1, line 14 are shown. Each mark represents one analysis run on one task set. The circle marks indicate runs where the shared bus was configured for FAIR arbitration, the triangles correspond to fixed priority-based arbitration and the squares

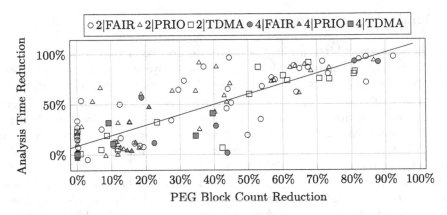

Fig. 5. Efficiency of the block exclusion criterion on example benchmarks for varying number of cores and arbitration policies. The solid line is a linear regression of the data points.

Table 1. Average analysis time and PEG sizes.

Schedule	Analysis	Duration	#PEBs
FAIR	C—N	4s	0
FAIR	P—O—N	1,695s	2,177
FAIR	P—B—N	583s	1,223
FAIR	C—T	6s	0
FAIR	P—O—T	2,065s	9,595
FAIR	P—B—T	801s	7,828
PRIO	P—O—N	1,438s	1,800
PRIO	P—B—N	514s	1,175
PRIO	P—O—T	1,971s	6,971
PRIO	P—B—T	808s	5,118

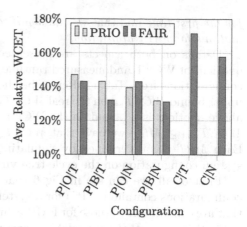

Fig. 6. Relative WCET results.

correspond to TDMA. Non-filled (filled) marks are analysis runs with the 2-core (4-core) system. The x-axis value is the number of PEG blocks that are generated during the analysis, when the BEC is used compared to the case when it is not used (100 %). On the y-axis the required analysis time is shown, also compared to the case that the BEC was not used (100 %). From the data points and the solid regression curve it is visible that the analysis time scales roughly linearly with the number of PEG blocks, which was expected, since the runtime of the main loop in Algorithm 1 depends on the total number of blocks. The variations stem from the convergence behavior of the individual benchmarks, i.e. how often loops have to be visited until the attached APSSs converge. More importantly, we can see from Fig. 5 that the BEC is effective, as on average it rules out 35.6 % of all blocks and leads to a reduction in analysis time of 49.7 %.

The average resulting analysis time is presented in Table 1. The column "Analysis" shows which type of WCET analysis was tested. We compare the classical multi-core WCET analysis [1] (abbr. "C") to our new parallelism analysis with (abbr. "P—B") and without (abbr. "P—O") usage of the block exclusion criterion. As already seen in Fig. 5, "P—B" is always superior to "P—O" but both are slower than the classical approach "C" by a factor of 130 on average. This is a result of the more complex system state and of the thousands of parallel interleavings that have to be explored, whereas the classical analysis only operates on the CFG of a single task and the state of a single core. The last element of the "Analysis" column shows whether the architecture was assumed to have *timing anomalies* (abbr. "T") or not (abbr. "N"). As presented in Sect. 5, this can be used to drastically reduce the PEG size, which is visible in Table 1 in column "#PEBs", which holds the average number of PEG blocks for this analysis scenario. The configurations where absence of timing anomalies was assumed ("N") produce far lower PEG sizes and analysis times than their counterparts ("T").

The benefits we get from the parallelism analysis ("P"-configurations) at the price of increased analysis times are that we can *analyze the PRIO arbitration for the first time* and that we can *significantly reduce the arbitration delay estimations for FAIR arbitration.*

Details on both aspects are presented in Fig. 6, where the average of the quotient of WCET and measured runtime (MRT) is shown for different analysis configurations from Table 1. Remember here, that we can only determine a safe upper bound $WCET_{est}$ on the real $WCET_{real}$ in all of our analyses. Therefore the above quotient is a bound on the WCET overestimation, since by $WCET_{est} \geq WCET_{real} \geq MRT$ we have that $WCET_{est} \div MRT \geq WCET_{est} \div WCET_{real}$. Each MRT was determined by simulating the task set execution for the given system configuration on the cycle-true virtual prototyping IDE CoMET [16].

First of all, we can see in Fig. 6 that the PEG-based WCET analyses (all configurations containing "P") for a system with PRIO arbitration yield results that are comparable to those for FAIR arbitration. The remaining overestimation is mostly due to other unavoidable sources of imprecision, like loose loop bounds and pipeline and value analysis overestimation. Also, we see that the restriction to timing-anomaly free architectures (all configurations with "N") enables not only reduced analysis times (cf. Table 1) but also tighter WCET estimations. The usage of the block exclusion criterion (configurations with "B") also leads to slightly decreased overestimation.

Finally, the "C"-configurations show the overestimation for the classical WCET analysis framework, which can only assume the maximum possible delay for every access in state-permeable arbitration policies. Our new parallelism-based analysis is able to clearly outperform this approach, being 32 % more accurate on average, but of course at the expense of increased analysis times.

7   Conclusions

We have presented a new type of WCET analysis which can precisely bound the runtime of safety-critical tasks running on complex multi-core systems. This is achieved by exploring all possible execution interleavings of a parallel periodic task set. A *parallel execution graph* (PEG) is employed to represent the interleavings in compressed form, a concept that was already used in [17]. What is genuine to the application of the PEG in WCET analysis is firstly that here we must work at the granularity of single machine cycles which drastically increases the graph size. But secondly and more importantly we can also use the timing information that we are generating for *pruning* parts of the graph which we prove to be not reachable in any real execution through the use of a new timing-based *block exclusion criterion.*

We tested this analysis on a prototype implementation. For a shared bus scheduled under a fair round-robin policy we observed WCET reductions of 32 % on average, compared to previous analysis approaches. For fixed priority-based scheduling no previous individual-access analysis methods exist. Here we could derive WCET values with a tightly bounded maximum overestimation of only 30–50 % on average, which is comparable to the single-core WCET overestimation ratio of our analyzer. In the future we plan to explore combinations of the block exclusion criterion and synchronization-aware analysis to further reduce the PEG size and lift the restriction that all tasks must have a uniform period. We also seek to evaluate the performance of the PEG-based analysis for systems with shared caches, for which up to now only pessimistic analyses existed.

Acknowledgments. This work was partially supported by EU COST Action IC1202: Timing Analysis On Code-Level (TACLe). The authors would also like to thank Synopsys for the provision of the virtual prototyping IDE CoMET.

References

1. Chattopadhyay, S., Kee, C., Roychoudhury, A., Kelter, T., Marwedel, P., Falk, H.: A unified WCET analysis framework for multi-core platforms. In: Real-Time and Embedded Technology and Applications Symposium (2012)
2. Falk, H., Lokuciejewski, P.: A compiler framework for the reduction of worst-case execution times. J. Real-Time Syst. **46**(2), 251–300 (2010)
3. Gustavsson, A.: Worst-case execution time analysis of parallel systems. In: Nyström, D., Nolte, T. (eds.) Real Time in Sweden 2011, pp. 104–107. Dag Nyström and Thomas Nolte, Sweden (2011)
4. Hahn, S., Reineke, J., Wilhelm, R.: Towards compositionality in execution time analysis - definition and challenges. In: International Workshop on Compositional Theory and Technology for Real-Time Embedded Systems, December 2013
5. Kelter, T., Falk, H., Marwedel, P., Chattopadhyay, S., Roychoudhury, A.: Bus-aware multicore WCET analysis through TDMA offset bounds. In: Euromicro Conference on Real-Time Systems, pp. 3–12. Porto, Portugal, July 2011
6. Kelter, T., Harde, T., Marwedel, P., Falk, H.: Evaluation of resource arbitration methods for multi-core real-time systems. In: International Workshop on Worst-Case Execution Time Analysis, July 2013
7. Kildall, G.A.: A unified approach to global program optimization. In: Symposium on Principles of Programming Languages, pp. 194–206. ACM, New York (1973)
8. Kleinsorge, J.C., Falk, H., Marwedel, P.: Simple analysis of partial worst-case execution paths on general control flow graphs. In: Proceedings of the International Conference on Embedded Software, pp. 1–10, September 2013
9. Knoop, J., Steffen, B., Vollmer, J.: Parallelism for free: efficient and optimal bitvector analyses for parallel programs. ACM Trans. Program. Lang. Syst. **18**(3), 268–299 (1996)
10. Li, Y., Suhendra, V., Liang, Y., Mitra, T., Roychoudhury, A.: Timing analysis of concurrent programs running on shared cache multi-cores. In: IEEE Real-Time Systems Symposium, pp. 57–67. IEEE Computer Society, Washington (2009)
11. Li, Y.T.S., Malik, S.: Performance analysis of embedded software using implicit path enumeration. In: Proceedings of the Annual ACM/IEEE Design Automation Conference, pp. 456–461. ACM, New York (1995)
12. Mittermayr, R., Blieberger, J.: Timing analysis of concurrent programs. In: International Workshop on Worst-Case Execution Time Analysis, pp. 59–68 (2012)
13. Potop-Butucaru, D., Puaut, I.: Integrated worst-case execution time estimation of multicore applications. In: Maiza, C. (ed.) International Workshop on Worst-Case Execution Time Analysis, pp. 21–31. Dagstuhl, Germany (2013)

14. Schliecker, S., Negrean, M., Nicolescu, G., Paulin, P., Ernst, R.: Reliable performance analysis of a multicore multithreaded system-on-chip. In: International Conference on Hardware/Software Codesign and System Synthesis, pp. 161–166. ACM, New York (2008)
15. Schranzhofer, A., Pellizzoni, R., Chen, J.J., Thiele, L., Caccamo, M.: Worst-case response time analysis of resource access models in multi-core systems. In: Design Automation Conference (2010)
16. Synopsys Inc.: CoMET System Engineering IDE. http://www.synopsys.com
17. Taylor, R.N.: A general-purpose algorithm for analyzing concurrent programs. Commun. ACM **26**(5), 361–376 (1983)
18. Valmari, A.: Eliminating redundant interleavings during concurrent program verification. In: Odijk, E., Rem, M., Syre, J.C. (eds.) Parallel Architectures and Languages Europe. LNCS, vol. 366, pp. 89–103. Springer, Heidelberg (1989)
19. Wilhelm, R., Engblom, J., Ermedahl, A., Holsti, N., Thesing, S., Whalley, D., Bernat, G., Ferdinand, C., Heckmann, R., Mitra, T., Mueller, F., Puaut, I., Puschner, P., Staschulat, J., Stenström, P.: The worst-case execution time problem - overview of methods and survey of tools. ACM Trans. Embed. Comput. Syst. **7**(3), 1–53 (2008)

Key-Secrecy of PACE with OTS/CafeOBJ

Dominik Klein[✉]

Bundesamt für Sicherheit in der Informationstechnik (BSI), Bonn, Germany
dominik.klein@bsi.bund.de

Abstract. The ICAO-standardized Password Authenticated Connection Establishment (PACE) protocol is used all over the world to secure access to electronic passports. Key-secrecy of PACE is proven by first modeling it as an Observational Transition System (OTS) in CafeOBJ, and then proving invariant properties by induction.

1 Introduction

Cryptographic primitives, such as encryption mechanisms, hash functions or message authentication codes, undergo the scrutiny of a large community of researchers. While their mathematical foundations might not yet be understood in full detail, there have been few sudden groundbreaking attacks on them. Using these primitives as building blocks to construct security protocols is, however, another difficult challenge. In fact, despite using well-known cryptographic primitives, erroneous protocol specifications and design decisions have often lead to attacks. A famous example is [16], and the survey [7] contains an impressive list of failed attempts to design secure protocols. Formally proving properties of a protocol to exclude subtle attacks is one important step in the construction of security protocols.

Password Authenticated Connection Establishment (PACE) [4,13] is a cryptographic protocol used all over the world for electronic passports. PACE establishes a secure communication channel between a terminal (trying to access data stored on the passport's RFID chip) and the passport itself. Ensuring trust in PACE is of uttermost importance due to several reasons: First, the predecessor of PACE, called Basic Access Control (BAC), is plagued with security concerns due to low-entropy passwords. Second, the contact-less RFID interface of electronic passports raises concerns of citizens that passports enable secret tracking or that criminals may remotely read out sensitive biometric information. Third, PACE is used in national id-cards that enable secure authentication for e-commerce.

CafeOBJ is an algebraic specification and programming language [8]. After specifying a formal model, e.g. of a cryptographic protocol such as PACE, CafeOBJ can also be used as an interactive theorem prover to show invariant properties of such a specified model: Mathematical proofs are written as *proof scores*, and a proof can be established by *executing* its proof score. This approach is used in this paper.

© Springer International Publishing Switzerland 2015
C. Artho and P.C. Ölveczky (Eds.): FTSCS 2014, CCIS 476, pp. 159–173, 2015.
DOI: 10.1007/978-3-319-17581-2_11

The contribution of this paper is threefold. First, key secrecy of PACE itself is shown, strengthening trust in the protocol. Second, while CafeOBJ has a proven track-record in the verification of security protocols [17–21, 23], the proof serves once more as a case study to show that theorem proving in CafeOBJ scales well beyond simple academic problems to real-world scenarios. Third, to the author's best knowledge, this proof is the first to model a protocol based on a Diffie-Hellman key-exchange in such detail in CafeOBJ. This might serve as a foundation for analyzing other DH-based protocols. The source code of the proof is available at https://github.com/d-klein/ots-proof.

The structure of this paper is as follows: In Sect. 2, the PACE protocol is introduced. A very brief recapitulation of modeling OTSs in CafeOBJ, and proving their invariants is given in Sect. 3. Section 4 provides an abstract version of PACE and shows how to model it as an OTS. The proof of key secrecy of PACE is shown in Sect. 5. Experiences and learned lessons are summarized in Sect. 6, and related work is reviewed in Sect. 7. Finally, concluding remarks are given in Sect. 8.

2 The PACE Key Agreement Protocol

To ensure compatibility with existing document formats and infrastructure, contactless RFID chips were chosen for electronic passports. This introduces two risks that need to be addressed: *Skimming*, i.e. an attacker reading out data from the passport without authorization, and *eavesdropping*, i.e. intercepting communication data during transmission. Note that skimming requires an online connection with the passport, whereas eavesdropped data can be analyzed offline after interception.

To prevent skimming, a terminal accessing data on the passport should prove that it is authorized to access the data. This can be done by e.g. reading information printed on the passport by OCR, and sending this data to the chip. The terminal thus demonstrates that it has physical access to the passport, and a passport holder can control electronic access to his passport by controlling physical access. Printed information on the passport often has low entropy. The machine-readable zone (MRZ) for example can be read by OCR and has 88 digits, but the vast majority of digits are not unique w.r.t. each passport, or can be easily guessed. Just hashing this printed data to directly derive a session key does not prevent sufficiently against offline attacks on eavesdropped transmission data, since the session key is the same for each session, and also has low entropy. Instead, a strong session key unique to each session is required to prevent (offline) analysis of eavesdropped transmission data.

The goal of the PACE key agreement protocol is to establish a secure, authenticated connection with a strong session key between the chip inside a passport and a corresponding terminal. PACE uses a pre-shared low entropy password to derive a strong session key by using a Diffie-Hellman key exchange [9]. The protocol is versatile in the sense that it allows to use either standard multiplicative groups of integers modulo p or groups based on elliptic curves. The latter is important in practice, since RFID chips have limited processing power.

The protocol works as follows: First, it is assumed that a common low entropy password π is known both by the chip and the terminal. Depending on the document type (international travel document, national id-card etc.) and use-case (border control, e-commerce) three solutions exist in practice: (1) The password is derived from the MRZ, (2) The password is derived from a Card Access Number (CAN) specifically printed on the document for this purpose or (3) The password is derived from a secret personal identification number (PIN) known only to the owner of the document. In all cases, the password is stored on the chip in a protected way. To read out data on the chip, the MRZ is optically read by the terminal, or the CAN or the PIN is entered manually.

In the next step, the chip sends both a random nonce s encrypted by a symmetric cipher with the hash $\mathcal{H}$ of π and the domain parameter D_{PICC} for the group operation to the terminal. Using a *mapping function* and the domain parameter, the nonce s is mapped to some generator g of the group $\langle g \rangle$. Both the terminal and the chip chose another nonce x resp. y and compute exponents, i.e. the group operation is applied with the nonce together with the generator to derive g^x resp. g^y. These are then shared, and a key $K = (g^x)^y = (g^y)^x$ and MAC and session-keys are derived. Knowledge of the sent exponents and the key is verified by exchanging MAC-tokens. See Fig. 1 for a brief overview of the protocol. For more detailed specifications, see [4].

3   OTS, CafeOBJ and Invariant-Proving

The PACE protocol is modeled as an Observational Transition System (OTS). For precise definitions and an introduction to OTSs, cf. [19]. Here, only a brief recapitulation on how OTSs are modeled in CafeOBJ is provided in order to give an intuition of the overall proof approach and proof structure. An OTS is a triple of a set of observable values, a set of initial states, and a set of conditional transition rules. A protocol can be modeled as an OTS, where in each state of the protocol, observations on this state can be made. The effect of a state change on the observations is described by transitions. An *invariant* is a property that holds (is observable) in all states reachable from the initial ones.

CafeOBJ is based on equational reasoning. Algebraic data types and operations on them are described by conditional rewrite rules. Rewrite rules are called equations in CafeOBJ, but they are applied directed from left to right. An OTS is modeled in CafeOBJ as follows:

- The state space is modeled as a *hidden sort H*.
- A data type D is described in order-sorted algebra with *visible sort V*.
- An observation is modeled as a CafeOBJ behavioral operator:

```
bop o : H V1 V2 ... VN -> V
```

V1,...,VN and V are visible sorts corresponding to data types $D_1, \ldots D_n$, and H is the hidden sort representing the state space. Intuitively, this equation describes that the observation V can be made in state H, where H is characterized by V1 ... VN.

Passport Chip (PICC)	Terminal (PCD)

shared password π

choose *nonce* $s \leftarrow \mathbb{Z}_q$
static domain parameter D_{PICC}

$z = \mathbf{enc}(\mathcal{H}(\pi), s)$

$$\xrightarrow{\quad D_{\text{PICC}}, z \quad}$$

$$s = \mathbf{dec}(\mathcal{H}(\pi), z)$$
$g = \mathbf{map}(D_{\text{PICC}}, s)$ $g = \mathbf{map}(D_{\text{PICC}}, s)$
choose $x \leftarrow \mathbb{Z}_q^*$ choose $y \leftarrow \mathbb{Z}_q^*$
$h_1 = g^x$ $h_2 = g^y$

$$\xrightarrow{\quad h_1 \quad}$$
$$\xleftarrow{\quad h_2 \quad}$$

abort, if $h_2 \notin \langle g \rangle$ or $h_1 \doteq h_2$ abort, if $h_2 \notin \langle g \rangle$ or $h_2 \doteq h_1$

$K = h_2^x = (g^y)^x$ $K = h_1^y = (g^x)^y$
$K_{\text{MAC}} = \mathcal{H}(K\|1)$ $K_{\text{MAC}} = \mathcal{H}(K\|1)$
$K_{\text{ENC}} = \mathcal{H}(K\|2)$ $K_{\text{ENC}} = \mathcal{H}(K\|2)$
$T_{\text{PICC}} = \mathbf{mac}(K_{\text{MAC}}, h_2)$ $T_{\text{PCD}} = \mathbf{mac}(K_{\text{MAC}}, h_1)$

$$\xrightarrow{\quad T_{\text{PICC}} \quad}$$
$$\xleftarrow{\quad T_{\text{PCD}} \quad}$$

abort, if $T_{\text{PCD}} \neq \mathbf{mac}(K_{\text{MAC}}, h_1)$ abort, if $T_{\text{PICC}} \neq \mathbf{mac}(K_{\text{MAC}}, h_2)$

Fig. 1. The PACE protocol.

- A transition is also modeled as a CafeOBJ behavioral operator:

```
bop t : H V1 V2 ... VM -> H
```

The first argument of t refers to the current state. The operator t — identified by the indices V1 ... VM — maps the current state to another state in the state space. How this transition operator affects the state space in particular, is defined in CafeOBJ with conditional equations of the form:

```
ceq o(t(X,Y1,...,YM),Z1,...,ZN) = changeval(X,Y1,...,YM,Z1,...ZN)
        if effective-condition(X,Y1,...,YM,Z1,...,ZN) .
```

```
ceq t(X,Y1,...,YM) = X
        if not effective-condition(X,Y1,...,YM,Z1,...,ZN) .
```

Here changeval is the operation that changes values of the observation to the ones of the successor state, and effective-condition evaluates whether the condition to apply the transition is met in the current state. If the observed values never change when applying the transition, one can combine the above simply to: eq o(t(X,Y1,...,YM),Z1,...,ZN) = o(X,Y1,...,YM).

CafeOBJ uses proof scores to prove invariants that hold in a model that is specified as described above. Proof scores define the proof obligations and induction hypothesis needed to proof invariants by induction.

Proof Scores. A proof score of an invariant consists of two parts: First, the induction hypothesis w.r.t. the predicate in the initial state is shown. Then the induction step follows. For each invariant $\text{pred}_i(s, \mathbf{x})$ a corresponding operator and an equation is defined:

```
op invI : H V1 V2 ... VN -> Bool .
eq invI(S,X1,...,XN) = ... .
```

In the definitions of visible sorts in the specification, also a constant `init` is defined, denoting an arbitrary initial state. Then to prove $\text{pred}_i(s, \mathbf{x})$, one fixes arbitrary objects v1,...,vN for the visible sorts V1,...,VN and issues a reduce command w.r.t. the initial state: `red invI(init,v1,...,vN)`.

For the induction step one has to show that if $\text{pred}_i(s, \mathbf{x})$ holds in state s, then it also holds in any possible next state s'. For each predicate one fixes arbitrary states s and s' by `ops s,s' : -> H`, defines an operator of form `op istepI : V1 V2 ... VN -> Bool` and an equation for the induction step:

```
eq istepI(X1,X2,...,XN) = invI(s,X1,,...,XN) implies invI(s',X1,...,XN).
```

Then one fixes arbitrary objects v1,...,vN for the visible sorts, defines how s' results from s by a transition t by `eq s' = t(s,...) .`, and issue a reduce command `red istepI(v1,...,vN)`. The reduce command uses the equations to obtain the equational normal form of an expression. If both for the initial state and the induction step rewriting to normal form reaches the constant `true`, the proof w.r.t. to transition t has succeeded. For a full proof, all defined transitions have to be considered.

Lemmata. Quite often the induction step cannot be shown directly, since the induction hypothesis is too weak. Then a lemma is needed. Let `invJ` be a predicate with free variables of visible sorts E1,...,EK, and let e1,...,eK denote either free variables of, or expressions (i.e. terms) of these sorts. One can strengthen the induction hypothesis by augmenting `invJ` in state s, i.e. by issuing `red invJ(s,e1,...eK) implies istepI(v1,...,vN)`. One advantage in OTS/CafeOBJ is that one can use `invJ` to strengthen the induction step in the proof of `invI` and vice-versa.

Case Analysis. Another proof technique is case analysis. Suppose for example that v1 is assumed to be of arbitrary form. For a constructor f, we can then distinguish the case that either v1 is constructed by f applied to some arbitrary vC, or that this is not the case. Then the induction step is split: One declares v1 = f(vC), and reduces `red istepI(v1,...)`. Then one does the same again, but declares (v1 = f(vC)) = `false` before reducing. Clearly all possible cases have been exhaustively considered, since it is always true that:

```
(v1 = f(vC)) or (not (v1 = f(vC)))
```

Of course it is possible to strengthen the induction hypothesis by more than one predicate, and to combine lemma application with case analysis.

4   Modeling PACE in CafeOBJ

The system is modeled in a way such that an unbounded number of principals interact with each other by sending messages. Honest principals behave according to protocol. Malicious ones can fake and forge messages. The malicious principals are modeled as the most general intruder according to the Dolev-Yao intruder model [10]. Moreover the following assumption are made:

1. Cryptographic primitives are sound. Random nonces are unique and cannot be guessed, encrypted messages can only be decoded by knowing the correct key, hashes are one-way and there are no collisions, and two message authentication codes are the same only if generated from the same message with the same key.
2. The intruder can glean any public information (i.e. messages, ciphers etc.) that is sent in the network.
3. The intruder can send two kinds of messages: He can use ciphers based on cryptographic primitives from existing messages as black boxes to send new fake messages, or he can use eavesdropped information to generate new messages from scratch. But, as noted above, he cannot eavesdrop information from ciphers based on cryptographic primitives without knowing the corresponding keys or passwords.

4.1   An Abstract Version of PACE

To abstract away from implementation-dependent information and those that cannot be captured in the Dolev-Yao model anyway, the following abstract version of the PACE protocol is used.

$$
\begin{aligned}
&\text{Message 1}: &&p \rightarrow q: &&\mathbf{enc}_\pi(n_s, D) \\
&\text{Message 2}: &&p \rightarrow q: &&*(n_a, G) \\
&\text{Message 3}: &&q \rightarrow p: &&*(n_b, G) \\
&\text{Message 4}: &&p \rightarrow q: &&\mathbf{mac}(\mathcal{H}(*(n_a, *(n_b, G))), *(n_b, G), D) \\
&\text{Message 5}: &&q \rightarrow p: &&\mathbf{mac}(\mathcal{H}(*(n_b, *(n_a, G))), *(n_a, G), D)
\end{aligned}
$$

It is assumed that a run of PACE is conducted by exchanging five messages. In the first step, a message is sent from a principal p to another one q. The message encrypts a random nonce n_s with the shared password π, with attached static domain parameters D. Next, p maps the nonce n_s from the first message with the domain parameters to a group generator G. Then p chooses a random nonce n_a, applies the operator $*$ to both n_a and G and sends the result $*(n_a, G)$ to q. In a similar manner, q chooses a random nonce n_b and sends $*(n_b, G)$ to p. Next, p computes the key $\mathcal{H}(*(n_a, *(n_b, G)))$. He then sends a message authentication code — encoded with that key — with the received exponent $*(n_b, G)$ and domain parameters D to q, in order to verify knowledge of both the received exponent and the generated key. Principal q does the same in reverse, and the common key $\mathcal{H}(*(n_a, *(n_b, G)))$ is used from now on to exchange encrypted messages.

4.2   Basic Data Types

The following algebraic data types, i.e. visible sorts and corresponding constructors are used:

- `Principal` denotes both honest and malicious principals in the network.
- `Random` denotes random nonces. Random nonces are supposed to be unique and unguessable.
- `Dompar` denotes the static domain parameters of PACE. Used domain parameters are not secret and known to every principal.
- `Mappoint` denotes a group generator. The constructor `maptopoint` of data type `Mappoint` takes as input a random nonce and static domain parameters and returns a group generator. It is supposed that `maptopoint` is a one-way function.
- `Expo` denotes an exponent of the form g^x, where the group generator g is generated by `maptopoint` using a random nonce and domain parameters as input.
- `Hash` denotes keys — it is supposed that hashing is the key derivation function. The constructor `hash` takes as input a random nonce and an exponent and returns a key.
- `Cipher1` denotes the cipher resulting from a symmetric encryption. Its constructor `enc` takes as input a random nonce and static domain parameters. It is implicitly assumed that a `Cipher1` is encoded with the shared password π in the following way: Given a `Cipher1`, every principal is able reconstruct the static domain parameters. But only if he knows the shared password π, he is able to decode the random nonce.
- `Cipher3` denotes message authentication codes. The constructor `mac` takes as input a hash, an exponent and domain parameters.

Three sorts and data types are defined for the messages in Sect. 4: Message 1 of Sect. 4 is of type `Message1`, messages 2 and 3 are of type `Message2`, and messages 4 and 5 are of type `Message3`. Here, `Message1` is a `Cipher1` attached with meta-information describing the creator, the (seemingly) sender, and the receiver of a message. For example

    me1(intruder,p,q,c)

denotes a `Message1` where c is a `Cipher1`, and the message is (seemingly) sent from principal p to q, but was actually created by the intruder, i.e. faked and injected in the network. Similar, a `Message3` is a `Cipher3` attached with corresponding meta-information. The data type `Message2` is constructed by attaching meta-information to an exponent. Moreover for the definition of the data structures two design decisions — cf. also Sect. 6 — should be noticed:

Modeling of the Shared Password π. PACE assumes a fixed shared password π known among honest principals. Knowledge of the password is modeled by a predicate `knowspi` where `knowspi(intruder) = false` is set. No specific data type is introduced for decryption of messages of type 1, instead it is just distinguished between messages that are created by an honest principal who does know π and the intruder, who does not.

Equality of Hashes. The equality operator $\_=\_$ for hashes is defined as

```
eq (H1 = H2) = (rand(H1) = rand(H2) and expo(H1) = expo(H2))
   or        (     rand(H1) = rand(expo(H2))
          and rand(H2) = rand(expo(H1))
          and point(expo(H1)) = point(expo(H2))) .
```

i.e. that $\mathcal{H}(*(n_a, *(n_b, G_1))) = \mathcal{H}(*(n_c, *(n_d, G_2)))$ if $G_1 = G_2$, $n_a = n_c$, $n_b = n_d$, or $G_1 = G_2$, $n_a = n_d$, $n_b = n_c$. This captures the equality of the keys generated during the key exchange.

4.3   Protocol Modeling

In order to collect all sent messages, all generated random nonces, and other information, the following definition of a *multiset* on an abstract level from [19] is reused. This definition is then later used as a parametrized module to define multisets containing the data-types defined in the previous section.

```
mod* SOUP (D :: EQTRIV) principal-sort Soup {
   [Elt.D < Soup]
   op empty : -> Soup {constr}
   op _ _ : Soup Soup -> Soup {constr assoc comm id: empty}
   op _\in_ : Elt.D Soup -> Bool
   var S : Soup
   vars E1 E2 : Elt.D
   eq E1 \in empty = false .
   eq E1 \in (E2 S) = (E1 = E2) or E1 \in S .
}
```

The operator \in defines membership in the multiset, and a space defines insertion. To collect all random nonces for example, one can define an observation bop rands : System -> RandSoup that takes as input a state, and returns as the observation a soup of random nonces. Given a random nonce r and a state s, one can test membership by r \in rands(s), and — for example describing the effects of a transition — insert r in the multiset by r rands(s). Observations and transitions are defined as follows:

```
-- observations
bop network  : System -> Network
bop rands    : System -> RandSoup
bop hashes   : System -> HashSoup
bop randsi   : System -> RandSoup
bop expos    : System -> ExpoSoup
bop cipher1s : System -> Cipher1Soup
```

```
bop cipher3s : System -> Cipher3Soup
-- transitions
bop sdm1  : System Principal Principal Random Dompar            -> System
bop sdm2  : System Principal Principal Random Message1          -> System
bop sdm3  : System Principal Principal Message1 Message2 Message2
                                                                -> System
-- faking and forging messages based on the gleaned info
bop fkm11 : System Principal Principal Cipher1                  -> System
bop fkm12 : System Principal Principal Random Dompar            -> System
bop fkm21 : System Principal Principal Expo                     -> System
bop fkm22 : System Principal Principal Random Random Dompar     -> System
bop fkm31 : System Principal Principal Cipher3                  -> System
bop fkm32 : System Principal Principal Random Expo Expo Dompar  -> System
```

Seven observers are used to collect information:

- **network** returns a multiset of *all* messages that have been sent so far.
- **rands** returns a multiset containing *all* random nonces that have been generated so far.
- **hashes** returns all *keys* resulting from the PACE protocol that have been gleaned or self-generated by the *intruder*. The name stems from the fact that one considers **hash** to be the key derivation function.
- **randsi** contains all *random nonces* gleaned or self-generated by the *intruder*.
- **expos** contains all exponents that have been inserted in the network and
- **cipher1s** and **cipher3s** collect *all* ciphertexts of messages of type 1 and messages of type 3 (i.e. mac-tokens).

The transitions **sdm1**, **sdm2**, and **sdm3** describe state transitions and their effects on observations when an honest principal sends a message of type 1, 2 or 3. Therefore the conditions on when these transitions are effective, capture precisely the behavior of an honest principal. For example **sdm1** is defined as:

```
eq c-sdm1(S,P,Q,R,D) = not(R \in rands(S)) .
ceq network(sdm1(S,P,Q,R,D))  = me1(P,P,Q,enc(R,D)) network(S)
     if c-sdm1(S,P,Q,R,D) .
```

Thus an honest principal p can add a message me1(P,P,Q,enc(R,D)) in state S — in message protocol notation $p \rightarrow q : \mathbf{enc}_\pi(R, D)$ — only to the network if the nonce R is fresh. Freshness means that R is not contained in the set of all nonces that have been generated before reaching state S. This freshness condition is modeled by the first equation.

The transitions **fkmXY** describe state transitions and their effects on observations when the intruder generates messages. Here one distinguishes two cases: (1) The intruder fakes an existing message by changing its source and destination (**fkmX1**) and (2) The intruder injects a new message in the network using information available to him (**fkmX2**). Therefore the effective conditions for these transitions are usually more lax than the ones for **sdmX**. For example the condition to fake a message of type 1

```
eq c-fkm11(S,P,Q,C1) = C1 \in cipher1s(S) .
```

is just that a cipher1 exists in the network. The intruder can then inject the message `me1(intruder,P,Q,C1)` with arbitrary source P and destination Q. Note that the meta information denoting the creator of the message cannot be altered by the intruder.

An example for the second case is the condition to construct an arbitrary new message of type 1

```
eq c-fkm12(S,P,Q,R,D) = (not (R \in rands(S))) or (R \in randsi(S)) .
```

Here the intruder can choose to either use a fresh random nonce, or one that he has gleaned or generated in an earlier state. He then injects the message `me1(intruder,P,Q,enc(R,D))` into the network.

5 Proving Key-Secrecy

Key secrecy is shown in the following sense: Suppose that one takes the perspective of an honest principal, i.e. one is either the passport or the terminal, and one behaves according to protocol. In particular it is assumed that

1. One has either sent a **Message1** with a nonce encrypted with the shared password π and domain parameters (passport) *or* one has received a **Message1** from a principal who knows π and decrypted it (terminal) and
2. One constructed a generator of the group with the nonce and the domain parameters from the above message, used the generator together with a fresh nonce to create an exponent, and sent it to the other party and
3. One *seemingly* (it is unknown who created the message) received an exponent back from that other party and
4. One *seemingly* received a MAC-token that, using ones secret nonce together with the received exponent as a key, validates that the other party knows ones sent exponent and the domain parameters.

Then the resulting key must *never* be known to the intruder. This can be almost verbatim translated into the next main theorem:

```
eq inv900(S,M1,M21,M22,M3,P,Q) =
  (M1 \in network(S) and M21 \in network(S)
   and M22 \in network(S) and M3 \in network(S)
   and sender(M3) = Q and receiver(M3) = P
   and creator(M21) = P and sender(M21) = P and receiver(M21) = Q
   and sender(M22) = Q and receiver(M22) = P
   and (not (creator(M21) = creator(M3)))
   and (not (P = Q)) and knowspi(P)
   and ((sender(M1) = P and creator(M1) = P and receiver(M1) = Q) or
        (sender(M1) = Q and receiver(M1) = P and knowspi(creator(M1))))
   and expo(M21) = expo(cipher3(M3))
   and dpar(cipher1(M1)) = dpar(point(expo(M21)))
   and rand(cipher1(M1)) = rand(point(expo(M21)))
   and dpar(cipher1(M1)) = dpar(cipher3(M3))
   and hash(cipher3(M3)) = hash(rand(expo(M21)),expo(M22)))
  implies
    not (hash(cipher3(M3)) \in hashes(S)) .
```

Application of Lemmata and Case Analysis. To prove key secrecy one needs additional invariants. Central to strengthening the induction hypothesis for `istep900` is the invariant that the assumptions of `inv900` imply that both principals have implicitly agreed upon the same generator g, which itself depends on the nonce exchanged in the first message. For brevity suppose that `assump(S,M1,M21,M22,P,Q)` is a predicate that denotes truth of the assumptions of invariant `inv900` above. The invariant can then be expressed as:

```
eq inv800(S,M1,M21,M22,M3,P,Q) = assump(S,M1,M21,M22,P,Q)
   implies rand(point(expo(M22))) = rand(point(expo(M21))) .
```

How such a lemma is used in the proof together with case analysis is illustrated, albeit for a simpler invariant. Frequent use of the following invariant as a lemma for others is made. It states that if one is in a state S, and a M1 of type `Message1` is in the network, then the random nonce of M1 has been used and is thus included in the collection of all random nonces `rands(S)`.

```
eq inv300(S,M1) = M1 \in network(S)
                  implies rand(cipher1(M1)) \in rands(S) .
```

`inv300` is proven inductively on the number of transitions. In the case of transition `fkm11` one performs case analysis w.r.t. its effective condition:

```
(c-fkm11(s,p10,q10,c11) = false) or (c-fkm11(s,p10,q10,c11) = true)
```

Here p10 and q10 denote arbitrary principals, and c11 denotes an arbitrary `cipher1`. For the first case, the proof directly succeeds:

```
open ISTEP
  ops p10 q10 : -> Principal .
  op m10 : -> Message1 .
  op c11 : -> Cipher1 .
  eq c-fkm11(s,p10,q10,c10) = false .
  eq s' = fkm11(s,p10,q10,r10,d10) .
  red istep300(m10) .
close
```

For the second case `c-fkm11(s,p10,q10,c11) = true`, one replaces the term with its definition `c11 \in cipher1s(s) = true` and performs another case analysis w.r.t. the equality `m10 = me1(intruder,p10,q10,c11)`.

```
open ISTEP
  ops p10 q10 : -> Principal .
  ops m10 : -> Message1 .
  op c11 : -> Cipher1 .
  eq c11 \in cipher1s(s) = true .
  eq m10 = me1(intruder,p10,q10,c11) .
  eq s' = fkm11(s,p10,q10,c11) .
***
close
```

If one directly tries to prove the induction step by reducing `red istep300(m10)` inserted at ***, CafeOBJ outputs

```
rand(c11) \in rands(s) xor
  me1(intruder,p10,q10,c11) \in network(s) xor ...
```

This indicates that if `me1(intruder,p10,q10,c11)` is not already included in and thus inserted in the network as a result of the transition `fkm11`, then `rand(c11) \in rands(s)` must be true for the induction step to hold. Therefore the induction hypothesis needs to be strengthened. One does so by introducing yet another invariant `inv150`, which states that if a `cipher1` is in the network, than its random nonce is included in the set of all used random nonces.

```
eq inv150(S,C1) = C1 \in cipher1s(S) implies rand(C1) \in rands(S) .
```

And indeed, applying `inv150` as a lemma at *** by inserting

```
red inv150(s,c11) implies istep300(m10)
```

successfully finishes the induction step. Therefore it has been verified that if a `Cipher1` exists, i.e. is included in the set of collected ciphers observable in state S in the network, then the random nonce of that cipher must be included in the set of collected nonces observable in that state.

6 Experience and Lessons Learned

From the experience of applying OTS/CafeOBJ to a rather large real-world example, three guidelines are formulated:

1. *Refine your specification.* When stuck in a proof attempt, it is worthwhile to reconsider the specification. Take for example the definition of equality of hashes. Initially equality was defined for two ciphers3's C1 and C2 intuitively as

   ```
   eq (C1 = C2) = (hash(C1) = hash(C2) and expo(C1) = expo(C2)
               and dpar(C1) = dpar(C2)).
   ```

   This has the awkward consequence that messages can no longer uniquely be identified: When a principal sends a message of type 3, implicitly *two* messages are added to the network, one w.r.t. each case of equality of the hash of the cipher. Then for example an invariant like

   ```
   m3 \in network(s) implies cipher3(m3) \in cipher3s(s)
   ```

   does not hold if we have `cipher3(m3) = mac(hash(r2,expo(r1,...)),...)` and `mac(hash(r1,expo(r2,...)),...) \in cipher3s(s)`. This makes reasoning during the induction steps quite unintuitive and led to defining equality of cipher3's as syntactic equality of normals forms, and formulating theorems accordingly when referring to multiple cipher3's with the same hash.

2. *Simplify your specification.* Trying to specify every detail naturally gives a proof that is most faithful to the real protocol. It however also leads to more involved proofs and case-analysis. For example, we purposely decided not to fully model the symmetric cipher used to encrypt the shared password π, but rather to model knowledge of π with a predicate.

3. *A deductive proof approach.* It is very simple in CafeOBJ to quickly add a lemma without proving it. Some invariants, like `inv900` in the current case, are quite involved, and it is likely that one encounters problems with the specification during the proof, and refines or simplifies the specification thereafter. This often also affects helper lemmata. It it thus very useful to focus on the proof of a complex invariant, thereby using several simpler, unproven lemmata, and only afterwards focus on the proof of the latter.

The main hindrance when conducting the proof is related to performance. Suppose one is proving an invariant of the form $a_1 \wedge a_2 \ldots \wedge a_n \implies b$, such as `inv900`. A direct proof attempt often does not terminate, due to the amount of branching. To get a terminating result, one can make a trivial case analysis w.r.t. a_i, e.g. distinguish the case for $\neg a_1$, for $a_1 \wedge \neg a_2$, and so on, to finally reach the case for $a_1 \wedge \ldots \wedge a_n$. Even then sometimes a proof attempt does not terminate, so additional assumptions and corresponding cases have to be added. Almost all cases are trivial – it is obvious that in the case with the assumption $\neg a_1$ the above invariant holds – but lead to a blow up of the size of the proofs. For example, our proof score consists of 38427 lines, of which the vast majority are for such trivial cases. Fortunately, the majority of these cases could be generated automatically by scripts. Nevertheless, tools that tie more directly with CafeOBJ, or come distributed with it, would be certainly helpful for an easier work-flow and increased productivity.

All in all, 40 invariants of the formalization of PACE were proven. The verification of all invariants together takes approximately two hours and eight minutes on an Intel Core i7-3520M @ 2.9 Ghz.

7   Related Work

Security Analysis of PACE. An inductive verification [5] of the PACE protocol has been conducted in the verification support environment (VSE) [14]. VSE has been developed in the 1990's by a consortium of German universities and industry to provide a tool to meet industry needs for the development of highly trustworthy systems. Since the proof source is not publicly published and the VSE tool and documentation is not available for download, a comparison is difficult. An independent verification of the proof however is important to ensure trust in the protocol, not only for users, but also for work in international standardization bodies. A pen-and-paper proof for security in the sense of Abdalla, Fouque and Pointcheval [1] has been given in [2]. In [6] attempts are made to merge the pen-and-paper proof with the VSE-proof.

Formal Analysis of Security Protocols. According to [4], the execution of the protocol, and thus the state space, is not bounded. An approach based on model-checking seems therefore not appropriate. Other than (classical) model-checking, a plethora of tools and approaches exist to formally analyze security protocols, and the reader is referred to [3] for a comprehensive overview. Compared to other tools, the choice of CafeOBJ was motivated rather from the perspective of a practitioner, and not necessarily due to other tools lacking features. In particular the OTS/CafeOBJ approach is well documented, has a proven track record w.r.t. security protocol verification [17–21,23], the CafeOBJ platform is very stable, and modeling of protocols is straight-forward. Also, it is not difficult to start with an abstract specification, and then add details and extend proofs later on.

The lack of automation in OTS/CafeOBJ is a double-edged sword. On one hand no hidden limitations exist, whereas most tools that aim for full automation make some assumptions to e.g. reduce the state space. It is sometimes not easy to anticipate in advance which of these limitations apply for the protocol one intends to prove. Moreover the manual approach forces oneself to recapitulate on the formalization and its appropriateness of capturing the protocol in question. On the other hand, the lack of automation is sometimes not time-effective and somewhat tedious. Constructing tools that not only offer a high level of automation, but also fully axiomatize Abelian group-theory to account for more in-depth algebraic attacks is an ongoing research-topic, with several tools, e.g. the Tamarin tool [24], which is based on multiset rewriting, or an extended version of ProVerif [15]. Maude, another member of the OBJ family, has been used for formal analysis of security protocols [22], and in particular the Maude-NPA [11] tool offers a narrowing based approach for Diffie-Hellman. Last, automation of the OTS/CafeOBJ approach itself has also recently been increased significantly [12].

All these approaches are natural candidates when extending the proof, e.g. by adding detail to the specification w.r.t. mapping a point and domain parameters to a group generator, or when extending to the protocol sequence to the full protocol sequence for extended access control

8   Conclusion and Future Work

Key secrecy has been successfully verified in CafeOBJ. This not only facilitates trust in the PACE protocol, but also represents one more case-study that shows that the OTS/CafeOBJ approach scales well beyond toy-examples like NS(L)PK to real-world scenarios. Also, the PACE proof can serve as a guide on how to model a DH-key exchange in CafeOBJ. Key-Secrecy however, is only one important property of PACE. Future directions include to extend the proof to mutual authentication, perfect forward secrecy, and the full EAC2 protocol stack, possibly with the help of the automated tools mentioned in Sect. 7.

References

1. Abdalla, M., Fouque, P.-A., Pointcheval, D.: Password-based authenticated key exchange in the three-party setting. In: Vaudenay, S. (ed.) PKC 2005. LNCS, vol. 3386, pp. 65–84. Springer, Heidelberg (2005)
2. Bender, J., Fischlin, M., Kügler, D.: Security analysis of the PACE key-agreement protocol. In: Samarati, P., Yung, M., Martinelli, F., Ardagna, C.A. (eds.) ISC 2009. LNCS, vol. 5735, pp. 33–48. Springer, Heidelberg (2009)

3. Blanchet, B.: Security protocol verification: symbolic and computational models. In: Degano, P., Guttman, J.D. (eds.) POST 2012. LNCS, vol. 7215, pp. 3–29. Springer, Heidelberg (2012)
4. BSI: Advanced security mechanisms for machine readable travel documents (2012)
5. Cheikhrouhou, L., Stephan, W.: Meilensteinreport: inductive verification of PACE. Technical report, DFKI GmbH (2010)
6. Cheikhrouhou, L., Stephan, W., Dagdelen, Ö., Fischlin, M., Ullmann, M.: Merging the cryptographic security analysis and the algebraic-logic security proof of PACE. Sicherheit. LNI, vol. 195, 83–94 (2012)
7. Clark, J., Jacob, J.: A survey of authentication protocol literature (1997)
8. Diaconescu, R., Futatsugi, K.: CafeOBJ Report: The Language, Proof Techniques and Methodologies for Object-oriented Algebraic Specification. AMAST Series in Computing, vol. 6. World Scientific, Singapore (1998)
9. Diffie, W., Hellman, M.E.: New directions in cryptography. IEEE Trans. Inf. Theory **22**(6), 644–654 (1976)
10. Dolev, D., Yao, A.C.C.: On the security of public key protocols. IEEE Trans. Inf. Theory **29**(2), 198–208 (1983)
11. Escobar, S., Meadows, C., Meseguer, J.: Maude-NPA: Cryptographic protocol analysis modulo equational properties. In: Aldini, A., Barthe, G., Gorrieri, R. (eds.) FOSAD 2007. LNCS, vol. 5705, pp. 1–50. Springer, Heidelberg (2009)
12. Găină, D., Zhang, M., Chiba, Y., Arimoto, Y.: Constructor-based inductive theorem prover. In: Heckel, R., Milius, S. (eds.) CALCO 2013. LNCS, vol. 8089, pp. 328–333. Springer, Heidelberg (2013)
13. ICAO: Doc 9303 - Machine readable travel documents
14. Koch, F.A., Ullmann, M., Wittmann, S.: Verification support environment. In: Alur, R., Henzinger, T.A. (eds.) CAV 1996. LNCS, vol. 1102, pp. 454–457. Springer, Heidelberg (1996)
15. Küsters, R., Truderung, T.: Using proverif to analyze protocols with Diffie-Hellman exponentiation. In: proceedings of the 22nd CSF (2009)
16. Lowe, G.: An attack on the needham-schroeder public-key authentication protocol. Inf. Process. Lett. **56**(3), 131–133 (1995)
17. Ogata, K., Futatsugi, K.: Rewriting-based verification of authentication protocols. Electron. Notes Theor. Comput. Sci. **71**, 208–222 (2002)
18. Ogata, K., Futatsugi, K.: Flaw and modification of the iKP electronic payment protocols. Inf. Process. Lett. **86**(2), 57–62 (2003)
19. Ogata, K., Futatsugi, K.: Proof scores in the OTS/cafeOBJ method. In: Najm, E., Nestmann, U., Stevens, P. (eds.) FMOODS 2003. LNCS, vol. 2884, pp. 170–184. Springer, Heidelberg (2003)
20. Ogata, K., Futatsugi, K.: Equational approach to formal analysis of TLS. In: Proceedings of the 25th ICDCS. IEEE Computer Society (2005)
21. Ogata, K., Futatsugi, K.: Proof score approach to analysis of electronic commerce protocols. Int. J. Softw. Eng. Knowl. Eng. **20**(2), 253–287 (2010)
22. Ölveczky, P.C., Grimeland, M.: Formal analysis of time-dependent cryptographic protocols in real-time maude. In: Proceedings of the 21st IPDPS (2007)
23. Ouranos, I., Ogata, K., Stefaneas, P.: Formal analysis of tesla protocol in the timed OTS/cafeOBJ method. In: Margaria, T., Steffen, B. (eds.) ISoLA 2012, Part II. LNCS, vol. 7610, pp. 126–142. Springer, Heidelberg (2012)
24. Schmidt, B., Meier, S., Cremers, C.J.F., Basin, D.A.: Automated analysis of Diffie-Hellman protocols and advanced security properties. In: Proceedings of the 25th CSF (2012)

Coalgebraic Semantic Model for the Clock Constraint Specification Language

Frédéric Mallet[1,2,3](✉) and Grygoriy Zholtkevych[4]

[1] University Nice Sophia Antipolis, CNRS, I3S, UMR 7271,
Sophia Antipolis, France
[2] INRIA Sophia Antipolis Méditerranée, Sophia Antipolis, France
[3] East China Normal University/Software Engineering Institute,
Shanghai, People's Republic of China
Frederic.Mallet@unice.fr
[4] Deparment of Theory and Application in Computerscience,
V.N. Karazin Kharkiv National University, Kharkiv, Ukraine

Abstract. The Clock Constraint Specification Language (CCSL) has initially been introduced as part of the UML Profile for MARTE dedicated to the modeling and analysis of real-time and embedded systems. CCSL proposes a set of simple patterns classically used to specify causal and temporal properties of (UML/EMF) models. The paper proposes a new semantic model for CCSL based on the notion of "clock coalgebra". Coalgebra promises to give a unified framework to study the behavior and semantics of reactive systems and, more generally, infinite data structures. They appear as being the adequate mathematical structure to capture the infinite nature of CCSL operators. This paper proposes a coalgebraic structure for CCSL, or rather a *natural* generalization of CCSL that we call *generalized* clock constraints: GenCCSL. We establish that GenCCSL covers the class of CCSL constraints and we give examples of GenCCSL constraints that cannot be expressed with *classical* CCSL. Then, we discuss the properties of the newly introduced class, including ways to detect valid and invalid GenCCSL behaviors, as well as deciding whether a GenCCSL constraint is also a CCSL one.

Keywords: Concurrent system · Behavior model · Clock model · Transition system · Coalgebra

1 Introduction

The UML profile for MARTE (Modeling and Analysis of Real-Time Embedded systems) [13] is dedicated to the modeling and analysis of real-time and embedded systems. Its time model [3] builds on the notion of *logical clock* that was concurrently made popular in distributed systems [8] and in synchronous languages [4]. Logical clocks offer a good abstraction to describe causal relationships between the occurrences of events in a distributed systems, but also synchronization constraints in synchronous (software or circuit) implementations. MARTE

C. Artho and P.C. Ölveczky (Eds.): FTSCS 2014, CCIS 476, pp. 174–188, 2015.
DOI: 10.1007/978-3-319-17581-2_12

offers a stereotype to identify clocks and then promotes the use of the Clock Constraint Specification Language (Annex C.3) as a concrete syntax to handle and constrain those clocks. An operational semantics of CCSL has been defined separately [1] as a basis for building a simulator, called TimeSquare [6]. Later, a denotational semantics was defined [9] in a bid to provide some exhaustive verification support for CCSL. The equivalence of these two semantics has also been proven [17]. CCSL operational semantics is inspired by the approach proposed by G. Plotkin for defining the operational semantics of software systems [14]. The theory of *universal coalgebra* [15] proposes another mathematical model to study the semantics of reactive systems and, more generally, of infinite data structures. It appears as being well fitted to deal with the infinite nature of CCSL operators.

This paper proposes a co-algebraic semantic model to reason on CCSL constraints. This opens the path to the use of co-algebraic bisimulation. It is used here to identify a lack of expressiveness in CCSL and define an extension, called GenCCSL.

We proceed by associating a coalgebra with each CCSL clock constraint. This is useful to identify valid schedules with tracks in the corresponding coalgebra. Such an identification embeds the class of clock constraints into a wider class of constraints, GenCCSL. The principal problem in this context is to understand whether this embedding is bijective or not. Showing that this embedding is not bijective leads us to conclude that CCSL is incomplete. We then discuss the properties of the constraints characterized by the generalized class, GenCCSL.

The remainder of the paper is as follows. Section 2 introduces the vocabulary, the syntax and the semantics of the considered CCSL constraints as well as the notion of coalgebra. Section 3 proposes our clock coalgebra. Section 4 presents the notion of stationary clock constraint and stresses the incompleteness of CCSL with regards to the proposed coalgebra. Section 5 discusses related works and sources of inspiration. Section 6 concludes and summarizes the main results.

2   Preliminaries

In this section we remind the notation and definitions of the key terms used.

A (logical) *clock* denotes a repetitive event of relevance for the system under consideration and its sequence of occurrences. For instance, if you consider a train system. A clock can be any command from the driver to control systems (brake pressed, power on...) or an event occurring (door opening, urgency brake requested...). If you rather consider a computer architecture, clocks can represent the processor clock, but also any kinds of requests on buses, fetch operations, interrupts...). We do not assume a regular rhythm in the occurrences (interrupt) but we do not preclude it (processor clock). The occurrences of the events, *i.e.,* the clocks, are also called its ticks. When the clock ticks, the event occurs. We do not need here any specific property on the clocks and therefore we do not give a formal definition. In the following, we consider that we operate on a set of clocks, $\mathcal{C}$.

2.1 Clock Constraints: Syntax

Syntactically a clock constraint is a finite set of primitive clock constraints, which are classified as clock relations and clock definitions.

There are four kinds of clock relations: `subclocking`, `exclusion`, `causality`, and `precedence`. All these relations are binary relations over clocks. The following notation is used to denote these relations between clocks $a \in C$ and $b \in C$:

$$a \boxed{\subseteq} b \qquad \text{denotes that clock } a \text{ is a subclock of clock } b,$$

$$a \boxed{\#} b \qquad \text{denotes that clock } a \text{ and } b \text{ are mutually exclusive},$$

$$a \boxed{\preccurlyeq} b \qquad \text{denotes that clock } a \text{ causes clock } b, \text{ and}$$

$$a \boxed{\prec} b \qquad \text{denotes that clock } a \text{ precedes clock } b.$$

Intuitively, the first two relations are synchronous constraints. `Subclock` allows a (sub)clock to tick only when its master (super)clock ticks. We say that the subclock is coarser than the superclock, and the superclock is finer than the subclock. The second one forbids two clocks to tick simultaneously, without giving a priority to either clock. The last two relations are asynchronous. `Causality` relates an effect to its cause, *e.g.*, the sending of a message in a queue and its reception. Its the classical symmetric and transitive causality relation of event structures [12]. If $a \boxed{\preccurlyeq} b$, we say that a is faster than b, or b is slower than a. `Precedence` is similar to `Causality` but excludes instantaneous communications. The formal definitions of these relations are given in the next subsection.

There is one kind of unary clock definition parametrized by a positive natural number, $n \in \mathbb{N}$.

$$b \triangleq a \, \$ \, n \qquad \text{denotes that clock } b \text{ is a } n\text{-times delay of clock } a.$$

Intuitively, b is the same clock as a except that the first n ticks are ignored. Finally, there are four kinds of binary clock definitions: `union`, `intersection`, `infimum`, and `supremum`. The following notation is used for these definitions

$$c \triangleq a \boxed{+} b \qquad \text{denotes that clock } c \text{ is a union of clocks } a \text{ and } b,$$

$$c \triangleq a \boxed{*} b \qquad \text{denotes that clock } c \text{ is an intersection of clocks } a \text{ and } b,$$

$$c \triangleq a \boxed{\wedge} b \qquad \text{denotes that clock } c \text{ is an infimum of clocks } a \text{ and } b, \text{ and}$$

$$c \triangleq a \boxed{\vee} b \qquad \text{denotes that clock } c \text{ is a supremum of clocks } a \text{ and } b.$$

Intuitively, the union of two clocks a and b is the coarsest clock c that is a super clock of both a and b. The intersection is the finest clock that is a subclock of both a and b. These two operators are related to the synchronous relation of subclocking. Let us take as an example, a system where a command is sent to two actuators. Let a and b be clocks that represent the instants at which the command is actually received by the actuators. Then, $a \boxed{+} b$ represent the instants at which a command is received on at least one actuator whereas $a \boxed{*} b$ represent the instants at which the command arrives simultaneously on the two actuators.

`Infimum` and `Supremum` play a dual role with the asynchronous relation of causality. The infimum of two clocks a and b is the slowest clock (with regards to causality) that is faster than both a and b. The supremum is the fastest clock slower than both a and b. Using the same example as before, $a \boxed{\wedge} b$ represents the instants of the earliest reception on either a or b. Sometimes a may receive the command first, sometimes it is b. On the other hand, $a \boxed{\vee} b$ represents the instants of the latest reception on either a or b.

2.2   Clock Constraints: Semantics

One way to define the semantics for a clock constraint system is to specify the corresponding set of schedules, *i.e.*, the scenarios of the valid system behavior. In general, for a clock system, there are several (infinitely many) valid schedules.

Definition 1. *Let $\mathcal{C}$ be a given finite set of clocks then a map $\sigma : \mathbb{N}_{>0} \to \mathcal{P}(\mathcal{C})$ is called a* schedule *and an element $\boldsymbol{\chi}^{\sigma}$ of $\mathbb{N}^{\mathcal{C}}$ is called a* configuration *for a given schedule σ. $\chi_a^{\sigma} \in \mathbb{N}$ is a component of $\boldsymbol{\chi}^{\sigma}$ that denotes the configuration of clock a.*[1]

Intuitively, a schedule is a sequence of steps. For a given step $t \in \mathbb{N}_{>0}$, $\sigma(t)$ is the set of clocks that tick simultaneously.

   With each schedule σ, the sequence of configurations $\langle \boldsymbol{\chi}^{\sigma}(t) \mid t \in \mathbb{N} \rangle$ can be defined in the following manner:

$$\boldsymbol{\chi}^{\sigma}(0) = \mathbf{0};$$

$$\chi_a^{\sigma}(t) = \begin{cases} \chi_a^{\sigma}(t-1), & \text{if } a \notin \sigma(t) \\ \chi_a^{\sigma}(t-1) + 1, & \text{if } a \in \sigma(t) \end{cases} \text{ for all } t \in \mathbb{N}_{>0}, a \in \mathcal{C}.$$

In other words, $\boldsymbol{\chi}^{\sigma}(t)$ counts the number of activations (ticks) of all the clocks at step t (for a given schedule).

   There is a close interrelation between schedules and sequences of configurations. This interrelation is established in the following simple proposition.

Proposition 1. *Let $\langle \boldsymbol{\chi}(t) \mid t \in \mathbb{N} \rangle$ be a sequence of configurations then there exists a schedule σ such that $\chi_a(t) = \chi_a^{\sigma}(t)$ for all $t \in \mathbb{N}$ and $a \in \mathcal{C}$ if and only if the following conditions hold*

$$\boldsymbol{\chi}(0) = \mathbf{0}$$

and

$$0 \leq \chi_a(t+1) - \chi_a(t) \leq 1 \text{ for all } t \in \mathbb{N} \text{ and } a \in \mathcal{C}.$$

Moreover, the schedule σ is uniquely determined by $\langle \boldsymbol{\chi}(t) \mid t \in \mathbb{N} \rangle$.

Proof. The proof is simple and we do not give it. But we specify the method to construct σ: $\sigma(t) = \{a \in \mathcal{C} \mid \chi_a(t) > \chi_a(t-1)\}$ for $t \in \mathbb{N}_{>0}$ □

Below, we define the semantics of a primitive clock constraint as a set of schedules that satisfy this constraint (similarly to [11]). We shall use the abbreviated notation $\sigma \models Cons$ to represent the statement "schedule σ satisfies clock constraint $Cons$" and $[\![Cons]\!]$ to refer to the set of all the schedules satisfying clock constraint $Cons$.

---

[1] Bold font denotes vectors. $\boldsymbol{\chi}^{\sigma} \in \mathbb{N}^{\mathcal{C}}$ whereas $\chi_a^{\sigma} \in \mathbb{N}$.

Subclocking. Let a and b be clocks belonging to $\mathcal{C}$ then we shall assume that $\sigma \models a \boxed{\subseteq} b$ means the validity of the following statement

$$a \in \sigma(t) \text{ implies } b \in \sigma(t) \text{ for all } t \in \mathbb{N}_{>0}.$$

Subclocking is the basic synchronous construct allowing one event to occur only if its master event also occurs.

Exclusion. Let a and b be clocks belonging to $\mathcal{C}$ then we shall assume that $\sigma \models a \boxed{\#} b$ means the validity of the following statement

$$a \notin \sigma(t) \text{ or } b \notin \sigma(t) \text{ for all } t \in \mathbb{N}_{>0}.$$

Exclusion, here, is a purely synchronous notion, which is very different from the notion of exclusion in event structures. Indeed, it prevents two clocks from ticking simultaneously. In event structures, two occurrences are exclusive of each other means that if one occurs, the other one will never be able to occur, ever.

Causality. Let a and b be clocks belonging to $\mathcal{C}$ then we shall assume that $\sigma \models a \boxed{\preccurlyeq} b$ means the validity of the following statement

$$\chi_a^\sigma(t) \geq \chi_b^\sigma(t) \text{ for all } t \in \mathbb{N}.$$

On the contrary, consality is a purely asynchronous notion, classical in process networks and Petri nets.

Precedence. Let a and b be clocks belonging to $\mathcal{C}$ then we shall assume that $\sigma \models a \boxed{\prec} b$ means the validity of the following statement

$$\chi_a^\sigma(t) = \chi_b^\sigma(t) \text{ implies } b \notin \sigma(t+1) \text{ for all } t \in \mathbb{N}.$$

Let us recall that $\chi^\sigma(0) = \mathbf{0}$ so the equality of configurations is at least achieved initially. Then a is bound to tick strictly faster than b unless they both never tick. This latter pathological case denotes a classical liveness problem in CCSL specifications. That is why we usually attempt to establish that all the clocks tick infinitely often.

Delay. Let a and b be clocks belonging to $\mathcal{C}$ then we say that b is delayed for $m \in \mathbb{N}$ compared to a (it is denoted by $b \triangleq a \,\$\, m$) and assume that $\sigma \models b \triangleq a \,\$\, m$ if the following statement is valid

$$\chi_b^\sigma(t) = \max(\chi_a^\sigma(t) - m, 0) \text{ for all } t \in \mathbb{N}$$

Union. Let a, b, and c be clocks belonging to $\mathcal{C}$ then we say that c is union of a and b and assume that $\sigma \models c \triangleq a \boxed{+} b$ if the following statement is valid

$$c \in \sigma(t) \text{ iff } a \in \sigma(t) \text{ or } b \in \sigma(t) \text{ for all } t \in \mathbb{N}_{>0}$$

Intersection. Let a, b, and c be clocks belonging to $\mathcal{C}$ then we say that c is intersection of a and b and assume that $\sigma \models c \triangleq a \boxed{*} b$ if the following statement is valid

$$c \in \sigma(t) \text{ iff } a \in \sigma(t) \text{ and } b \in \sigma(t) \text{ for all } t \in \mathbb{N}_{>0}$$

Infimum. Let a, b, and c be clocks belonging to $\mathcal{C}$ then we say that c is infimum of a and b and assume that $\sigma \models c \triangleq a \boxed{\wedge} b$ if the following statement is valid

$$\chi_c^\sigma(t) = \max(\chi_a^\sigma(t), \chi_b^\sigma(t)) \text{ for all } t \in \mathbb{N}$$

Supremum. Let a, b, and c be clocks belonging to $\mathcal{C}$ then we say that c is supremum of a and b and assume that $\sigma \models c \triangleq a \boxed{\vee} b$ if the following statement is valid

$$\chi_c^\sigma(t) = \min(\chi_a^\sigma(t), \chi_b^\sigma(t)) \text{ for all } t \in \mathbb{N}$$

Definition 2. *If S is a finite set of primitive clock constraints described above then $\sigma \models S$ means that $\sigma \models \gamma$ for each $\gamma \in S$ and $[\![S]\!]$ denotes the set of all schedules σ such that $\sigma \models S$.*

2.3 Coalgebra as a Tool to Model Computer Systems

Gordon Plotkin explains [14] that transition structures are adequate models of computer systems: "In discrete (digital) computer systems behaviour consists of elementary steps which are occurrences of operations. Such elementary steps are called here, (and also in many other situations in Computer Science) transitions (= moves). Thus a transition step from one configuration to another and as a first idea we take it to be a binary relation between configurations." In [15] it has been shown that considering transition systems as a coalgebra gives useful, non-trivial results. It allows mathematical reasoning on infinite data structures, such as the behavior of reactive systems and it paves the way to co-algebra homomorphism and bisimulation. This is essential to prove the semantic preservation when transforming MARTE/CCSL into other formal models. In this paper, we rely on it to define a notion of incompleteness for CCSL and propose an extension, called GenCCSL.

We give in this subsection a minimally needed review of the definitions and notations used on transition systems and coalgebra. We then define a *clock coalgebra* for MARTE/CCSL.

Definition 3. *A transition system is a structure $\langle \Gamma, \longrightarrow \rangle$ where Γ is a set (of elements, γ, called configurations) and $\longrightarrow \subset \Gamma \times \Gamma$ is a binary relation (called the transition relation). Read $\gamma \longrightarrow \gamma'$ as saying that there is a transition from configuration γ to configuration γ'.*

Using the notion of coalgebra we obtain an alternative way to describe transition systems.

Definition 4. *A (powerset) coalgebra* [15] *is a structure* $\langle \Gamma, \alpha \rangle$ *where* α *is a map from* Γ *into the set of all subsets of* Γ, $\mathcal{P}(\Gamma)$. *In this context* Γ *is called the carrier of the coalgebra.*

It is evident that any transition system $\langle \Gamma, \longrightarrow \rangle$ determines the coalgebra $\langle \Gamma, \alpha \rangle$, where $\gamma' \in \alpha(\gamma)$ if and only if $\gamma \longrightarrow \gamma'$, and conversely, any coalgebra $\langle \Gamma, \alpha \rangle$ determines the transition system $\langle \Gamma, \longrightarrow \rangle$, where $\gamma \longrightarrow \gamma'$ if and only if $\gamma' \in \alpha(\gamma)$.

Definition 5. *Let* $\langle \Gamma, \alpha \rangle$ *be a coalgebra,* B *be a subset of* Γ *then the structure* $\langle B, \alpha \rangle$ *is called a subcoalgebra of* $\langle \Gamma, \alpha \rangle$ *if the embedding* $\alpha(\gamma) \subset B$ *is true for each* $\gamma \in B$.

One can check that any coalgebra $\langle \Gamma, \alpha \rangle$ is a subcoalgebra of itself and the intersection of a family of subcoalgebras is a subcoalgebra too. Hence, for each subset $X \subset \Gamma$ there exists a least one subcoalgebra whose carrier contains X. In this case, the carrier of this subcoalgebra is denoted by $\langle X \rangle$.

   To calculate $\langle X \rangle$ one can use Tarski's fixed point theorem [16] for the monotonic operator Ψ_X on the lattice $\mathcal{P}_X(\Gamma)$, where $\mathcal{P}_X(\Gamma)$ is the set of all Γ subsets that cover X. This operator is defined by the following formula

$$\Psi_X(V) = V \cup \{\gamma' \in \Gamma \mid (\exists \gamma \in V)\ \gamma' \in \alpha(\gamma)\}.$$

Calculation Schema. To calculate $\langle X \rangle$ one can build the following sequence of sets

$$V_0 = X,$$

and for $n > 0$

$$V_n = V_{n-1} \cup \{\gamma' \in \Gamma \mid (\exists \gamma \in V_{n-1})\ \gamma' \in \alpha(\gamma)\};$$

then

$$\langle X \rangle = \bigcup_{n \geq 0} V_n.$$

This computational schema ensures that an element $\gamma \in \Gamma$ belongs to $\langle X \rangle$ if and only if there exists a finite sequence $\gamma_0, \ldots, \gamma_{n-1}, \gamma_n$ formed by elements of Γ such that

$$\gamma_0 \in X \text{ and } \gamma_n = \gamma; \tag{1}$$
$$\gamma_k \in \alpha(\gamma_{k-1}) \text{ for } k = 1, \ldots, n. \tag{2}$$

Finite or infinite Γ-valued sequences satisfying (2) are used below therefore we give them the name "tracks".

   Hence, conditions (1) and (2) mean that an element $\gamma \in \Gamma$ belongs to $\langle X \rangle$ if and only if there exists a track that links some element of X and γ.

3   Clock Constraints and Coalgebras

In this section interrelations between clock constraints and powerset coalgebras are studied.

Below we assume that some finite set of clocks $\mathcal{C}$ has been given.

Let us define the constraint-free coalgebra over a clock set $\mathcal{C}$ as the coalgebra with the carrier $\mathbb{N}^{\mathcal{C}}$ and the map $\alpha : \mathbb{N}^{\mathcal{C}} \to \mathcal{P}(\mathbb{N}^{\mathcal{C}})$ defined by the formula:

$$\chi' \in \alpha(\chi) \quad \text{if and only if} \quad 0 \leq \chi'_a - \chi_a \leq 1 \quad \text{for all} \quad a \in \mathcal{C}.$$

It is evident that for any $\chi \in \mathbb{N}^{\mathcal{C}}$ the map α is represented in the form

$$\alpha(\chi) = \chi + \{0, 1\}^{\mathcal{C}}.$$

The following statement is, in fact, a reformulation of Proposition 1, which states that a clock can only tick once at each instant and that all the evolutions are possible when no constraint is specified.

Proposition 2. *Let* $\langle \chi(t) \mid t \in \mathbb{N} \rangle$ *be a sequence of configurations then there exists a schedule* σ *such that* $\chi_a(t) = \chi_a^{\sigma}(t)$ *for all* $t \in \mathbb{N}$ *and* $a \in \mathcal{C}$ *if and only if this sequence is a track in the coalgebra* $\langle \mathbb{N}^{\mathcal{C}}, \alpha \rangle$ *such that* $\chi(0) = \mathbf{0}$.

A track $\langle \chi(t) \mid t \in \mathbb{N} \rangle$ is called *initial* if the condition $\chi(0) = \mathbf{0}$ holds.

The natural and simplest way to take into account some constraints is to specify a map $\triangle : \mathbb{N}^{\mathcal{C}} \to \mathcal{P}(\{0, 1\}^{\mathcal{C}})$ such that $\mathbf{0} \in \triangle(\chi)$ for any $\chi \in \mathbb{N}^{\mathcal{C}}$ and to define

$$\alpha_{\triangle}(\chi) = \chi + \triangle(\chi).$$

A map $\triangle : \mathbb{N}^{\mathcal{C}} \to \mathcal{P}(\{0, 1\}^{\mathcal{C}})$ that satisfies the condition $\mathbf{0} \in \triangle(\chi)$ for any $\chi \in \mathbb{N}^{\mathcal{C}}$ is called an *actuation distribution* on $\mathcal{C}$. The actuation distribution captures the set of sets of clocks that are allowed to tick simultaneously at one instant given a configuration.

Definition 6. *Let* $\triangle : \mathbb{N}^{\mathcal{C}} \to \mathcal{P}(\{0, 1\}^{\mathcal{C}})$ *be an actuation distribution and* $\langle \mathbb{N}^{\mathcal{C}}, \alpha_{\triangle} \rangle$ *be a coalgebra, where* $\alpha_{\triangle}(\chi) = \chi + \triangle(\chi)$, *then an element of* $\mathbb{N}^{\mathcal{C}}$ *is called* $\triangle$-*reachable configuration if it belongs to the carrier of the minimal subcoalgebra containing* $\mathbf{0}$.

Such a set of reachable configurations is denoted below by $R(\triangle)$.

Definition 7. *Let* $\triangle : \mathbb{N}^{\mathcal{C}} \to \mathcal{P}(\{0, 1\}^{\mathcal{C}})$ *be an actuation distribution then the coalgebra* $\langle R(\triangle), \alpha_{\triangle} \rangle$ *is called the* clock coalgebra *associated with* $\triangle$.

Proposition 3. *Let* $\triangle : \mathbb{N}^{\mathcal{C}} \to \mathcal{P}(\{0, 1\}^{\mathcal{C}})$ *be an actuation distribution and* $\langle \chi(t) \mid t \in \mathbb{N} \rangle$ *be an initial track in the coalgebra* $\langle \mathbb{N}^{\mathcal{C}}, \alpha_{\triangle} \rangle$ *if and only if it is an initial track in the subcoalgebra* $\langle R(\triangle), \alpha_{\triangle} \rangle$.

Proof. This is immediate consequence of the definition of initial tracks.   □

3.1   Structure of Actuation Distributions

The set $\mathcal{P}\left(\{0,1\}^{\mathcal{C}}\right)$ is finite therefore there exists a finite partition of the set $\mathbb{N}^{\mathcal{C}}$ such that an actuation distribution $\triangle$ is constant on each atom of the partition. One can extract the coarsest of such partitions.

Hence, if we fix some actuation distribution $\triangle$ and denote by $\Pi_\triangle$ the coarsest partition of $\mathbb{N}^{\mathcal{C}}$ such that $\triangle$ is constant on any atom of the partition then we can assume that each such atom can be represented by a formula of some formal arithmetical system.

If $\Pi_\triangle$ has k atoms and $\lambda_1(\boldsymbol{\chi}), \ldots, \lambda_k(\boldsymbol{\chi})$ are formulae, which represent the corresponding atoms, then the following conditions hold

$$\lambda_1(\boldsymbol{\chi}) \vee \cdots \vee \lambda_k(\boldsymbol{\chi}) \equiv \mathfrak{t}, \tag{3}$$

$$\lambda_i(\boldsymbol{\chi}) \wedge \lambda_j(\boldsymbol{\chi}) \equiv \mathfrak{f} \text{ for } i \neq j \text{ and } 1 \leq i,j \leq k, \tag{4}$$

where $\mathfrak{t}$ is true and $\mathfrak{f}$ is false.

Further, let us denote by $\triangle_i$ the value of $\triangle(\boldsymbol{\chi})$ under condition that $\lambda_i(\boldsymbol{\chi}) = \mathfrak{t}$ where $i = 1, \ldots, k$. Then $\mathbf{0} \in \triangle_i \subset \{0,1\}^{\mathcal{C}}$ and it can be represented by the boolean function $\delta_i(\boldsymbol{\tau})$ over a boolean vector $\boldsymbol{\tau} = \langle \tau_c \mid c \in \mathcal{C} \rangle$ determined by the following condition

$$\delta_i(\boldsymbol{\tau}) = 1 \text{ if and only if } \boldsymbol{\tau} \in \triangle_i.$$

The condition $\mathbf{0} \in \triangle_i$ ensures validity of the equation

$$\delta_i(\mathbf{0}) = 1. \tag{5}$$

Hence, the following proposition describes the structure of an actuation distribution.

Proposition 4. *Each actuation distribution $\triangle$ can be represented as a set of rules*

$$\lambda_i(\boldsymbol{\chi}) \implies \delta_i(\boldsymbol{\tau}) \text{ where } i = 1, \ldots, k$$

such that formulae $\lambda_1, \ldots, \lambda_k$ satisfy conditions (3) and (4) and boolean functions $\delta_1, \ldots, \delta_k$ satisfy condition (5).

3.2   Coalgebras for Primitive Clock Constraints

In this subsection coalgebras associated with primitive clock constraints are computed. To do this we use the computational scheme presented in Sec. 2.3.

Proposition 5 (Clock Relations). *Let $a, b \in \mathcal{C}$ and Rel be a clock relation between clocks a and b then*

case $Rel = \{a \boxed{\subseteq} b\}$: *if $\triangle$ is defined by the following rule*

$$\mathfrak{t} \longrightarrow \tau_a \rightarrow \tau_b$$

then $\langle \boldsymbol{\chi}(t) \mid t \in \mathbb{N} \rangle$ is a track in the coalgebra $\langle R(\triangle), \alpha_\triangle \rangle$ if and only if there exists a schedule σ such that $\sigma \models Rel$ and $\boldsymbol{\chi}^\sigma(t) = \boldsymbol{\chi}(t)$ for all $t \in \mathbb{N}$;

case $Rel = \{a \boxed{\#} b\}$: *if* $\triangle$ *is defined by the following rule*

$$t \Longrightarrow \neg\tau_a \vee \neg\tau_b$$

then $\langle \chi(t) \mid t \in \mathbb{N} \rangle$ *is a track in the coalgebra* $\langle R(\triangle), \alpha_\triangle \rangle$ *if and only if there exists a schedule* σ *such that* $\sigma \models Rel$ *and* $\chi^\sigma(t) = \chi(t)$ *for all* $t \in \mathbb{N}$;
case $Rel = \{a \boxed{\preccurlyeq} b\}$: *if* $\triangle$ *is defined by the following set of rules*

$$\{\chi_a = \chi_b \Longrightarrow \tau_b \to \tau_a\}$$

then $\langle \chi(t) \mid t \in \mathbb{N} \rangle$ *is a track in the coalgebra* $\langle R(\triangle), \alpha_\triangle \rangle$ *if and only if there exists a schedule* σ *such that* $\sigma \models Rel$ *and* $\chi^\sigma(t) = \chi(t)$ *for all* $t \in \mathbb{N}$;
case $Rel = \{a \boxed{\prec} b\}$: *if* $\triangle$ *is defined by the following set of rules*

$$\{\chi_a = \chi_b \Longrightarrow \neg\tau_b\}$$

then $\langle \chi(t) \mid t \in \mathbb{N} \rangle$ *is a track in the coalgebra* $\langle R(\triangle), \alpha_\triangle \rangle$ *if and only if there exists a schedule* σ *such that* $\sigma \models Rel$ *and* $\chi^\sigma(t) = \chi(t)$ *for all* $t \in \mathbb{N}$.

Proof. Let us define the function $n : \mathbb{N}^\mathcal{C} \to \mathbb{N}$ in the following manner

$$n(\chi) = \min\{m \in \mathbb{N} \mid \chi \in V_m\},$$

where $\langle V_n \mid n \in \mathbb{N} \rangle$ is the series of sets defined by the computational schema from Sect. 2.3. Using Proposition 3, and mathematical induction by $n(\chi)$ one can check that

$$R(\triangle) = \begin{cases} \{\chi \in \mathbb{N}^\mathcal{C} \mid \chi_a \leq \chi_b\}, & \text{for the case of subclocking} \\ \mathbb{N}^\mathcal{C}, & \text{for the case of exclusion} \\ \{\chi \in \mathbb{N}^\mathcal{C} \mid \chi_a \geq \chi_b\}, & \text{for the case of causality and precedence} \end{cases}$$

Further, checking that any track in the coalgebra $\langle R(\triangle), \alpha_\triangle \rangle$ corresponds to some schedule σ such that $\sigma \models Rel$ and conversely is an easy exercise.   □

Proposition 6 (Delay). *Let* $a, b \in \mathcal{C}$ *and* $Expr = \{b \triangleq a \$ m\}$ *for some natural* m *then if* $\triangle$ *is defined by the following set of rules*

$$\{\chi_a < m \Longrightarrow \neg\tau_b, \ \chi_a \geq m \Longrightarrow \tau_a \leftrightarrow \tau_b\}$$

then $\langle \chi(t) \mid t \in \mathbb{N} \rangle$ *is a track in the coalgebra* $\langle R(\triangle), \alpha_\triangle \rangle$ *if and only if there exists a schedule* σ *such that* $\sigma \models Expr$ *and* $\chi^\sigma(t) = \chi(t)$ *for all* $t \in \mathbb{N}$.

Proof. Acting as in the proof of the previous proposition one can establish that

$$R(\triangle) = \{\chi \in \mathbb{N}^\mathcal{C} \mid \chi_a \leq m, \ \chi_b = 0\} \cup \{\chi \in \mathbb{N}^\mathcal{C} \mid \chi_a > m, \ \chi_b = \chi_a - m\}.$$

Further reasoning are similar to the reasoning in the previous proof.   □

Proposition 7 (Binary Clock Definitions). *Let* $a, b, c \in \mathcal{C}$ *and* C *be a binary definition of clock* c *using clocks* a *and* b *then*

case $Expr = \{c \triangleq a \boxed{+} b\}$: *if $\triangle$ is defined by the following rule*

$$\mathfrak{t} \Longrightarrow \tau_c \leftrightarrow \tau_a \vee \tau_b$$

then $\langle \chi(t) \mid t \in \mathbb{N} \rangle$ is a track in the coalgebra $\langle R(\triangle), \alpha_\triangle \rangle$ if and only if there exists a schedule σ such that $\sigma \models Expr$ and $\chi^\sigma(t) = \chi(t)$ for all $t \in \mathbb{N}$;

case $Expr = \{c \triangleq a \boxed{*} b\}$: *if $\triangle$ is defined by the following rule*

$$\mathfrak{t} \Longrightarrow \tau_c \leftrightarrow \tau_a \wedge \tau_b$$

then $\langle \chi(t) \mid t \in \mathbb{N} \rangle$ is a track in the coalgebra $\langle R(\triangle), \alpha_\triangle \rangle$ if and only if there exists a schedule σ such that $\sigma \models Expr$ and $\chi^\sigma(t) = \chi(t)$ for all $t \in \mathbb{N}$;

case $Expr = \{c \triangleq a \boxed{\wedge} b\}$: *if $\triangle$ is defined by the following set of rules*

$$\{\chi_a < \chi_b \Longrightarrow \tau_c \leftrightarrow \tau_b, \ \chi_a = \chi_b \Longrightarrow \tau_c \leftrightarrow \tau_a \vee \tau_b, \ \chi_a > \chi_b \Longrightarrow \tau_c \leftrightarrow \tau_a\}$$

then $\langle \chi(t) \mid t \in \mathbb{N} \rangle$ is a track in the coalgebra $\langle R(\triangle), \alpha_\triangle \rangle$ if and only if there exists a schedule σ such that $\sigma \models Expr$ and $\chi^\sigma(t) = \chi(t)$ for all $t \in \mathbb{N}$;

case $Expr = \{c \triangleq a \boxed{\vee} b\}$: *if $\triangle$ is defined by the following set of rules*

$$\{\chi_a < \chi_b \Longrightarrow \tau_c \leftrightarrow \tau_a, \ \chi_a = \chi_b \Longrightarrow \tau_c \leftrightarrow \tau_a \wedge \tau_b, \ \chi_a > \chi_b \Longrightarrow \tau_c \leftrightarrow \tau_b\}$$

then $\langle \chi(t) \mid t \in \mathbb{N} \rangle$ is a track in the coalgebra $\langle R(\triangle), \alpha_\triangle \rangle$ if and only if there exists a schedule σ such that $\sigma \models Expr$ and $\chi^\sigma(t) = \chi(t)$ for all $t \in \mathbb{N}$.

Proof. Acting as in the proof of Proposition 5 one can establish that

$$R(\triangle) = \begin{cases} \{\chi \in \mathbb{N}^C \mid \chi_b \leq \chi_a \leq \chi_c \leq \chi_a + \chi_b\} \cup \\ \quad \{\chi \in \mathbb{N}^C \mid \chi_a < \chi_b \leq \chi_c \leq \chi_a + \chi_b\}, \text{ in the case of union} \\ \{\chi \in \mathbb{N}^C \mid \chi_c \leq \chi_a \leq \chi_b\} \cup \\ \quad \{\chi \in \mathbb{N}^C \mid \chi_c \leq \chi_b \leq \chi_a\}, \text{ in the case of intersection} \\ \{\chi \in \mathbb{N}^C \mid \chi_a \leq \chi_b, \chi_c = \chi_b\} \cup \\ \quad \{\chi \in \mathbb{N}^C \mid \chi_a > \chi_b, \chi_c = \chi_a\}, \text{ in the case of infimum} \\ \{\chi \in \mathbb{N}^C \mid \chi_a \leq \chi_b, \chi_c = \chi_a\} \cup \\ \quad \{\chi \in \mathbb{N}^C \mid \chi_a > \chi_b, \chi_c = \chi_b\}, \text{ in the case of supremum} \end{cases}$$

Further reasonings are the same as in the previous propositions. $\square$

4   Stationary Clock Constraints

Actuation distributions of some clock constraints do not depend on the current configuration as one can see from previous considerations. It motivates the following definition.

Definition 8. *An actuation distribution $\triangle : \mathbb{N}^C \to \{0, 1\}^C$ is called stationary if the map $\triangle$ is a constant map.*

Some primitive clock constraints, such as subclocking, exclusion, union and intersection, represent stationary actuation distributions. Therefore the question whether any stationary actuation distribution is represented by a set of stationary primitive clock constraints is interesting.

The following proposition demonstrates that it is true for 2-clock systems.

Proposition 8. *Let $C = \{a, b\}$ then any corresponding stationary actuation distribution can be expressed by a set of subclocking and exclusion relations.*

Proof. Let us represent a vector $\tau \in \mathbb{N}^C$ as $\tau = (\tau_a, \tau_b)$ the all possible stationary actuation distributions for C can be listed in the following manner.

1	$\triangle = \{0, 1\}^C$	constraint free
2	$\triangle = \{(0,0), (0,1), (1,1)\}$	$a \boxed{\subseteq} b$
3	$\triangle = \{(0,0), (1,0), (1,1)\}$	$b \boxed{\subseteq} a$
4	$\triangle = \{(0,0), (1,0), (0,1)\}$	$a \boxed{\#} b$
5	$\triangle = \{(0,0), (0,1)\}$	$a \boxed{\subseteq} b \wedge a \boxed{\#} b$
6	$\triangle = \{(0,0), (1,0)\}$	$b \boxed{\subseteq} a \wedge a \boxed{\#} b$
7	$\triangle = \{(0,0), (1,1)\}$	$a \boxed{\subseteq} b \wedge b \boxed{\subseteq} a$
8	$\triangle = \{(0,0)\}$	$a \boxed{\subseteq} b \wedge b \boxed{\subseteq} a \wedge a \boxed{\#} b$

Hence, we have built all the possible cases.   □

However, this gives, in fact, the only example of completeness of stationary primitive clock constraints to represent stationary actuation distributions.

Theorem 1. *If $|C| > 2$ then there exists at least one stationary actuation distribution that cannot be represented as a set of stationary primitive clock constraints.*

Proof. Analyzing definitions collected in Sect. 3.2 one can see that subclocking relations, exclusion relations, union definitions, and intersection definitions form an exhaustive list of stationary primitive clock constraints.

Further suppose that $|C| = n$ and $n > 2$. Firstly, note that $\triangle$ for a stationary primitive clock relation contains at most $3 \cdot 2^{n-2}$ vectors.

Secondly, let us calculate the number of vectors that can belong to $\triangle$ considering only either union or intersection definitions when $n = 3$. To do it, let us denote $C = \{a, b, c\}$ then actuation vectors τ be represented as $\tau = \{\tau_a, \tau_b, \tau_c\}$ and all possible actuation distributions for a stationary definitions are listed as follows

$$c \triangleq a \boxed{+} b \qquad \triangle = \{(0,0,0), (1,0,1), (0,1,1), (1,1,1)\}$$
$$c \triangleq a \boxed{*} b \qquad \triangle = \{(0,0,0), (1,0,0), (0,1,0), (1,1,1)\}$$

Using this fact one can claim that for $n \geq 3$, $\triangle$ for stationary clock definitions contains at most $4 \cdot 2^{n-3} = 2^{n-1}$ vectors.

Thirdly, $\triangle$ for any clock constraint represented by a set of stationary clock relations and clock definitions is equal to the intersection of the corresponding $\triangle$-s, thus the studied $\triangle$ contains at most $3 \cdot 2^{n-2}$ vectors.

Further, $\triangle$ other arbitrary stationary constraints can contain from one to $2^n - 1$ vectors. Hence, all $\triangle$-s that contain from $3 \cdot 2^{n-2} + 1$ to $2^n - 1$ vectors cannot be represented by a set of clock relations or/and clock definitions. To demonstrate that such constraints exist let us calculate the number of elements in the set

$$\{k \in \mathbb{N} \mid 3 \cdot 2^{n-2} + 1 \leq k \leq 2^n - 1\}.$$

One can easily check that $2^{n-1} - 1$ is always in the set for $n \geq 3$.   □

Example 1. If $\triangle = \{\tau \in \{0,1\}^{\mathcal{C}} \mid (\exists c \in \mathcal{C})\, \tau_c = 0\}$ then it cannot be represented as a set of stationary clock relations and clock definitions.

Intuitively, this example shows that one cannot explicitly prevent one specific clock from ticking with classical CCSL. This is a pathological example that illustrates the incompleteness of CCSL. By relying on a co-algebra, we extend the family of constraints that can be built and we can also highlight what cannot be done with CCSL.

5   Related Work

CCSL operational semantics is inspired by the approach proposed by G. Plotkin for defining the operational semantics of software systems [14]. In [15] it is proposed to use the concept of "universal coalgebra" for studying Plotkin's semantic model. This is the main inspiration for our work.

Co-inductive structures have already been used in the context of logic programming for modeling complex real-time systems (see for instance, [7]). However, they were mainly used as a way to handle infinite structures, where infinity came from the dense nature of time and of its continuous evolution, such as in timed pushdown automata [5]. We use them here to handle systems that are discrete (but still infinite) in nature and to prove that CCSL is not rich enough to capture all that could be built by the coalgebraic structure. We then propose to build a generalized and complete constraint language as an extension of CCSL.

Transformation based approaches have been proposed for mapping CCSL or a subset of it, into different semantic domains such as VHDL, Petri nets, and Promela. André et al. [2] have presented an automatic transformation of a CCSL specification into VHDL code. The proposed transformation assembles instances of pre-built VHDL components while preserving the polychronous semantics of CCSL. The generated code can be integrated in the VHDL design and verification flow. Mallet and André have proposed a formal semantics to a kernel subset of CCSL, and presented an equivalent interpretation of the kernel in two different formal languages, namely Signal and Time Petri nets [10]. In their work, relevant examples have been used to show instances when Petri-nets are suitable to express CCSL constraints, as well as instances where synchronous languages are more appropriate. Our contribution is very different in nature, since rather than restricting the scope of CCSL to allow verification, we here attempt to generalize the language and find a wider semantic domain that still brings useful information about the constraint system.

6 Conclusion

In the paper we have presented a new semantic domain used to study the expressiveness of the MARTE CCSL constraint language. CCSL constraints are encoded using a clock co-algebra that is later used to identify what can be expressed in CCSL and more importantly what cannot be expressed.

In Subsect. 3.1, a coalgebraic structure of clocks has been studied. The obtained results show that computability of constraint preconditions is necessary for verifying the validity of a schedule for a constraint. Taking into account that any precondition is a predicate of natural variables the question about a choice of formal arithmetic system for specifying such a precondition arises.

Besides, this new structure defines a class of constraints covering classical CCSL constraints. This result is given in Subsect. 3.2. Theorem 1 shows that the newly defined class of clock constraints is strictly larger than the class of CCSL constraints. This semantic domain therefore defines a class of *generalized* clock constraints. We then study the relationships between this generalized class and the classical class of clock constraints.

Using a coalgebraic structure to capture clock constraints is a first step to allow for the bisimulation of CCSL specifications. This is important since CCSL was meant to provide a reference semantic domain for MARTE time model. Such MARTE/CCSL models are then doomed to be transformed into other formal modeling languages amenable to analysis. Bisimulation would then provide a support for verifying the correctness of the transformation.

References

1. André, C.: Syntax and semantics of the Clock Constraint Specification Language (CCSL). Research report 6925, INRIA, May 2009. http://hal.inria.fr/inria-00384077/
2. André, C., Mallet, F., DeAntoni, J.: VHDL observers for clock constraint checking. In: International Symposium on Industrial Embedded Systems (SIES), pp. 98–107. IEEE, Trento, Italy, July 2010. http://dx.doi.org/10.1109/SIES.2010.5551372
3. André, C., Mallet, F., de Simone, R.: Modeling time(s). In: Engels, G., Opdyke, B., Schmidt, D.C., Weil, F. (eds.) MODELS 2007. LNCS, vol. 4735, pp. 559–573. Springer, Heidelberg (2007). http://dx.doi.org/10.1007/978-3-540-75209-7 38
4. Benveniste, A., Caspi, P., Edwards, S.A., Halbwachs, N., Le Guernic, P., de Simone, R.: The synchronous languages 12 years later. Proc. IEEE **91**(1), 64–83 (2003)
5. Dang, Z.: Binary reachability analysis of pushdown timed automata with dense clocks. In: Berry, G., Comon, H., Finkel, A. (eds.) CAV 2001. LNCS, vol. 2102, pp. 506–518. Springer, Heidelberg (2001)

6. DeAntoni, J., Mallet, F.: TimeSquare: treat your models with logical time. In: Furia, C.A., Nanz, S. (eds.) TOOLS 2012. LNCS, vol. 7304, pp. 34–41. Springer, Heidelberg (2012). http://dx.doi.org/10.1007/978-3-642-30561-0 4
7. Gupta, G., Saeedloei, N., DeVries, B., Min, R., Marple, K., Kluźniak, F.: Infinite computation, co-induction and computational logic. In: Corradini, A., Klin, B., Cîrstea, C. (eds.) CALCO 2011. LNCS, vol. 6859, pp. 40–54. Springer, Heidelberg (2011)
8. Lamport, L.: Time, clocks, and the ordering of events in a distributed system. Commun. ACM **21**(7), 558–565 (1978)
9. Mallet, F.: Logical Time @ Work for the Modeling and Analysis of Embedded Systems. LAMBERT Academic Publishing, January 2011, ISBN: 978-3-8433-9388-1
10. Mallet, F., André, C.: On the semantics of UML/Marte clock constraints. In: 2009 IEEE International Symposium on Object/Component/Service-Oriented Real-Time Distributed Computing, ISORC, pp. 305–312. IEEE Computer Press, Tokyo, March 2009. http://dx.doi.org/10.1109/ISORC.2009.27
11. Mallet, F., Millo, J.V., de Simone, R.: Safe CCSL specifications and marked graphs. In: 11th ACM/IEEE International Conference on Formal Methods and Models for Codesign, MEMOCODE, pp. 157–166. IEEE (2013). http://ieeexplore.ieee.org/xpl/freeabs_all.jsp?arnumber=6670955
12. Nielsen, M., Plotkin, G.D., Winskel, G.: Petri nets, event structures and domains. In: Kahn, G. (ed.) Semantics of Concurrent Computation. LNCS, vol. 70. Springer, Heidelberg (1979). http://dx.doi.org/10.1007/BFb0022474
13. OMG: UML Profile for MARTE, v1.0. Object Management Group, November 2009, formal/2009-11-02
14. Plotkin, G.D.: A structural approach to operational semantics. J. Log. Algebr. Program. **60–61**, 17–139 (2004)
15. Rutten, J.J.M.M.: Universal coalgebra: a theory of systems. Theor. Comput. Sci. **249**(1), 3–80 (2000). http://dx.doi.org/10.1016/S0304-3975(00)00056-6
16. Tarski, A.: A lattice-theoretical fixpoint theorem and its applications. Pacific J. Math. **5**(2), 285–309 (1955). http://projecteuclid.org/euclid.pjm/1103044538
17. Zholtkevych, G., Mallet, F., Zaretska, I., Zholtkevych, G.: Two semantic models for clock relations in the clock constraint specification language. In: Ermolayev, V., Mayr, H.C., Nikitchenko, M., Spivakovsky, A., Zholtkevych, G. (eds.) ICTERI 2013. CCIS, vol. 412, pp. 190–209. Springer, Heidelberg (2013). http://dx.doi.org/10.1007/978-3-319-03998-5 10

Analyzing Industrial Architectural Models by Simulation and Model-Checking

Raluca Marinescu[1]([✉]), Henrik Kaijser[2], Marius Mikučionis[3],
Cristina Seceleanu[1], Henrik Lönn[2], and Alexandre David[3]

[1] Mälardalen University, Västerås, Sweden
{raluca.marinescu,cristina.seceleanu}@mdh.se
[2] Volvo Group Trucks Technology, Gothenburg, Sweden
{henrik.kaijser,henrik.lonn}@volvo.com
[3] Aalborg University, Aalborg, Denmark
{marius,adavid}@cs.aau.dk

Abstract. The software architecture of any automotive system has to be decided well in advance of production, so it is very desirable to assess its quality in order to obtain quick indications of errors at early design phases. In this paper, we present a constellation of analysis techniques for architectural models described in EAST-ADL. The methods are complementary in terms of covering EAST-ADL model analysis against a rich set of requirements, and in terms of the varying degree of confidence in the provided guarantees. Based on the needs of the current model-driven development in a chosen automotive context, we propose three analysis techniques of EAST-ADL architectural models, in an attempt to tackle some of the exposed design needs: simulation of EAST-ADL functions in Simulink, model-checking EAST-ADL models with timed automata semantics, and statistical model-checking in UPPAAL, applied on an automatically generated network of timed automata. An industrial Brake-by-Wire prototype is the case study on which we show the potential of simulating EAST-ADL models in Simulink, model-checking downscale EAST-ADL models, as well statistical model-checking of full model versions, in order to tame verification scalability problems.

1 Introduction

Mechanical and hydraulic systems in current vehicles are being replaced by electrical/electronic systems that can implement highly complex functions like cruise control and automatic braking. In order to deal with this complexity, the automotive industry has moved towards a model-based development process, during which high-level system models are designed and analyzed against requirements. Since many automotive systems are safety-critical, new standards such as ISO26262 place requirements on the quality of software. Consequently, companies that wish to adopt such standards will need to use methods and tools fit for guaranteeing such quality on each level of design abstraction.

Simulink [2], a model-based tool for design, simulation, and code generation of embedded systems, is already a well-established practice in the automotive

© Springer International Publishing Switzerland 2015
C. Artho and P.C. Ölveczky (Eds.): FTSCS 2014, CCIS 476, pp. 189–205, 2015.
DOI: 10.1007/978-3-319-17581-2_13

domain. Simulink is typically used to define and assess system behavior in an early phase, or to create a detailed behavioral behavioral definition of the system in order to automatically generate the corresponding code. Architectural description languages, on the other hand, can be introduced earlier in the development, to provide models that could handle the complex software architecture of automotive systems. Compared to the current state-of-practice, architectural models offer a well-defined and standardized structure that deals with all the related information (e.g. functions, timing, triggering) of safety-critical systems [8]. A candidate for this task is EAST-ADL [7], an architectural description language dedicated to the modeling and development of automotive embedded systems. The use of such modeling notations enables the application of verification techniques early in the industrial development process, in an attempt to gain early-phase indications of possible functional and timing errors.

In this paper, we propose a constellation of complementary verification techniques that can be applied on EAST-ADL models to deliver various types of model correctness assurance. We start by briefly presenting the EAST-ADL architectural language and the tools involved in the verification process (see Sect. 2), and we discuss the current state-of-practice in the development of automotive systems as used nowadays by the automotive industry (see Sect. 3). Next, we present our simulation and model-checking methodology (see Sect. 4), and we show the verification techniques based on the: (i) simulation of EAST-ADL models from a set of predefined verification cases with Simulink (see Sect. 6), (ii) symbolic simulation and formal verification of EAST-ADL with UPPAAL, and (iii) statistical model-checking of the architectural model with UPPAAL SMC (see Sect. 8). In order to enable the verification of architectural models in EAST-ADL, we also contribute with a timed automata (TA) semantics that we propose for the EAST-ADL components (see Sect. 7). We show how the formal techniques underlying the tools complement each other, by applying the EAST-ADL to Simulink, and EAST-ADL to UPPAAL-TA transformations to analyze the Brake-by-Wire (BBW) industrial system (see Sect. 5). Such an endeavor exposes also the advantages and limitations of each framework, when used on an industrial system model, which can serve as a guiding result especially if safety standards such as ISO26262 are to be adopted. We end this paper by discussing similar related works (see Sect. 9), and by presenting our conclusions (see Sect. 10). The actual contribution of this paper consists of introducing two new transformations, one from EAST-ADL models to Simulink models, and one from EAST-ADL models to EAST-ADL models, together with the application of simulation, model-checking and statistical model-checking on an industrial architectural model.

2   Brief Overview of the EAST-ADL Language

EAST-ADL [7] is an AUTOSAR [4] compatible architectural description language for automotive electronic systems. The functionality of the system is defined at four levels of abstraction, as follows. The *Vehicle Level* is the highest level of abstraction and describes the electronic features as they are perceived externally. Next, the *Analysis Level* allows an abstract functional representation of the architecture without prescribing a specific hardware topology. The *Design Level* presents a detailed functional representation of the architecture, plus the allocation of these elements on to the hardware platform. Last, the *Implementation Level* describes the implementation of the system using AUTOSAR elements. At each abstraction level, the system model relies on the definition of a set of *FunctionTypes* representing components that describe the functional structure of the system. Each of these *FunctionTypes* has: (i) a set of *FlowPorts* that provide and receive data, (ii) a *FunctionTrigger* that can be either time-based or event-based, and (iii) a *FunctionBehavior*. The system is modeled as a set of interconnected *FunctionPrototypes*, where each *FunctionPrototype* is an instantiation of the corresponding *FunctionType*. The execution of each *FunctionPrototype* is based on the "read-execute-write" semantics, which enables semantically sound analysis and behavioral composition, and makes the function execution independent of the notation used, when defining its internal behavior. The *FunctionBehavior* is defined using different notations and tools, e.g., Simulink or UPPAAL PORT timed automata (TA) [13]. At each level of abstraction, the above structural elements of the system can be extended with annotations for orthogonal aspects like requirements, timing properties, generic constraints. etc. EAST-ADL also provides means to describe different validation and verification activities as *VVCases* for different levels of abstraction.

In the following section, we present a typical automotive development process and we try to identify different needs and gaps that need to be addressed.

3   The Current Development Process in an Automotive Context

We have identified four main groups of actors who are involved in a typical automotive development process: the *Client*, the *System Engineers*, the *Software Developers*, and the *Verification Engineers*. As depicted in Fig. 1, the *Client* compiles a set of informal, natural language requirements describing the new system that needs to be implemented. The *System Engineers* break down these requirements in incremental steps, passing the current requirement set from one engineer to the other for further decomposition. The *Software Developers* decompose further these requirements while considering implementation elements like

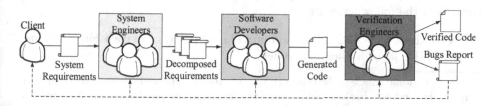

Fig. 1. A typical automotive development process.

the system architecture. This new set of requirements, consisting of one requirement document per system component, is divided among the *Software Developers*, who create a model-based implementation of the components in the system. The components may be modeled using the Simulink tool, and the code is automatically generated based on these models. This code is integrated as the behavior of an AUTOSAR software component and, where necessary, adjusted by the *Software Developers*. In order to ensure correct behavior, model-in-the-loop and software-in-the-loop analysis are used. Once a software component has been implemented, it can be deployed on an electronic control unit (ECU) for component testing. Finally, the *Verification Engineers* perform testing at the system level directly on the platform, using manually written tests. Any bugs discovered in the implementation or any problems in the requirements are reported back to the person responsible for the implementation or requirement, respectively. Since models start to be included in the industrial development process, there is also an increased need of stronger evidence of model correctness with respect to functional or timing requirements.

For the development process described above, different state-of-the-art techniques could facilitate model integration and verification, as follows:

– Introducing architectural languages (like EAST-ADL) will keep track of requirements, features, functions, and hardware topology in an integrated model, making the design decisions consistent and traceable.
– Providing the behavior for architectural components based on formal definitions like TA, together with typical Simulink definitions, will enable alternative representations of the same function, hence providing a more comprehensive assessment of the system.
– Applying formal verification techniques, like model-checking, on the system's formalized structural and behavioral model will provide correctness assurances regarding important properties.

In order to adopt these steps, an integrated system model is needed, such that different verification techniques can be applied consistently, on the same system description, at various levels of abstraction.

4   Our Methodology for Analyzing Architectural Models

In this section, we propose a methodology for simulation and model-checking of EAST-ADL models, which is depicted in Fig. 2. Our verification methodology consists of the following steps:

– Create the EAST-ADL model and provide the behavior of each *FunctionType* as a FMU[1] [3] or a Simulink model;

---

[1] The Functional Mock-up Interface (FMI) is a tool-independent standard to support behavior models using a combination of xml-files and compiled C-code. The standard defines the concept of a Functional Mock-up Unit (FMU), as a software component that implements the FMI standard.

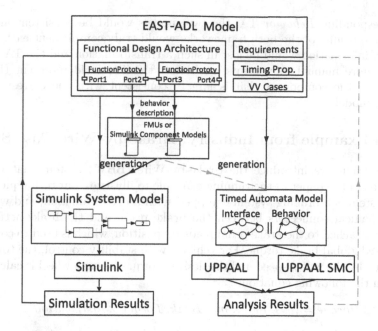

Fig. 2. Our simulation and model-checking methodology.

- Select the verification method:
  1. Simulation: by implementing an automatic transformation from the architectural model to a Simulink model and calling the Simulink tool, we can provide verification through simulation;
  2. Model-checking: by implementing an automatic transformation from the architectural model to a network of TA, we can use the UPPAAL or UPPAAL SMC model-checker to formally verify the system;
- Return the verification results back to the EAST-ADL model for possible improvements of the design.

There are several differences between the two frameworks. The simulation method requires the EAST-ADL model to be extended with verification and validation elements as *VVCases*, which describe the part of the model to be analyzed, together with the definition of monitor *FunctionTypes*, stimuli data, and the requirements to be verified. The behavioral model of the monitor is provided as an FMU or a Simulink model. The transformation to the network of TA provides formal semantics for the architectural model in terms of timed transition systems [5]. In order to preserve the informal semantics of the architectural language, the transformation produces a network of two synchronized TA for each EAST-ADL *FunctionPrototype*: an *Interface* TA with the elements provided in the architectural model and a *Behavior* TA.

The parts represented with a dotted line in Fig. 2 have not been implemented in the current version of the transformation. By extending our methodology to include an automatic transformation from the Simulink component model to the corresponding *Behavior* TA, the two models would be consistent and the verification results of the both frameworks would truly complement each other. However, information would be lost in such a transformation and the TA model would require manual refinements, such that the TA could represent the key behavior of the component that is largely consistent with the corresponding Simulink model.

5   An Example from Industry: Brake-by-Wire Case Study

In this section, we introduce the Brake-by-Wire (BBW) system that will be used through the paper as the running example to illustrate our techniques. The BBW system is a braking system equipped with an ABS function, and without any mechanical connectors between the brake pedal and the brake actuators. A sensor attached to the brake pedal reads its position, which is used to compute the desired global brake torque. For vehicles with stability control, the torque is influenced by the wheel speed and the desired torque for each wheel is calculated based on the following equation:

$$torque = (pos/100) \times maxBrakeTorque \times distribution \tag{1}$$

where *pos* is the pedal position with values $\in [0,100]$, *maxBrakeTorque* is the maximum global brake torque, and *distribution* is the static distribution factor. The ABS algorithm computes the slip rate s based on the following equation:

$$s = (v - w \times R)/v \tag{2}$$

where v is the speed of the vehicle, w is the speed of the wheel, and R is the radius of the wheel. The friction coefficient has a nonlinear relationship with the slip rate: when s starts increasing, the friction coefficient also increases, and its value reaches the peak when s is around 0.2. After that, further increase in s reduces the friction coefficient of the wheel. For this reason, if s is greater than 0.2 the brake actuator is released and no brake is applied, otherwise the requested brake torque is used.

Figure 3 presents the EAST-ADL model of the BBW system at the *Design Level*, and a set of requirements has been provided (to describe the functionality of this system at this level), as follows:

D$_1$ The torque on the wheel shall be defined as: $(pos/100) \times maxBrakeTorque \times distribution$.

D$_2$ If *VehicleSpeedIn* > *ABSVehicleSpeedThrsh* and s > *ABSSlipRateThrsh*, then *ABSBrakeTorqueOut* shall be set to 0Nm.

D$_3$ If s <= *ABSSlipRateThrsh* or *VehicleSpeedIn* <= *ABSVehicleSpeedThrsh*, then *ABSBrakeTorqueOut* shall be set to *RequestedTorqueIn*.

D$_4$ Investigate the latency between the wheel sensor and the brake pedal actuator.

The goal of this work is to show how one can verify the above requirements on the EAST-ADL description, using various verification techniques that we present in the following.

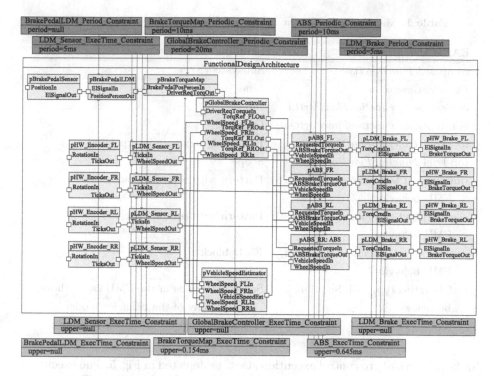

Fig. 3. The EAST-ADL model of the BBW system at design level.

6 Simulation of EAST-ADL Functional Architecture in Simulink

In this section we describe the simulation method proposed in Sect. 4, which has been implemented as an EATOP [1] plug-in called FMUSim that synthesizes a Simulink model and configures it according to the properties in the EAST-ADL model. The model transformation preserves the compositional hierarchy of the EAST-ADL model in EATOP, and is implemented as a one-to-one mapping between EAST-ADL elements and Simulink elements, as depicted in Table 1.

In order to simulate a time-trigged EAST-ADL function, the FMU block needs to be sampled once per period. However, the FMU blocks provided by the FMI Toolbox are continuous and cannot be sampled directly. As depicted in Fig. 4, the solution chosen in this implementation is to add a pulse generator and a subsystem *InputData* that is acting as a flip-flop clocked on the positive flank of the pulse. Since the execution of a Simulink block is instantaneous, another flip-flop *OutputData* is added, which is clocked on the negative flank of the pulse, such that the execution time of the FMU becomes equal to the pulse width. Similarly, in order to simulate an event-triggered EAST-ADL function, we reuse the negative flank of the trigger pulse from another time-triggered function that acts as the event source. The negative flank of *EventTriggerIn* is used to clock a

Table 1. Mapping rules for the EAST-ADL to Simulink transformation.

EAST-ADL element	Simulink element(s)
composed *FunctionType*	Subsystem
FunctionConnector	Line
non-top-level *FunctionFlowPortIn*	Inport
non-top-level *FunctionFlowPortOut*	Outport
top-level *FunctionFlowPortIn*	Repeating sequence interpolated
top-level *FunctionFlowPortOut*	Scope
time-trigged leaf *FunctionType* with FMU behavior	Pattern with several elements
event-trigged leaf *FunctionType* with FMU behavior	Pattern with several elements
continuous leaf *FunctionType* with FMU behavior	FMU block
leaf *FunctionType* with Simulink behavior	Same pattern as in the FMU cases above, but a copy of the behavior model is inserted instead of the FMU block

flip-flop *InputData* to control execution start, as depicted in Fig. 5. The execution period of the function is then simulated by adding a flip-flop *OutputData*, which is clocked on a step down that is generated at a time equal to the worst-case execution time (WCET) after the function starts executing. The clock signal is exported as *EventTriggerOut* for the pattern to be repeatable. This means that it is possible to simulate a chain of event-trigged functions with the pattern.

In this transformation, we have not addressed the nondeterminism or the possible interleavings of the *FunctionPrototypes*'s execution. Since we are performing simulations on the transformed model, the current execution pattern is one of infinitely many interleavings and event sequences, which means that some errors may be overlooked. To represent deviating clock speeds and arbitrary start-up time, an arbitrary component could be added by the transformation to the offset and period times, and a deterministic yet random sequence would secure repeatability of the simulation runs. Multiple runs with randomized parametrization would increase confidence through the extended state space covered. However, these extensions to the method are not in the scope of this paper.

Application on the BBW Case Study. We have applied the transformation described above on the BBW case study. The resulting model contains one FMU for each leaf EAST-ADL *FunctionPrototype*, plus the required monitors for the *VVCase* specified in the EAST-ADL model.

As depicted in Fig. 6, *pBrakeTorqueRRMonitor* is a complex monitor despite the fact that it verifies a simple linear function like requirement D_1 for the rear right wheel. The time until a new pedal position has propagated through the system and has given rise to a new torque value *GBC_TorqueReq_RR* varies

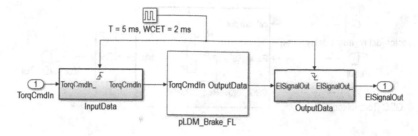

Fig. 4. Simulink pattern for modeling time-trigged execution of an EAST-ADL function with execution time. The block *pLDM_Brake_FL* represents the FMU.

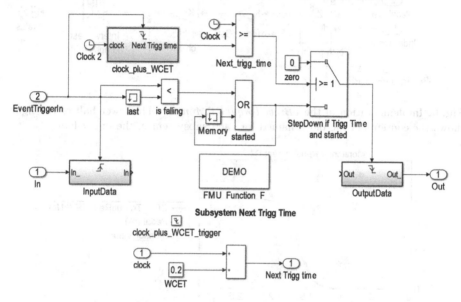

Fig. 5. Simulink pattern for modeling event-trigged execution of an EAST-ADL function with execution time. The block *FMU Function F* represents the FMU.

between *delay_min* and *delay_max* [ms]. As shown in Fig. 7, the torque requested by the brake controller on the rear right wheel is a linear scaling of the pedal position delayed by the propagation time. The boolean monitor function "looks back" in time according to the delay interval, and is able to find a pedal position corresponding to the requested torque at all evaluated time points. The result shows that requirement D_1 is satisfied to the extent guaranteed by the simulation technique.

7   Formal Semantics of EAST-ADL as a Network of Timed Automata

To formally verify that the architectural model meets its requirements, we need to exhaustively explore all the function blocks in the model. In this context, we

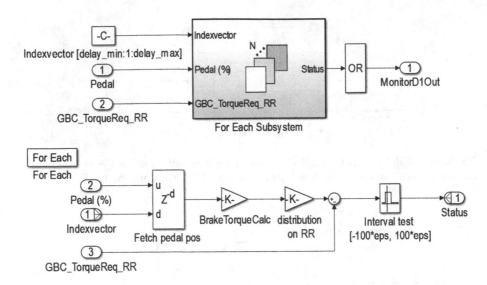

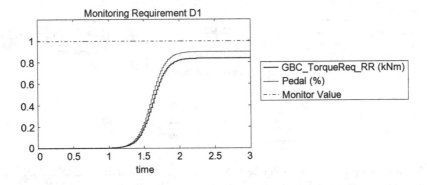

Fig. 6. Implementation of the *pBrakeTorqueRRMonitor*. The lower half of the figure shows the contents of the block named for each subsystem in the upper half.

Fig. 7. Simulation results provided by the *pBrakeTorqueRRMonitor*.

need to represent the execution semantics of the EAST-ADL function blocks using a network of TA (see Fig. 2), which has a well-defined formal semantics in terms of timed transition systems [5]. We have developed an automatic transformation, considering a subset of the EAST-ADL elements, which we define as a tuple:

$$EAST - ADL_{DesignLevel} \triangleq \langle F_P, Con, DP, Trigg, TC \rangle,$$

where F_P is the set of *FunctionPrototypes*, *Con* is the set of connectors between the F_P, DP is the set of data ports, defined as the union of input ports and output ports, *Trigg* is the set of triggering elements, defined as the union of events and periodic triggers, and TC the set of the model's timing constraints.

In a similar manner, the TA is defined as a tuple:

$$TA \triangleq \langle L, l_0, C, A, E, I \rangle,$$

where L is a finite set of locations, $l_0 \in L$ is the initial location, C is a set of clocks, A is a set of possible actions, E is a set of edges between two locations, and I is a set of invariants attached to the locations.

The transformation is a one-to-one function $\pi : \text{EAST-ADL}_{DesignLevel} \rightarrow \text{TA}$, which maps each element in the $\text{EAST-ADL}_{DesignLevel}$ to a TA element. The mapping rules are:

- Each function F_P is defined in terms of a network of two TA, as shown in Fig. 8. To preserve the "read-execute-write" semantics of EAST-ADL, the *Interface* TA (see Fig. 8a) has four locations: (i) *Idle*, (ii) a *Read* location that allows the update of the variables according to the values on the input ports, independent of other computations, (iii) an *Exec* location that triggers the *Behavior* TA (see Fig. 8b) that models the desired behavior of F_P, and (iv) a *Write* location that allows the update of the output ports according to the values of the computed internal variables, respectively, independent of other computations.
- Each input and output port DP is mapped to a global variable in the TA network, respectively.
- Each connector *Con* from output port $Port_{out1}$ of F_{P1} to input port $Port_{in2}$ of F_{P2} is transformed into an assignment $Port_{in2} := Port_{out1}$, along the edge from *Idle* to *Read*;
- The triggering of each interface TA is based on the triggering $Trigg$ associated to the EAST-ADL F_P. Concretely, this creates two possible instantiations of the *Interface* TA: (i) for timed-triggered F_P the transformation produces a local clock, plus invariants and guards on TA (see Fig. 9a), and (ii) for event-triggered F_P the transformation produces a set of dedicated variables that need to be constantly updated and reset, respectively (see Fig. 10a).
- Other timing annotations TC, e.g., the execution time, can be included in the timing behavior of the TA model.

Once we obtain the network of TA corresponding to the EAST-ADL model, one manually edits the *Behavior* TA to match the desired behavior of the corresponding *FunctionPrototype*. Formal analysis techniques like model-checking and statistical model-checking are then applied to verify the resulting model. In the next section we apply such transformation on the BBW EAST-ADL model, to enable the latter's verification.

8   Analysis of EAST-ADL Models Using Model-Checking and Statistical Model Checking

We have applied our method on the BBW architecture, and generated a network of 50 TA, by transforming each of the 25 F_P of Fig. 3 into a network of two

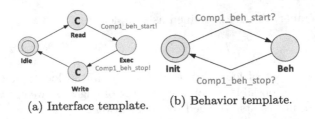

(a) Interface template.   (b) Behavior template.

Fig. 8. The generic TA semantics of an EAST-ADL F_P.

synchronized TA, respectively. In Figs. 9 and 10, we exemplify the transformation of two F_P as follows: Fig. 9a presents the interface of the time-triggered $pABS\_FL$ F_P, automatically generated from the EAST-ADL model, Fig. 9b presents the behavior of the $pABS\_FL$ F_P obtained after manually editing the dedicated TA template (see Fig. 8b); Fig. 10a shows the interface of the event-triggered $pVehicleSpeedEstimator$ F_P, whereas Fig. 10b shows the behavior of the $pVehicle$ $SpeedEstimator$ F_P, after manually editing the dedicated TA template. On this formal model, we have applied model-checking and statistical model-checking techniques to validate the original EAST-ADL model against the requirements introduced in Sect. 5.

Model-checking with UPPAAL. With UPPAAL, we have simulated and we have attempted to verify the previously described network of TA. However, the size of the model has lead to a state space explosion. On a computer with 1.8 Ghz Intel processor and 8 GB memory, the verifier could explore only 10 962 377 states before it had run out of memory. This is not surprising, since the BBW system is subject to an enormous state-space explosion due to large number to TA in the network, each with its clock and its set of variable created based o the ports of the corresponding *FunctionPrototype*.

Consequently, we have used UPPAAL to verify a simplified version of the BBW system with one wheel only. Properties D_2 and D_3 are formalized as TCTL properties [5], as follows:

D_2 $A[]$ $pABS\_FL\_VehicleSpeedIn > speed\_thrshld$ *and* $pABS\_FL\_s == true$
   imply $pABS\_FL\_ABSBrakeTorqueOut == 0$.

D_3 $A[]$ $pABS\_FL\_VehicleSpeedIn <= speed\_thrshld$ *or* $pABS\_FL\_s == false$
   imply $pABS\_FL\_ABSBrakeTorqueOut == pABS\_FL\_RequestedTorqueIn$.

Both properties have been verified and hold on the model. For property D_2 the verification took 13,7 s and used 26 900 KB of memory. For property D_3 the verification took 9,1 s and used 26 916 KB of memory.

Statistical Model-Checking with UPPAAL SMC. TA is a suitable formalism for analyzing architectural models like EAST-ADL, and enables symbolic model-checking techniques to provide a rigorous proof of verifying or refuting a TCTL property. However, such techniques suffer from state-space explosion in terms of number of parallel components in the model, which is the case with complex, industrial systems. One possible solution is the use of a statistical

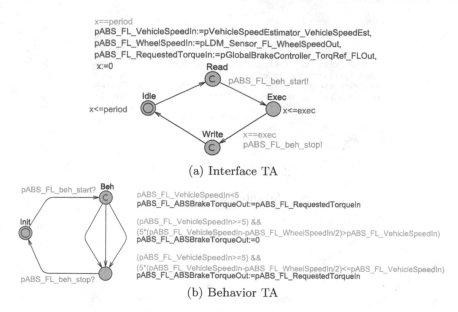

(a) Interface TA

(b) Behavior TA

Fig. 9. The TA model for the *pABS_FL* EAST-ADL F_P.

model-checking engine to generate stochastic simulations and employ statistical methods to estimate probabilities and probability distributions over time with given confidence levels. The UPPAAL modeling language has been extended with probabilistic and dynamical constructs, given a stochastic semantics of timed automata networks [9], and the tool has been equipped with statistical model-checking (SMC) algorithms [10] to decide qualitative properties in terms of probabilities and cost. The symbolic and statistical techniques complement each other: SMC can show results only up to a specified level of confidence and never for certain like symbolic techniques, but it is a cheap way to generate and confirm safety counter-examples where symbolic techniques may employ expensive over-approximation [11]. Here, we attempt to analyze requirement D_4.

Since UPPAAL SMC works on stochastic models, we have manually added probabilistic extensions to the four-wheels BBW model that contains the timed behavior. Figure 11a and b show exponential rates added to locations *Idle* and *Exec* of one Encoder component of Fig. 3. The rate of 1 means that the component may potentially stay in the location forever, but it will stay there for 1 time unit on average which is consistent with the timed behavior. Further, we are interested in latency between pressing the pedal and applying the brakes, hence we added a monitoring stop-watch automaton shown in Fig. 11c. The monitoring automaton has a stop-watch L that is stopped originally in location *Wait* by specifying that the derivative is zero: $L' == 0$. The stop-watch is started when synchronization *pBrakePedalSensor_beh_start?* is received (the derivative $L' == 1$ is implicit in timed automata). The stop-watch is stopped again when any of the wheels receive the synchronization braking signal, like *pHW_Brake_FL_beh_start?* or *pHW_Brake_FR_beh_start?* (the synchronizations

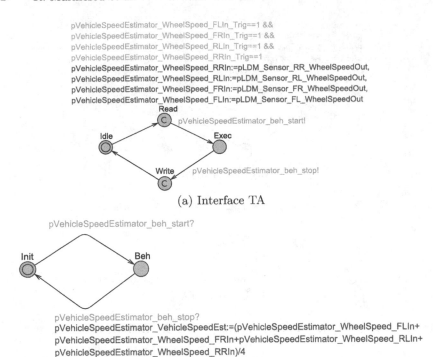

(a) Interface TA

(b) Behavior TA

Fig. 10. The TA model for the *pVehicleSpeedEstimator* EAST-ADL F_P.

are on different edges that are drawn on top of each other to minimize cluttering). The latency can be estimated by the following query: $Pr[bm.L <= 1000](<> bm.Done)$ that asks what is the probability that the brake monitor process bm will end up in location *Done* in terms of the stop-watch L value. The result is shown in Fig. 11d. The average latency is 5 time units but it tends to be high even though our added stochastic delay assumptions are decreasing towards infinity, which is a worrying behavior. The good news is that it seems to be strictly limited by 6 time units and no simulation has been observed greater or equal than 6 time units, which is on the other hand surprising, as the model contains components with unlimited delays.

9   Related Work

Several researchers have looked into the formal analysis and verification of EAST-ADL models. Kang et al. [13] propose a component-based analysis framework for the EAST-ADL models extended with TA semantics based on the UPPAAL PORT model-checker. Mallet et al. [14] describe the use of UML MARTE profile for the timing analysis of EAST-ADL. In addition, Feng et al. [12] propose a translation of EAST-ADL activity diagrams into the input language of SPIN for formal verification. More recently, Qureshi et al. [15] describe a model-to-model

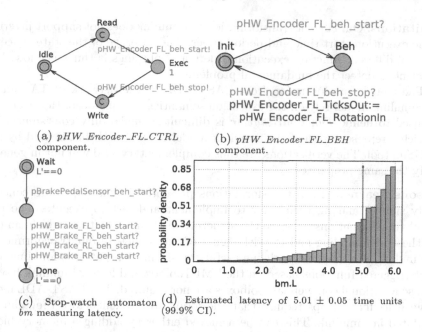

(a) *pHW_Encoder_FL_CTRL* component.

(b) *pHW_Encoder_FL_BEH* component.

(c) Stop-watch automaton *bm* measuring latency.

(d) Estimated latency of 5.01 ± 0.05 time units (99.9% CI).

Fig. 11. The components decorated with stochastic extensions and estimated latency between pressing the pedal and applying brakes.

transformation from' EAST-ADL to timed automata towards formal verification based on timing constraints using UPPAAL. Closely related to our work, in the context of model-driven development, Biehl et al. [6] propose a modular approach for data integration, together with their experiences from applying this approach for the verification of EAST-ADL models. The latter is focused on introducing a systematic solution for model-based tool integration, whereas our work is focused on the analysis of industrial systems through complementary methodologies that provide various degrees of assurance.

10   Conclusions and Discussion

In this paper, we have presented a set of analysis techniques dedicated to the simulation and verification of automotive embedded systems specified in the EAST-ADL architectural language. In order to provide different correctness guarantees, we present three techniques that enable the transformation in, and analysis of EAST-ADL models with: (i) Simulink, a design and simulation tool used extensively in industry, (ii) UPPAAL for model-checking purposes, and (iii) UPPAAL SMC, a new extension of UPPAAL with statistical model-checking capabilities. We report our analysis results by applying all these frameworks on the industrial BBW case study. As future work, we intend to investigate the possible integration and application of these frameworks into the large-vehicle industrial development process.

Limitations. Our current transformation to Simulink does not support jittering of the execution start time and period times. The coverage of the state space in terms of different function execution orders and phasings is thus very low, but sufficient to detect the fundamental problems.

The model transformation from EAST-ADL to the network of TA and to the Simulink model rely on the execution semantics of EAST-ADL. However, the TA used to define *FunctionBehavior* is difficult to make fully consistent with the richer representation of the Simulink model or the FMU that is used by the FMUSim tool. The verifications are thus complementary, and will not in general verify the same properties.

Lessons Learned. Both transformations presented in the paper are conceptually simple, making them easy to implement and fast to execute. The two model transformations preserve the structure of the architecture, which simplifies the understanding and the debugging of the model. In our transformation to Simulink, it is possible to define useful transformation patterns for time and event triggered functions based on the FMI Toolbox and legacy Simulink blocks only, so additional commercial toolboxes are not required. The EAST-ADL models with feedback loops require that the loops are broken before they can be simulated in Simulink. This can be achieved either by adding a memory block somewhere in each loop or latching the subsystem ports of at least one subsystem in each loop. Moreover, the network of TA can be easily used for statistical model-checking with UPPAAL SMC, ensuring formal verification of the model even if the analysis with UPPAAL leads to a state-space explosion.

Acknowledgment. The research leading to these results has received funding from the ARTEMIS Joint Undertaking under grant agreement number 269335, and from VINNOVA, the Swedish Governmental Agency for Innovation Systems, within the MBAT project.

References

1. Eclipse. The EAST-ADL Tool Platform (EATOP) Editor Tool (2014). http://www.eclipse.org/proposals/modeling.eatop/
2. Mathworks. The MATLAB Simulink Design Tool (2014). http://www.mathworks.se/products/simulink/
3. Modelica Association Project. The Functional Mock-up Interface (FMI) Standard (2014). http://www.fmi-standard.org/
4. The AUTomotive Open System ARchitecture (AUTOSAR) (2014). http://www.autosar.org/
5. Alur, R.: Timed automata. In: Halbwachs, N., Peled, D.A. (eds.) CAV 1999. LNCS, vol. 1633, pp. 8–22. Springer, Heidelberg (1999)
6. Biehl, M., Sjöstedt, C.-J., Törngren, M.: A modular tool integration approach-experiences from two case studies. In: 3rd Workshop on Model-Driven Tool & Process Integration at the European Conference on Modelling Foundations and Applications (2010)

7. Blom, H., Lönn, H., Hagl, F., Papadopoulos, Y., Reiser, M.-O., Sjöstedt, C.-J., Chen, D.J., Tagliabò, F., Torchiaro, S., Tucci, S.: EAST-ADL: An architecture description language for automotive software-intensive systems. EAST-ADL WhitePaper, vol. 1 (2013)
8. Cuenot, P., Chen, D., Gerard, S., Lonn, H., Reiser, M.-O., Servat, D., Sjostedt, C.-J., Kolagari, R.T., Torngren, M., Weber, M.: Managing complexity of automotive electronics using the EAST-ADL. In: 12th IEEE International Conference on Engineering Complex Computer Systems, pp. 353–358. IEEE (2007)
9. David, A., Larsen, K.G., Legay, A., Mikučionis, M., Poulsen, D.B., van Vliet, J., Wang, Z.: Statistical model checking for networks of priced timed automata. In: Fahrenberg, U., Tripakis, S. (eds.) FORMATS 2011. LNCS, vol. 6919, pp. 80–96. Springer, Heidelberg (2011)
10. David, A., Larsen, K.G., Legay, A., Mikučionis, M., Wang, Z.: Time for statistical model checking of real-time systems. In: Gopalakrishnan, G., Qadeer, S. (eds.) CAV 2011. LNCS, vol. 6806, pp. 349–355. Springer, Heidelberg (2011)
11. David, A., Larsen, K.G., Legay, A., Mikučionis, M.: Schedulability of herschel-planck revisited using statistical model checking. In: Margaria, T., Steffen, B. (eds.) ISoLA 2012, Part II. LNCS, vol. 7610, pp. 293–307. Springer, Heidelberg (2012)
12. Feng, L., Chen, D., Lönn, H., Torngren, M.: Verifying system behaviors in EAST-ADL2 with the SPIN model checker. In: International Conference on Mechatronics and Automation, pp. 144–149 (2010)
13. Kang, E.-Y., Enoiu, E.P., Marinescu, R., Seceleanu, C., Schobbens, P.-Y., Pettersson, P.: A methodology for formal analysis and verification of EAST-ADL models. Reliab. Eng. Syst. Saf. Int. J. 120, 127–138 (2013)
14. Mallet, F., Peraldi-Frati, M.-A., André, C.: Marte CCSL to execute EAST-ADL timing requirements. In: International Symposium on Object/Component/Service-Oriented Real-Time Distributed Computing, pp. 249–253. IEEE (2009)
15. Qureshi, T.N., Chen, D.-J., Persson, M., Trngren, M.: On integrating EAST-ADL and UPPAAL for embedded system architecture verification. In: Sangiovanni-Vincentelli, A. (ed.) Embedded Systems Development, vol. 20. Springer, New York (2014)

Specifying and Verifying Concurrent C Programs with TLA+

Amira Methni[1,4](✉), Matthieu Lemerre[2], Belgacem Ben Hedia[1],
Serge Haddad[3], and Kamel Barkaoui[4]

[1] Embedded Real-Time System Lab, CEA, LIST, 91191 Gif-sur-yvette, France
{amira.methni,belgacem.ben-hedia}@cea.fr
[2] Software Safety Lab, CEA, LIST, 91191 Gif-sur-yvette, France
matthieu.lemerre@cea.fr
[3] LSV, ENS Cachan, CNRS&INRIA, Paris, France
haddad@lsv.ens-cachan.fr
[4] CNAM, CEDRIC, Paris, France
barkaoui@cnam.fr

Abstract. Verifying software systems automatically from their source
code rather than modelling them in a dedicated language gives more confidence in establishing their properties. Here we propose a formal specification and verification approach for concurrent C programs directly
based on the semantics of C. We define a set of translation rules and
implement it in a tool (C2TLA+) that automatically translates C code
into a TLA+ specification. The TLC model checker can use this specification to generate a model, allowing to check the absence of runtime errors
and dead code in the C program in a given configuration. In addition, we
show how translated specifications interact with manually written ones
to: check the C code against safety or liveness properties; provide concurrency primitives or model hardware that cannot be expressed in C;
and use abstract versions of translated C functions to address the state
explosion problem. All these verifications have been conducted on an
industrial case study, which is a part of the microkernel of the PharOS
real-time system.

1 Introduction

Most software systems like the Linux kernel or the Apache Webserver are implemented in a low level language such as C, which is one of the most used programming languages in industry. Verifying C code is challenging, in particular
due to the presence of pointers and pointer arithmetic.

Moreover, C software systems are often concurrent, and traditional testing
techniques are not efficient to check the correctness of the implementation. Thus,
the use of formal verification techniques is essential. We address these issues in
the context of formal verification of operating systems microkernels written in
C code. In this paper, we focus on the model checking technique, a popular technique for the verification of correctness properties of finite-state systems. Given
a set of properties expressed in a temporal logic and a model, it automatically

© Springer International Publishing Switzerland 2015
C. Artho and P.C. Ölveczky (Eds.): FTSCS 2014, CCIS 476, pp. 206–222, 2015.
DOI: 10.1007/978-3-319-17581-2_14

analyzes the state space of the model and checks whether the model satisfies the properties [6]. To apply this technique to the verification of C programs, the target modeling language should express all C features, handle concurrency, allow to state the properties that we want to verify, and its tools should scale up to large systems.

Contribution. Our main contribution is to provide a formal specification and verification approach of C concurrent programs, based on both axiomatic (e.g., pre-post conditions) and operational (executable model) specification of a C implementation. We use TLA+ [17] as a formal specification language for writing our specifications. In this approach, we translate a C code to an executable TLA+ specification using the C2TLA+ tool that we present in the paper. The generated specifications can be checked for runtime errors in the C code. We show how the specifications thus generated can be completed with manually written TLA+ specifications: to provide concurrency primitives, to model hardware that cannot be expressed in C, to check the C code against safety or liveness properties and to provide an abstract operational specification. In the latter case, the operational specification can be used in place of the C code in order to verify the whole system. Preliminary experiments hint that this could considerably lessen the state explosion problem. These examples are presented in a concrete case study, which is part of the microkernel of the real-time operating system PharOS [19].

Outline. The rest of the paper is organized as follows. We discuss related work in Sect. 2. We give an overview of TLA+ in Sect. 3. Section 4 presents the global approach and focus on the translation from C to TLA+. Section 5 presents a concrete application of the approach on the case study. Section 6 concludes and presents future research directions.

2 Related Work

There are a variety of formal verification techniques. Among them there are deductive verification techniques using theorem proving such as VCC [7]. These techniques provide a rigorous approach but usually require a lot of human effort and user expertise. Model checking is an automatic technique which requires less human effort because it is fully automated once the system and its properties are specified. But, it is restricted to finite-state systems. In what follows we focus on the model checking tools for C programs related to our work.

SLAM [2] was the first model checker for C programs to implement the *Counterexample Guided Abstraction Refinement* (CEGAR) approach [5]. This approach has been used later in the BLAST [11] toolkit. SLAM and BLAST have been used to check device drivers but they are only used for sequential C programs.

Besides CEGAR based tools, an approach consists to transform the C code into the input language of a model checker. Modex [14] can automatically extract a Promela model from a C code implementation. The Promela code generated is then checked with the SPIN [12] model checker. Promela is a simple language that does not handle pointer and has no procedure calls. Modex handles these missing features by including embedded declarations and statements inside Promela specifications. The embedded code fragments can not be checked by the SPIN and can contain a division by zero error, or null pointer dereference. To mitigate this problem, Modex instruments additional checks using assertions. But, not all errors can be anticipated and the model checker can crash [13].

CBMC [4] is a bounded model checker for ANSI C programs that translates a program into a formula (in Static Single Assignment form) which is then fed to a SAT or SMT solver to check its satisfiability. It can be used to verify array bounds, pointer safety, exceptions and user-specified assertions. On the other hand, CBMC explores program behavior exhaustively but only up to a given depth, i. e., it is restricted to programs without deep loops [10]. PlusCal [18] is a high-level language for expressing multiprocess algorithms. A PlusCal algorithm can be automatically translated into a TLA+ specification. PlusCal-2 [1] improves Lamport's PlusCal language by adding new constructs like hierarchical processes and specifying atomicity for some part of the code. Moreover, it does not support some constructs of imperative programming like pointer-based structures and does not handle function calls. PlusCal is also an algorithm language that can be used to replace pseudo code but cannot be used in the final implementation.

In this work, we use TLA+ as formal framework which provides an expressive power to specify the semantics of a programming language. It is supported by the TLC model checker and the TLAPS [8] prover. Moreover, TLA+ is a logic that can reason about concurrent systems and can express safety and liveness properties unlike SLAM, BLAST and CBMC which have limited support for concurrent properties as they only check safety properties. Furthermore, TLA+ provides a mechanism for structuring large specifications using a refinement process between different levels of abstraction unlike Spin and CBMC.

3   An Overview of TLA+

TLA+ [17] is the specification language of the Temporal Logic of Actions (TLA). TLA is a variant of linear temporal logic introduced by Lamport [16] for specifying and reasoning about concurrent systems. The syntax of TLA is given in Fig. 1 (the symbol $\triangleq$ means *equal by definition*). Readers interested in a more detailed presentation of TLA+ can refer to Lamport's book [17].

TLA+ specifies a system by describing its possible behaviors. A *behavior* is an infinite sequence of states. A *state* is an assignment of values to variables. A *state function* is a nonboolean expression built from constants, variables and constant operators and it assigns a value to each state. For example, $y + 2$ is a state function that assigns to state s two plus the value that s assigns to the variable y. An *action* is a boolean expression containing constants, variables and primed variables (adorned with "'" operator). Unprimed variables refer to variable values in the actual state and primed variables refer to their values in

$\langle formula \rangle$ $\triangleq$ $\langle predicate \rangle$ | $\Box[\langle action \rangle]_{\langle state\ function \rangle}$ | $\neg \langle formula \rangle$
                    | $\langle formula \rangle \wedge \langle formula \rangle$ | $\Box \langle formula \rangle$

$\langle action \rangle$ $\triangleq$ boolean valued expression containing constant symbols, variables,
                   and primed variables

$\langle predicate \rangle$ $\triangleq$ $\langle formula \rangle$ with no primed variables | ENABLED $\langle action \rangle$

$\langle state\ function \rangle$ $\triangleq$ nonboolean expression containing constant symbols and variables

Fig. 1. TLA syntax [17]

the next-state. Thus, an action represents a relation between old states and new states. A *state predicate* (or predicate for short) is an action with no primed variables.

TLA+ formulas are built up from actions and predicates using boolean operators ($\neg$ and $\wedge$ and others that can be derived from these two), quantification over logical variables ($\forall, \exists$), and the unary temporal operator $\Box$ (*always*) of linear temporal logic [20].

The behaviors satisfying this specification are the ones that represent correct behaviors of the system, where a behavior represents a conceivable history of a universe that may contain the system.

The predicate "ENABLED $\mathcal{A}$", where $\mathcal{A}$ is an action, is defined to be true in a state s iff there exists some state t such that the pair of states $\langle s, t \rangle$ satisfies $\mathcal{A}$. The formula $[\mathcal{A}]_{vars}$, where $\mathcal{A}$ is an action and *vars* the tuple of all system variables, is equal to $(\mathcal{A} \vee (vars' = vars))$ where $vars'$ is the expression obtained by priming all variables in *vars*. It asserts that every step (pair of successive states) is either an $\mathcal{A}$ step or else leaves the values of all variables *vars* unchanged. TLA+ defines the abbreviation "UNCHANGED *vars*" to denote that $vars' = vars$. While TLA+ permits a variety of specification styles, the specification that we use is defined by:

$$Spec \triangleq Init \wedge \Box[Next]_{vars} \wedge Fairness \qquad (1)$$

where:

- *Init* is a state predicate describing the possible initial states by assigning values to all system variables,
- *Next* is an action representing the program's next-state relation,
- *vars* is the tuple of all variables,
- *Fairness* is an optional formula representing weak or strong assumptions about the execution of actions.

Formula *Spec* is true of a behavior σ iff *Init* is true of the first state of σ and every step of σ is either a *Next* step or a "stuttering step", in which none of the specified variables change their values, and *Fairness* holds.

The TLA+ formula $Spec \Rightarrow \phi$ is valid when the model represented by *Spec* satisfies the property ϕ, or implements the model ϕ.

TLA+ has a model checker called TLC that can be used to check the validity of safety and liveness properties. TLC handles specifications that have the standard form of the formula (1). It requires a configuration file which defines the

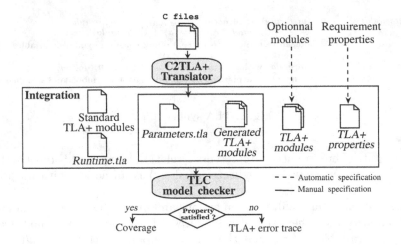

Fig. 2. Specification and verification process

finite-state instance to analyze. TLC begins by generating all states satisfying the initial predicate *Init*. Then, it generates every possible next-state t such that the pair of states $\langle s, t \rangle$ satisfies *Next* and the *Fairness* constraints, looking for a state where an invariant is violated. Finally, it checks temporal properties over the state space.

4   Specification and Verification Process

4.1   Proposed Approach

Approach Workflow. The specification and verification process is illustrated in Fig. 2. The first step of the process is to translate from an implementation provided by one or more .c files a TLA+ specification using our translator C2TLA+. Before translation, the C files are parsed and normalized according to CIL (C Intermediate Language) [21]. Normalization to CIL makes programs more amenable to analysis and transformation. In particular, all expressions containing side-effects are put into separate statements (introducing temporary variables); initializers for local variables are turned into assignments; all forms of loops (`while`, `for` and `do-while`) are normalized as a single `while(1)` looping construct plus explicit `goto` statement.

After obtaining the Abstract Syntax Tree (AST) of the C program, C2TLA+ generates the TLA+ specification according to a set of translation rules described in Subsect. 4.2. The whole system is composed of TLA+ modules resulting from C translation or manual specification that come from different sources:

- Several standard modules are provided with TLA+. They contain the definition of basic operators. Like *Head*, *Tail*, *Len* (for length), ∘ (for concatenation), and *SubSeq* (for subsequence) that are defined in *Sequences* module.

- The *Runtime* module contains the TLA+ definition of arithmetic, logical and relational operators used by C2TLA+, as well as the definition of *load()* and *store()* for loading/storing an lvalue in the memory.
- Modules resulting from translation. C2TLA+ generates for each .c file a TLA+ module and the *Parameters* module which contains the definition of constants, type sizes, offsets of member fields and variables used by the translation. It also defines the initial predicate *Init*, the action *Next* and the specification formula *Spec*. For simplicity, we assume that the size of an integer or a pointer is 1 (one memory cell).
- Optional manual modules can be specified by the user. They provide concurrency primitives or hardware that can not be expressed in C, or an abstract model.

The set of properties is manually specified. Then, all the modules are integrated to form the complete specification, which is given to TLC to generate the model and check the properties (or refinements) to be verified. If a property is not satisfied, TLC reports a trace that leads to the bad state. TLC also provides coverage information, i.e., the number of times each action was "executed" to construct a new state. Using this information, we can identify actions that are never "executed" and which might indicate an error in the specification. Both the trace and coverage information can be translated back to C.

The Considered Subset of C. We restrict ourselves to a subset of C resulting from the simplifications done by CIL. Table 1 gives the BNF representation of the AST of CIL for this subset. The considered aspects include basic data-types (int, struct, enum), integer operations, arrays, pointers, pointer arithmetic, all kinds of control flow statements, function calls and recursion. Currently, we do not handle float types, non-portable conversions between objects of different types, dynamic allocation, function calls through pointers, and assignment of structs (not needed by our case study), but the translator could be updated to handle them.

4.2 Memory Layout of Concurrent C Program

A concurrent program consists in several interleaved sequences of operations called *processes* (corresponding to threads in C). C2TLA+ attributes a unique identifier to each process, and defines the constant *ProcSet* to be the set of all process identifiers.

The memory layout of a C program in C2TLA+ is organized into four regions:

- A region that contains global (and static) variables. This region is represented by a an array, called *mem*, that maps addresses to values. This memory region is shared by all processes.
- A region that contains local variables and function parameters. It is represented by the TLA+ variable *stack_data*. This region is represented by a 2-dimensional array: one dimension corresponds to the process *id* (the stack

Table 1. BNF representation of the AST of CIL for the considered subset of C (The symbols $+_{pa}/-_{pp}$ denote the addition/substraction between a pointer and an integer. $-_{pp}$ denotes the substraction between two pointers. ε is a terminal symbol that denotes an empty element).

```
<prg>                                    ::=<decls> (<fun_def>)*
<decls>                                  ::= εdecl | <decl> <decls>
<decl>                                   ::=<type> VAR_ID ;
<params>                                 ::= εparam | <param> <params>
<param>                                  ::=<type> VAR_ID ,
<fun_def>                                ::=<type> FUN_ID (<params>) { <decl> <stmt> }
<type>                                   ::=   int | <type> * | struct { (<type> VAR_ID ;)* };
                                         | enum { ENUM_ID , (ENUM_ID)* };
<stmt>                                   ::=   { (<stmt>;)* } | while(1) <stmt>
                                         | if <expr> <stmt> (else <stmt>)? | <lval> = <expr>
                                         | <lval> = FUN_ID ( (<expr>,)* ) | LABEL_ID: <stmt>
                                         | goto LABEL_ID | break | continue | return (<expr>)?
                                         | εstmt  \* Skip instruction *\
<expr>                                   ::=   <expr> <bin_op> <expr> | <un_op> <expr>
                                         | <expr> +pa<expr> | <expr> -pa<expr>
                                         | <expr> -pp<expr> | & <expr> | <lval> | CONSTANT
<lval>                                   ::=   VAR_ID <offs> | (* <expr> ) <offs>
<offs>                                   ::=   .FIELD_ID <offs> | [ <expr> ] <offs> | εoffs
<bin_op>                                 ::=   * | + | - | % | / | > | >= | < | <= | == | != | && | ||
<un_op>                                  ::=   !
{VAR, FUN, ENUM, LABEL, FIELD}_ID        ::=   [a-zA-Z][0-9a-zA-Z_]*
CONSTANT                                 ::=   [1-9]([0-9])*
```

is not shared between processes); the other to addresses (i. e., offsets in the stack). The stack of each function is divided into *stack frames* whose boundaries (for each process) are given in another variable, *stack_regs*. Each stack frame corresponds to a call to a function which has not yet returned. Note that this representation allows a function to access variables in its callers (through pointers), which is frequent in C.

- A region that stores the program counter of each process; i.e., which statement is being executed. This information needs to be saved and restored on function calls and returns. Rather than saving the program counter together with the data (in the *stack_data* variable), we find it simpler to organize the registers of the program as a stack. We define the TLA+ variable *stack_regs*, associating to each process a stack of records. Each record contains two fields:

  - *pc*, the program counter, points to the current statement of the function being executed, represented by a tuple ⟨function name, label⟩;
  - *fp*, the frame pointer, contains the base offset of the current stack frame.

Note that we do not need to store the stack pointer, which is already given using "*Len(stack_data)*". Each element of the stack of records represents the registers of a function in the callstack; in particular, "*Head(stack_regs[id])*" represents the registers of the function being currently executed by the process *id*.

- A region that contains the values returned by a process. It is modeled using an array called *ret*, indexed by the process identifier.

C2TLA+ maps each C variable to unique TLA+ constant modeled by a record composed with two fields. The first one, *loc*, determines the memory region

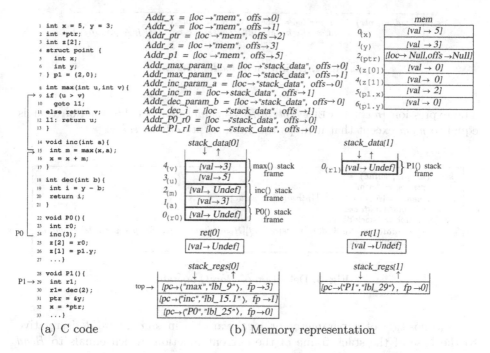

```
1  int x = 5, y = 3;
2  int *ptr;
3  int z[2];
4  struct point {
5      int x;
6      int y;
7  } p1 = (2,0);

8  int max(int u,int v){
9      if (u > v)
10         goto 11;
11     else return v;
12  11: return u;
13  }

14  void inc(int a){
15     int m = max(x,a);
16     x = x + m;
17  }

18  int dec(int b){
19     int i = y - b;
20     return i;
21  }

22  void P0(){
23     int r0;
24     inc(3);
25     z[2] = r0;
26     z[1] = p1.y;
27     ...}

28  void P1(){
29     int r1;
30     r1= dec(2);
31     ptr = &y;
32     x = *ptr;
33     ...}
```

PO (brace covering lines 22-27)
P1 (arrow at line 29)
(arrow at line 9)
(arrow at line 15)

$Addr\_x = [loc \to "mem",\ offs \to 0]$
$Addr\_y = [loc \to "mem",\ offs \to 1]$
$Addr\_ptr = [loc \to "mem",\ offs \to 2]$
$Addr\_z = [loc \to "mem",\ offs \to 3]$
$Addr\_p1 = [loc \to "mem",\ offs \to 5]$
$Addr\_max\_param\_u = [loc \to "stack\_data",\ offs \to 0]$
$Addr\_max\_param\_v = [loc \to "stack\_data",\ offs \to 1]$
$Addr\_inc\_param\_a = [loc \to "stack\_data",\ offs \to 0]$
$Addr\_inc\_m = [loc \to "stack\_data",\ offs \to 1]$
$Addr\_dec\_param\_b = [loc \to "stack\_data",\ offs \to 0]$
$Addr\_dec\_i = [loc \to "stack\_data",\ offs \to 1]$
$Addr\_P0\_r0 = [loc \to "stack\_data",\ offs \to 0]$
$Addr\_P1\_r1 = [loc \to "stack\_data",\ offs \to 0]$

mem
$0_{(x)}$ [val → 5]
$1_{(y)}$ [val → 3]
$2_{(ptr)}$ [loc→ Null,offs →Null]
$3_{(z[0])}$ [val → 0]
$4_{(z[1])}$ [val → 0]
$5_{(p1.x)}$ [val → 2]
$6_{(p1.y)}$ [val → 0]

stack_data[0]
$4_{(v)}$ [val→3] } max() stack frame
$3_{(u)}$ [val→5]
$2_{(m)}$ [val→ Undef] } inc() stack frame
$1_{(a)}$ [val→3]
$0_{(r0)}$ [val→ Undef] } P0() stack frame

ret[0]
[val→ Undef]

stack_data[1]
$0_{(r1)}$ [val→ Undef] } P1() stack frame

ret[1]
[val →Undef]

stack_regs[0]
top → [pc→("max","lbl_9"), fp →3]
       [pc→("inc","lbl_15.1"), fp →1]
       [pc→("P0","lbl_25"), fp →0]

stack_regs[1]
[pc→("P1","lbl_29"), fp →0]

(a) C code   (b) Memory representation

Fig. 3. Example of a C code in which one process (with *id* equals 0) executes function
P0() and the second one executes function P1(). The arrows in the C code indicate
which statement the process *id* is executing. The top of the *stack_regs[0]* indicates that
process 0 is executing the statement with label 9 of function max().

where the variable is stored (*mem* or *stack_data*). The other one, *offs*, defines
the offset of the data in the memory region. Fig. 3 provides a snapshot of the
memory on a C code example. The TLA+ expression $[loc \mapsto "mem", offs \mapsto 0]$
denotes the record *Addr_x* such that *Addr_x.loc* equals "*mem*" and *Addr_x.offs*
equals 0. *offs* for a local variable is relative to the start of the stack frame of the
current function, while *offs* for a global variable is the absolute index in *mem*.

C2TLA+ assigns to global (and static) variables not explicitly initialized
the value 0 for integers, and $[loc \mapsto Null, offs \mapsto Null]$ for pointers. For local
variables, it assigns the *Undef* value. *Null* and *Undef* are TLA+ "model values",
which are an unspecified values that TLC considers to be unequal to any value
that can be expressed in TLA+.

Loading and Assignment. An lvalue is a kind of expression that is evaluated to
an address and which refers to a region of storage. Accessing the value stored in
this region is performed using the *load()* operator (defined in Fig. 4) which uses
the TLA+ construct IF/THEN/ELSE.

The left-hand operand of an assignment must be an lvalue. The assignment in C2TLA+ is performed by the *store()* operator defined in Fig. 5, which
assigns to the lvalue *ptr* the *value* of the right-hand operand of the assignment.

$$load(id,\ ptr) \triangleq \text{IF } ptr.loc = \text{"mem" THEN } mem[ptr.offs]$$
$$\text{ELSE } stack\_data[id][Head(stack\_regs[id]).fp + ptr.offs]$$

Fig. 4. Definition of *load()* operator

The expression $[mem \text{ EXCEPT } ![ptr.offs] = value]$ denotes the function that is equal to *mem* except that it maps the value of *ptr.offs* to *value*.

$$store(id,\ ptr,\ value) \triangleq$$
$$\lor\ \land ptr.loc = \text{"mem"}$$
$$\land mem' = [mem \text{ EXCEPT } ![ptr.offs] = value]$$
$$\land \text{UNCHANGED } stack\_data$$
$$\lor\ \land ptr.loc = \text{"stack\_data"}$$
$$\land stack\_data' = [stack\_data \text{ EXCEPT } ![id][Head(stack\_regs[id]).fp + ptr.offs] = value]$$
$$\land \text{UNCHANGED } mem$$

Fig. 5. Definition of *store()* operator

The position of a parameter or local variable in *stack_data[id]* is relative to the base of the stack frame of the current function, which equals to *Head (stack_regs[id]).fp*.

Arrays, Pointer Arithmetic and Structure Member. Accessing an array element in C2TLA+ requires computing the offset using the size of the elements, the index and the base address of the array. For example, accessing to z[a] is translated into:

$$load(id, [loc \mapsto Addr\_z.loc,\ offs \mapsto (Addr\_z.offs + (load(id, Addr\_a) * Size\_of\_int))])$$

The same kind of computation is used to perform pointer arithmetic. Similarly, accessing a structure member is achieved by shifting the base address of the structure with the constant accumulated size of all previous members. For example, accessing to point.y is translated into:

$$load(id, [loc \mapsto Addr\_point.loc,\ offs \mapsto (Addr\_point.offs + Offset\_point\_y)])$$

4.3   Intra-procedural Control Flow

Function Definition. Each C function definition is translated into an operator with the process identifier *id* as argument. The function body is translated into the disjunction of the translation of each statement it contains. A C statement is translated into the conjunction of actions that are done simultaneously. At a given state one and only one action is true (i.e., feasible). The translation of function dec() of the example is as follows:

$$
\begin{aligned}
dec(id) \triangleq{} &\vee \wedge Head(stack\_regs[id]).pc = \langle\text{``dec''},\text{``lbl\_19''}\,\rangle\\
& \wedge store(id, Addr\_dec\_i, minus(load(id, Addr\_y), load(id, Addr\_dec\_param\_b)))\\
& \wedge stack\_regs' = [stack\_regs \text{ EXCEPT } ![id] = \\
& \langle[pc \mapsto \langle\text{``dec''}, \text{``lbl\_20''}\rangle, fp \mapsto Head(stack\_regs[id]).fp]\rangle \circ Tail(stack\_regs[id])]\\
& \wedge \text{UNCHANGED } \langle ret\rangle\\
&\vee \wedge Head(stack\_regs[id]).pc = \langle\text{``dec''},\text{``lbl\_20''}\rangle\\
& \wedge stack\_regs' = \ldots
\end{aligned}
$$

The translation of each statement s simultaneously asserts that the program counter points to s; performs the action corresponding to that statement; and updates the program counter to point to the next statement to execute.

Jump Statements. The translation of `goto/break/continue` statements consists in updating *stack_regs[id]* to the successor statement. The `goto l1` statement in function `max()` is translated as:

$$
\begin{aligned}
&\vee \wedge Head(stack\_regs[id]).pc = \langle\text{``max''}, \text{``lbl\_10''}\rangle\\
& \wedge stack\_regs' = [stack\_regs \text{ EXCEPT } ![id] = \\
& \langle[pc \mapsto \langle\text{``max''}, \text{``lbl\_12''}\rangle, fp \mapsto Head(stack\_regs[id]).fp]\rangle \circ Tail(stack\_regs[id])]\\
& \wedge \text{UNCHANGED } \langle mem, stack\_data, ret\rangle
\end{aligned}
$$

Selection Statements. C integer expressions used in `if` condition are normalized by C2TLA+. Selection statement causes the program control (i. e., *stack_regs[id]*) to be transferred to a specific block based upon whether the guard expression is true or not. The translation of `if` statement in function `max()` is as follows:

$$
\begin{aligned}
&\vee \wedge Head(stack\_regs[id]).pc = \langle\text{``max''}, \text{``lbl\_9''}\rangle\\
& \wedge \text{IF } ((Gt(load(id, Addr\_max\_param\_u)), (load(id, Addr\_max\_param\_v))) \neq [val \mapsto 0])\\
& \text{THEN } stack\_regs' = [stack\_regs \text{ EXCEPT } ![id] = \\
&\phantom{\vee\wedge\text{THEN}} \langle[pc \mapsto \langle\text{``max''}, \text{``lbl\_10''}\rangle, fp \mapsto Head(stack\_regs[id]).fp]\rangle \circ Tail(stack\_regs[id])]\\
& \text{ELSE } stack\_regs' = [stack\_regs \text{ EXCEPT } ![id] = \\
&\phantom{\vee\wedge\text{ELSE}} \langle[pc \mapsto \langle\text{``max''}, \text{``lbl\_11''}\rangle, fp \mapsto Head(stack\_regs[id]).fp]\rangle \circ Tail(stack\_regs[id])]\\
& \wedge \text{UNCHANGED } \langle mem, stack\_data, ret\rangle
\end{aligned}
$$

Iteration Statement. All loops in C are normalized by CIL as a single `while(1)` looping construct (plus eventual `if` and `break` statements), that we translate like other jump statements.

4.4   Inter-procedural Control Flow

Function Call. The function call is translated in two actions. Before calling a function f, its stack frame is pushed onto the *stack_data[id]* which obeys the LIFO order. The *stack_regs[id]* is updated by changing its head to a record whose *pc* field points to the action done once the call has finished. At the top of *stack_regs[id]* is pushed a record with *pc* pointing to the first statement of the called function, and *fp* to the new stack frame. Once the function returns, the second action copies the return value. For instance, the translation of `r1 = dec(2)` is as follows:

$$\begin{aligned}
&\lor \land Head(\ stack\_regs[id]).pc = \langle\,\text{"P1"},\ \text{"lbl\_30"}\,\rangle \\
&\quad \land stack\_data' = [stack\_data \text{ EXCEPT }!\,[id] = stack\_data[id] \circ \langle[val \mapsto 2],\ [val \mapsto Undef]\rangle] \\
&\quad \land stack\_regs' = [stack\_regs \text{ EXCEPT }!\,[id] \\
&\qquad = \langle[pc \mapsto \langle\,\text{"dec"},\text{"lbl\_19"}\,\rangle, fp \mapsto Len(stack\_data[id]) + 1]\,\rangle \\
&\qquad \circ \langle[pc \mapsto \langle\,\text{"P1"},\text{"lbl\_30.1"}\,\rangle,\ fp \mapsto Head(stack\_regs[id]).fp]\rangle \circ Tail(stack\_regs[id])] \\
&\quad \land \text{UNCHANGED } \langle mem,\ ret\rangle \\
&\lor \land Head(\ stack\_regs[id]).pc = \langle\,\text{"P1"},\ \text{"lbl\_30.1"}\,\rangle \\
&\quad \land store(id,\ Addr\_P1\_r1,\ ret[id]) \\
&\quad \land stack\_regs' = [stack\_regs \text{ EXCEPT }!\,[id] = \\
&\qquad \langle[pc \mapsto \langle\,\text{"P1"},\text{"lbl\_31"}\,\rangle,\ fp \mapsto Head(stack\_reg[id]).fp]\rangle \circ Tail(stack\_regs[id])] \\
&\quad \land \text{UNCHANGED } \langle ret\rangle
\end{aligned}$$

Return Statement. Once the function returns, the top of the *stack_regs[id]* is popped and its stack frame is removed from *stack_data[id]* using the *SubSeq* operator. The returned value is stored on *ret[id]*. The **return i** statement of function **dec()** is translated as follows:

$$\begin{aligned}
&\lor \land Head(stack\_regs[id]).pc = \langle\,\text{"dec"},\ \text{"lbl\_20"}\,\rangle \\
&\quad \land stack\_regs' = [stack\_regs \text{ EXCEPT }!\,[id] = Tail(stack\_regs[id])] \\
&\quad \land stack\_data' = [stack\_data \text{ EXCEPT }!\,[id] = \\
&\qquad SubSeq(stack\_data[id],\ 1,\ Head(stack\_regs[id]).fp - 1)] \\
&\quad \land ret' = [ret \text{ EXCEPT }!\,[id] = load(id,\ Addr\_dec\_i)] \\
&\quad \land \text{UNCHANGED } \langle mem\rangle
\end{aligned}$$

4.5 Generating the Specification

In addition to generating constants and variables declarations, C2TLA+ also defines in *Parameters* module the main specification by generating:

- The *Init* predicate that initializes all variables of the system.
- The tuple of all variables $vars \triangleq \langle mem,\ stack\_data,\ stack\_regs,\ ret\rangle$.
- *process*(*id*), that defines the next-state action of process *id*. It asserts that one of the functions is being executed until *stack_regs[id]* becomes empty. For the C code example, it is defined as:

$$\begin{aligned}
process(id) \triangleq\ &\land stack\_regs[id] \neq \langle\rangle \\
&\land (\ max(id) \lor inc(id) \lor dec(id) \lor P0(id) \lor P1(id)\ )
\end{aligned}$$

- The next-state action *Next* of all processes, that states that one of the process that has not finished is nondeterministically chosen to execute one step.

$$\begin{aligned}
Next \triangleq\ &\lor \exists\ id \in ProcSet : process(id) \\
&\lor (\forall\ id \in ProcSet : (stack\_regs[id] = \langle\rangle) \land (\text{UNCHANGED } vars))
\end{aligned}$$

- The complete specification $Spec \triangleq Init \land \Box[Next]_{vars} \land WF_{vars}(Next)$. It is necessary to consider the fairness assumptions if we want to check liveness properties. We assume only weak fairness assumptions.

The specification can be checked by TLC without manually defining anything by the user. Errors that occur because TLC could not evaluate an expression correspond to a runtime error in the C code, like dereferencing a null pointer, and are reported to the user. C2TLA+ also generates the *Termination* property which asserts that all processes have their stack pointer eventually empty. This property is useful in some test cases.

$$Termination \triangleq \Diamond(\forall \; id \in ProcSet \; : \; Head(stack\_regs[id]).pc = \langle\rangle)$$

5 Implementation and Experiments

C2TLA+ is developed as a Frama-C [9] plugin, implemented in OCaml. Frama-C uses CIL to reorganize and simplify C code, produces an Abstract Syntax Tree (AST) and passes it to the C2TLA+ translator. We have used C2TLA+ in a case study, described in Sect. 5.1. We use this case study as an example to describe the interactions between generated specifications and manually specified ones.

5.1 Case Study Description

We have applied our approach and tools (C2TLA+, TLC) on a critical part of the microkernel of the PharOS [19] real-time operating system (RTOS). This part contains approximately 600 lines of code and consists in a distributed version of the scheduling algorithm of the RTOS tasks. It implements a variant of the EDF (Earliest-Deadline First) scheduling algorithm. It runs on a dual-core system and consists of two processes: one running on the *control core* and the other on the *executing core*. The two processes share a set of task lists. Concurrent access to shared data is ensured by lock-free synchronization. Figure 6(a) presents the architecture of the modules of the microkernel that are of interest to us:

date provides the current date of the system. The considered implementation uses Lamport's algorithm of concurrent reading and writing of clocks [15]. This allows to read a concrete clock value, even if this value is concurrently updated.

spinlock implements lock-based concurrency primitive using "compare-and-swap" primitive.

tasklist implements the life-cycle of a task as given in Fig. 6(b). Tasks can be in several states, each state corresponds to a data structure listing the tasks in that state. The incoming/outgoing edge denotes insertion/removal operation. Tasks are characterized by their *start time* and *deadline*.

scheduler is at the top-level. It performs inter-core notifications to awake processes when they have things to do. This module is not considered in translation because we do not provide support for interruptions yet.

5.2 TLA+ Modules of the Model

C2TLA+ takes as inputs the C source code of these modules. By applying our approach, we obtain the TLA+ modules of Fig. 7.

C2TLA+ generates the *Parameters* module and a TLA+ module for each C input file. These modules can interact with manually specified TLA+ modules.

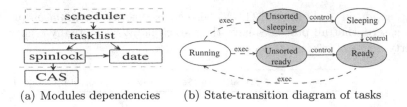

(a) Modules dependencies   (b) State-transition diagram of tasks

Fig. 6. Case study description

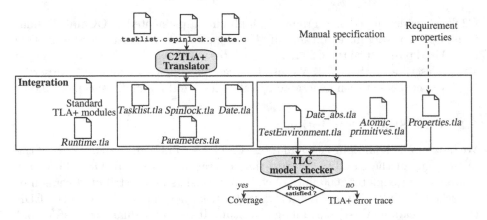

Fig. 7. TLA+ modules of the case study

Test Environment. The test environment represents the entry point of the model. It simulates the main *scheduler* module by calling the *tasklist* API and it is manually specified in the *TestEnvironment* TLA+ module.

Interacting with Manually TLA+ Specifications.

Specifying Concurrency Primitives. The *spinlock* module contains the definition of "acquire" and "release" operations which use the "compare-and-swap" (CAS) primitive. Fig. 8(a) shows the pseudo code version of this primitive. As this operation is performed atomically, we cannot translate it with C2TLA+. Such primitives are specified manually, respecting the calling conventions of Subsect. 4.4 and are declared in the C code using `__attribute__` annotation mechanism to define the TLA+ module where the primitives are specified. For instance, CAS is specified in the *Atomic_primitives* module as shown in Fig. 8(b). Other primitives could be added to *Atomic_primitives* which could be provided as a standard module.

Using an Abstract Model. The implementation of read and write operations on clock, in *date* module, is performed on several instructions. The possible interleaving of these instructions multiplies the number of states of the model. To cope with this problem, we write an abstract TLA+ version of *date*, called

```
int CAS (int *,int , int) __attribute__
((Atomic_primitives,alias("CAS")));
...
int CAS(int *addr, int old, int new)
{
 atomic {
  int temp = *addr;
  if (temp == old)
  {
   *addr = new;
   return 0;
  }
  else return 1;}
}
```

(a) Pseudo code

$$CAS(id) \triangleq$$
$$\land Head(stack\_regs[id]).pc = \langle \text{"CAS"}, \text{"lbl\_1"} \rangle$$
$$\land \text{IF } (load(id, load(id, Addr\_CAS\_param\_addr)) = load(id, Addr\_CAS\_param\_old))$$
$$\text{THEN } \land mem' = [mem \text{ EXCEPT}$$
$$![load(id, Addr\_CAS\_param\_addr).offs] = load(id, Addr\_CAS\_param\_new)]$$
$$\land ret' = [ret \text{ EXCEPT } ![id] = [val \mapsto 1]]$$
$$\text{ELSE } \land ret' = [ret \text{ EXCEPT } ![id] = [val \mapsto 0]]$$
$$\land \text{UNCHANGED } \langle mem \rangle$$
$$\land stack\_regs' = [stack\_regs \text{ EXCEPT } ![id] = Tail(stack\_regs[id])]$$
$$\land stack\_data' = [stack\_data \text{ EXCEPT } ![id] = SubSeq(stack\_data[id], 1, Head(stack\_regs[id]).fp - 1)]$$

(b) TLA+ code

Fig. 8. CAS definition

Date_abs which reads and writes the whole date atomically. Using this version considerably decreases the state space (see Table 2). We also verify that *Date* (the translated module) is a refinement of *Date_abs*.

5.3 Specifying and Verifying Properties

We verified various properties of the system. Here we provide some examples. We have checked that all spinlocks protect the critical sections, i.e., statements of the two processes cannot be executed simultaneously.

$$Mutex(sc1, sc2) \triangleq$$
$$\Box((Head(stack\_regs[\text{"exec\_core"}]).pc = sc1) \Rightarrow (Head(stack\_regs[\text{"control\_core"}]).pc \neq sc2))$$

An important invariant of the system is that the tasks in the ready list are sorted by their deadlines; this is necessary to implement the EDF algorithm. To state this invariant, we first define a recursive operator *getSeqDeadlines* which maps the C linked list to a more abstract TLA+ sequence. The property is simpler to state on this abstract sequence by defining the *IsSortedSeq()* operator.

$$getSeqDeadlines[ptr \in SetAddr] \triangleq$$
$$\text{IF } (ptr \neq [loc \mapsto Null, offs \mapsto Null])$$
$$\text{THEN } \langle load(id, [loc \mapsto ptr.loc, offs \mapsto (ptr.offs + Offset\_task\_deadline)]) \rangle$$
$$\quad \circ getSeqDeadlines[load(\text{"unsued"}, [loc \mapsto ptr.loc, offs \mapsto (ptr.offs + Offset\_task\_next)])]$$
$$\text{ELSE } \langle \rangle$$
$$IsSortedSeq(S) \triangleq$$
$$S \neq \langle \rangle \Rightarrow (\forall i \in 1 .. Len(S), j \in 1 .. Len(S) : (i \neq j) \land (i \leq j) \Rightarrow (S[i].val \leq S[j].val))$$

The property applied on *ready* list is expressed as follows:

$$\Box IsSortedSeq(getSeqDeadlines[load(\text{"unsued"}, Addr\_readyList)])$$

We have also checked some liveness properties, for instance, that if a thread entered its critical section, it will eventually leave it. This property can be expressed by comparing the program counter of the process to the statement labels of the functions "spinlock_acquire" and "spinlock_release". For example, for the *executing core*, the property is expressed as:

$$\square((Head(stack\_regs["\text{exec\_core}"]).pc = \langle "spinlock\_acquire", "lbl\_2" \rangle) \Rightarrow$$
$$\lozenge(Head(stack\_regs["\text{exec\_core}"]).pc = \langle "spinlock\_release", "lbl\_15" \rangle))$$

In order to use the abstract model *Date_abs* instead of *Date*, we have to check that the *Date* model is a refinement of the *Date_abs* model. For this, we have to map states in *Date* model with those of *Date_abs* model by substituting constants and variables used in *Date_abs* with those of *Date*. The refinement is expressed in TLA+ as logical implication. Verifying this refinement is satisfying that the specification of *Date* implies this substitution.

5.4   Verification and Discussion

We integrated the modules together and we performed model checking on two complete specifications. The first specification uses the translated *Date* module and the second one uses the abstract *Date_abs* module. The experiment was performed on an Intel Core Pentium i7-2760QM with 8 cores (2.40 GHz each) machine, with 8 Gb of RAM memory. We model checked the two specifications by considering four possible values of the clock. The executing core updates the *start time* and *deadline* of the task that has run and inserts it into the *unsorted* lists. Table 2 provides the generated states and the model checking time according to the number of tasks, for the two considered specifications.

Table 2. Runtimes of model checking (time in seconds)

Tasks	Specification using			
	Date		*Date_abs*	
	State space	Time	State space	Time
1	5.986.509	227	718.084	20
2	>501.876.263	>10.800	5.450.732	64
3	-	-	45.201.603	960
4	-	-	138.679.106	2.400

For two tasks, the specification using *Date* module takes more than 3 h to be model checked. Using an abstract model significantly reduces the size of the state space and the time required for model checking.

We have successfully checked that the correctness properties (defined in Sub-Sect. 5.3) are satisfied by the model. One of the motivations for verifying this code was to check that the fine-grained locking constructs were properly used. We checked that changing the locks in the source code leads to TLC finding that some invariants become violated. In that case, we obtain the error trace that explains how the error can happen and TLC reports that the coverage is incomplete.

6 Conclusion and Future Work

We have sketched an approach for specifying and verifying C code based on an automated translation from C to TLA+. The main advantage of our approach is the ability to make generated TLA+ specifications from a C implementation interact with more abstract, potentially already existing manually specified TLA+ specifications. We use the TLC model checker to verify a part of the implementation of an RTOS microkernel against safety and liveness properties expressed in TLA+. We also checked that a generated specification was a refinement of an abstract TLA+ specification, and showed that we could successfully use abstraction to reduce the size of the state space.

We plan to extend this work on several interesting directions. We would like to extend the translator to handle a bigger subset of C and to generate TLA+ properties from the ACSL [3] specification language used in Frama-C. We want to update the translator so that the generated TLA+ specification catches all C runtime errors. It would be interesting to benefit from Frama-C analysis of shared variables by several processes to generate TLA+ code with less interleaving between the processes, to reduce the state space. We also plan to further study the use of TLA+ modules with different levels of refinement. Finally, we aim to use the TLA+ proof system [8] to prove properties on an abstract specification of PharOS and prove that the specification generated by C2TLA+ is a refinement of this abstract specification.

References

1. Akhtar, S., Merz, S., Quinson, M.: A high-level language for modeling algorithms and their properties. In: Davies, J. (ed.) SBMF 2010. LNCS, vol. 6527, pp. 49–63. Springer, Heidelberg (2011)
2. Ball, T., Rajamani, S.K.: The SLAM project: debugging system software via static analysis. SIGPLAN Not. **37**(1), 1–3 (2002)
3. Baudin, P., Filliâtre, J.C., Marché, C., Monate, B., Moy, Y., Prevosto, V.: ACSL: ANSI/ISO C Specification Language, version 1.4 (2009). http://frama-c.cea.fr/acsl.html
4. Clarke, E., Kroning, D., Lerda, F.: A tool for checking ANSI-C programs. In: Jensen, K., Podelski, A. (eds.) TACAS 2004. LNCS, vol. 2988, pp. 168–176. Springer, Heidelberg (2004)
5. Clarke, E.M., Grumberg, O., Jha, S., Lu, Y., Veith, H.: Counterexample-guided abstraction refinement. In: Emerson, E.A., Sistla, A.P. (eds.) CAV 2000. LNCS, vol. 1855, pp. 154–169. Springer, Heidelberg (2000)
6. Clarke Jr., E.M., Grumberg, O., Peled, D.A.: Model Checking. MIT Press, Cambridge (1999)

7. Cohen, E., Dahlweid, M., Hillebrand, M., Leinenbach, D., Moskal, M., Santen, T., Schulte, W., Tobies, S.: VCC: a practical system for verifying concurrent C. In: Berghofer, S., Nipkow, T., Urban, C., Wenzel, M. (eds.) TPHOLs 2009. LNCS, vol. 5674, pp. 23–42. Springer, Heidelberg (2009)

8. Cousineau, D., Doligez, D., Lamport, L., Merz, S., Ricketts, D., Vanzetto, H.: TLA$^+$ Proofs. In: Giannakopoulou, D., Méry, D. (eds.) FM 2012. LNCS, vol. 7436, pp. 147–154. Springer, Heidelberg (2012)

9. Cuoq, P., Kirchner, F., Kosmatov, N., Prevosto, V., Signoles, J., Yakobowski, B.: Frama-C: a software analysis perspective. In: Eleftherakis, G., Hinchey, M., Holcombe, M. (eds.) SEFM 2012. LNCS, vol. 7504, pp. 233–247. Springer, Heidelberg (2012)

10. D'Silva, V., Kroening, D., Weissenbacher, G.: A survey of automated techniques for formal software verification. IEEE Trans. Comput. Aided Des. Integr. Circuits Syst. (TCAD) **27**(7), 1165–1178 (2008)

11. Henzinger, T.A., Jhala, R., Majumdar, R., Sutre, G.: Software verification with BLAST. In: Ball, T., Rajamani, S.K. (eds.) SPIN 2003. LNCS, vol. 2648, pp. 235–239. Springer, Heidelberg (2003)

12. Holzmann, G.J.: The model checker SPIN. IEEE Trans. Softw. Eng. **23**(5), 279–295 (1997)

13. Holzmann, G.J.: Trends in software verification. In: Araki, K., Gnesi, S., Mandrioli, D. (eds.) FME 2003. LNCS, vol. 2805, pp. 40–50. Springer, Heidelberg (2003)

14. Holzmann, G.J., Smith, M.H.: An automated verification method for distributed systems software based on model extraction. IEEE Trans. Soft. Eng. **28**, 364–377 (2002)

15. Lamport, L.: Concurrent reading and writing of clocks. ACM Trans. Comput. Syst. **8**(4), 305–310 (1990)

16. Lamport, L.: The temporal logic of actions. ACM Trans. Program. Lang. Syst. **16**(3), 872–923 (1994)

17. Lamport, L.: Specifying Systems: The TLA+ Language and Tools for Hardware and Software Engineers. Addison-Wesley, MA (2002)

18. Lamport, L.: The PlusCal algorithm language. In: Leucker, M., Morgan, C. (eds.) ICTAC 2009. LNCS, vol. 5684, pp. 36–60. Springer, Heidelberg (2009)

19. Lemerre, M., Ohayon, E., Chabrol, D., Jan, M., Jacques, M.B.: Method and tools for mixed-criticality real-time applications within PharOS. In: Proceedings of AMICS 2011: 1st International Workshop on Architectures and Applications for Mixed-Criticality Systems (2011)

20. Manna, Z., Pnueli, A.: The Temporal Logic of Reactive and Concurrent Systems. Springer, New York (1992)

21. Necula, G.C., Mcpeak, S., Rahul, S.P., Weimer, W.: CIL: intermediate language and tools for analysis and transformation of C programs. In: International Conference on Compiler Construction. pp. 213–228 (2002)

Formal Modeling and Verification of Interlocking Systems Featuring Sequential Release

Linh H. Vu[1]([✉]), Anne E. Haxthausen[1], and Jan Peleska[2]

[1] DTU Compute, Technical University of Denmark, Kongens Lyngby, Denmark
{lvho,aeha}@dtu.dk
[2] Department of Mathematics and Computer Science, University of Bremen,
Bremen, Germany
jp@informatik.uni-bremen.de

Abstract. In this paper, we present a method and an associated tool suite for formal verification of the new ETCS level 2 based Danish railway interlocking systems. We have made a generic and reconfigurable model of the system behavior and generic high-level safety properties. This model accommodates *sequential release* – a feature in the new Danish interlocking systems. The generic model and safety properties can be instantiated with interlocking configuration data, resulting in a concrete model in the form of a Kripke structure, and in high-level safety properties expressed as state invariants. Using SMT based bounded model checking (BMC) and inductive reasoning, we are able to verify the properties for model instances corresponding to railway networks of industrial size. Experiments also show that BMC is efficient for finding bugs in the railway interlocking designs.

Keywords: Railway interlocking systems · Formal verification · Bounded model checking · Inductive reasoning · RobustRails · Safety-critical systems

1 Introduction

An interlocking system is responsible for guiding trains safely through a given railway network. It is a vital part of any railway signaling system and has the highest safety integrity level (SIL4) according to the CENELEC 50128 standard [5]. Conventionally, the development and verification process of interlocking systems is informal and mostly manual, hence time-consuming, costly, and error-prone. Thus, automated verification of interlocking systems is an active research topic, investigated by several research groups, see e.g. [8–10,14,15,23]. As part of the RobustRailS research project[1], our work aims at establishing a

---

L.H. Vu and A.E. Haxthausen—The authors' research has been funded by the RobustRailS project granted by the Danish Council for Strategic Research.

J. Peleska—The author's research has been partially funded by ITEA2 project openETCS under grant agreement 11025.

[1] http://robustrails.man.dtu.dk.

C. Artho and P.C. Ölveczky (Eds.): FTSCS 2014, CCIS 476, pp. 223–238, 2015.
DOI: 10.1007/978-3-319-17581-2_15

holistic method supporting the verification of such systems. The method should be formal and facilitate automation in order to provide a better verification process compared to the conventional one. In Denmark, in the period of 2009–2021, new interlocking systems that are compatible with standardized European Train Control System (ETCS) Level 2 [4] will be deployed in the entire country within the context of the Danish Signalling Programme[2]. In the context of the RobustRailS project accompanying the signalling programme on a scientific level, the proposed method will be applied to these new systems.

The main contributions presented in this paper are as follows. (1) We present a formal model of the behavior of ETCS Level 2 compatible interlocking systems. (2) The model accommodates sequential release: this is a method for incrementally releasing route portions that have been traversed by the associated train, with the objective to increase the level of concurrency in route allocation and, consequently, the train throughput. (3) The state space encodings allow for high-level safety properties and state transition relations to be processed in a highly efficient manner by SMT solvers supporting bit vector and integer arithmetics. (4) A verification technique combining induction with bounded model checking (BMC) using novel SMT solvers enables the verification of safety properties for railway network instances of industrial size.

The paper is organized as follows: Sect. 2 gives a brief introduction to the new Danish route-based interlocking systems. The proposed method is described in Sect. 3. Section 4 presents the formal, generic model in the form of a Kripke structure, while the safety properties are formalized in Sect. 5. Section 6 describes the verification strategy. The experimental results are shown in Sect. 7. Related work and concluding remarks are presented in Sects. 8 and 9, respectively.

2   The New Danish Route-Based Interlocking Systems

A railway network in ETCS Level 2 consists of a number of track-side elements of different types[3]: linear sections, points, marker boards. Figure 1 shows an example layout of a railway network having six linear sections (b10,t10,t12,t14,t20, b14), two points (t11,t13), and eight marker boards (mb10..mb21). A linear section is a section with up to two neighbors: one in the *up* end, and one in the *down* end[4], e.g. the linear section t12 in Fig. 1 has t13 and t11 as neighbors at its up end and down end, respectively. A point can have up to three neighbors: one at the *stem*, one at the *plus* end, and one at the *minus* end, e.g. point t11 in Fig. 1 has t10, t12, and t20 as neighbors at its stem, plus, and minus ends, respectively. Linear sections and points are collectively called detection sections, as they are used by interlocking systems to detect the presence of trains in a railway network. A point can be switched between two positions: PLUS and MINUS.

---

[2] http://www.bane.dk/signalprogrammet.

[3] Here we only show types that are relevant for the work presented in this paper.

[4] In Denmark, *up* and *down* denote the directions in which the distance from a reference location is *increasing* and *decreasing*, respectively. The location is the same for both up and down, e.g. an end of a line.

When it is in the PLUS (MINUS) position, traffic can run from its *stem* to its *plus* (*minus*) end and vice versa. A marker board is installed along a section, and it is used as reference location for an intended travel direction that it is facing, e.g. mb13 in Fig. 1 is installed along section t12, and it is intended for travel direction up. Contrary to legacy systems, in ETCS Level 2, there are no physical signals, but *virtual signals* associated with marker boards. A virtual signal can be OPEN or CLOSED, respectively, allowing or disallowing traffic to pass the associated marker board. For simplicity, the terms *virtual signals*, *signals*, and *marker boards* are used interchangeably throughout this paper.

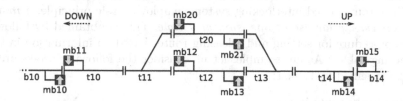

Fig. 1. An example railway network layout

An interlocking system monitors constantly the status of track-side elements, and sets them to appropriate states in order to allow trains traveling safely through the given railway network. The new Danish interlocking systems are route-based. An *interlocking table* specifies the routes in the given network layout and the conditions for setting these routes. A *route* is a path from a *source* signal to a *destination* signal.

In railway signaling terminology, *setting* a route denotes the process of allocating the resources – i.e. sections, points, signals – for the route, and then locking it exclusively for only one train when the resources are allocated. The specification of a route and conditions for setting and releasing it include the following information: *(a)* a list of the detection sections in the route's *path, (b)* a list of the detection sections which are used as *overlaps* – buffer space in case trains overshoot the route's path, *(c)* required positions of *points*[5] used by the route, *(d)* a set of *protecting signals* used for flank or front protection [19] for the route, and *(e)* a set of *conflicting routes* which must not be set while the current route is set.

Table 1 shows an excerpt of an interlocking table for the network shown in Fig. 1. As can be seen, one of the routes has id 1a, goes from mb10 to mb13 via three sections t10, t11 and t12, and has no overlap. It requires point t11 (on its path) to be in PLUS position and point t13 (outside its path) to be in MINUS position (as a protecting point). The route has mb11, mb12 and mb20 as protecting signals, and it is in conflict with routes 1b, 2a, 2b, 3, 4, 5a, 5b, 6b, and 7.

---

[5] This includes points in the path and overlaps, and points used for flank and front protection. For detail about flank and front protection, see [19].

Table 1. Excerpt of the interlocking table for the network layout in Fig. 1. The overlaps column is omitted as it is empty for all of the routes. (p means PLUS, m means MINUS.)

Id	Source	Dest.	Points	Signals	Path	Conflicts
1a	mb10	mb13	t11:p;t13:m	mb11;mb12;mb20	t10;t11;t12	1b;2a;2b;3;4;5a;5b;6b;7
..	...	...	...	...	...	...
7	mb20	mb11	t11:m	mb10;mb12	t11;t10	1a;1b;2a;2b;3;5b;6a

Interlocking Principles. In order to prevent collision and derailment of trains, traditional route-based interlocking systems employ a basic principle: *a route is locked exclusively for use of one train at a time.* This is obtained by following a strict procedure for setting and releasing routes based on information in their interlocking tables. As an example, let us consider the following procedure for route 1a specified in Table 1:

(0) Initially the route is *free.*
(1) When a request for setting the route is received by the interlocking system, the route is *marked* as requested.
(2) The interlocking system checks the status of different track-side elements in the system to figure out whether it can start *allocating* resources for route 1a, e.g. sections t10, t11 and t12 must be vacant, and conflicting routes must not be allocated or locked. If so, the interlocking commands points and signals to their required positions according to the route's specification, e.g. it commands the point t11 to switch to PLUS, t13 to switch to MINUS, and the protecting signals mb11, mb12 and mb20 to change to CLOSED.
(3) The interlocking system constantly monitors the status of the track-side elements. When the signals and points have changed their states as commanded in step 2, the route is *locked* and its source signal mb10 is set to OPEN, allowing a train to enter the route.
(4) When the locked route is *used*, i.e. a train enters it, the source signal mb10 is set to CLOSED preventing other trains from entering.
(5) The route is *released* (set back to *free*) when the train has finished using it, i.e. the train has passed mb13, or the train has come to standstill in front of mb13.

Sequential Release. The new Danish interlocking systems employ *sequential release* (also known as sectional release) [19]. This feature results in two major changes:

(a) With sequential release, the interlocking can release an element in a locked route as soon as the train has passed it, instead of waiting until the train has finished using the route and then releasing the route as a whole. Consequently, the capacity increases.
(b) As a direct result of (a), a route may be allocated (in step (2) above) while some of its conflicting routes are still in use by trains, instead of waiting

for all of its conflicting routes to be released as in traditional route-based interlocking systems. For example, when a train has passed section t11 while going along route 1a, t11 will be released and then route 7 going in the opposite direction (see Table 1) can be allocated (assuming that other conditions for this are fulfilled).

3 Verification Method

The verification process is shown in Fig. 2. The verification process begins with the configuration data of an interlocking system, consisting of a network layout and an interlocking table. The configuration data are described in a domain-specific language [22] (DSL) having an XML representation[6]. After being parsed into an internal representation, a static checker verifies whether the configuration data is statically well-formed according to the static semantics of the DSL. As an option the user may not provide an interlocking table, but instead use an interlocking table generator (ITG) to get a table created automatically. Instantiating a generic model of the dynamic behavior of the Danish interlocking systems with the well-formed configuration data results in a model instance in the form of a Kripke structure. Similarly, the concrete safety-properties expressed as state invariants are also generated from the generic safety- properties. The model instance is then checked against the concrete properties using a combination of BMC and inductive reasoning. If the model instance does not satisfy the properties, counter-examples will be generated. An interface for visualizing the counter-examples at the DSL level is under development.

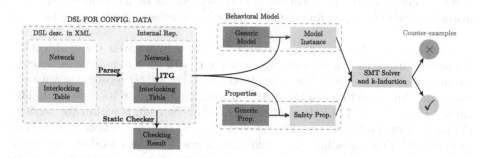

Fig. 2. Verification process

The tool-chain associated with the method has been implemented using the RT-Tester tool-box [17,21]. The bounded model checker in RT-Tester uses the SONOLAR SMT solver [18] to compute counter-examples for induction and base cases. RT-Tester has been selected because (1) it is an integrated model-based testing and BMC tool, and (2) its SMT solver also supports floating point arithmetic. The first property is crucial for us, because our objective is to complement

---

[6] A graphical representation and editor is currently under development.

the model verification with HW/SW integration tests. The second capability is vital, because we also plan to extend the model by real-time aspects, such as train velocity and braking curves.

4 Kripke Structure Encodings of Interlocking Systems

The dynamic behavior of an interlocking system is formalized as a Kripke structure $K = (S, s_0, R, L, AP)$ with state space S, initial state $s_0 \in S$, transition relation $R \subseteq S \times S$, and labeling function $L : S \to 2^{AP}$, where AP is the set of atomic propositions and 2^{AP} is the power set of AP. The labeling function L maps a state s to the set $L(s)$ of atomic propositions that hold in s. Due to the limited space of this paper and the complexity of the Kripke encodings, in the following subsections, we only outline how the state space S and the transition relation R of a Kripke structure are encoded.

4.1 State Space

In order to encode the states of an interlocking system, a finite set $V = \{v_0, \ldots, v_n\}$ of variables is defined to represent the current status of different components in the system such as a track element or a route. Each variable $v \in V$ has an associated finite domain $D_v \subset \mathbb{N}_0$. The state space is the set of all valuation functions $s : V \to \bigcup_{v \in V} D_v$ for which $s(v) \in D_v$ for all $v \in V$. The initial state s_0 is the (safe) state in which all detection sections are vacant, all signals are closed, all routes are free, and there are no trains in the network. In our encodings, s_0 is the state in which all variables are evaluated to 0. For readability, sometimes we use named constants instead of their corresponding integral values in the subsequent paragraphs.

Vacancy Status. The vacancy status of a section in a given travel direction is encoded using the three least significant bits HTO of a non-negative integer variable as shown in Fig. 3. For example, the variable $l.U2D$ records the vacancy status of a linear section l in the direction from its up end to its down end. The value 1 of the bits H, T, O indicate: (H) the head of the train is within the section, (T) the tail of the train is within the section, and (O) the section is occupied, respectively. This encoding offers two advantages: *(a)* the encoding can cover the case where a train occupies more than one detection section (e.g., when it is crossing the joint between two sections), and *(b)* the safety properties can be expressed efficiently using arithmetic operations on integer variables as shown in Sect. 5.

Fig. 3. A variable recording occupancy status of a detection section

Lockable Elements. In order to accommodate sequential release into our model, we consider a linear or point section as a *lockable element*. The status of a lockable element e is encoded by two variables: *(1) e.MODE* – indicating the mode of the element, and *(2) e.PREV* – this variable is set to 1 when the previous section in the same route has been released, otherwise $e.PREV = 0$. An element can be in one of the following modes: FREE (the element is not *exclusively* locked by a route, or used by any train), EXLCK (the element is *exclusively* locked for a route), or USED (the element has been used, i.e., occupied, by a train after it was *exclusively* locked for a route).

Point Positions. The position of a point p is encoded by two variables: *(1) p.POS* – the actual position of the point, and *(2) p.CMD* – the point position commanded by the interlocking. The value of $p.POS$ can be one of the following[7]: PLUS(0), MINUS(1), or INTERMEDIATE(2) (the position where the point is switching from one side to the other). The value of $p.CMD$ can only be PLUS or MINUS (as the interlocking *cannot* command a point to switch to the INTERMEDIATE position).

Signal Aspects. The aspect of a signal s is encoded by two variables: *(1) s.ACT* – the actual aspect of the virtual signal, its value can be OPEN or CLOSED, and *(2) s.CMD* – the aspect as commanded by the interlocking, the possible values of this variable have the same meaning as the ones of $s.ACT$. The $s.ACT$ variable represents the aspect of the signal as "seen" by the train, while $s.CMD$ is the aspect of the signal as seen by the interlocking. The values of these two variables may be different because of the delay in the communication between the interlocking system and the trains.

Routes. For each route r, a variable $r.MODE$ is used to encode the current mode of that route. A route can be in one of the following modes: FREE, MARKED, ALLOCATING, LOCKED, or USED.

4.2   Transition Relation

The transition relation $R \subseteq S \times S$ can be represented symbolically by a predicate Φ with free variables in $V \cup V'$, where $V' = \{v' \mid v \in V\}$ is the set of next-state variables. A pair of states $(s, s') \in R$, if and only if Φ evaluates to true when replacing every $v \in V$ occurring in Φ with $s(v)$ and every $v' \in V'$ occurring in Φ with $s'(v)$. In order to specify Φ, we divide the transitions in an interlocking system into four types as in the following, each type is represented collectively in a predicate with free variables in $V \cup V'$.

(0) route dispatching transitions represented collectively by the predicate Φ_d;
(1) interlocking transitions – e.g., setting mode of a route – represented by the predicate Φ_ι;

---

[7] The notation *name(integer-value)* means that *name* is the name of constant having the value *integer-value*.

(2) track element transitions – e.g., switching a point or a signal – represented by the predicate Φ_ϵ; and

(3) train movement transitions represented by the predicate Φ_τ.

Transitions of type (0) are not prioritized, i.e., they can be chosen whenever they are enabled, independently from other transitions. On the other hand, transitions of types (1), (2), and (3) are prioritized in the descending order that they appear in the list, i.e., transitions of type (1) has the highest priority and transitions of type (3) has the lowest. Whenever two transitions of different priorities are both enabled, the one with higher priority will be chosen. Transitions with the same priority are chosen non-deterministically if they are enabled at the same time. This priority of transitions is based on the intuition that in practice, the events in the interlocking control logic occur at significantly higher speed than the ones occurring in a track element. An analogous argument applies to events related to track elements and others related to train movements. With these types of transitions, the transition relation of an interlocking system can be specified as in the following

$$\Phi \equiv \Phi_d \vee \text{ITE}(\iota, \Phi_\iota, \text{ITE}(\epsilon, \Phi_\epsilon, \Phi_\tau)) \tag{1}$$

where $\text{ITE}(c, i, e)$ is the *if-then-else* function: if c holds then the value of the function is i, otherwise it is e; ι expresses whether an interlocking transition is enabled; and ϵ expresses whether a track element transition is enabled. The route dispatching transition relation Φ_d is put outside of the ITE function in (1) in order to allow the routes to be dispatched arbitrarily. If route dispatching transitions were given the same or higher priority as the one of interlocking control logic transitions, all routes which could be dispatched would have to be dispatched before track elements or trains could make any transition. On the other hand, if route dispatching were given lower priority than interlocking control logic transitions, then a route could not be dispatched if another route is processed by the interlocking.

Route Dispatching. A route can be dispatched arbitrarily whenever its mode is FREE. This means that multiple routes can be dispatched at the same time.

Life-cycle of a Route. Figure 4 shows the "life-cycle" of a route, i.e., its different modes and the transitions from one mode to another. This "life-cycle" reflects the procedure for setting and sequentially releasing a route as described in Sect. 2. The transitions labeled (1), (2), (3), (4), and (6) in Fig. 4 correspond to items (1) – (5) in the procedure presented in Sect. 2 for setting and releasing a route. Transition (5) models the sequential release that can take place while the route stays in USED mode: as the train moves along the route, its elements are released sequentially as soon as the train has passed them. Transition (2) is adapted to sequential release: allocation is now also allowed when a conflicting route is in the USED mode, as long as elements shared with the given route have been sequentially released.

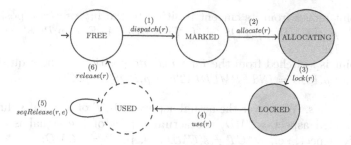

Fig. 4. A life-cycle of a route

Life-cycle of a Lockable Element. Figure 5 depicts the "life-cycle" of a *lockable element* within the network controlled by the interlocking system. Each node in the diagram is labeled with information about the status of the element e: (a) whether the element is vacant, (b) its current mode, and (c) the value of the $PREV$ variable indicating whether the previous element $prev(r, e)$ of e in the route r has been released. An element e is initially in a state in which it is vacant, in FREE mode, and its $PREV$ variable is 0. (1) When the interlocking system is allocating a route r that uses e, it sets the mode of the element to EXLCK, meaning that the element is locked exclusively for r. (2) The element becomes occupied, i.e., not vacant, as a train enters. (3) After that, e's mode is set to USED. (4) When the train leaves the previous element $prev(r, e)$ of e in the route r, $prev(r, e)$ is released, and it informs e by setting the variable $e.PREV$ to 1. (5) When the train leaves e, the latter becomes vacant again, (6) e is released and the next element $next(r, e)$ in the same route is informed by setting $next(r, e).PREV$ to 1.

Switching Points. A point p can be switched if it is requested to be switched to a position $p.CMD$ that is different from its current position $p.POS$. The point switching process occurs in two steps:

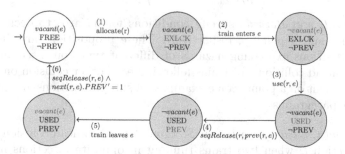

Fig. 5. "Life-cycle" of a lockable element e. $vacant(e)$ is a formula over variables encoding e's vacancy status shown in Sect. 4.1.

(1) the point moves from its current position to the *intermediate* position, i.e.,
$p.POS \neq p.CMD \wedge p.POS \neq INTERMEDIATE \wedge p.POS' = INTER\text{-}MEDIATE$,

(2) the point is switched from the *intermediate* position to the requested position, i.e., $p.POS = INTERMEDIATE \wedge p.POS' = p.CMD$.

Switching Signals. Whenever the actual aspect $s.ACT$ of a signal s differs from the commanded aspect $s.CMD$, the actual aspect of the signal is set to the commanded aspect, i.e., $s.ACT \neq s.CMD \wedge s.ACT' = s.CMD$.

Train Movements. Trains are not explicitly specified in our model, in the sense that there are no explicit train objects. Instead, train movements and other aspects are implicitly modeled via the occupancy status of train detection sections, inspired by the "rubber-band" model described in [1]. This implicit model is advantageous when compared to the explicit one, because it models arbitrary numbers of trains of arbitrary length. In the implicit model of train movements, train length – in terms of numbers of sections that a train occupies – may vary as trains move. This variation reflects the actual view of interlocking systems of the train length: although trains have fixed geometric length, their length – in terms of the number of sections that they occupy – as seen by the interlocking systems is not fixed.

5   High-Level Safety Properties

Interlocking systems must at least guarantee the high-level safety properties of non-collision and non-derailment. These properties can be expressed as state invariants over the vacancy status variables of linear and point sections in the given network. Basically, an interlocking system is safe if no hazardous situations occur on any linear or point section at any time. Thus, the high- level safety properties can be expressed formally by the following state invariant

$$\phi = \neg(\bigvee_{l:Linear} Hazard_l \vee \bigvee_{p:Point} Hazard_p) \tag{2}$$

where $Hazard_l$ and $Hazard_p$ specify conditions for hazards to occur on a linear section l and a point p, respectively. These propositions are disjunctions of sub-propositions expressing hazards of different types on a section such as: (a) head-to-head collision, (b) trains following each other collision on a section, or (c) derailment on a point. Some examples of sub-propositions are given in the subsequent paragraphs.

Head-to-Head Collision on a Linear Section. A head-to-head collision occurs on a linear section l, when two trains running in opposite directions meet. This situation is expressed by the following formula where $l.D2U$ ($l.U2D$) is the variable encoding the vacancy status of the section in the travel direction from down (up) to up (down).

$$l.D2U * l.U2D > 0 \tag{3}$$

As $l.D2U * l.U2D > 0$ iff $l.D2U > 0$ and $l.U2D > 0$, the formula expresses that the section is occupied in both down-to-up ($l.D2U > 0$) and up-to-down ($l.U2D > 0$) directions. Collisions of type (b) are formulated in the similar way.

Derailment on a Point. A derailment occurs when a train traverses a point p which is not locked in the correct position for the travel direction of the train. This situation is expressed by the following formula where $p.POS$ is the point's actual position, $p.S2PM$, $p.P2S$, and $p.M2S$ are variables encoding the vacancy status of the point in the travel direction entering the point from its stem, plus, or minus ends, respectively, & and $\gg$ are *bit-wise and* and *arithmetic bit shift right* operators, respectively.

$$p.POS * p.P2S + (1 - (p.POS \ \& \ 1)) * p.M2S + (p.POS \gg 1) * p.S2PM > 0 \quad (4)$$

Formula (4) captures the following cases: (a) a train is entering a point from its plus end ($p.P2S > 0$) while the point is in not in the plus position ($p.POS > 0$), (b) a train is entering a point from its minus end ($p.M2S > 0$) while the point is not in the minus position ($1 - (p.POS \ \& \ 1) > 0$), and (c) a train is entering a point from its stem end ($p.S2PM > 0$) while the point is in the intermediate position ($(p.POS \gg 1) > 0$).

6   Verification of Safety Properties

When a model K (see Sect. 4) and a proposition ϕ expressing high-level safety properties (see Sect. 5) have been generated, the next task according to our method is to prove the absence of hazardous situations, i.e., to prove that ϕ holds in all reachable states of K. This is written $K \models G(\phi)$ where G is *Globally* temporal operator in Linear Temporal Logic (LTL). The following subsections describe our approach for verifying this.

6.1   Verification Strategy

We employ a strategy combining BMC and *k-induction* techniques similar to the one in [13]. The verification procedure is performed in two steps: *(i) base case:* prove that ϕ holds for $k > 0$ consecutive states[8], starting from the initial state s_0, and *(ii) induction case:* prove that if ϕ holds for $k > 0$ consecutive states, starting from an arbitrary state s_n, then ϕ will also hold in the $(k+1)^{th}$ state. Both the base case and the induction case are transformed to problems of finding counter-examples for their negated formulas using an SMT solver. If no counter-examples are found, then the cases have been proved.

---

[8] Two states are consecutive, if there is a transition from the first to the second according to the model K.

6.2   Invariant Strengthening

As pointed out in [3], when ϕ is not strong enough to be inductive, counter-examples are found for the induction case. These counter- examples are often *spurious*, i.e., they start from an unreachable state and do not correspond to any actual run of the system. In order to make ϕ inductive, it is strengthened with an extra invariant ψ, i.e., one should prove $\phi \wedge \psi$ instead of ϕ. ψ is called the *strengthening invariant*, which eliminates the spurious counter-examples. An example of such strengthening properties is given in the following.

Train Integrity. Some states of the variables expressing the train occupancy status of the track sections (see Sect. 4) are not feasible as they correspond to situations that are not physically possible. An example of an infeasible state is one in which the variables express that a section s is occupied in one direction by a train without the head being on the section, but the next section in that travel direction is unoccupied.

The train integrity conditions can be formalized as a conjunction of formulas over the track vacancy variables. For each travel direction (*up* and *down*), there is a formula for each section s that has a next section in the given travel direction. The pattern of such a formula depends on the other sections the current section is connected to in the given travel direction. For instance, for travel direction *up* and a linear section s that has a linear section s' as neighbor in travel direction *up*, the formula will take the following form:

$$(s.D2U \ \& \ 0b101) = 0b001 \iff (s'.D2U \ \& \ 0b011) = 0b001 \tag{5}$$

where $\&$ is the *bit-wise and* operator. This formula expresses that section s is occupied by a train in direction *up* (the O bit of $s.D2U$ is 1) without the head being on the section (the H bit of $s.D2U$ is 0), if and only if section s' is occupied by a train in direction *up* (the O bit of $s'.D2U$ is 1) without a tail being on the section (the T bit of $s'.D2U$ is 0). Formula (5) shows the expressiveness of our state encodings allowing properties to be efficiently formulated in compact formulas.

7   Experiments

We have used the tool-chain to verify the safety properties for model instances of a number of railway networks, ranging from a trivial tiny toy network to a large station (Køge) extracted from the early deployment line of the new Danish signalling systems.

In our first trials of verifying the models, we used simple induction (k-induction with $k = 1$), but we got spurious counter-examples. To avoid that we tried to increase k and strengthen the invariant to be verified. It turned out that the verification time increased significantly as k increased, making it impossible to verify even the small networks. However, we were able to derive strengthening properties ψ (see Sect. 6) for which the verification could be done just using simple induction.

Table 2. Verification results for different networks using simple induction ($k = 1$). Toy, cross, and mini are made-up trivial networks, while Gadstrup-Havdrup (Gt-Hd) and Køge are extracted from the early deployment line in the Danish Signalling Programme. (BR: branching ratio)

Case	Linears	Points	Signals	Routes	BR	Vars	Time(sec)	Memory(MB)
Toy	6	1	6	4	0.17	47	2	63
Cross	8	2	8	10	0.25	72	9	137
Mini	6	2	8	12	0.33	66	11	128
Gt-Hd	21	5	24	33	0.24	200	146	626
Køge	57	23	60	73	0.40	582	3868	4457

(Not for all applications this is possible, see, e.g., [13]). Table 2 shows the results of the final verification. Each row of the table lists the size of a network in terms of the number of linear sections, points, signals, and routes in the configuration, and the number of generated variables in the corresponding model instance. The two last columns show the approximate accumulated verification time and memory usage. All experiments have been performed on Intel(R) Core(TM) i7-3520 M CPU @ 2.90 GHz, 8 GB RAM, Ubuntu 14.04 LTS, Linux 3.14.1-031401-generic x86_64 kernel.

The *branching ratio* of a network (BR in Table 2) is defined as the ratio of the number of points to the number of linear sections in that network. The larger the branching ratio is, the more complex the corresponding network is in terms of branching. The size of the formula Φ specifying the transition relation as well as the size of the formulas ϕ and ψ specifying the state invariants grow as the size of the network grows. Our experiments show that the formulas grow much more when the network's branching ratio also increases, than when the branching ratio is nearly the same (as it is, e.g., the case when chaining multiple simple stations). This is due to the fact that the interdependency between variables in the model also increases when BR increases.

We also injected errors into models. Counter examples for these were normally found in relatively short time. This appears to be a general trend when dealing with interlocking systems [16]. In a few cases, it took long time to find counter examples. Such examples usually represent very subtle errors in the model or the configuration data, which may be easily overlooked by inspection.

8 Related Work

In recent years, the railway domain has become one of the most promising application domains of formal methods. Several research groups have investigated how formal methods would help efficiently producing more robust railway control systems. An overview of recent trends can be found in [7], and recommendations and best-practices for efficient development and verification of safe railway control systems are summarized in [12]. Re-configurable systems and automated verification are among these recommendations that we have followed.

Model checking is a promising technique for verifying safety properties of interlocking systems thanks to its capability to be fully automated. Unfortunately, due to the state explosion problem, the technique is only able to verify applications of small size [8]. Several techniques have been proposed in order to push the applicability bounds toward industrial size. Winter et al. suggest using ordering strategies optimized for interlocking models [23]. A number of high-level abstractions for reducing the complexity of interlocking models are presented in [15]. In [6], Fantechi et al. suggest a distributed interlocking model whose verification can be divided into small tasks and verified in parallel. SAT-based model checking and slicing technique are used in [16]. In order to remedy the problem with state space explosion in the global model checking approach, we have recently for some other applications [13,14] used BMC instead. In the current work, a combination of SMT-based BMC with inductive reasoning allowed us to verify safety properties without having to explore the whole state space, hence we were able to push the bounds even further to handle larger networks of industrial size. As an alternative to the model checking approach, theorem proving based techniques have also shown success in the railway domain, see, e.g., [2,11], but are less automated.

Although sequential release has been used in some interlocking systems, we have not found any published formal models of interlocking systems that integrate this feature. In [20], the conditions for elements to be unlocked and reused in sequential releases are pre-computed and specified in the interlocking tables. In our approach, sequential release is integrated into the behavioral model rather than into the configuration data. This reduces the complexity of the configuration data and makes interlocking configuration data relatively independent from the chosen interlocking approaches.

9   Conclusion and Future Work

This paper presented a fully automated, formal method and an associated tool suite for verifying the forthcoming new ETCS Level 2 based Danish railway interlocking systems featuring sequential release. A formal model for these systems was outlined. A novelty in our contribution is that the system is part of an ETCS Level 2 based signalling system in which there are no physical signals along the tracks; instead, movement authorities are communicated via onboard computers. By introducing the concept of virtual signals, we have been able to handle the assignment of movement authorities in a way that is very similar to the situations where conventional signals are used. Another novelty is that the formal model features sequential release. As a consequence, the model is more complex than those supporting route-based release only, because additional variables and transitions are required. Therefore the verification becomes more challenging. In spite of this difficulty, using a combination of SMT-based BMC and inductive reasoning, we were able to successfully verify safety properties for systems controlling large networks of realistic size. This was enabled by encodings of the state space, the transition relation, and of the safety properties that can be efficiently evaluated by SMT solvers supporting bit vector and integer arithmetics.

In order to compare our verification approach to the approaches that use BDD-based symbolic model checking, a translation from our model to NuSMV – a well-known BDD-based symbolic model checker – is currently in progress. For future work, we will benchmark how sequential release affects the complexity, and hence verification challenges, of interlocking models. Furthermore, we will investigate advanced techniques for automating the process of discovering strengthening invariants, or reducing the size of the networks that need to be modeled. For the current model there are potential overlaps between the strengthening invariants, which should be eliminated in order to reduce the size of the formula to be solved by the SMT solver.

Acknowledgments. The authors would like to thank Ross Edwin Gammon and Nikhil Mohan Pande from Banedanmark (Railnet Denmark) and Jan Bertelsen from Thales for helping us with their expertise about Danish interlocking systems and always being helpful when we had questions; and Dr.-Ing. Uwe Schulze and Florian Lapschies from University of Bremen for their help with the implementation in the RT-Tester tool-chain.

References

1. Aanæs, M., Thai, H.P.: Modelling and verification of relay interlocking systems. Master's thesis, Technical University of Denmark, DTU Informatics (2012). Series: IMM-MSC-2012-14
2. Behnia, S., Mammar, A., Mota, J.-M., Breton, N., Caspi, P., Raymond, P.: Industrialising a proof-based verification approach of computerised interlocking systems. In: Allan, J., Arias, E., Brebbia, C.A., Goodman, C., Rumsey, A.F., Sciutto, G., Tomii, N. (eds.) Eleventh International Conference on Computer System Design and Operation in the Railway and Other Transit Systems (COMPRAIL 2008). WIT Press (2008)
3. de Moura, L., Rueß, H., Sorea, M.: Bounded model checking and induction: from refutation to verification. In: Hunt Jr, W.A., Somenzi, F. (eds.) CAV 2003. LNCS, vol. 2725, pp. 14–26. Springer, Heidelberg (2003)
4. ERTMS: Annex A for ETCS Baseline 3 and GSM-R Baseline 0, April 2012
5. CENELEC European Committee for Electrotechnical Standardization. EN 50128:2011 - Railway applications - Communications, signalling and processing systems - Software for railway control and protection systems (2011)
6. Fantechi, A.: Distributing the challenge of model checking interlocking control tables. In: Margaria, T., Steffen, B. (eds.) ISoLA 2012, Part II. LNCS, vol. 7610, pp. 276–289. Springer, Heidelberg (2012)
7. Fantechi, A.: Twenty-five years of formal methods and railways: what next? In: Counsell, S., Núñez, M. (eds.) SEFM 2013. LNCS, vol. 8368, pp. 167–183. Springer, Heidelberg (2014)
8. Ferrari, A., Magnani, G., Grasso, D., Fantechi, A.: Model checking interlocking control tables. In: Schnieder, E., Tarnai, G. (eds.) FORMS/FORMAT 2010 - Formal Methods for Automation and Safety in Railway and Automotive Systems, pp. 107–115. Springer, Heidelberg (2010)

9. Hvid Hansen, H., Ketema, J., Luttik, B., Mousavi, M.R., van de Pol, J., dos Santos, O.M.: Automated verification of executable UML models. In: Aichernig, B.K., de Boer, F.S., Bonsangue, M.M. (eds.) Formal Methods for Components and Objects. LNCS, vol. 6957, pp. 225–250. Springer, Heidelberg (2011)
10. Haxthausen, A.E., Le Bliguet, M., Kjær, A.A.: Modelling and verification of relay interlocking systems. In: Choppy, C., Sokolsky, O. (eds.) Monterey Workshop 2008. LNCS, vol. 6028, pp. 141–153. Springer, Heidelberg (2010)
11. Haxthausen, A.E., Peleska, J.: Formal development and verification of a distributed railway control systems. IEEE Trans. Softw. Eng. **26**, 687–701 (2000)
12. Haxthausen, A.E., Peleska, J.: Efficient development and verification of safe railway control software. In: Reinhardt, C., Shroeder, K. (eds.) Railways: Types, Design and Safety Issues, pp. 127–148. Nova Science Publishers Inc, New York (2013)
13. Haxthausen, A.E., Peleska, J., Kinder, S.: A formal approach for the construction and verification of railway control systems. Formal Aspects Comput. **23**, 191–219 (2011). Springer
14. Haxthausen, A.E., Peleska, J., Pinger, R.: Applied bounded model checking for interlocking system designs. In: Counsell, S., Núñez, M. (eds.) SEFM 2013. LNCS, vol. 8368, pp. 205–220. Springer, Heidelberg (2014)
15. James, P., Moller, F., Nguyen, H.N., Roggenbach, M., Schneider, S., Treharne, H., Trumble, M., Williams, D.: Verification of scheme plans using CSP—B. In: Counsell, S., Núñez, M. (eds.) SEFM 2013. LNCS, vol. 8368, pp. 189–204. Springer, Heidelberg (2014)
16. James, P., Roggenbach, M.: Automatically verifying railway interlockings using sat-based model checking. In: Proceedings of the Electronic Communications of the EASST, vol. 35, EASST (2011)
17. Peleska, J.: Industrial-strength model-based testing - state of the art and current challenges. In: Petrenko, A.K., Schlingloff, H. (eds.) Proceedings of the 8th Workshop on Model-Based Testing, Electronic Proceedings in Theoretical Computer Science, vol. 111, pp. 3–28. Open Publishing Association, Rome, Italy (2013)
18. Peleska, J., Vorobev, E., Lapschies, F.: Automated test case generation with SMT-solving and abstract interpretation. In: Bobaru, M., Havelund, K., Holzmann, G.J., Joshi, R. (eds.) NFM 2011. LNCS, vol. 6617, pp. 298–312. Springer, Heidelberg (2011)
19. Theeg, G., Vlasenko, S.V., Anders, E.: Railway Signalling & Interlocking: International Compendium. Eurailpress, Germany (2009)
20. Tombs, D., Robinson, N., Nikandros, G.: Signalling control table generation and verification. In: CORE 2002: Cost Efficient Railways through Engineering, p. 415. Railway Technical Society of Australasia/Rail Track Association of Australia (2002)
21. Verified Systems International GmbH: RT-Tester Model-Based Test Case and Test Data Generator - RTT-MBT - User Manual (2013)
22. Vu, L.H., Haxthausen, A.E., Peleska, J.: A domain-specific language for railway interlocking systems. In: Schnieder, E., Tarnai, G. (eds.) FORMS/FORMAT 2014–10th Symposium on Formal Methods for Automation and Safety in Railway and Automotive Systems, pp. 200–209. Institute for Traffic Safety and Automation Engineering, Technische Universität Braunschweig (2014)
23. Winter, K.: Optimising ordering strategies for symbolic model checking of railway interlockings. In: Margaria, T., Steffen, B. (eds.) ISoLA 2012, Part II. LNCS, vol. 7610, pp. 246–260. Springer, Heidelberg (2012)

A Spin-Based Approach for Checking OSEK/VDX Applications

Haitao Zhang$^{(\boxtimes)}$, Toshiaki Aoki, and Yuki Chiba

Japan Advanced Institute of Science and Technology, Nomi, Japan
{zhanghaitao,toshiaki,chiba}@jaist.ac.jp

Abstract. OSEK/VDX, a standard of automobile OS, has been widely adopted by many manufacturers to design and develop a vehicle-mounted OS. With the increasing functionalities in vehicles, more and more applications are developed based on the OSEK/VDX OS. However, how to ensure the reliability of the developed OSEK/VDX applications is becoming a challenge for developers. As to ensure the reliability of the developed OSEK/VDX applications, model checking as an exhaustive checking technique can be applied to verify the developed OSEK/VDX applications. In our previous work, we have proposed a bounded model checking approach to verify the OSEK/VDX applications. In this paper, we describe and develop an alternative approach to verify the OSEK/VDX applications based on the Spin. There are two motivations in this paper, one is to show how to use Spin to verify the OSEK/VDX applications, and the other is to investigate the effectiveness of our bounded model checking approach and Spin-based approach based on the experiments.

Keywords: OSEK/VDX applications · Scheduler · Spin model checker

1 Introduction

OSEK/VDX [11,13], a standard of automobile OS, is proposed by German and France automobile manufacturers in 1994. The original motivation of OSEK/VDX standard is to resolve the problem of increasing software content in automobiles and to deliver high-quality products. With the development of OSEK/VDX OS standard, it has been widely adopted by many automobile manufacturers to design and develop a vehicle-mounted OS, such as BMW, Opel, and Volkswagen. As to enhance the driving fun and safety, more and more applications are developed based on the OSEK/VDX OS. However, with the increasing complexity in the development, how to ensure the reliability of the developed OSEK/VDX applications is becoming a challenge for developers.

To ensure the reliability of the developed OSEK/VDX applications, model checking [2,3] as an exhaustive technique can be applied to verify the OSEK/VDX applications. There are many model checking methods that have been applied to verify the sequential software [18] and multi-threaded software [14,15]. However, it is difficult to directly use these existing model checking methods

© Springer International Publishing Switzerland 2015
C. Artho and P.C. Ölveczky (Eds.): FTSCS 2014, CCIS 476, pp. 239–255, 2015.
DOI: 10.1007/978-3-319-17581-2_16

to verify the OSEK/VDX applications, since the execution characteristics of OSEK/VDX applications are different from sequential software and general multi-threaded software such as SystemC programs. For example, when an application runs on the OSEK/VDX OS,

- tasks within the application are concurrently executed and the running task can be explicitly determined by OSEK/VDX scheduler according to the task priority and configuration data.
- tasks within application can invoke service APIs to interact with OSEK/VDX OS for changing task states, setting a synchronization event, and accessing a shared resource.
- the invoked service APIs may lead to context switch of tasks.

According to these execution characteristics, we can easily find that the checking process on OSEK/VDX applications is different from checking sequential software and multi-threaded software, since the OSEK/VDX application is like a multi-threaded software compared with sequential software, and moreover, in contrast with multi-threaded software, OSEK/VDX application can interact with OSEK/VDX OS via service APIs, and its executions are conducted by a deterministic scheduler[1] (in OSEK/VDX OS, the *static priority scheduling policy* is adopted to dispatch tasks within the application).

As to apply model checking technique to verify the OSEK/VDX applications, in our previous work [7,8], we have proposed a technique named execution path generator (EPG) to verify the design model of developed OSEK/VDX applications based on the SMT-based bounded model checking (BMC) [5]. Particularly, in order to accurately construct a transitions system for the OSEK/VDX application and avoid the behaviors of OS model to be poured into the transition system, an OS model corresponding to the OSEK/VDX specification is embedded in the EPG to respond to the invoked service APIs and compute the running task. We have conducted many experiments using EPG technique, the experiment results show that, although the EPG technique can handle the complex applications which contain a lot of tasks and APIs, it will spend much time checking the applications which hold a lot of loops. Furthermore, the EPG technique for now cannot check the applications which contain interruptions. Therefore, in this paper we develop an alternative approach to check the OSEK/VDX applications based on the Spin model checker [6], and we want to investigate the effectiveness of Spin-based approach and EPG technique based on the experiments.

As to accurately check an OSEK/VDX application using Spin model checker, in our Spin-based approach a synchronization model (SynM) is used to simulate the executions of the target application. In the SynM, all of the tasks and interrupt service routines (ISRs) within the target application are regarded as **process**, and the OSEK/VDX OS model as a special **process** is employed to

---

[1] In general multi-threaded software such as SystemC programs, the executions of threads are conducted by a non-deterministic scheduler. As to completely check the multi-threaded software, all of the possible interleavings of threads are taken into account in the checking process.

responding to the invoked service APIs and conducting the executions of tasks, and moreover, the `channel` within `promela` is used to implement the interactive behaviors between application model and OS model via service APIs.

We have implemented our SynM in Spin model checker and conducted many experiments using Spin based on the several OSEK/VDX applications. The experiment results show that, our Spin-based approach is capable of checking the safety properties related to variables, service APIs, OS data, and mutual exclusion in the checking process, and moreover, the Spin-based approach also can be used to check the applications which hold ISRs. In addition, in the experiments we also investigated the effectiveness of the Spin-based approach and EPG technique. The investigation results show that, (i) for the simple application which contains a few tasks (less than 15) but many loops, Spin-based approach is faster than EPG technique in the verification. However, (ii) for the complex application which contains many tasks and APIs, the EPG technique is more efficient to check these applications compared with Spin-based approach.

The rest of the paper is structured as follows. The preliminaries for OSEK/VDX OS and applications are presented in Sect. 2. Based on the discussion about the execution characteristics of OSEK/VDX applications, the Spin-based approach is presented in Sect. 3. As to evaluate our approach, some experiments are carried out in Sect. 4. Related work is discussed in Sect. 5. Conclusion and future work are shown in the last section.

2   Preliminaries

2.1   OSEK/VDX OS

A general OSEK/VDX OS consists of a scheduler module, event process module, resource process module, alarm process module, and interruption process module. Based on these system modules, OSEK/VDX OS supports a standardized application interfaces (APIs) for user to develop customized applications. In our research, we focus on the applications that communicate with scheduler module, event process module, resource process module, and interruption process module. The structure of OSEK/VDX OS with an application is shown in Fig. 1.

Scheduluer Module: OSEK/VDX OS can process two types of tasks, basic task and extended task. The states of a basic task consist of *running* state, *suspended* state, and *ready* state. Compared with basic task, the extended task can hold synchronization events and has a unique state called *waiting* state. In the scheduling process, the *static priority scheduling policy* with non-preemptive and full-preemptive strategies is adopted by scheduler to conduct the executions of tasks, and moreover, scheduler manages a ready queue to indicate the execution order of tasks. Besides, scheduler can respond to four service APIs (*TerminateTask*, *ActivateTask*, *ChainTask*, and *Schedule*) that can be invoked by tasks to switch task states. For instance, if the service API *ActivateTask*(*tk1*) is invoked by running task, and task *tk1* is currently in the *suspended* state, scheduler will move task *tk1* from *suspended* state to *ready* state.

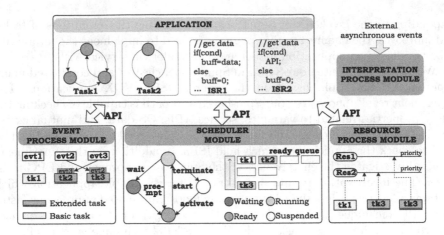

Fig. 1. The structure of OSEK/VDX OS with an application.

Event Process Module: In the event process module, OSEK/VDX OS provides a synchronization mechanism for implementing synchronous executions between tasks. Particularly, only extended tasks can hold a definite number of events, and events are the criteria for the switching of task states from *running* state to *waiting* state or from *waiting* state to *ready* state. There are three service APIs (*SetEvent*, *WaitEvent*, and *ClearEvent*) that can be responded by event process module, and tasks can invoke these service APIs to implement the synchronous executions. E.g., when the running task *tk1* waits for the event *evt1* using service API *WaitEvent(evt1)*, task *tk1* cannot continue until the event *evt1* is set by other tasks (basic tasks or extended tasks) using service API *SetEvent(tk1,evt1)*.

Resource Process Module: The priority inversion and deadlock are two typical problems of common synchronization mechanism when several tasks access the same shared resource with different priorities. In order to avoid these two problems, OSEK/VDX OS adopts the *Priority Ceiling Protocol* [4] to coordinate the behaviors of accessing shared resources in the resource process module. The resource process module supports two service APIs (*GetResource* and *ReleaseResource*) which can be invoked by tasks to access a shared resource according to the ceiling priority of the accessed resource. For example, if the service API *GetResource(res1)* is invoked by *running* task, and the priority of the task is lower than the ceiling priority of the resource *res1*, the priority of the task will be raised to the ceiling priority of the resource *res1*, and the priority of the task will be reset to the priority before requiring the resource *res1* when *ReleaseResource(res1)* is invoked by the task. Note that, the ceiling priority of a shared resource is lower than the lowest priority of all tasks that do not access the resource, and higher than the priority of all tasks that access the resource.

Interruption Process Module: The interrupt service routines (ISRs) play an important role in the OSEK/VDX applications, such as responding to an

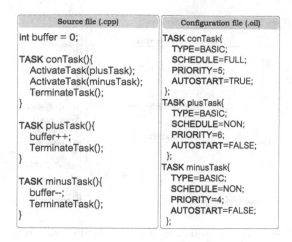

Fig. 2. The simple application.

external event or receiving data from a sensor. In OSEK/VDX OS, the interruption process module supports two categories of ISRs (ISR categories 1 and 2) for applications. The features of ISRs within OSEK/VDX OS are as follow. (*i*) The impulse signals of ISRs are triggered by the external asynchronous events. (*ii*) The ISRs can interrupt the non-preemptive and full-preemptive tasks, and a lower priority ISR can be interrupted by a higher priority ISR. (*iii*) In contrast with category 1 ISR, the category 2 ISR can invoke service APIs to activate a task, set an event to an extended task, and access a shared resource. (*iv*) The rescheduling will happen if a category 2 ISR have been terminated and no other ISR is activated.

2.2 OSEK/VDX Application and Execution Characteristics

An application developed based on OSEK/VDX OS consists of two files, one is the source file, and the other is the configuration file. The source file, which can be developed by C++ language, is used to present the concrete behaviors of the application. The configuration file is used to define tasks, events, resources, and ISRs. A simple OSEK/VDX application without ISRs is shown in Fig. 2.

As to clearly comprehend the execution characteristics of OSEK/VDX applications, an example is discussed in this part. In the simple application shown in Fig. 2, since only the attribute AUTOSTART[2] of *conTask* is set to be TRUE, *conTask* will be firstly moved to *running* state by scheduler and then *conTask* is executed. As shown in Fig. 3, when the service API *ActivateTask(plusTask)* is invoked by *conTask*, scheduler will be loaded to respond to the API. For this moment, the running task *conTask* will be preempted by *plusTask* since the

---

[2] AUTOSTART: if the attribute AUTOSTART of a task is set to be TRUE, the task starts from *ready* state in the initial state. Otherwise, the task starts from *suspended* state.

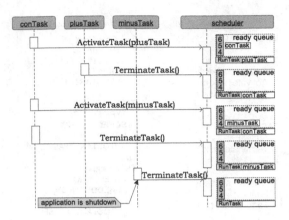

Fig. 3. The execution sequences of the application shown in Fig. 2.

priority of *plusTask* is higher than *conTask* and the attribute SCHEDUL[3] of *conTask* is set to be FULL (if a task is activated, the task will be moved from *suspended* to *ready* state by scheduler). Currently, the task *plusTask* gets run-unit to run, and goes to *suspended* state when the service API *TerminateTask()* is invoked (the service API *TerminateTask()* is used to terminate the executions of a task, and terminated tasks will be moved from *running* state to *suspended* state by scheduler. If the running task is terminated, scheduler then dispatches the head task in the ready queue to run). When *plusTask* is terminated, *conTask* will be moved to *running* state again and continue its executions from preempted point. Then, *minusTask* is activated by *conTask*, and will be run when the service API *TerminateTask()* is invoked by *conTask* (*conTask* cannot be preempted by *minusTask*, since the priority of *minusTask* is lesser than *conTask*).

According to the executions of the given example, we can find the following execution characteristics, (*i*) which task within the application is to be run is determined by scheduler according to the ready queue and configuration file of the application, (*ii*) task states can be changed by invoked service APIs, (*iii*) the invoked service APIs may lead to context switch of tasks. Based on the listed characteristics, we can easily find that the execution characteristics of OSEK/VDX applications are different from sequential software and multi-threaded software. In order to employ Spin model checker to accurately verify the OSEK/VDX applications, there are two challenges that should be addressed, e.g., (*i*) how to implement the scheduling behaviors, (*ii*) how to implement the interactive behaviors between tasks and scheduler via service APIs. As to overcome these two challenges, we develop a synchronization model to simulate the executions of the OSEK/VDX applications, which will be demonstrated in the next section.

---

[3] SCHEDUL: if the attribute SCHEDUL of a task is set to be FULL, the task can be preempted by higher priority tasks. Otherwise, the task will not leave *running* state until the service API *TerminateTask*, *ChainTask* or *Schedule* is invoked, or waits for an event.

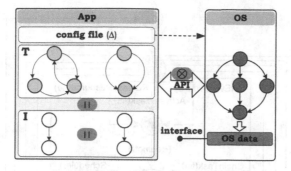

Fig. 4. The synchronization model (SynM).

3   The Spin-Based Checking Approach

3.1   The Synchronization Model

To accurately check OSEK/VDX applications using Spin model checker, the key work is how to construct a checking model. Based on the given example shown in Fig. 2, we have found that the running task within the application is determined by the scheduler according to the ready queue and task configuration data. Thus, as to accurately simulate the executions of tasks, the best way is to construct an OS model (such as scheduler model) in the checking model to conduct the executions of tasks.

In our approach, a synchronization model (SynM) is constructed to simulate the executions of target application, which is shown in Fig. 4. The SynM is a combination of OS model $\mathcal{OS}$ and application model App. Where, the OS model corresponding to the OSEK/VDX specification is employed to conduct the executions of the application and respond to the invoked service APIs. The application model $App = \{\Delta,\ T,\ I\}$ is the set of components, Δ is the configuration file of application, $T = \{t_1,\ t_2, \cdots\}$ is the finite set of tasks defined in the application, $I = \{isr_1,\ isr_2, \cdots\}$ is the finite set of interrupt service routines (ISRs) defined in the application (note that, in the SynM all of the tasks, ISRs and OS model are regarded as **process**). Furthermore, the application model and OS model will synchronously execute via service APIs. The execution characteristics of SynM are stated in the following.

When an application runs on the OSEK/VDX OS, the head task in the ready queue will be dispatched to run if the run-unit is idle. The other tasks in the *ready* state, *suspended* state and *waiting* state will not be run until the running chance is given by scheduler. Thus, the first execution characteristic of SynM is as follows.

– *a task $t \in T$ can be run iff its ID equals to the running task ID that is computed by OS model, and the remanent tasks $A' = T \backslash \{t\}$ are restrained to execute.*

Once a service API is invoked by the application, the OS will be loaded to run for responding to the invoked service API (the executions of the application

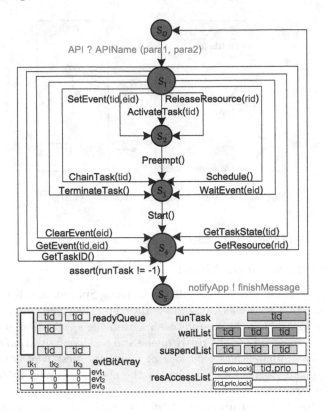

Fig. 5. OS model.

will be preempted by OS). When OS has already completed its executions, the
run-unit is released, and then the application will be continued again. According
to the described execution characteristics, the following three execution characteristics are poured into the SynM for simulating the interactive executions
between OS model and application model.

– *application model App and OS model OS are synchronously executed via
  APIs.*
– *when a service API is invoked by running task t or isr, the task t or isr will
  stop its execution to wait for the executions of OS model.*
– *once OS model receives an invoked service API from App, OS model will
  be executed for responding to the invoked service API and computing the
  running task ID. If OS model has completed its executions, application model
  App will be executed from the stopped point, and then OS model waits for
  the next service API from application model.*

As to completely simulate the ISRs, in our SynM all of the possible interleavings between running task and ISRs are considered due to the non-deterministic
occurring time and execution order of ISRs. Substantially, in the checking process,

the executions between ISRs and currently running task can be considered as the concurrent program. In SynM, we stipulate that ISRs I and running task t are concurrently executed, and $\forall isr_i, isr_j \in I$ are also concurrently executed. In addition, in order to avoid the executions of ISRs to be interleaved by tasks, the behaviors of ISRs are designated as an `atomic` sequence. Here, a shortcoming is involved in our approach because of the `atomic` sequence, that is, our approach does not allow higher priority ISRs to interrupt the lower priority ISRs. Based on the above analysis, the following one execution characteristic is put into SynM.

- $\forall isr \in I$ and running task $t \in T$ are concurrently executed, and $\forall isr_i, isr_j \in I$ are concurrently executed in the SynM. Note that the behaviors of ISRs are designated as `atomic` sequence.

Furthermore, as to support the checking process on the given property related to task states, event states, and shared resource states, an interface corresponding to OS data is provided by SynM.

3.2   Implementation in Spin

According to the SynM, we can easily simulate the executions of an OSEK/VDX application. As to conveniently use Spin to check OSEK/VDX applications based on the SynM, we have constructed an OS model using `promela` language according to the OSEK/VDX specification, and moreover, three interface functions are supported by the constructed OS model for easily constructing the application model according to the given application. The OS model and interface functions are stated in the following.

OS Model: The OS model is developed based on the our previous work [9], which has been adopted by Japan automobile manufacturers to test the developed OSEK/VDX OS. As shown in Fig. 5, the OS model is a tuple $\mathcal{OS} = (S, s_0, D, F, \Sigma)$, which is a combination of scheduler model, event process model and resource process model. Where, S is the finite set of states, $s_0 \in S$ is the initial state. $D = \{runTask, readyQueue, suspendList, waitList, evtBitArray, resAccessList\}$ is the set of data structures. F is the set of functions. $\Sigma \subseteq S \times F \times S$ is the set of transition relations.

In the OS model, D is the interface of OS data shown in SynM. Where, $runTask$ which is a variable is used to store the running task tid ($tid \in \mathbb{N}$ is the identifier of tasks). Since several tasks can share a same priority in the OSEK/VDX OS, the $readyQueue$ which is composed of queues with different priorities is used to store the tid of $ready$ tasks. The data structures $suspendList$ and $waitList$ are used to store the tid of tasks in the $suspended$ state and $waiting$ state, respectively. $evtBitArray$ which is a matrix is used to store the event states of extended tasks ($eid \in \mathbb{N}$ is the identifier of events). $resAccessList$ which is composed of lists is used to indicate the state of resources accessed by tasks ($rid \in \mathbb{N}$ is the identifier of resources). In the function set F, `API?APIName(para1,para2)` and `notifyApp!finishMessage` are the synchronization functions, their implementations specified in `promela` are shown in Fig. 6. Here, `API?APIName(para1,`

```
mtype {TerminateTask, ActivateTask, ChainTask,
       Schedule, SetEvent, GetEvent, ClearEvent,
       WaitEvent, GetResource, ReleaseResource,
       GetTaskState, GetTaskID
};
mtype APIName;
int   para1, para2;
bool  finishMessage;
chan  API = [0] of {mtype, int, int};
chan  notifyApp = [0] of {bool};
```

Fig. 6. The synchronization functions specified in promela.

```
inline waitForRun(_tid){
  (runTask == _tid);
}
```

Fig. 7. The inline function waitForRun(_tid) specified in promela.

para2) is used to receive the invoked service APIs from application model (where, APIName is the name of invoked service API, para1 and para2 are the parameters in the service APIs). notifyApp!finishMessage is used to notify the application model that OS model has already completed its executions. In addition, the assertion $assert(runTask \mathrel{!=} -1)$ is used to terminate the checking process if there is no running task (where, "−1" represents that running task is idle). The other functions in F such as ChainTask(tid) and TerminateTask(), which are the standardized functions defined in OSEK/VDX specification, are used to operate the system data D according to the invoked service APIs.

Interface Functions: The first interface function waitForRun() shown in Fig. 7 is used to restrain the executions of the tasks whose *tid* are not equal to *runTask*.

The second interface function taskAPI() shown in Fig. 8, which can be invoked by tasks, is used to simulate the behaviors of service APIs, in which API!_APIName (_para1,_para2) and notifyAPP?finishMessage are used to implement the interactive executions between OS model and tasks, (_tid == *runTask*) is employed to simulate the context switch of tasks caused by the invoked service API (the parameter _tid is the host task ID). In addition, since category 2 ISRs can invoke service APIs to access a shared resource, it may lead to the mutual exclusion problem when running task and ISRs want to access the same shared resource. Therefore, the if branches are used to change the state of shared resources for restraining the executions of ISRs when running task is holding the shared resource, where the variable *lock* is used to label the resource state.

Like tasks, for the category 2 ISRs, we also provide an interface function to implement the interactive executions between OS model and ISRs, which is shown in Fig. 9. In the function, the variable *lock* is used to implement the mutual exclusion behaviors between ISRs and tasks. Note that the functions shown in Figs. 8 and 9 are only used to restraint the executions of ISRs when running task and ISRs want to access the same resource, the behaviors between tasks or ISRs for accessing shared resources are coordinated by the resource process model and atomic sequence, respectively.

```
inline taskAPI(_tid,_APIName,_para1,_para2){
  atomic{
  if
  ::_APIName == GetResource ->
     resAccessList[_para1].lock=true;
  ::_APIName == ReleaseResource ->
     resAccessList[_para1].lock=false;
  fi;
  API ! _APIName(_para1,_para2);
  notifyAPP ? finishMessage;
  (_tid == runTask);
  }
}
```

Fig. 8. The inline function `taskAPI` specified in `promela`.

```
inline ISRAPI(_APIName,_para1,_para2){
  atomic
  {
  if
  ::_APIName == GetResource ->
     (resAccessList[_para1].lock == false);
     resAccessList[_para1].lock=true;
  ::_APIName == ReleaseResource ->
     resAccessList[_para1].lock=false;
  ::else ->
     API ! _APIName(_para1,_para2);
     notifyAPP ? finishMessage;
  fi;
  }
}
```

Fig. 9. The inline function `ISRAPI` specified in `promela`.

Checking Application Using Spin: Based on the OS model and supported interface functions, we can easily construct an application model for the given application and check the constructed application model using Spin model checker. E.g., the application model of the example shown in Fig. 2 has been presented in Fig. 10. Note that, for the configuration file, our OS model also provides an interface function for inputting the configuration data. The OS model is available at the osek-spin homepage.[4] In addition, since the category 2 ISRs can invoked service APIs to set an event to an extended task or activate a task from *suspendList*, it will possibly lead to a rescheduling point. Therefore, when we check the application which contains category 2 ISR, we should insert the function `waitForRun(_tid)` into each transition of tasks to simulate the context switch of tasks.

3.3 Given Property

Based on the OS model and supported interface functions, we can accurately check an OSEK/VDX application using Spin model checker. In this section, we

[4] http://www.jaist.ac.jp/~s1220209/osek-spin.htm.

```
#include "OSmodel.h"
proctype conTask() {
 start:
 waitForRun(conTask.tid);
     taskAPI(conTask.tid, ActivateTask, plusTask.tid,-1);
     taskAPI(conTask.tid, ActivateTask, minusTask.tid,-1);
     taskAPI(conTask.tid,TerminateTask, -1,-1);
 goto start;
}
proctype plusTask() {
 start:
 waitForRun(plusTask.tid);
     buffer=buffer+1;
     taskAPI(plusTask.tid, TerminateTask, -1,-1);
 goto start;
}
proctype minusTask() {
 start:
     waitForRun(minusTask.tid);
     buffer=buffer-1;
     taskAPI(minusTask.tid, TerminateTask, -1,-1);
 goto start;
}
init {
run OSModel(); run conTask(); run plusTask();   run minusTask();
}
```

Fig. 10. The application model of the example shown in Fig. 2.

will talk about what kinds of given properties can be checked by our approach in the practical checking process.

Variable Property: In the practical checking process, sometimes we want to check whether the executions of target application have already reached a specified state via asserting the values of variables declared in an application. Based on the SynM, we can find that all of the executions of target application can be checked by Spin model checker. Thus, our approach can be used to check variable property using assertion statement.

LTL Property: In addition to assertions, the given property which holds temporal operators is frequently used to check an application in the practical checking process. For instance, we want to check whether the value of a variable will be changed to be zero in the future. Since Spin model checker can accept the given property specified in Linear Temporal Logic (LTL), our approach thus can be used to check the LTL property.

Service API Property: The service API is also an interesting checking point for the OSEK/VDX applications, since service APIs perform an important part in the interaction between application and OSEK/VDX OS. In the checking process, we usually want to check whether a service API will be invoked by tasks. In our approach, the service API is represented as a set {APIName,para1,para2} of variables in promela. Therefore, our approach can check the service API property.

OS Data Property: When an application runs on the OSEK/VDX OS, it is difficult to judge the execution situations of the application since the executions of OSEK/VDX applications are conducted by the scheduler, and tasks within application can invoke service APIs to synchronously execute and access shared resources. As to clearly detect the execution situations of an application, the states of tasks, events and shared resources are often considered as a checking point. To check this type of property (which is named as OS data property in our paper), an interface with respect to OS data such as the data in the ready queue is provided by OS model in our approach. E.g., we can use the LTL property shown in formula (1) to check whether the task *tid* will be run after *ActivateTask(tid)* is invoked.

$$\Diamond \, ((\texttt{APIName} == ActivateTask \,\&\&\, \texttt{para1} == tid)$$
$$\&\& \, \texttt{X}(runTask == tid)) \qquad (1)$$

Mutual Exclusion Property: Furthermore, the checking process on mutual exclusion property also will be carried out in the practical checking process, since tasks and ISRs within application can enter a critical section for accessing a shared resource using service APIs *GetResource(rid)* and *ReleaseResource(rid)*. Informally, mutual exclusion contains two properties, one is *exclusiveness*, the other is *liveness*. In our approach, the task *tid* of accessing shared resources is recorded by *resAccessList* of OS model. Thus, our approach can be used to check these two properties. For instance, we can use the LTL properties shown in formula (2) and (3) to check the *exclusiveness* property and *liveness* property respectively, where we suppose task *tk1* and task *tk2* will access the same shared resource *rid*, IN represents matching task *tid* in list, n is the number of tasks defined in the application.

$$! \Diamond (tk1.tid \text{ IN } resAccessList[rid].list[0:n] \,\&\&$$
$$tk2.tid \text{ IN } resAccessList[rid].list[0:n]) \qquad (2)$$
$$\Diamond (tk1.tid \text{ IN } resAccessList[rid].list[0:n]) \qquad (3)$$

4   Experiment and Discussion

As to show the practicality of our approach, some experiments are carried out in this part. In the experiments, as to comprehensively investigate the effectiveness our approach, the applications which hold different task number, API number and loop number are selected as our benchmarks. Moreover, we also compared the Spin-based approach with osek-bmc[5] which is an implementation of our EPG technique. In the experiments, we investigate four aspects, including task number, API number, loop number, and ISR number. jSpin is selected as the experiment platform, and the "C complier" is configured to "-DVECTORSZ=16384 -DBITSTATE", the max depth is set to "20,000,000". In the EPG technique,

---

[5] osek-bmc is available at http://www.jaist.ac.jp/~s1220209/Index.htm.

the max depth is set to "20,000,000", and the loop bound is set to 40. All of the experiment results have been listed in Table 1. In the results table, #t is the number of tasks, #l is the number of loops, #s is the number of explored states. "Mb" is the memory consumption measured in Mbyte, "time" is the time consumption measured in second. The benchmarks used in the experiments are available at http://www.jaist.ac.jp/~s1220209/osek-spin.htm.

4.1 Experiment Results

There are some noticeable results in the Table 1. In all of the conducted experiments (lines 1–18), Spin-based approach will check more states than `osek-bmc`. Moreover, if we increase the task number and APIs number, Spin will run out of memory and time (e.g., line 4 and 10). Compared with Spin-based approach, `osek-bmc` can successfully check these examples with small states, and spends lower cost (time and memory) than Spin. It is easy to explain why `osek-bmc` is excellent in the verification. In EPG technique, the OS model is embedded in the checking algorithm level for avoiding the transitions of OS model to be verified in the checking process. However, in Spin-based approach, since the OS model is a part of constructed checking model, Spin will not only check the behaviors of tasks but also verify the OS model behaviors, and moreover, all of the states with respect to both tasks and OS model states will be stored in the memory in the checking process. Therefore, Spin-based approach will spend more time and memory checking the same applications compared with EPG technique.

However, if the target application contains a few tasks but many loops (lines 11–18), Spin-based approach will defeat `osek-bmc` in time consumption. This is because, in EPG technique, since the different APIs in different branches will lead to different task execution sequences, the transition system of the target application is constructed based on the execution paths. Therefore, when the target application holds a lot of loops, `osek-bmc` will check a large number of execution paths and a large number of the same sub-paths will be repeatedly verified in the verification, which will slow down the performance of `osek-bmc`. In contrast with EPG technique, in Spin-based approach, loops will not be unfold in the checking process, and moreover, we do not need to set an appropriate bound for loops. These efforts will make Spin-based approach more efficient than EPG technique. Furthermore, based on the conducted experiments (lines 19–24), we can find that the Spin-based approach is capable of checking the applications which holds ISRs (EPG technique for now cannot check ISRs).

4.2 Discussion

Based on the shown experiments, there are several important investigation results can be considered in the practical verification of OSEK/VDX applications. (*i*) For the simple applications which contain a few tasks (less than 15) but many loops, the Spin-based approach is capable of checking this kind of applications in the practical verification. However, (*ii*) for the complex applications which hold a lot of tasks and APIs, we should use `osek-bmc` to verify these

Table 1. Comparison between Spin-based approach and EPG technique

Benchmark	Size			#API	Spin-based approach				osek-bmc/EPG			
	#t	#l	loop bound		#s	Mb	Time (s)	Result	#s	Mb	Time (s)	Result
1 passCnt1	4	0	-	4	480	755	0.19	sat	18	2.13	0.093	sat
2 passCnt2	10	0	-	10	137225	768	3.76	sat	46	2.13	0.097	sat
3 passCnt3_bug	15	0	-	15	670176	798	17.6	unsat	29	2.14	0.231	unsat
4 passCnt4_bug	20	0	-	20	-	M.O.	T.O.	-	41	2.15	0.301	unsat
6 msgp4_bug	18	0	-	35	-	-	T.O.	-	145	2.22	0.571	unsat
7 increAPI1_bug	10	1	10	200	2955686	832	59.9	unsat	333	2.23	2.923	unsat
8 increAPI2_bug	10	1	20	400	5905975	891	116	unsat	663	2.24	6.130	unsat
9 increAPI3_bug	10	1	30	600	8897424	937	174	unsat	993	2.27	10.24	unsat
10 increAPI4_bug	10	1	40	800	-	M.O.	-	-	1323	2.31	15.23	unsat
11 token2_bug	6	6	40	161	34371	765	1.12	unsat	2283	2.23	139	unsat
12 token3_safe	9	9	40	161	46990	769	1.26	sat	6417	2.41	192	sat
13 cyclic1	6	16	5	86	4025	757	0.26	sat	992	2.41	10.76	sat
14 cyclic2	9	28	10	289	21803	761	1.31	sat	3276	2.61	60.59	sat
15 cyclic3	12	40	10	412	116432	768	3.97	sat	4680	2.80	94.94	sat
16 cyclic4	15	56	10	575	1110057	799	29.4	sat	6552	3.06	198.4	sat
17 acc_res1_safe	2	3	10	4	13907	759	0.46	sat	3491	2.32	88.8	sat
18 acc_res2_safe	13	13	10	480	483126	762	12.2	sat	-	-	T.O.	-
19 passCnt1_1ISR	4	0	-	4	500	761	0.18	unsat				
20 passCnt1_2ISR	4	0	-	4	724	762	0.19	unsat				
21 passCnt1_3ISR	4	0	-	4	9656	763	0.43	unsat				
22 passCnt2_1ISR	10	0	-	10	131037	769	3.56	unsat				
23 passCnt2_2ISR	10	0	-	10	146770	772	3.93	unsat				
24 passCnt2_3ISR	10	0	-	10	666960	775	17.2	unsat				

applications. Furthermore, (*iii*) if the target application holds a lot of tasks, APIs and loops, we can firstly use Spin-based approach to check the application until Spin-based approach runs out of the memory, and then use `osek-bmc` to continue the checking process.

5 Related Work

With the development of OSEK/VDX OS standard, OSEK/VDX has been widely applied in the development of vehicle-mounted OS. For the developed OSEK/VDX OS and its applications, how to ensure the reliability is becoming challenge for developers with the continuously increasing complexity in the development process. To the scope of checking developed OSEK/VDX OS, there are some invaluable methods, e.g., Jiang Chen and Toshiaki Aoki have proposed a method [9] to generate the highly reliable test-cases for checking whether developed OS conforms to the OSEK/VDX OS standard based on the Spin model checker. As to support an environment of OSEK/VDX OS for model checking, an UML-based method for producing `promela` scripts of OSEK/VDX OS is also proposed in paper [10]. In addition, for the Trampoline [1] which is an open source RTOS developed based on the OSEK/VDX OS standard, Yunja Choi proposed a method [17] to convert the Trampoline kernel into formal models and an incremental verification approach is applied in the verification. Furthermore, a CSP-based approach for checking the code-level OSEK/VDX OS is also addressed in the paper [16].

To the developed applications, the paper [12] has proposed a method to check the timing property based on the UPPAAL. However, to the best of our knowledge, there is no work that considers a formal method to check the safety property of OSEK/VDX applications except our previous works. The main contribution of our paper is that we successfully apply Spin to check the OSEK/VDX applications based on our SynM. The advantages of our approach are as follow. (i) Our approach can accurately check the OSEK/VDX applications, since the OS model as a special process is used to respond to service APIs and compute the running task in the checking process. (ii) The checking process on ISRs is taken into account in our approach.

6   Conclusion and Future Work

In this paper, we presented an approach to check OSEK/VDX applications based on the Spin model checker. In our approach, as to accurately check OSEK/VDX applications using Spin model checker, a synchronization model is employed to simulate the executions of OSEK/VDX applications. We have implemented our approach in Spin model checker and conducted many experiments, the experiment results show that our Spin-based approach is capable of checking the safety property of OSEK/VDX applications. We have also investigated the effectiveness of the Spin-based approach and EPG technique based on the many experiments. The investigation results show that, (i) for the simple application which contains a few tasks (less than 15) but many loops, Spin-based approach is faster than EPG technique in the verification. However, (ii) for the complex application which contains many tasks and APIs, the EPG technique is more efficient to check these applications compared with Spin-based approach.

In the future, there is an important work that will be carried out based on the drawbacks of our approach. In the conducted experiments, we find that, in our Spin-based approach the OS model will be involved in the verification compared with EPG technique. Therefore, as to efficiently check OSEK/VDX applications using Spin, we will translate the behaviors of OSEK/VDX applications into the sequential C program based on the EPG technique.

References

1. Trampoline. http://trampoline.rts-software.org/
2. Clarke, E.M., Emerson, E.A.: Model checking: algorithmic verification and debugging. Commun. ACM **152**(11), 74–84 (2009)
3. Clarke, E.M., Grumberg, O., Long, D.E.: Model checking and abstraction. ACM Trans Program. Lang. Syst. **16**(5), 1512–1542 (1994)

4. Burns, A., Wellings, A.: Real-Time Systems and Programming Languages, 4th edn. Addison Wesley Longmain, New York (2009)
5. Biere, A., Clarke, E.M., Zhu, Y.: Bounded model checking. Adv. Comput. **58**(11), 117–148 (2003)
6. Holzmann, G.J.: The Spin Model Checker: Primer and Reference Manual. Lucent Technologies Inc., Bell Laboratories, Boston, USA (2003)
7. Zhang, H., Aoki, T., et al.: An approach for checking OSEK/VDX applications. In: 13th QSIC, pp. 113–116 (2013)
8. Zhang, H., Aoki, T., Lin, H.-H., et al.: SMT-based bounded model checking for OSEK/VDX applications. In: 20th APSEC, vol. 2(4), pp. 307–314 (2013)
9. Chen, J., Aoki, T.: Conformance testing for OSEK/VDX operating system using model checking. In: 18th Asia Pacific, pp. 274–281 (2011)
10. Yatake, K., Aoki, T.: Automatic generation of model checking scripts based on environment modeling. In: van de Pol, J., Weber, M. (eds.) Model Checking Software. LNCS, vol. 6349, pp. 58–75. Springer, Heidelberg (2010)
11. Lemieux, J.: Programming in the OSEK/VDX Environment. CMP, Suite 200 Lawrence, KS 66046, USA (2001)
12. Waszniowski, L., Hanzlek, Z.: Formal verification of multitasking applications based on timed automata model. Real-Time Syst. **38**(1), 39–65 (2008)
13. OSEK/VDX Group: OSEK/VDX operating system specification 2.2.3. http://portal.osek-vdx.org/
14. Stoller, S.D.: Model-checking multi-threaded distributed java programs. In: 7th International SPIN Workshop, pp. 224–244 (2000)
15. Qadeer, S., Rehof, J.: Context-bounded model checking of concurrent software. In: Halbwachs, N., Zuck, L.D. (eds.) TACAS 2005. LNCS, vol. 3440, pp. 93–107. Springer, Heidelberg (2005)
16. Huang, Y., Zhao, Y., et al.: Modeling and verifying the code-level OSEK/VDX operating system with CSP. In: 5th Theoretical Aspects of Software Engineering (TASE), pp. 142–149 (2011)
17. Choi, Y.: Safety analysis of trampoline os using model checking: an experience report. In: Software Reliability Engineering (ISSRE), pp. 200–209 (2011)
18. Yang, Z., Wang, C., Gupta, A., et al.: Model checking sequential software programs via mixed symbolic analysis. ACM Trans. Des. Autom. Electron. Syst. **14**(1), 1–26 (2009)

Author Index

Printed in the United States
By Bookmasters